T0327332

MANAGING AND MEASURING PERFORMANCE IN PUBLIC AND NONPROFIT ORGANIZATIONS

MANAGING AND MEASURING PERFORMANCE IN PUBLIC AND NONPROFIT ORGANIZATIONS

An Integrated Approach

SECOND EDITION

Theodore H. Poister
Maria P. Aristigueta
Jeremy L. Hall

JB JOSSEY-BASS™
A Wiley Brand

Cover design by Wiley
Cover image: © iStock.com / aleksandarvelasevic

Published by Jossey-Bass
A Wiley Brand
One Montgomery Street, Suite 1200, San Francisco, CA 94104-4594—www.josseybass.com

Jossey-Bass books and products are available through most bookstores. To contact Jossey-Bass
directly call our Customer Care Department within the U.S. at 800-956-7739, outside the U.S.
at 317-572-3986, or fax 317-572-4002.

Wiley publishes in a variety of print and electronic formats and by print-on-demand. Some
material included with standard print versions of this book may not be included in e-books or
in print-on-demand. If this book refers to media such as a CD or DVD that is not included in
the version you purchased, you may download this material at http://booksupport.wiley.com.
For more information about Wiley products, visit www.wiley.com.

Library of Congress Cataloging-in-Publication Data
Poister, Theodore H.
[Measuring performance in public and nonprofit organizations]
Managing and measuring performance in public and nonprofit organizations: an integrated
approach / Theodore H. Poister, Maria P. Aristigueta, Jeremy L. Hall. – Second edition.
pages cm
Revised edition of Poister's Measuring performance in public and nonprofit organizations.
Includes bibliographical references and index.
ISBN 978-1-118-43905-0 (hardback)
1. Organizational effectiveness–Measurement. 2. Organizational effectiveness–Management.
3. Nonprofit organizations. 4. Public administration. 5. Performance–Measurement.
6. Performance–Management   I. Aristigueta, Maria Pilar   II. Hall, Jeremy L.   III. Title.
HD58.9.P65 2015
658.4'013–dc23
2014021079

Printed in the United States of America
SECOND EDITION
HB Printing   10 9 8 7 6 5 4 3 2 1

CONTENTS

PART 3: STRATEGIC APPLICATIONS OF PERFORMANCE MANAGEMENT PRINCIPLES   197

PART 4: DESIGN AND IMPLEMENTATION OF PERFORMANCE MANAGEMENT PROCESSES   411

To my wonderful granddaughters,
Susannah Grace and Caroline Elizabeth Tusher
Who light up my life and make it all the more worthwhile.—Ted Poister

To my husband, Don Coons,
For his unwavering love, patience, and support.—Maria Aristigueta

To my niece, Kadence Olivia Dick,
Who brightens each day and always motivates me to perform
at my best.—Jeremy L. Hall

PREFACE

This is the second edition of *Measuring Performance in Public and Nonprofit Organizations*, a sole-authored book published in 2003. Over the intervening ten years, the emphasis on performance management in government has grown tremendously, and in the eyes of both its champions and its critics, it is clear that public and nonprofit organizations are operating in an era of performance. Performance management systems, which set clear goals and objectives and use systematic performance information to manage more effectively in order to achieve them, are ubiquitous in government at all levels in the United States and many other countries, and the adoption of such systems has proliferated rapidly in the nonprofit sector as well.

If the missions and goals of public and nonprofit organizations are worthwhile—if they indeed add public value to the societies and communities they serve—then performance is of paramount importance. And it is important to understand that high levels of performance do not just occur on their own, and there are many barriers to improving performance in most settings. Numerous stakeholders have a vested interest in performance management, including legislative bodies, other elected officials, chief executive officers, managers and employees, agencies in higher levels of government, customers and constituents, and relevant professional organizations. In the nonprofit sector, boards of directors, administrators, managers, employees, volunteers, customers and clients, advocacy groups, and funding organizations all have a stake in the effective use of performance measures to improve decisions, manage more effectively, and improve performance and accountability.

While the adoption of performance measurement systems has been pervasive in the public and nonprofit sectors, however, they are not always well conceived and constructed, these systems may not be used, and they are often not integrated into management and decision systems effectively. Moreover, the jury is still out regarding the extent to which performance management systems actually make a difference and help contribute to improved program and agency performance. It is not at all surprising, then, that performance management is a dominant topic in the current literature and research in the field of public management as well as in professional graduate education programs preparing students for careers as leaders in the public service.

The purpose of this book is not to promote performance management but rather to help readers understand what performance management systems are and how they function, and to design and implement them effectively. Although the title has been changed from the first edition to emphasize the broader focus on performance *management itself* rather than performance *measurement* as the central element of the process and two coauthors have been added, this book still bears a strong connection to the first edition in terms of approach, orientation, and organization. All chapters have been revised and updated extensively to reflect the substantial evolution and expansion of the field over the past ten years, the current context within which performance management is conducted, and newer approaches and practices aimed at making the enterprise more effective.

The organization of the book is similar to that of the first edition. The two chapters in part 1 introduce the field and provide an overview of the process for developing useful performance management systems. The five chapters in part 2 focus on the methodology of performance measurement in terms of developing performance frameworks, tying measures to goals and objectives, redefining performance measures as operational performance indicators, reporting performance data, and analyzing performances. The chapters in part 3 discuss the development and application of performance management principles in a variety of decision-making venues, including strategic planning and management, performance-informed budgeting, the management of programs and organizations, quality and process improvement, and comparative performance measurement and benchmarking. In addition, two new chapters have been added to this section, focusing on performance-based contracts and grants management and the stakeholder engagement processes. Part 4 concludes the book with a single summary chapter that discusses the design and implementation of effective performance management systems.

As with the first edition, this book is written with two audiences in mind. Although it is not explicitly designed as a textbook, it works well as a text or supplemental reading for primarily graduate courses in planning, public policy, and program evaluation, in addition to public and nonprofit management that have a performance-based orientation. It is also designed to serve as a resource to provide guidance for managers, professional staff, consultants, and others in designing and implementing effective performance management systems. The response to the first edition over the past ten years seems to indicate that it was useful for both the academic and practitioner communities, and we hope that will be the case with this edition as well.

ACKNOWLEDGMENTS

Many people have contributed directly or indirectly to this book by providing opportunities for me to develop performance management systems, allowing access to existing systems, or serving as mentors by sharing with me their knowledge and experiences regarding the design, implementation, and use of performance measures to manage more effectively. These individuals, many of them long-time friends, include the late Thomas D. Larson, former secretary of transportation in Pennsylvania and former administrator of the Federal Highway Administration; the late Richard H. Harris Jr., director of the Center for Performance Excellence in the Pennsylvania Department of Transportation (PennDOT); Joe Robinson Jr., former director of PennDOT's Performance Improvement and Metrics Division; David Margolis, director of the Bureau of Fiscal Management at PennDOT; William E. Nichols Jr., general manager of River Valley Transit (RVT) in Williamsport, Pennsylvania; Kevin Kilpatrick, planning and grants administrator at RVT; James Lyle, former director of business process improvement at the Georgia Department of Administrative Services and executive director of Georgia Public Television; Gerald Gillette, former principal operations analyst in the Office of Child Support Enforcement of the Georgia Department of Human Resources; the late Terry Lathrop, former deputy director of the City of Charlotte, North Carolina, Department of Transportation; the late Patrick Manion, former deputy city manager of Phoenix, Arizona; Stuart Berman, former chief of the Epidemiology and Surveillance Branch, Division of STD Prevention of the US Centers for Disease Control; Earl Mahfuz, former treasurer of the Georgia Department of Transportation (GDOT); Jim Davis, former director of strategic development at GDOT; Amy DeGroff, program evaluation team leader, and Janet Royalty, data manager, at the Division of Cancer Prevention and Control at the Centers for Disease Prevention, and Kristy Joseph, unit manager in the Division of GLobal Health Protection at the Centers for Disease Control; Joey Ridenour, executive director of the Arizona State Board of Nursing; and Lindsey Erickson, project manager at the National Council of State Boards of Nursing (NCSBN), and all the members of the CORE Committee at NCSBN. I have enjoyed working with all these people and appreciate all I have learned from them regarding performance management.

In addition, numerous students in the master's program in public administration at Georgia State University over the years, as well as participants in numerous professional development programs I have conducted for the Evaluators' Institute in San Francisco, Chicago, Atlanta, Toronto, and Washington, DC, have provided insight regarding problems, challenges, and strategies for success in working with performance measures. I have also enjoyed and benefited from collaborating with good friends John Thomas and David Van Slyke, a colleague and former colleague at Georgia State, respectively, as well as former and current graduate students at Georgia State, including Lauren Edwards, Obed Pasha, Anita Berryman, and Robert Weishan, on a number of performance management–related projects. I wish them all well in their future endeavors in this area.

Finally, I express my sincere appreciation for Maria Aristigueta and Jeremy Hall, who have joined me in writing this second edition. I marvel at their heroic efforts in meeting demanding deadlines, lacking the head start that I had with this project, and, more important, their fresh perspective and differing orientations, exposures, and insights have made many meaningful contributions to this edition. I have enjoyed working with them both, and I look forward to the prospect of further collaboration with them on performance management or related topics in the future.

August 2014   Ted Poister
                                                                                        Alpharetta, Georgia

I am deeply grateful to Ted Poister for the opportunity to collaborate with him on the second edition of this book. He is a wonderful role model for those of us interested in performance and a wealth of knowledge. He is also exemplary in bridging the theory-practice divide so important to the advancement of this field. In addition, Ted Poister and Jeremy Hall are a pleasure to work with.

In the early 1990s, I was fortunate to have Joseph Wholey as a professor and dissertation adviser at the University of Southern California. Because he is firm believer in the use of performance for program improvement and a leader in the field of performance management, I benefited greatly from the chance to work with him. Like Ted, he saw great value in practice and considered it the laboratory for the field.

I am also indebted to my colleagues and staff at the University of Delaware who provide the environment and encouragement for excellence every step of the way. I am particularly grateful to the graduate students in my performance management course who have participated in case studies and contributed to my knowledge of current practices in the field. I have especially benefited from the assistance from Lorelly Solano, Christopher Kelly, and William Morrett.

Finally, I express gratitude to my family for their patience as I spent many weekends and evenings writing to meet the tight deadlines for this book. I am particularly grateful to my husband, Don Coons, for his unwavering love and support and to whom I dedicate my contributions to this book.

August 2014   Maria P. Aristigueta
                                                                                             Newark, Delaware

I express my sincere gratitude to a number of individuals who shaped my interest in performance management and have facilitated my work along the way. Of particular note, Ed Jennings (University of Kentucky Martin School) helped me to develop my first analytical framework from the performance perspective. I also extend thanks to Merl Hackbart, also at the Martin School, for providing me with a solid foundation in public budgeting; although I may not use it as often as I would like, that background certainly came in handy on this project. I owe a debt of gratitude to my dean, Marc Holzer, for supporting this endeavor and, more important, allowing me the opportunity to carry my interests in performance management into the classroom. I thank Michael Hail for introducing me to the world of grant management in 1998 and working with me to develop those skills over the fifteen years since then. And I thank my family for their enduring support during many long nights and weekends as this project came together. Most of all, I appreciate Ted Poister for being a supportive voice in the field for those of us who study performance issues and for allowing me the opportunity to join him and Maria Aristigueta on this project.

August 2014   Jeremy L. Hall
                                                                  Science Hill, Kentucky

PART ONE

INTRODUCTION TO PERFORMANCE MEASUREMENT

Performance management—the process of defining, monitoring, and using objective indicators of the performance of organizations and programs to inform management and decision making on a regular basis—is of vital concern to managers in government and the nonprofit sector. The chapters in part 1 discuss the scope and evolution of performance management in these fields and locate it in the context of results-oriented approaches to management. They also convey the variety of purposes that can be served by measurement systems and a sense of why performance management is so important. A crucial point made in part 1 is that performance measurement systems are usually not stand-alone systems. Rather, they are essential to support and strengthen other management and decision-making processes, such as planning, budgeting, the management of organizations and employees, program management, process improvement, grants and contract management, and comparative benchmarking. Thus, it is imperative for system designers to clarify a system's intended uses at the outset and to tailor the system to serve those needs. These chapters also discuss the limitations of performance management systems, as well as the challenges and difficulties inherent in developing them, and they present a holistic process for designing and implementing effective performance measurement systems.

## CHAPTER ONE

INTRODUCTION TO PERFORMANCE MEASUREMENT AND MANAGEMENT

Performance management focuses organizations on results through the use of performance information in various decision-making venues. The practice of performance management had its origin in the early twentieth century, and through sporadic and varied implementation efforts, it has appeared in numerous permutations in a variety of settings at the municipal, state, and national levels. In spite of this lengthy history, it has been only since the 1980s that performance management has evolved into a burgeoning field of practice that permeates public and nonprofit administration at all levels and locations around the globe. It has been said that performance is pervasive (Radin, 2006), and that is a fair assessment. This book sets out to provide a clear understanding of the concept and practice of performance management in modern governance, which incorporates the current reality that public goods and services are provided by public, nonprofit, and private organizations and various combinations of these.

The scope of performance management is wide. It has become a central part of governance and decision making at all levels of government—domestic and international—and has begun to permeate nonprofit practice as well. Carolyn Heinrich (2007) refers to the rise of performance management as follows: "The rise of the development of performance management systems and practices has been nothing short of meteoric; both nationally and locally, performance management is now a goal or function of most governmental and nongovernmental organizations, and in many countries, legislation and cabinet-level entities have been created to support it" (256).

To extend our understanding, we first situate performance management within the broader field of public management, the implementation side of the public policy process. It is carried out by public servants in local, state, and federal governments in the United States and other governments around the globe. Public management encompasses the work of the bureaucracy, and as such it has increased in size and scope over time. The Progressive movement of the 1920s heralded an era of professional government based on rational principles. One manifestation of that shift was the development of the federal civil service system. The social, economic, and environmental policy programs of the 1960s expanded the scope of public management again. Now government has given way to the broader concept of governance, which takes into account the fact that public goods and services are increasingly delivered by third parties, including private sector firms, other levels of government, and nonprofit organizations (Frederickson & Frederickson, 2006).

Throughout these periods, there have been numerous reform efforts grounded in rationality—attempts to make government decisions and administration less political, and less subjective, through the use of objective decision strategies. Deborah Stone (1997) referred to this as the government rationality movement. But each rationality-based approach could also be viewed as reform oriented, intended to better hold bureaucrats accountable. Program evaluation, zero-based budgeting, strategic planning, and, of course, performance measurement all offer examples of such rationality-oriented reform strategies, though this is only a partial list. As Dubnick and Frederickson (2011) observed, there has been undue emphasis on implementing new reform strategies without sufficient attention to their potential problems. Romzek (2000) tells us that new reform strategies always introduce new accountability requirements that are added to, rather than replace, the old ones. Moynihan (2008) reflects on the relative ease associated with adopting performance measurement symbolically without the substantive commitment necessary to bring about the expected results. Adding a new layer of accountability expectations on top of existing systems without consideration for the integration of the new systems with the old creates myriad complex and confusing accountability expectations for those charged with implementing them. As one such reform strategy, performance measurement has at times fallen victim to the same pressures as other reform efforts.

In recent years, we have begun to develop a better understanding of what is necessary for performance measurement to generate the results it has promised. We distinguish between performance measurement and performance management in the literature and in practice. *Performance measurement* refers to the collection of data on key performance indicators; it is a relatively simple exercise, though practice has shown it to be difficult for governments with low technical capacity and stakeholder support (Berman & Wang, 2000) and difficult to implement under conditions of goal multiplicity or confusion (Koppell, 2005). *Performance management* refers to a strategic daily use of performance information by managers to correct problems before they manifest in performance deficiencies. Moynihan (2008), in a seminal investigation into performance measurement efforts at the state level, introduced the *performance management doctrine*, which offers three salient indicators of the sophistication of a performance measurement effort that characterize a shift from simple performance measurement to performance management: movement away from output measures toward outcome measures, the use of performance information in decision making, and the devolution of discretion to street level managers in exchange for responsibility for agency performance.

The challenge of performance management is thus to demonstrate outcomes resulting from the resources that the program, agency, or organization has consumed to appropriate managers, stakeholders, clients, and citizens. Performance management also strives to improve performance over time by using performance information to identify and correct deficiencies in the production process. The exact users of performance information vary from setting to setting, and so will their information needs, as we will see throughout the book. This implies that performance management systems need to be custom designed according to the purposes they serve. Over time, performance measurement has become further integrated into decision making, with data collected at various points suited to providing meaningful reports to support these purposes at the appropriate times. Poister (2010) advocates for three overlapping transitions: from strategic planning to strategic management, from performance measurement to performance management, and from using such tools independently toward better integration of strategic management and performance management.

As we explore the mechanics of performance management in detail, a number of questions from public management practice and research help to structure our understanding of performance management:

- How does performance management fit within understood accountability frameworks?
- How extensively has performance management been implemented at various levels of government?
- What factors explain when and where performance management is adopted?
- Under what conditions is performance management effective?
- What is the relationship between capacity and performance, and what forms of organizational capacity are necessary to implement performance management effectively?
- What special conditions affect the use of performance management in networked or intergovernmental settings where authority is shared and goal ambiguity exists?

And, of course, the most important question in this field of study is this:

- Does performance management actually improve performance?

Public Management, Performance Management, and Accountability

This chapter introduces the concept of performance management and situates it within the broader field of public management. In the balance of this chapter, we review the history of the development of performance management from its origins to the present. We discuss the current state of performance management in both government and nonprofit sectors and the characteristics that have come to be associated with effective performance management in those settings. We explore the limitations of performance management; present a brief assessment of the major questions that currently motivate research in the field; and conclude the chapter with a quick synopsis of the significant applications of performance management in practice, such as budgeting and grant and contract management.

Performance Measurement and Performance Management Defined

Performance measurement has been defined by several notable scholars. Hatry (2006) considers performance measurement to consist of "regular measurement of the results (outcomes) and efficiency of services or programs" (2006, 3). Poister defined it as the "process of defining, monitoring, and using objective indicators of the performance of organizations and programs on a regular basis" (2008, 1). We adopt the following definition of performance measurement in this book: *performance measurement is the systematic, orderly collection of quantitative data along a set of key indicators of organizational (or program) performance.* The advancement to performance management requires expanding our definition to the following: *performance management is the collection and purposive use of quantitative performance information to support management decisions that advance the accomplishment of organizational (or program) strategic goals.*

The performance management framework organizes institutional thinking strategically toward key performance goals and strives to orient decision making toward greater use of performance information to stimulate improvement. This is an ongoing cycle of key organizational management processes, all of which interact in meaningful ways with performance measurement. Our conceptual framework is based on ongoing interplay among performance measurement and reporting, strategic planning and other types of planning, budgeting, ongoing management, and performance measurement and reporting, as shown in figure 1.1.

FIGURE 1.1 THE PERFORMANCE MANAGEMENT FRAMEWORK

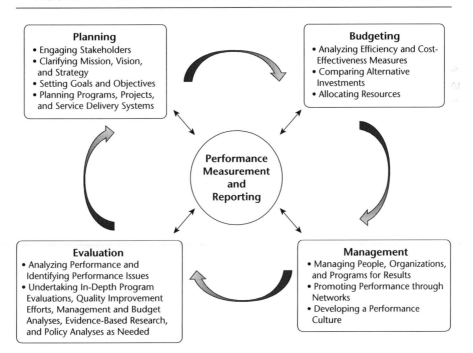

Planning
- Engaging Stakeholders
- Clarifying Mission, Vision, and Strategy
- Setting Goals and Objectives
- Planning Programs, Projects, and Service Delivery Systems

Budgeting
- Analyzing Efficiency and Cost-Effectiveness Measures
- Comparing Alternative Investments
- Allocating Resources

Performance Measurement and Reporting

Evaluation
- Analyzing Performance and Identifying Performance Issues
- Undertaking In-Depth Program Evaluations, Quality Improvement Efforts, Management and Budget Analyses, Evidence-Based Research, and Policy Analyses as Needed

Management
- Managing People, Organizations, and Programs for Results
- Promoting Performance through Networks
- Developing a Performance Culture

Performance measurement and reporting is the central element in the performance management model and is the unique feature that defines it as a performance-based approach to managing. Key sets of measures of agency and program performance are observed at periodic intervals and reported to appropriate managers or other decision makers in order to inform the planning, budgeting, management, and evaluation functions from a performance perspective. In addition, these other functions influence the performance measurement process, and thus the linkages between performance measurement and these other functions are all bidirectional.

At a strategic level, planning engages and solicits feedback from stakeholders, clarifies an agency's mission and vision, establishes strategic goals and objectives, and develops strategic initiatives. Within the framework of strategy that is developed, or even in its absence, other efforts develop plans for programs, projects, service delivery systems, and organizational processes. In a performance management framework, all of these planning activities are informed by data produced by ongoing performance measurement processes that provide information regarding current performance trends and current levels. In turn, the planning activities often identify performance measures needed to monitor goal attainment and the kinds of results that plans are designed to produce, and these measures are likely to become part of ongoing performance measurement processes.

Budgeting concerns the allocation of resources to fund programmatic activities and organizational processes. These decisions tend to be based on a mix of policy preferences, idealism, tradition, and political realities, but in a performance management mode, they are also informed, perhaps even influenced, by performance information relating resources to be expended to the results expected to be produced. Thus, performance-oriented budgeting is more likely to take efficiency and cost-effectiveness measures into account in comparing alternative investment packages and allocating resources with an eye toward the amount of products or services to be delivered or the results or outcomes to be produced. Budget decisions along these lines also influence the kinds of indicators that are emphasized in performance measurement systems.

The management component of figure 1.1 focuses on the implementation and management of strategies, programs, projects, services, and new initiatives on an ongoing basis. In a performance context, this emphasizes managing, motivating, and incentivizing people, organization units, and programs with an eye toward achieving desired results. This approach to management is also more likely to emphasize the development and maintenance of performance-oriented organization cultures and, where appropriate, promote performance orientations and approaches through extended networks on which producing desired results depends. Such management approaches may suggest additional kinds of performance indicators regarding employee productivity, quality, organization climate, or customer service, for example, to be monitored on a regular basis.

Finally, the evaluation component of the model focuses principally on analyzing the performance data being reported, identifying performance issues, and assessing their implications for improving performance. However, at times other types of evaluative effort are required. Sometimes assessments based on the performance data and other information suggest the need to undertake more in-depth evaluative activity, such as formal program evaluations, quality or process improvement studies, management and budget analyses, policy analyses, or evidence-based research. While the information generated by the more routine performance measurement and reporting processes certainly feeds into and informs program evaluations and these other more in-depth evaluative efforts, the latter may well suggest additions to or revisions in the indicators monitored through the ongoing performance measurement process.

Although the performance management model shown in figure 1.1 constitutes a conceptual cycle of activities and decision making, it is not intended to represent steps in a process that follow one another in regular cycles over time. Rather, as a report by the National Performance Management Advisory Commission (2010) points out, the processes included in the model operate on different time lines with planning on a long-term basis (perhaps two to five or more years), budgeting focusing on one or two years, ongoing management operating on a day-to-day basis, and many evaluation efforts undertaken sporadically. And performance measurement and reporting processes typically focus on regular weekly, monthly, quarterly, or annual intervals. Nevertheless, while it can be messy, performance management can be held together by the measurement and reporting function at the center of the model, coupled with a disciplined approach to aligning plans, budgets, management practices, and evaluation activities around common goals and objectives and their accompanying performance measures.

When the adoption of performance measurement and management is substantive and not simply symbolic, the purpose of these practices is rather straightforward. Performance measurement strives to document the level of performance achieved during a specified period of time using measures (and indicators) selected to reflect the purposes of the performance measurement effort. In other words, performance measurement might track inputs, activity levels, outputs, or outcomes; it might use measures of efficiency, effectiveness, equity, cost-effectiveness, or customer satisfaction, for example; and it might be collected to inform internal audiences such as employees or managers or external audiences that include political principals and stakeholder groups. The purpose of performance measurement determines the set of measures and indicators selected, as well as the timing of data collection, the methods of analysis to be used, and the reporting formats and frequencies. Performance management is the strategic use of this performance information in management decision making to maximize key organizational goals through a variety of decision-making areas, including management, budgeting, personnel, contracts, and quality and process improvement. Through informed decisions about common management functions, including staffing and budgeting, for example, performance management allows managers to right the course as deviations are detected that may jeopardize expected performance levels. A good performance management system relies on the collection of valid, reliable, and timely performance information; direction of that information to appropriate users at appropriate times with appropriate discretion to act; and the use of that information to make changes, minor or major, using the tools at their disposal.

The most common goals of performance measurement and management are to reduce costs (increase efficiency), increase effectiveness (or cost-effectiveness), maintain equity, and deliver high-quality products that are met with high levels of customer satisfaction. At a deeper level, the purposes may include accountability to citizens, justifying increased resources, and political and popular support, among others. Deeper still, the goal may be to remain competitive with benchmark cities, attract residents and businesses, and portray the image of a progressive community with a high quality of life.

The first edition of this book referred primarily to performance measurement, because that was the state of the art at that time. Now the field has evolved into a more sophisticated, more strategic approach to management, making the term *performance management* more applicable. Moynihan (2008) describes what he calls the *performance management doctrine*, which has three primary components that distinguish it from simple performance measurement. Let's begin there: performance measurement is the quantitative tracking of agency or program performance, usually accompanied by a reporting effort to either internal users or to the public. Moynihan (2008) indicates that performance management must evolve from this point of origin by (1) shifting from a focus on outputs—the direct results of agency activities—toward a focus on outcomes—the end result of the agency's actions on its goals; (2) developing a culture where performance information is used to inform agency decision making, not simply collected in a separate process; and (3) devolving decision-making discretion to frontline managers in exchange for responsibility for outcomes. To summarize, performance management refers to the integration of performance information with other management processes, including human resources, budgeting, and general management.

Performance information is useful to determine what an organization has done with the resources it has been given in a particular period of time, linking it closely with the responsiveness dimension of accountability. Over time our ability to measure and track performance has improved and become increasingly sophisticated. We examine the details of these improvements later in the book, but this refers generally to the exercise of metrics that consider outcomes and impacts rather than inputs and outputs, and engage in comparison and analysis against past performance and peers.

While most of the early literature on performance measurement was largely descriptive or conceptual (Altman, 1979; Hatry, 1980; Poister, 1982, 1983), a number of more recent books and articles examine the performance movement in depth. These writers can be generally organized into three groups: the proponents (such as Wholey & Hatry, 1992; Behn, 2003), the pragmatists (such as Moynihan, 2008; Frederickson & Frederickson, 2006), and the skeptics (Radin, 2006, for example). A limited number of studies examine the effectiveness of performance measurement or management efforts on actual performance levels. This more recent literature has mixed findings, as we discuss in chapter 15.

Public Management and Performance Management

Public management refers broadly to the management of public organizations to achieve public purposes. The field of practice and study has shifted over time with prominent changes in public bureaucratic institutions through the establishment of a series of new traditions of public management, including strategic planning, performance management, privatization and contracting, and a stronger focus on market-based approaches. Many of these are components of the new public management movement, though other traditions evolved independently. There has been an increase of professionalization within the civil service, with the result that principal-agent relationships that reinforce a command-and-control structure are no longer seen as the only factor necessary to understand agency or employee actions.

New Public Management (Hood, 1991) refocused public sector management toward greater efficiency, highlighting the use of market-based practices borrowed from private sector management, including contracting out and outsourcing. The result has been an explosion of strategic planning, which brings a strong goal orientation, as well as efforts to assess performance and adjust strategy to increase it. The movement calls for greater managerial discretion in exchange for greater responsibility for outcomes. It suggests the use of incentives rather than principal-agent relationships as the mechanism of control.

Bob Behn, in a widely cited *Public Administration Review* article from 1995, raised three "big questions" for public management:

(1) How can public managers break the micromanagement cycle— an excess of procedural rules which prevents agencies from producing results, which leads to more procedural rules, which leads to...
(2) How can public managers motivate people to work energetically and intelligently toward achieving public purposes? And
(3) How can public managers measure the achievements of their agencies in ways that help to increase those achievements? (315)

Each of these questions highlights the role of managers in bringing about improved performance, and the questions collectively suggest that performance is at the core of public management. Performance management, then, is a management approach that we ought to develop with an eye toward reducing unnecessary rules; it offers a prospect for reducing micromanagement. Motivation of individuals working within an organization is a core component of performance management (Behn, 2003). And finally, measuring achievements in order to bring about performance improvement means that we need to measure things that matter, at an appropriate time, and in a way that can be linked directly to actionable management decisions. Within the framework of micromanagement, Behn (1995) identifies a number of more specific management questions, most of which have more than a tangential connection to performance measurement, including trust, governance, entrepreneurship.

Behn (2003) offers another look at performance measurement from the perspective of its many overlapping purposes. He identifies eight specific managerial purposes where performance measurement may play a meaningful role: to evaluate, control, budget, motivate, promote, celebrate, learn, and improve. Behn sees improvement as the central purpose, with the preceding seven serving subordinate roles that are pursued with the overall goal of improving performance.

Whereas Behn (2003) focuses on managerial purposes that performance measurement may serve, Hatry (1999) describes a number of managerial functions that performance information can support in different decision venues: (1) responding to elected officials' and the public's demands for accountability, (2) making budget requests, (3) internal budgeting, (4) triggering in-depth examinations of performance problems and possible corrections, (5) motivating, (6) contracting, (7) evaluating, (8) supporting strategic planning, (9) communicating better with the public to build public trust, and (10) improving (Hatry, 1999). As with Behn (2003), Hatry (1999) emphasizes the role of performance improvement as the principal concern of performance measurement.

Performance management not only supports public management but helps to define and structure it in an era when performance is customarily the foremost goal of public management. By providing managers with information at key decision junctures, strategic choices will result in improvement along those performance dimensions that are prioritized.

Performance Management and Accountability

To fully understand the concept of performance management, we need to begin with the reason for such broad interest in the topic, which can be summed up in a single word: *accountability*. Hatry (2006) indicates that a major use of performance information is "to establish accountability" (3). Accountability itself is a broad concept that refers to a number of more specific forms or conceptual dimensions. Several authors have attempted to clarify the various types of accountability expectations that public managers face on a daily basis to better understand their behavior and to temper our expectations for success with the reality of modern public and nonprofit administration. Yang (2012) refers to accountability as a hallmark of modern democratic governance and a central concept in public management. Dubnick and Yang (2011) suggest that all major schools of thought in public administration are arguably about accountability and all major debates about government reforms are related to accountability.

Accountability systems are often the source of important public sector problems. As Yang (2012) notes, balancing multiple expectations resulting from different forms of accountability is easily said but not easily done. He identifies six conclusions about the accountability literature: conflicts among accountability pressures can lead to problems; overreliance on particular types of accountability can lead to problems; there is no perfect accountability model, and each can devolve into an unproductive or illegitimate reality; principal-agent-based accountability is limited; third-party governance and hybrid organizations such as public-private partnerships require special accountability capacities; and, importantly, "managerial reforms such as performance measurement and reinvention have complications in traditional forms of accountability" (260). Let's examine a few prominent accountability frameworks to get a sense of the relationship of performance measurement and management to public accountability.

Koppell (2005) refers to five distinct dimensions of accountability that might be explored: transparency, liability, controllability, responsibility, and responsiveness. He suggests that the first two are foundational requirements necessary to realize the remaining three. *Transparency* refers to our ability to see what government did and how it did it; this is a form of accountability to citizens and stakeholders at large. *Liability* refers to the penalties that are imposed for failure to adhere to the high standards of public law and administration. The remaining three dimensions are much more relevant to our topic of inquiry, however. *Controllability* refers to the ability of policymakers and decision makers to sway the bureaucracy into conformity with their expectations. This is what we think of as political control in political science, but it is broadly applicable to decision-making (legislative and executive, such as the president, Congress, and boards of directors) bodies and the implementing administrations they oversee. Inertia, culture, information asymmetry, and a variety of other factors have been shown to limit controllability, reducing the ability of those leaders to fulfill their policy agendas. Performance measurement requirements offer one mechanism (alongside oversight and others) for policy leaders to exert stronger vertical control over the actions of the administration. By clearly defining what is expected, measuring actual performance, comparing it to established targets or benchmarks, and providing proper positive and negative incentives, performance measurement promises to enhance controllability.

The *responsibility* dimension of accountability refers to an organization's accountability to the structural requirements that constitute its mandates. These typically take the form of laws, statutes, ordinances, and so on. The key question of interest is simple: Did the agency or organization follow the rules? Accountability here can be supplemented by a proper accounting of activities and outcomes that were accomplished. To be brief, performance monitoring can allow us to determine whether an agency fulfilled its obligation under the law by providing data against which to base judgments.

But the real home of performance measurement and management for accountability rests soundly in the dimension that Koppell (2005) refers to as *responsiveness*. Here we are concerned with the needs and demands of citizens and stakeholders. What do they need? What do they expect from the agency or organization? This dimension is neatly intertwined with the organization's mission—its reason for being. So with an understanding that performance measurement is an approach to enhancing accountability, we need to go a step further and clearly distinguish performance measurement from performance management.

Other models, such as Yang (2012), explicitly link accountability systems, felt accountability, and performance. Accountability, according to Yang (2012), is emergent, and not simply a set of rules or tools. The interplay of structure and agency (what Heinrich, 2007, and Lynn, & Hill, 2008, would refer to as *craft*) result in an accountability reality that changes and shifts over time. The felt accountability dimension is important because it helps to explain how actors perceive, prioritize, and respond to multiple accountability pressures. This means that we can best understand accountability by exploring the information and signals that bureaucratic actors receive and how they respond. In other words, the accountability that such an actor feels is more important than the structures or rules that are in place, especially in a system with multiple such overlapping rules and structures that have been added as reforms over time. This perspective makes it possible to understand accountability in networked and contracted governance arrangements as well.

FIGURE 1.2 ROMZEK AND DUBNICK'S TYPES
OF ACCOUNTABILITY SYSTEMS

		Source of Agency Control	
		INTERNAL	EXTERNAL
Degree of Control Over Agency Actions	HIGH	1. Bureaucratic	2. Legal
	LOW	3. Professional	4. Political

Source: Romzek and Dubnick (1987, 229).

Romzek and Dubnick (1987) identify four types of accountability that public agency managers typically use to manage the accountability expectations they face: legal, political, bureaucratic, and professional. It is important to understand that these varied types of accountability are sometimes found to be in conflict with one another, such as in the case they present of NASA and the space shuttle *Challenger* disaster. The interplay of two factors defines these four distinct accountability systems: "(1) Whether the ability to define and control expectations is held by some specified entity inside or outside the agency; and (2) the degree of control that entity is given over defining those agency's expectations" (Romzek & Dubnick, 1987, 228). They present this as a two-by-two table to reveal the interplay of the two factors (see figure 1.2). The act of performance management most closely resembles their conceptualization of professional accountability. As Romzek and Dubnick (1987) put it:

Those employees expect to be held fully accountable for their actions and insist that agency leaders trust them to do the best job possible. If they fail to meet job performance expectations, it is assumed they can be reprimanded or fired. Otherwise they expect to be given sufficient discretion to get the job done. Thus, professional accountability is characterized by placement of control over organizational activities in the hands of the employee with the expertise or special skills to get the job done. The key to the professional accountability system, therefore, is deference to expertise within the agency. (229)

Deference to expertise, of course, mirrors Moynihan's (2008) charge for greater managerial discretion in exchange for performance-based accountability.

If we perceive performance measurement and management—management reforms aimed at improving accountability—through these frameworks, we can see the potential for conflict and confusion. In public sector environments where there are multiple principals, there are often overlapping and conflicting goals and, consequently, conflicting performance expectations. Everything we understand about accountability helps us to better understand the challenges and opportunities associated with performance management.

Performance Management Institutionalization

How extensive has been the adoption of performance measurement or management? That is a challenging question because of differences in the degree of adoption versus implementation. As Moynihan (2008) indicates, adoption is easy but implementation is more difficult. We also find differences in the extent to which utilization has evolved in different levels of government. Increased use has been accompanied by increased institutionalization through legislative or executive mandate as well.

Great strides in federal program performance management were not realized until the advent of the government performance review and subsequent legislation. The federal government's formal adoption of performance measurement began in 1993 with passage of the Government Performance and Results Act (GPRA). GPRA mandated strategic planning within agencies, establishment of clear objectives and performance targets, and measurement of actual performance against those targets as part of the annual budget process. Its implementation continues to evolve with each transition of presidential power. Under the George W. Bush administration, the requirements of GPRA were fulfilled under the Program Assessment Rating Tool (better known as the PART initiative) beginning in July 2002. This program-focused approach examined and rated program performance according to a five-point scale: effective, moderately effective, adequate, ineffective, and results not demonstrated (figure 1.3). (In the way of performance reporting and transparency, results were reported through a central web portal at www.ExpectMore.gov.) PART was intended to "inform and improve agency GPRA plans and reports, and establish a meaningful systematic link between GPRA and the budget process" (Strategisys, 2014).

FIGURE 1.3 PART PROGRAM IMPROVEMENT OVER TIME

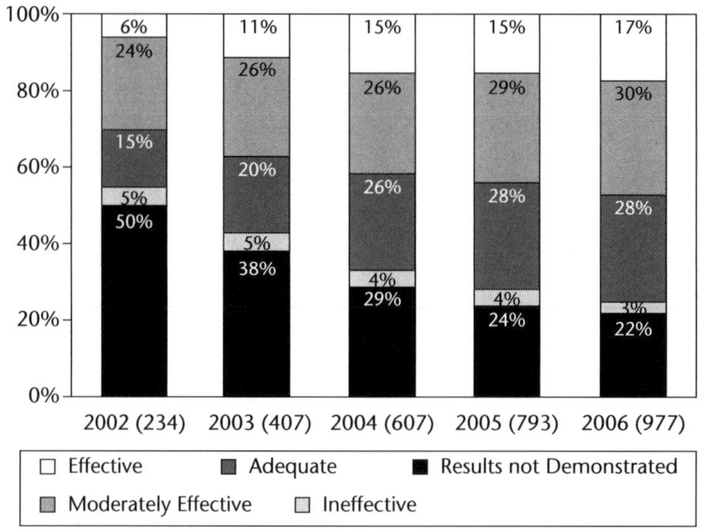

	2002 (234)	2003 (407)	2004 (607)	2005 (793)	2006 (977)
Effective	6%	11%	15%	15%	17%
Moderately Effective	24%	26%	26%	29%	30%
Adequate	15%	20%	26%	28%	28%
Ineffective	5%	5%	4%	4%	3%
Results not Demonstrated	50%	38%	29%	24%	22%

☐ Effective   ■ Adequate   ■ Results not Demonstrated

■ Moderately Effective   ☐ Ineffective

Note: Parenthetical numbers refer to the total number of programs evaluated during the stated year.

Source: http://www.whitehouse.gov/sites/default/files/omb/budget/fy2009/pdf/spec.pdf.

Aggregate results were shown to improve over time. Research has found that PART was a success in many regards. In a Government Accountability Office report, Posner (2004) writes that PART "illustrated the potential to build on GPRA's foundation to more actively promote the use of performance information in budget decisions" (summary). As is often the case with performance information, PART supplied new performance information to decision makers, but that information lacked demand and utilization in the decision-making process. As Posner (2004) put it, "GPRA expanded the supply of performance information generated by federal agencies, although as the PART assessments demonstrate, more must be done to develop credible performance information. However, improving the supply of performance information is in and of itself insufficient to sustain performance management and achieve real improvements in management and program results. Rather, it needs to be accompanied by a demand for that information by decision makers and managers alike" (2).

PART Description

The Program Assessment Rating Tool (PART) is a questionnaire designed to help assess the management and performance of programs. It is used to evaluate a program's purpose, design, planning, management, results, and accountability to determine its overall effectiveness.

Based on the evaluation, recommendations are made to improve program results.

To reflect that federal programs deliver goods and services using different mechanisms, PART also has customized questions depending on the type of program. The seven PART categories are direct federal, competitive grant, block/formula grant, regulatory, capital assets and service acquisition, credit, and research and development.

Each PART questionnaire has twenty-five questions divided into four sections.

- Section 1 asks whether a program's purpose is clear and whether it is well designed to achieve its objectives.
- Section 2 involves strategic planning, and weighs whether the agency establishes valid annual and long-term goals for its programs.
- Section 3 rates the management of an agency's program, including financial oversight and program improvement efforts.
- Section 4 focuses on results that programs can report with accuracy and consistency.

The answers to questions in each of the four sections result in a numerical score for each section from 0 to 100 (the best score). Because reporting a single weighted numerical rating could suggest false precision or draw attention away from the very areas most in need of improvement, numerical scores are translated into qualitative ratings. The bands and associated ratings are as follows:

Rating Range

Effective	85–100
Moderately effective	70–84
Adequate	50–69
Ineffective	0–49

Source: http://georgewbush-whitehouse.archives.gov/omb/expectmore/part.html.

Mullen (2006) reports that PART was successful in three broad areas: (1) helping structure and discipline the Office of Management and Budget's (OMB) use of performance information over a broad range of programs, questions, and evidence; (2) making use of performance information more transparent through public reporting of judgments and explicit recommendations to change management practices and program design; and (3) stimulating agencies' interest in performance and budget integration and improving evidence demonstrating program results. According to the United States Government Accountability Office (2005), the PART process has aided OMB's ability to oversee agencies, concentrated agency efforts on improving program management, and developing or strengthening an evaluation culture within agencies. Early evidence suggested positive benefits for program management and hierarchical control over agencies, but what about the effect of performance information on budgets? Research here shows the initiative to be a success as well. Olsen and Levy (2004) find that PART has a positive effect on the allocation of resources with the effect of a one standard deviation increase in the PART score resulting in a 9 percent increase in the president's proposed funding. Figure 1.3 shows the extent of aggregate program improvement over time.

As is so often the case with presidential initiatives, the transition to the Obama administration saw the abandonment of the PART initiative. Congress at the time of this transition was also at work on amendments to GPRA, which ultimately became law in 2010 as the Government Performance and Results Modernization Act (GPRAMA). GPRA had been passed in 1993 and phased in over a four-year period, followed by thirteen years of full implementation. GPRAMA offers the first substantial revision to the law. A recent Congressional Research Service report examined the key modifications to the act along with the key considerations for Congress (Brass, 2012). Brass (2012) describes the modifications under GPRAMA as follows:

> After a four-year phase-in period for GPRA 1993 and 13 years of the law's full implementation, GPRAMA makes substantial changes. Among other things, GPRAMA
>
> • Continues three agency-level products from GPRA 1993, but with changes
> • Establishes new products and processes that focus on goal-setting and performance measurement in policy areas that cut across agencies

- Brings attention to using goals and measures during policy implementation
- Increases reporting on the Internet
- Requires individuals to be responsible for some goals and management tasks

In making these changes, GPRAMA aligns the timing of many products to coincide with presidential terms and budget proposals. The law also includes more central roles for the Office of Management and Budget (OMB), an entity that often seeks to advance the President's policy preferences. GPRAMA also contains more specific requirements for consultations with Congress. By design, many of GPRAMA's products are required to be submitted to Congress for scrutiny and potential use. (1)

Under GPRAMA, many processes and procedures are continued from GPRA, while new processes, procedures, and products have been added. One key difference is that GPRAMA institutionalizes responsibility for performance assessment at the individual level. Furthermore, it creates new agency-level and federal-wide systems. Congress is reluctant to abandon its oversight role, and management-oriented laws like GPRAMA are no exception. Brass (2012) raises a number of important issues for Congress to consider during the implementation of the new act that point to clear concerns that congressional and presidential purposes may differ:

- Are agencies' and OMB's consultations with Congress working well? Are agencies and OMB defining goals and assessing performance in ways that reflect underlying statutes and congressional intent?
- Are the representations that agencies and OMB make about government performance perceived by Congress, federal personnel, and the public as credible and useful? What are the implications of evidence that is presented?
- Are agencies and OMB implementing GPRAMA with desired levels of transparency and public participation?
- Are agencies, OMB, and Congress focusing effectively on crosscutting policy areas to better coordinate efforts and reduce any unnecessary duplication?

- Are agencies and OMB implementing GPRAMA in a responsive, effective manner? Is GPRAMA working well? If not, what might be done? (Brass, 2012, summary)

Most states have formal statewide performance management systems (Moynihan, 2008). Most of these systems have centralized administration and are connected to the state budget process to provide the capacity to collect data uniformly and better connect performance information with the budget process. These systems take various forms and are instituted through varied laws that reflect state purposes and political realities. One example of a strong central system that connects strategic planning, performance measurement, and the budget process comes from Texas, where the comptroller of public accounts corrals state agencies into consistent processes and guidelines. To reveal the complexity of such a system, figure 1.4 provides an overview of the biennial performance management cycle

FIGURE 1.4 TEXAS'S STRATEGIC PLANNING, PERFORMANCE BUDGETING, AND PERFORMANCE MONITORING SYSTEM

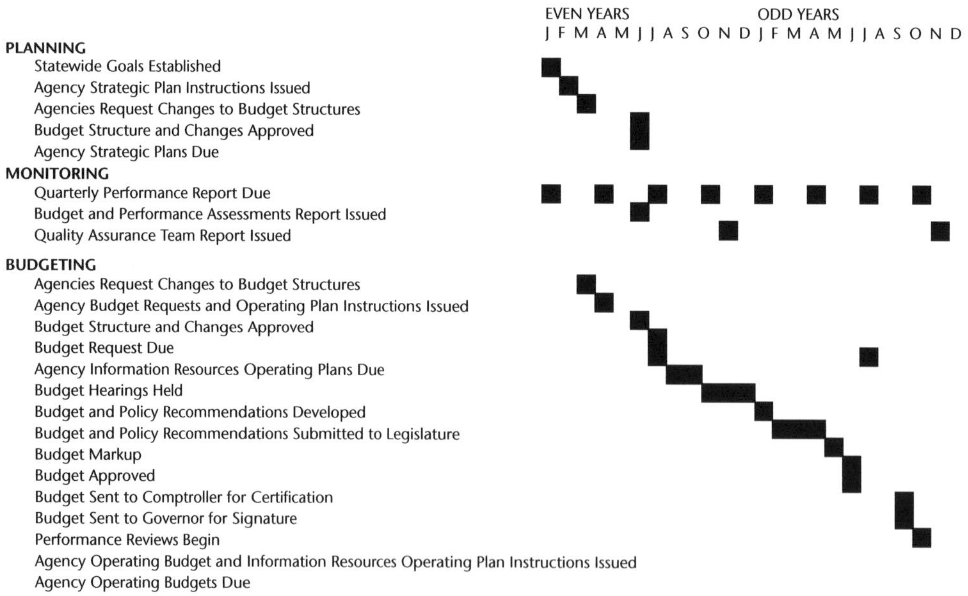

EVEN YEARS   ODD YEARS
J F M A M J J A S O N D J F M A M J J A S O N D

PLANNING
Statewide Goals Established
Agency Strategic Plan Instructions Issued
Agencies Request Changes to Budget Structures
Budget Structure and Changes Approved
Agency Strategic Plans Due
MONITORING
Quarterly Performance Report Due
Budget and Performance Assessments Report Issued
Quality Assurance Team Report Issued

BUDGETING
Agencies Request Changes to Budget Structures
Agency Budget Requests and Operating Plan Instructions Issued
Budget Structure and Changes Approved
Budget Request Due
Agency Information Resources Operating Plans Due
Budget Hearings Held
Budget and Policy Recommendations Developed
Budget and Policy Recommendations Submitted to Legislature
Budget Markup
Budget Approved
Budget Sent to Comptroller for Certification
Budget Sent to Governor for Signature
Performance Reviews Begin
Agency Operating Budget and Information Resources Operating Plan Instructions Issued
Agency Operating Budgets Due

Source: http://www.spartnerships.com/promos/2010lege-files/cd_handout/7_Budget%20Cycle%20 Diagram.pdf, retrieved March 11, 2014.

in Texas. Texas has one of the oldest and strongest state performance systems, established by Governor Ann Richards in collaboration with the Texas legislative budget board in 1992 in the wake of fiscal pressure from the preceding decade.

While states have large budgets and stronger capacity, performance management utilization rates are lower for cities (Poister & Streib, 1999; Moynihan & Pandey, 2010) and lower still for counties (Berman & Wang, 2000). Of course, there is little research into county administration, which seem to constitute the "dark continent" of public administration research (Snider, 1952). It is accurate to say that performance measurement and management are higher where capacity levels are higher, which biases implementation levels toward larger governments. CompStat was the original big city performance management system, first developed in the New York City Police Department under Commissioner William Bratton and Mayor Rudolph Giuliani in 1994, and attributed with reducing crime by over 60 percent in the first year of use. The approach has been expanded in focus and replicated in somewhat smaller cities over time.

The CitiStat program, as another example, originated in Baltimore as a mayoral initiative by Mayor Martin O'Malley after he took office in 1999; the program resulted in over $13 million in savings to the city the first year. Hall (2008) has found a strong relationship between capacity and actual performance levels, but here we are interested in the capacity to implement performance measurement within the organization. Such capacity includes a supportive environment, organizational culture (Moynihan & Pandey, 2010), and technical or administrative capacities (Berman & Wang, 2000). Strong executive leadership seems to be a common characteristic among municipal performance management system adoptions.

Performance management, then, may have its genesis in legislative mandates or executive mandates, but judicial action may also lead to institutionalized performance management. For example, a judicial consent decree entered between the Los Angeles police department and the US Department of Justice required the implementation of a performance evaluation system to monitor conformity with the substantive requirements of the agreement (United States v. City of Los Angeles, California, Board of Police Commissioners of the City of Los Angeles, and the Los Angeles Police Department, 2000). The source of a mandate or a performance initiative can vary considerably. In the nonprofit sector, such mandates may be the initiative of an executive director, a policy mandate made by the board of directors, or even a requirement imposed by a third party, such as a funding agency or grant-making foundation.

Benefits of Performance Management

Whereas many management approaches seem to come and go in government, sometimes resembling flavor-of-the-month fads, from all appearances, the interest in performance management is here to stay. This is because the use of performance information has a commonsense logic that is irrefutable: that agencies have a greater probability of achieving their goals and objectives if they use performance measures to monitor their progress along these lines and then take follow-up actions as necessary to ensure success. Conversely, managing programs or agencies without performance measures has been likened to flying blind, with no instruments to indicate where the enterprise is heading.

When performance measurement systems are designed and implemented effectively, they provide a tool for managers to maintain control over their organizations and a mechanism for governing bodies and funding agencies to hold organizations accountable for producing the desired kinds of results. Performance measures are critical elements of many kinds of results-oriented management approaches, including strategic management, results-based budgeting, performance management systems, process improvement efforts, performance contracting, and employee incentive systems. In addition, they produce data that can contribute to more informed decision making. Measures of output, productivity, efficiency, effectiveness, service quality, and customer satisfaction provide information that public and nonprofit organizations can use to manage their programs and operations more effectively. They can also help managers reward success and take corrective action to avoid replicating failure.

Performance measures focus attention throughout the organization on the priorities set by governing bodies or top management and can act as catalysts that bring about performance improvements. That is, everything else being equal, managers and employees will tend to perform toward the measures because they would rather "look good" than not look so good on established measures. Thus, appropriately configured performance measures motivate managers and employees to work harder and smarter to accomplish organizational goals and objectives. Finally, measurement systems can be used to communicate the results produced by the organization to an array of external as well as internal audiences, and at times they can help the organization make its case, for example, in supporting budget requests to governing bodies or grant applications to funding agencies.

Challenges of Performance Management

These benefits do not materialize automatically. Designing and implementing effective performance measurement systems is a challenging business in terms of both addressing a number of methodological issues and managing organizational and institutional change. Although many public and nonprofit agencies have workable systems in place, others see their measurement systems fall apart before being completed, and still others end up installing systems that are not particularly helpful or are simply not used effectively. This often happens because the measurement systems were not designed appropriately to serve a particular purpose or because they were not implemented effectively in ways that build commitment and lead to their effective use.

Among the important challenges to performance measurement and management are a number of sage criticisms levied by prominent scholars in the field. Moynihan (2008) argues that the symbolic rather than substantive use of performance information is little more than window dressing. For performance measurement to generate impacts, he says, it must be used substantively to guide action. Piotrowski and Rosenbloom (2002) raise concern for those aspects of performance that have not been measured, including democratic and constitutional values such as transparency, equity, or fairness. Radin (2006) echoes these concerns, arguing that performance measurement in general has focused on efficiency to the exclusion of other values and measures. And Frederickson and Frederickson (2006) raise our awareness that in contracted or other forms of third-party governance, each step removed from the policy source is an opportunity for mission creep to allow the goals that are emphasized during implementation to vary from those intended by the original policy.

It also becomes more and more problematic to collect information consistently from these implementing organizations whose rewards are not dependent on the timely collection of reliable performance information. Hall and Jennings (2011) examine the case of the American Recovery and Reinvestment Act (ARRA) as a pilot project for collecting information all the way down to the lowest subcontractor level (Jennings, Hall, & Zhang, 2012). They highlight the magnitude of the endeavor, but also the simplicity of its measurement task, which led to a focus on jobs and salaries rather than the substantive outcomes of the numerous federal projects that were funded.

Frederickson and Frederickson's (2006) arguments about third-party implementation raise our awareness of another challenge for performance measurement and management. In any environment with multiple actors, particularly multiple principals, there is potential for goal multiplicity and confusion. In many cases, there can even be goal conflict. The result is confusion over what should be measured and what measure reflects organization success. For example, in environmental policy, we might measure pollution levels as an indicator of regulatory performance. However, opponents (who may share legislative or executive power), witnessing a closure of businesses and resulting job loss, begin to suggest economic variables as valid indicators of environmental regulatory performance. While some might argue for balance, the mission-driven environmental agency is more likely to concentrate on measures that more closely reflect the organization's logic, neglecting the pesky side effects. And the agency could not be blamed for highlighting performance information that portrayed it in the most positive light; after all, its budget may be influenced by those very performance measures.

We see in such situations that performance measurement creates incentives, often perverse incentives. A number of potential pitfalls may result from such gaming. Some examples are measuring those aspects of performance that portray the agency in the best light, or adjusting strategies to generate the highest perceived output through processes such as creaming. For example, if an agency provides adult education and literacy services, and the funding agency requires that a single performance indicator be collected—in this case, the number of participants earning the GED (Graduation Equivalency Diploma)—the agency faces a choice. It could recruit and train individuals with the greatest need (let's say those with eight-grade education levels) or target individuals who dropped out their senior year of high school and required the least amount of training to pass the GED. The creaming approach allows the organization to demonstrate high levels of outcomes for minimal service and cost; meanwhile, needy potential participants remain unserved. Over time, the result is goal displacement, which means that the organization begins to perform to the measure rather than to the mission. Readers are probably familiar with the expression "teaching to the test," which reflects goal displacement in the form of teachers who prepare students for an examination rather than their level of learning as preparation for higher education or careers. Gaming is a real concern, and it is usually combated through increasingly sophisticated measures over time. Another concern is the use of performance information as a punitive tool. It is often through no fault of the agency that performance faltered; in many cases environmental factors can influence performance beyond the agency's control. One prominent example is the effect of the economy on crime.

Distinguishing Performance Management from Its Cousins

Because of their common focus on greater accountability through an emphasis on outcomes, some scholars have referred to various management reforms as "cousins," including performance measurement, policy analysis, program evaluation, and now evidence-based practice (Frederickson & Frederickson, 2006). The two most commonly considered in concert are program evaluation and performance measurement, largely because the use of performance measurement has displaced much of the management emphasis on program evaluation over the past two decades. More recent attention has considered the compatibility of performance measurement and evidence-based practice. In each case, the two practices serve different purposes, and each provides value in informing decisions at different levels. Hall (2013) offered the stages heuristic of the policy process as a conceptual tool for exploring the points at which each of several results-oriented management tools (strategic planning, policy analysis, performance measurement, and program evaluation) could be drawn on to inform management decisions. The foundational skills necessary to use one tool are often largely transferable to the other.

James McDavid and Laura Hawthorn (2006) tackled the distinction—and integration—of program evaluation and performance measurement in great detail. Among evaluators, there is a sense that program evaluation is more sophisticated methodologically, more conclusive in its findings, and more useful in determining the actual value of a program than performance measurement. These views are not unfounded; program evaluation has traditionally relied on sophisticated research designs, complex methodologies, and highly rigorous experimental or quasi-experimental assessments that are typically beyond the purview of performance measurement. Yet program evaluation typically provides those results only after a full implementation cycle has transpired, whereas performance measurement has the potential to offer ongoing performance feedback, though such feedback will not have the same level of validity or reliability as a more formal evaluation research design. But McDavid and Hawthorn argue that the tools can be integrated in important ways. For one, they both rely on a common understanding of program theory from which key conceptual measures are derived—that is, the logic of process through which a program converts inputs and resources to outputs and outcomes through its various activities. In addition to logic models, McDavid and Hawthorn argue for greater care in measurement and research design in performance measurement so that the data collected for performance measurement purposes can be later used in evaluations, but also so that the confidence in reported performance results can be increased through greater reliability and validity. The result is that managers should be able to participate in the evaluation of their own programs.

Carolyn Heinrich (2007) explored the challenges and prospects for using both performance management and evidence-based policy in an article in the *American Review of Public Administration*. She notes in particular that "differences and tensions between these movements—such as their methods and standards for assembling and analyzing data, and the strategic timing and use of this information to influence policy and hold public managers accountable for performance—could limit their success" (255). She defines evidence-based policy as a process "in which policies and practices are based on or determined by scientifically rigorous evidence" (255). Heinrich notes that in principle, "evidence-based policy and performance management appear to share an elemental goal: to improve government effectiveness by developing and using a more rigorous base of information and scientific evidence to guide decisions about program design, funding, implementation, and management"; but in practice, "there are some important differences and tensions between the approaches of these two movements to achieving this common objective such as their methods and standards for assembling and analyzing data, and the strategic timing and use of this information to influence policy and/or hold public managers accountable for performance" (256).

As with the distinction between program evaluation and performance measurement, we encounter similar concerns between evidence-based practice and performance measurement. Commenting on the opportunity presented by the increasing quality of data available, Heinrich (2007) concludes:

> If their use continues, "high-stakes" performance management systems need to incorporate ample buffers for errors and imprecision in data collection and analysis and allow time for careful case reviews before sanctions are applied or bonuses awarded. In general, we would be

better served if our demands for performance accountability were less focused on identifying which entities achieve "bottom-line" results and more on producing information that enlightens public managers as to how they can improve performance. (274)

Hall and Jennings (2008) characterize evidence-based practice as a research-informed subset of best practices alongside promising practices, which do not hold up to the same standards of methodological rigor. They further explain that the necessary level of evidence should be commensurate with the level of risk involved for a particular policy choice. In later research (Jennings & Hall, 2012) they characterize evidence-based policies, programs, and practices as similar outcomes of the same evidence-based approach to decision making. Ultimately, evidence-based practice "is about using scientific evidence to produce better public program outcomes" (Jennings & Hall, 2012, 246).

Recognizing that there is some room for interpretation when it comes to the quality of evidence being used across functional areas, the principal distinctions between evidence-based practice and performance management are the level of methodological rigor employed (and the consequences for validity and reliability) and the timing of use for decision purposes. Whereas performance measurement offers the greatest utility during implementation, evidence-based policy and practice look to inform the choice of policy or program before implementation. Again, evidence-based practice employs methodologies that are typically more rigorous than those used in performance measurement to ensure higher levels of validity and reliability. The methodological distinction between these analytical approaches highlights another challenge: keeping data within the realm of manager comprehension and action. Program evaluation and evidence-based practice both risk alienating managers who may not be familiar with or able to comfortably interpret their results.

If we think about these various results-oriented management strategies collectively, as Hall (2013) suggests, we begin to see the opportunities for sorting out their complexity to better use them in concert and capitalize on their areas of overlap. So if strategic planning defines strategy and goals, evidence-based practice can help to select programs or policies with the greatest likelihood of success, performance management can monitor progress during implementation, and program evaluation can offer a retrospective assessment of the results actually attributable to the program. Figure 1.5 shows these relationships in conjunction with the stages of the policy process. Figure 1.6 reveals a potential cyclical relationship among

FIGURE 1.5 RESULTS-ORIENTED MANAGEMENT TOOLS AND THE POLICY STAGES HEURISTIC

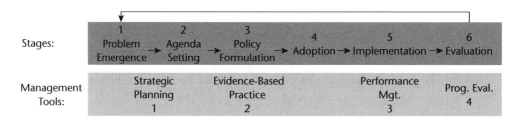

FIGURE 1.6 DATA AGGREGATION AND UTILIZATION OVER TIME ACROSS MANAGEMENT PRACTICES

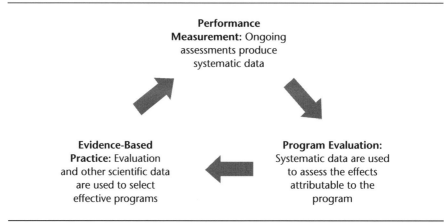

Source: Hall (2013).

performance measurement, program evaluation, and evidence-based practice as data are accumulated and analyzed for various purposes over time.

Outline of the Book

This chapter has offered an introduction to the concepts of performance measurement and performance management, situated them within the broader public management and accountability literatures, and highlighted the key purposes, benefits, and problems associated with performance management in practice. The remainder of the book provides an in-depth examination of the steps necessary to develop and implement a full-scale performance management system, highlighting particular areas of specialized application.

Chapter 2 completes part 1 with an overview of the development of performance management systems. The chapters in part 2 explain each step in the performance measurement process: developing a performance framework (chapter 3), clarifying agency goals and objectives (chapter 4), operationalizing performance indicators (chapter 5), reporting performance information (chapter 6), and analyzing performance information (chapter 7). Part 3 examines the strategic application of performance management principles to core management functions and unique circumstances: strategic management (chapter 8), performance budgeting (chapter 9), managing organizational units, programs, and employees (chapter 10), managing grants and contracts (chapter 11), improving quality, productivity, and customer service (chapter 12), soliciting stakeholder feedback (chapter 13), and benchmarking to improve public practice (chapter 14). Part 4, chapter 15, offers a concluding review of the barriers to effective use of performance management and a forward-looking examination of the prospects for expanded performance management utilization in the public and nonprofit sectors.

Collectively these chapters touch on all the elements of the performance management model shown in figure 1.1 and discussed earlier in this chapter. For the most part, the chapters in part 2 focus on the performance measurement and reporting process in the center of the model, addressing the development of performance frameworks, definition of operational indicators, and the design of formats to report performance data, while chapter 7, on analyzing performance data, relates more directly to the evaluation component of the model. Chapter 8, on strategic planning and management, clearly focuses on the planning component in the model, and chapter 13, on obtaining stakeholder feedback, also relates to planning, while chapter 9 focuses on the budgeting component. Chapter 10, on managing organizations, programs, and people, focuses most directly on the ongoing management component of the model, although it also relates to the evaluation component in part through its discussion of the use of program evaluation and evidence-based research in managing programs. Chapter 11, on managing grants and contracts, and chapter 12, on quality and process improvement, also relate to ongoing agency and program management, as does chapter 14 on benchmarking practices. Chapter 15, which focuses on prospects for performance management, relates to the entire model.

References

Altman, S. (1979). Performance monitoring systems for public managers. *Public Administration Review, 39*(1), 31–35.

Behn, R. D. (1995). The big questions of public management. *Public Administration Review, 55,* 313–324.

Behn, R. D. (2003). Why measure performance? Different purposes require different measures. *Public Administration Review, 63,* 586–606.

Berman, E., & Wang, X. (2000). Performance measurement in US counties: Capacity for reform. *Public Administration Review, 60,* 409–420.

Brass, C. T. (2012). *Changes to the Government Performance and Results Act (GPRA): Overview of the new framework of products and processes.* Congressional Research Service. http://fas.org/sgp/crs/misc/R42379.pdf

Dubnick, M. J., & Frederickson, H. G. (2011). *Accountable governance: Problems and promises.* New York: M. E. Sharpe.

Dubnick, M., & Yang, K. (2011). The pursuit of accountability: Promise, problems, and prospects. In D. Menzel & H. White (Eds.), *The state of public administration* (pp. 171–186). Armonk, NY: M. E. Sharpe.

Frederickson, D. G., & Frederickson, H. G. (2006). *Measuring the performance of the hollow state.* Washington, DC: Georgetown University Press.

Hall, J. L. (2008). The forgotten regional organizations: Creating capacity for economic development. *Public Administration Review, 68*(1), 110–125.

Hall, J. L. (2013). *Performance measurement and evidence-based practice: A practical guide to strategies of management reform.* Paper presented at the Annual Meeting of the American Society for Public Administration, New Orleans, LA.

Hall, J. L., & Jennings, E. T. (2008). Taking chances: Evaluating risk as a guide to better use of best practices. *Public Administration Review, 68,* 695–708.

Hall, J. L., & Jennings, E. T. (2011). The American Recovery and Reinvestment Act (ARRA). *Public Performance and Management Review, 35,* 202–226.

Hatry, H. P. (1980). Performance measurement principles and techniques: An overview for local government. *Public Productivity Review, 4,* 312–339.

Hatry, H. P. (1999). *Performance measurement: Getting results.* Washington, DC: Urban Institute.

Hatry, H. P. (2006). *Performance measurement: Getting results.* Washington, DC: Urban Institute.

Heinrich, C. J. (2007). Evidence-based policy and performance management challenges and prospects in two parallel movements. *American Review of Public Administration, 37,* 255–277.

Hood, C. (1991). A public management for all seasons? *Public Administration, 69*(1), 3–19.

Jennings, E. T., & Hall, J. L. (2012). Evidence-based practice and the use of information in state agency decision making. *Journal of Public Administration Research and Theory, 22,* 245–266.

Jennings, E. T., Hall, J. L., & Zhang, Z. (2012). The American Recovery and Reinvestment Act and state accountability. *Public Performance and Management Review, 35,* 527–549.

Koppell, J.G.S. (2005). Pathologies of accountability: ICANN and the challenge of "multiple accountabilities disorder." *Public Administration Review, 65*(1), 94–108.

Laurence, E. Lynn, Jr. & Hill, Carolyn J. (2008). *Public Management: A Three-Dimensional Approach.* CQ Press: Washington, DC.

McDavid, J. C., & Hawthorn, L. R. (Eds.). (2006). *Program evaluation and performance measurement: An introduction to practice.* Thousand Oaks, CA: Sage.

Moynihan, D. P. (2008). *The dynamics of performance management: Constructing information and reform.* Washington, DC: Georgetown University Press.

Moynihan, D. P., & Pandey, S. K. (2010). The big question for performance management: Why do managers use performance information? *Journal of Public Administration Research and Theory, 20,* 849–866.

Mullen, P. R. (2006). Performance-based budgeting: The contribution of the program assessment rating tool. *Public Budgeting & Finance, 26*(4), 79–88.

National Performance Management Advisory Commission. (2010). *A performance management framework for state and local government: From measurement and reporting to management and improving.* Chicago: National Performance Management Advisory Commission.

Olsen, R., & Levy, D. (2004). Program performance and the president's budget: Do OMB's PART scores really matter. *Mathematica Policy Research.* http://www.mathematica-mpr.com/publications/PDFs/OMBbudgeting.pdf

Piotrowski, S. J., & Rosenbloom, D. H. (2002). Nonmission-based values in results–oriented public management: The case of freedom of information. *Public Administration Review, 62,* 643–657.

Poister, T. H. (1982). Performance monitoring in the evaluation process. *Evaluation Review, 6,* 601–623.

Poister, T. H. (1983). *Performance monitoring.* Lexington, MA: Lexington Books.

Poister, T. H. (2008). *Measuring performance in public and nonprofit organizations.* Hoboken, NJ: Wiley.

Poister, T. H. (2010). The future of strategic planning in the public sector: Linking strategic management and performance. *Public Administration Review, 70*(s1): s246–s254.

Poister, T. H., & Streib, G. (1999). Performance measurement in municipal government: Assessing the state of the practice. *Public Administration Review, 59,* 325–335.

Posner, P. L. (2004). OMB's program assessment rating tool presents opportunities and challenges for budget and performance integration. United States Government Accountability Office. GAO-04–439T. http://www.gao.gov/assets/120/110571.pdf

Radin, B. (2006). *Challenging the performance movement: Accountability, complexity, and democratic values.* Washington, DC: Georgetown University Press.

Romzek, B. S. (2000). Dynamics of public sector accountability in an era of reform. *International Review of Administrative Sciences, 66*(1), 21–44.

Romzek, B. S., & Dubnick, M. J. (1987). Accountability in the public sector: Lessons from the Challenger tragedy. *Public Administration Review,* pp. 227–238.

Snider, C. F. (1952). American county government: A mid-century review. *American Political Science Review, 46,* 66–80.

Stone, D. A. (1997). *Policy paradox: The art of political decision making.* New York: W. W. Norton.

Strategisys. (2014). OMB's program assessment rating tool (PART). http://strategisys.com/omb_part

United States Government Accountability Office. (2005). PART focuses attention on program performance, but more can be done to engage Congress. GAO-06-28. http://www.gao.gov/new.items/d0628.pdf

United States v. City of Los Angeles, California, Board of Police Commissioners of the City of Los Angeles, and the Los Angeles Police Department. (2000). Consent decree. http://www.lapdonline.org/assets/pdf/final_consent_decree.pdf

Wholey, J. S., & Hatry, H. P. (1992). The case for performance monitoring. *Public Administration Review, 52,* 604–610.

Yang, K. (2012). Further understanding accountability in public organizations' actionable knowledge and the structure-agency duality. *Administration and Society, 44,* 255–284.

## CHAPTER TWO

DEVELOPING EFFECTIVE PERFORMANCE MANAGEMENT SYSTEMS

How do you go about creating and installing a performance management system in a public or nonprofit organization? How can you ensure that such a system is designed to meet the needs it is intended to serve? What are the essential steps in the design and implementation process?

The Design and Implementation Process

Those who have responsibility for developing performance management systems must proceed deliberately and systematically if they are to develop systems that are used effectively for their intended purposes. This chapter presents a step-by-step process for developing a performance management system that can help manage agencies and programs more effectively.

As we discussed in chapter 1, *performance management is the purposive use of quantitative performance information to support management decisions that advance the accomplishment of organizational (or program) goals.* The performance management framework organizes institutional thinking strategically toward key performance goals and strives to orient decision-making and policymaking processes toward greater use of performance information to stimulate learning and improvement. This is an ongoing cycle of key organizational management processes that interact in meaningful ways with performance measurement.

Performance measurement and *performance management* are often used interchangeably, although they are distinctly different. Performance measurement helps managers monitor performance. Many governments and nonprofits have tracked inputs and outputs and, to a lesser extent, efficiency and effectiveness. These data have been reported at regular intervals and communicated to stakeholders. This type of measurement is a critical component of performance management. However, measuring and reporting alone rarely lead to organizational learning and improved performance outcomes. Performance management, however, encompasses an array of practices designed to create a performance culture. Performance management systematically uses measurement and data analysis as well as other management tools to facilitate moving from measurement and reporting to learning and improving results.

Performance management systems come in all shapes and sizes. They may be comprehensive systems that include strategic planning, performance measurement, performance-based budgeting, and performance evaluations or those that establish goals and monitor detailed indicators of a production process or service delivery operation within one particular agency every week; others track a few global measures for an entire state or the nation as a whole on an annual basis. Some performance measurement systems are intended to focus primarily on efficiency and productivity within work units, whereas others are designed to monitor the outcomes produced by major public programs. Still others serve to track the quality of the services provided by an agency and the extent to which clients are satisfied with these services. What differentiates these programs as performance management is that the data are used to manage, make decisions, and improve programs.

Yet all of these different kinds of performance management and measurement systems can be developed with a common design and implementation process. The key is to tailor the process to both the specific purpose for which a particular system is being designed and to the program or agency whose performance is being measured. Figure 2.1 outlines a process for designing and implementing effective performance management systems. It begins with clarifying the purpose of the system and securing management commitment and proceeds through a sequence of essential steps to full-scale implementation and evaluation.

FIGURE 2.1 PROCESS FOR DESIGNING AND IMPLEMENTING PERFORMANCE MANAGEMENT SYSTEMS

1. • Clarify the purpose of the system
2. • Assess organizational readiness
3. • Identify external stakeholders
4. • Organize the system development process
5. • Identify key purposes and parameters for initiating performance management
6. • Define the components for the performance management system, performance criteria, and use
7. • Define, evaluate, and select indicators
8. • Develop data collection procedures
9. • Specify system design
10. • Conduct a pilot if necessary
11. • Implement full-scale system
12. • Use, modify, and evaluate the system
13. • Share the results with stakeholders

Step One: Clarify the Purpose of the System

Before getting started, it is important to clarify the purpose of the system. Questions that should be answered include these:

- Is it to support implementation and management of an agency's strategic agenda, manage employees, manage programs, manage organizations, support quality improvement efforts, manage grants and contracts, or inform budget decision making?
- How will the performance measures be used to help manage more effectively?
- With whom will the data be shared?
- Who will be involved in regular reviews of the performance information?

- How will the information be provided to the decision makers?
- What kinds of decisions and actions are the performance data expected to inform—for example, goals, priorities, resource allocation and utilization, operating procedures, program design and operation, work processes, personnel, organization design and functioning?
- What kinds of incentives are being used explicitly or implicitly to encourage working harder and smarter to strengthen performance?

Step Two: Assess Organizational Readiness

The second step in the process is to secure management commitment to the design, implementation, and use of the performance management system. If those who have responsibility for managing the agency, organizational units, or particular programs do not intend to use the management system or are not committed to sponsoring its development and providing support for its design and implementation, the effort will have little chance of success. Thus, it is critical at the outset to make sure that the managers of the department, agency, division, or program in question—those whose support for a performance management system will be essential for it to be used effectively—are on board with the effort and committed to supporting its development and use in the organization. It is important to have the commitment of those at various levels in the organization, including those who are expected to be users of the system and those who will need to provide the resources and ensure the organizational arrangements needed to maintain the system.

Organizations should be assessed on readiness that allow for levels of more or less complex systems to management performance (Van Dooren, Bouckaert, & Halligan, 2010). Niven (2003) provides ten criteria for evaluating the organization's readiness to implement and sustain performance management:

1. A clearly defined strategy
2. Strong, committed sponsorship or a champion
3. A clear and urgent need
4. The support of midlevel managers
5. An appropriately defined scale and scope
6. A strong team with available resources
7. A culture of measurement
8. Alignment between management and information technology
9. Availability of quality data
10. A solid technical infrastructure

Step Three: Identify External Stakeholders

It will be helpful to have commitments from external stakeholders—for example, customer groups, advocacy groups, and professional groups. If agreement can be developed among the key players regarding the usefulness and importance of a system, with support for it ensured along the way, the effort is ultimately much more likely to produce an effective management system. If such commitments are not forthcoming at the outset, it is probably not a workable situation for developing a useful system. (More on external stakeholders will be found in chapter 13.)

Step Four: Organize the System Development Process

Along with a commitment from higher levels of management, the individual or group of people who will take the lead in developing the management system must also organize the process for doing so. Typically this means formally recognizing the individual or team that will have overall responsibility for developing the system, adopting a design and implementation process to use (like the one shown in figure 2.1), and identifying individuals or work units that may be involved in specific parts of that process. This step includes decisions about all those who will be involved in various steps in the process—managers, employees, staff, analysts, consultants, clients, and others. It also includes developing a schedule for undertaking and completing various steps in the process. Beyond timetables and delivery dates, the individual or team taking the lead responsibility might find it helpful to manage the overall effort as a project. We return to issues concerning the management of the design and implementation process in chapter 15.

Step Five: Identify Key Purposes and Parameters for Initiating Performance Management

The fifth step in the process is to build on step two and clarify the purpose of the management system and the parameters within which it is to be designed. Purpose is best thought of in terms of use:

- Who are the intended users of this system, and what kinds of information do they need from it?
- Will this system be used simply for reporting and informational purposes, or is it intended to generate data that will assist in making better decisions or managing more effectively?

- Is it being designed to monitor progress in implementing an agency's strategic initiatives, inform the budgeting process, manage people and work units more effectively, support quality improvement efforts, or compare your agency's performance against other similar organizations?
- What kinds of performance data can best support these processes, and how frequently do they need to be observed?

Chapters 8 through 14 discuss the design and use of performance measures for these purposes, and it becomes clear that systems developed to support different management processes will themselves be very different in terms of focus, the kinds of measures that are used, the level of detail involved, the frequency of reporting performance data, and the way in which the system is used. Thus, it is essential to be clear about the purpose of a performance measurement system at the outset so that it can be designed to maximum advantage.

Beyond the questions of purpose and connections between the performance measurement system and other management and decision-making processes, system parameters are often thought of in terms of both scope and constraints. Thus, system designers must address the following kinds of questions early on in the process:

- What is the scope of the new system?
- Will it focus on organizational units or on programs?
- Will it cover a particular operating unit, a division, or the entire organization?
- Do we need data for individual field offices, for example, or can the data simply be rolled up and tracked for a single, larger entity?
- Should the measures comprehend the entire, multifaceted program or just one particular service delivery system?
- Who are the most important decision makers regarding these agencies or programs, and what kinds of performance data do they need?
- Are there multiple audiences for the performance data to be generated by this system, possibly including internal and external stakeholders?
- Are reports produced by this system likely to be going to more than one level of management?
- What are the resource constraints within which this measurement system will be expected to function?
- What level of effort can be invested in support of this system, and to what extent will resources be available to support new data collection efforts that might have to be designed specifically for this system?

- Are any barriers to the development of a workable performance measurement system apparent at the outset?
- Are some data that would obviously be desirable to support this system simply not available?
- Would the cost of some preferred data elements clearly exceed available resources? If so, are there likely to be acceptable alternatives?
- Is there likely to be resistance to this system on the part of managers, employees, or other stakeholders whose support and cooperation are essential for success? Can we find ways to overcome this problem?

The answers to these kinds of questions will have a great influence on the system's design, so they will need to be addressed very carefully. Sometimes these parameters are clear from external mandates for performance management systems, such as legislation of reporting requirements for jurisdiction-wide performance and accountability or monitoring requirements of grants programs managed by higher levels of government. In other cases, establishing the focus may be a matter of working closely with the managers who are commissioning a performance management system in order to clarify purpose and parameters before proceeding to the design stage.

Step Six: Define the Components for the Performance Management System, Performance Criteria, and Use

There are several performance management systems that many governments and nonprofits are using, including strategic planning based on mission, mandates, goals, objectives, strategies, and measures found in chapter 8 of this book; the balanced scorecard found in chapter 8; and the Stat system approach (e.g., CompStat and CitiStat) found in chapter 13. Organizations may adopt one of these approaches fully or partially, or select elements from several to create their own unique system. For example, the State of Delaware is among governments that use the framework in the Malcolm Baldrige National Quality Award program, focusing on leadership, strategic planning, customer focus, measurement, process management, and improving results. This model recommends a structured approach to management based on criteria set up for receiving the Baldrige Award.

Important areas to consider, according to Kamensky and Fountain (2008), include:

- Leadership meetings for discussions of the performance of the various programs
- The commitment of program managers and key contributors to the system
- Links to resources, with discussion that includes whether the performance information will be used in the budget decisions
- The role of granters or networks in delivering the services and how their performance will be used in the system
- Stakeholder feedback and how it will be used to inform performance
- Evaluation of programs to improve performance
- How nonachieving programs will be handled

This sixth step also requires the identification of the intended outcomes, use, and other performance criteria to be monitored by the measurement system:

- What are the key dimensions of performance of the agency or program that you should be tracking?
- What services are being provided, and who are the customers?
- What kind of results are you looking for?
- How do effectiveness, efficiency, quality, productivity, customer satisfaction, and cost-effectiveness criteria translate into this program area?
- How will this information be used? Will it inform budget decisions?

Chapter 3 is devoted to the subject of identifying program outcomes and other performance criteria. It introduces the concept of logic models that outline programmatic activity, immediate products, intermediate outcomes, and ultimate results and the presumed cause-and-effect relationships among these elements. Analysts, consultants, and other system designers can review program plans and prior research and can work with managers and program delivery staff, as well as with clients, and sometimes other external stakeholders, to clarify what these elements really are. Once a program logic model has been developed and validated with these groups, the relevant performance criteria can be derived directly from the model.

Remember that the ultimate purpose of these systems is program improvement. How will this information be used to improve programs? Chapter 4 elaborates on the all-important linkage of performance measures to goals and objectives. Chapter 9 addresses the use of performance information in budgeting.

Step Seven: Define, Evaluate, and Select Indicators

When consensus has been developed on what aspects of performance should be incorporated in a particular performance management system, the question of how to measure these criteria may begin to be addressed. As discussed in chapter 5, this involves defining, evaluating, and then selecting preferred performance indicators. Questions to consider include these:

- How should certain measures be specified?
- What about the reliability and validity of proposed indicators?
- How can you capture certain data elements, and to what extent will this entail collecting original data from new data sources?
- Is the value of these indicators worth the investment of time, money, and effort that will be required to collect the data?
- Will these measures set up appropriate incentives that will help to improve performance, or could they actually be counterproductive?

This is usually the most methodologically involved step in the process of designing performance management systems. It cuts to the heart of the issue: How will you measure the performance of this agency or program on an ongoing basis? The ideas come from prior research and other measurement systems, as well as from goals, objectives, and standards and from the logical extension of the definition of what constitutes strong performance for a particular program. Sometimes it is possible to identify alternative indicators for particular measures, and in fact the use of multiple or cascading measures is well advised. In addition, there are often trade-offs between the quality of a particular indicator and the practical issues in trying to operationalize it. Thus, as discussed in chapter 5, it is important to identify potential measures and then evaluate each one on a series of criteria in order to decide which to include in the monitoring system.

Step Eight: Develop Data Collection Procedures

Given a set of indicators to be incorporated in a performance management system, the next step in the design process is to develop procedures for collecting and processing the data on a regular basis. The data for performance monitoring systems come from a wide variety of sources, including agency records, program operating data, existing management information systems, direct observation, tests, clinical examinations, various types of surveys, and other special measurement tools. As discussed in chapter 7, in circumstances where the raw data already reside in established data files maintained for other purposes, the data collection procedures involve extracting the required data elements from these existing databases. Within a given agency, this is usually accomplished by programming computer software to export and import specific data elements from one database to another. Sometimes, particularly with respect to grant programs, for example, procedures must be developed for collecting data from a number of other agencies and aggregating them in a common database. Increasingly this is accomplished through interactive computer software over the Internet.

In other instances, operationalizing performance indicators requires collecting original data specifically for the purposes of performance measurement. With respect to tests, which may be needed to rate client or even employee proficiency in any number of skill areas or tasks as well as in educational programs, there are often a number of standard instruments to choose from or adapt; in other cases, new instruments have to be developed. This is also the case with respect to the kinds of medical, psychiatric, or psychological examinations that are often needed to gauge the outcomes of health care or other kinds of individual or community-based programs. Similarly, instruments may need to be developed for direct observation surveys in which trained observers rate particular kinds of physical conditions or behavioral patterns.

Some performance measures rely on surveys of clients or other stakeholders, and these require decisions about the survey mode—personal interview, telephone, mail-out, individual or group administered, or computer based—as well as the adaptation or design of specific survey instruments. In addition to instrument design, these kinds of performance measures require the development of protocols for administering tests, clinical examinations, and surveys so as to ensure the validity of the indicators as well as their reliability through uniform data collection procedures. Furthermore, the development of procedures for collecting original data, especially through surveys and other kinds of client follow-up, often requires decisions about sampling strategies.

With regard to both existing data and procedures for collecting original data specifically for performance measurement systems, we need to be concerned with quality assurance. As mentioned in chapter 1, performance management systems are worthwhile only if managers and decision makers actually use them for program improvement, and this will happen only if the intended users have faith in the reliability of the data. If data collection procedures are sloppy, the data will be less than reliable, and managers will not have confidence in them. Worse, if the data are biased somehow because, for example, records are falsified or people responsible for data entry in the field tend to include some cases but systematically exclude others, the resulting performance data will be distorted and misleading. As will be discussed in chapter 7, there needs to be provision for some kind of spot checking or systematic data audit to ensure the integrity of the data being collected.

Step Nine: Specify System Design

At some point in the design process, you must make decisions about how the performance management system will operate. One of these decisions concerns reporting frequencies and channels—that is, how often particular indicators will be reported to different intended users. As will become clear in chapters 8 through 14, how you make this decision will depend primarily on the specific purpose of a monitoring system. For example, performance measures developed to gauge the outcomes of an agency's strategic initiatives might be reported annually, whereas indicators used to track the outputs and labor productivity of a service delivery system in order to optimize workload management might well be tracked weekly. In addition to reporting frequency, there is the issue of which data elements go to which users. In some cases, for instance, detailed data broken down by work units might be reported to operating-level managers, while data on the same indicators might be rolled up and reported in the aggregate to senior-level executives.

System design also entails determining what kinds of analysis the performance data should facilitate and what kinds of reporting formats should be emphasized. As discussed in chapter 6, performance measures do not convey information unless the data are reported in some kind of context through comparisons over time, against targets or standards, among organizational or programmatic units, or against external benchmarks. What kind of breakouts and comparisons should you employ? In deciding which analytical frameworks to emphasize, you should use the criterion of maximizing the usefulness of the performance data in terms of the overall purpose of the monitoring system. As illustrated in chapter 7, a great variety of reporting formats is available for presenting performance data, ranging from spreadsheet tables, graphs, and symbols to pictorial and dashboard displays; the objective should be to employ elements of any or all of these to present the data in the most intelligible and meaningful manner.

Furthermore, computer software applications have to be developed to support the performance management system from data entry and data processing through to the generation and distribution of reports, which increasingly can be done electronically. As discussed in chapter 7, a variety of software packages may be useful along these lines, including spreadsheet, database management, and graphical programs, as well as special software packages available commercially that have been designed specifically to support performance monitoring systems. Often some combination of these packages can be used most effectively. Thus, system designers have to determine whether their performance monitoring system would function more effectively with existing software adapted to support the system or with original software developed expressly for that system.

A final element of system specification is to assign personnel responsibilities for maintaining the performance management system when it is put into use. As discussed in chapter 15, this includes assigning responsibilities for data entry, which might well be dispersed among various operating units or field offices (or both), as well as for data processing, quality assurance, and reporting. Usually primary responsibility for supporting the system is assigned to a staff unit concerned with planning and evaluation, management information systems, budget and finance, management analysis, quality improvement, or customer service, depending on the principal use for which the system is designed. In addition, clarification of who is responsible for reviewing and using the performance data is needed, and establishment of deadlines within reporting cycles for data entry, processing, distribution of reports, and review.

Step Ten: Conduct a Pilot If Necessary

Sometimes it is possible to move directly from design to implementation of performance management systems, particularly in small agencies where responsibilities for inputting data and maintaining the system will not be fragmented or with simple, straightforward systems in which there are no unanswered questions about feasibility. However, in some cases, it may be a good idea to pilot the system, or elements of it at least, before committing to full-scale implementation. Most often, pilots are conducted when there is a need to test the feasibility of collecting certain kinds of data, demonstrate the workability of the administrative arrangements for more complex systems, get a clearer idea of the level of effort involved in implementing a new system, testing the software platform, or simply validating newly designed surveys or other data collection instruments. When there are real concerns about these kinds of issues, it often makes sense to conduct a pilot, perhaps on a smaller scale or sample basis, to get a better understanding of how well a system works and of particular problems that need to be addressed before implementing the system across the board. You can then make appropriate adjustments to the mix of indicators, data collection efforts, and software applications in order to increase the probability that the system will work effectively.

Step Eleven: Implement Full-Scale System

With or without benefit of a pilot, implementing any new management system presents challenges. Implementation of a performance management system means collecting and processing all the required data within deadlines, running the data and disseminating performance reports to the designated users on a timely basis, and reviewing the data to track performance and use this information as an additional input for decision making. It also includes initiating quality assurance procedures and instituting checks in data collection procedures where practical to identify stray values and otherwise erroneous data.

With larger or more complex systems, especially those involving data input from numerous people in the field, some training may well be essential for reliable data. As discussed in chapter 15, the most important factor for guaranteeing the successful implementation of a new monitoring system is a clear commitment from top management, or the highest management level that has commissioned a particular system, to providing reliable data and using the system effectively as a management tool.

Step Twelve: Use, Modify, and Evaluate the System

No matter how carefully a system may have been implemented, problems are likely to emerge in terms of data completeness, quality control, software applications, or the generation of reports. The level of effort required to support the system, particularly in terms of data collection and data entry, may also be a real concern as well as an unknown at the outset. Thus, over the first few cycles—typically months, quarters, or years—it is important to closely monitor the operation of the system itself and evaluate how well it is working. And when implementation and maintenance problems are identified, they need to be resolved quickly and effectively.

Managers must begin to assess the usefulness of the measurement system as a tool for managing more effectively and improving decisions, performance, and accountability. If a performance management system is not providing worthwhile information and helping gain a good reading on performance and improve substantive results, managers should look for ways to strengthen the measures and the data or even the overall system. This is often a matter of fine-tuning particular indicators or data collection procedures, adding or eliminating certain measures, or making adjustments in reporting frequencies or presentation formats to provide more useful information, but it could also involve more basic changes in how the data are reported and used in management and decision-making processes. Depending on what the performance data show, experience in using the system might suggest the need to modify targets or performance standards or even to make changes in the programmatic goals and objectives that the measurement system is built around.

Evaluation must be a component of performance management because understanding the casual relationship between the activities the organization carries out and the results it achieves is necessary to learning, improvement, and accountability. It is the follow-up step whereby the results of programs and expenditures can be assessed according to expected results. Evaluations, discussed in chapter 10, rely on developing evaluation objectives that program results can be measured against. A basic performance evaluation has the following phases:

- Define the evaluation question.
- Establish a data collection strategy based on the question.
- Collect the data, which may require more than a single tool or method.
- Analyze and report the findings, and make recommendations for program improvement.

Data validation, discussed in chapter 7, is an important component of evaluation, and a performance management system will not function well without valid and reliable data. Staff must be trained in both the importance of having reliable data and how to test for reliability. If the validity of data is not addressed, performance management systems could create and communicate inaccurate pictures of actual performance.

Step Thirteen: Share the Results with Stakeholders

Stakeholder involvement is an important component of performance management. As discussed in chapter 13, developing a stakeholder feedback effort will help all parties gain understanding and develop and maintain support for the public and nonprofit programs. By inviting feedback and questions, not just providing information, a good communication process can counter inaccurate information and faulty perceptions by rapidly identifying inaccuracies and making sure that accurate and relevant information is provided. It is important to note that stakeholders may also consist of other public, nonprofit, and private sector actors, as many public services are the joint efforts of collaborations between governmental and nongovernmental actors.

A Flexible Process

Developing a performance management systems is both an art and a science. It is a science because it must flow systematically from the purpose of the system and the parameters within which it must be designed and because the particulars of the system must be based on an objective logic underlying the operation of the agency, program, or service delivery system to be monitored. However, it is also an art because it is a creative process in terms of defining measures, reporting formats, and software applications and it must be carried out in a way that is sensitive to the needs of people who will be using it and that will build credibility and support for the system along the way.

There is perhaps no precise "one right way" to develop a performance management system. Success will stem in part from tailoring the design and implementation process to the particular needs of the organization or program in question. Although the steps outlined in this chapter are presented in a logical sequence, this should not be viewed as a rigid process. Indeed, as is true of any other creative effort, designing and implementing performance measurement systems may at times be more iterative than sequential. Although the steps presented in figure 2.1 are all essential, integrating them is much more important than performing them in a particular sequence.

Utilization is the primary test of the worth of any performance management system. Thus, performing all the steps in the design and implementation process with a clear focus on the purpose of a particular monitoring system and an eye on the needs of its intended users is critical to ensuring that the performance measures add value to the agency or the program. To this end, soliciting input along the way from people who will be working with the system—field personnel, systems specialists, analysts, and managers—as well as others who might have a stake in the system, such as clients or governing boards, can be invaluable in building credibility and ownership of the system once it is in place.

References

Kamensky, J., & Fountain, J. (2008). Creating and sustaining a results-oriented performance management framework. In P. DeLancer Julnes, F. Berry, M. Aristigueta, & K. Yang (Eds.), *International handbook of practice-based performance management* (pp. 489–508). Thousand Oaks, CA: Sage.

Niven, P. (2003). *Balanced scorecard step by step for government and nonprofit agencies.* Hoboken, NJ: Wiley.

Van Dooren, W. Bouckaert, G., & Halligan, J. (2010). *Performance management in the public sector.* Abingdon, Oxon, OX: Routledge.

PART TWO

METHODOLOGICAL ELEMENTS OF PERFORMANCE MEASUREMENT

Performance management can be challenging from a methodological perspective, and the chapters in part 2 address key methodological concerns in some detail. Focusing on performance measurement as the critical element of the larger performance management process, the first question to be addressed is what to measure. Chapter 3 discusses the use of program logic models to identify outcomes and other performance criteria and then presents various classes of measures, including measures of output, efficiency, productivity, effectiveness, service quality, customer satisfaction, and cost-effectiveness. Chapter 4 focuses on tying performance measures to programmatic or organizational goals and objectives.

Second is the question of how to measure these various dimensions of performance. Chapter 5 discusses the definition and systematic assessment of operational indicators in terms of validity and reliability, timeliness, usefulness, and a number of other criteria.

Third is the question of what to do with the performance data once they have been collected. Chapter 6 illustrates a number of kinds of tabular, graphical, and pictorial formats for displaying performance data as interesting and useful information. Finally, chapter 7 discusses the analysis of performance data, emphasizing the importance of comparisons—of current performance levels against past or recent trends, of actual performance against targets, across organizational or programmatic units, or against other agencies or programs, for example—as well as more in-depth analytics in order to provide real information in an appropriate context.

## CHAPTER THREE

DEVELOPING A PERFORMANCE FRAMEWORK

Program Logic Models and Performance Measures

What are the aspects of program or organizational performance that would be important to monitor on a regular basis in a performance management system? What does the effectiveness of a particular public program or the quality of the services it provides entail? What does efficiency mean with respect to a given program, or the productivity of employees working in a service delivery system?

In order for a measurement system to be useful, it must focus on the most appropriate aspects of performance. To ensure that a measurement system is results oriented as opposed to being data driven, it should be guided by a clear performance framework, a structure that identifies the parameters of program or organizational performance and may outline the presumed relationships among them. This chapter addresses the what of performance measurement: What are the important dimensions of program performance to address, and what are the principal kinds of performance measures to track them? More specifically, the chapter discusses one principal type of performance framework, program logic models. These logic models focus primarily on program performance, reflect a results-oriented perspective, and are appropriate for programs delivered by both public and nonprofit organizations. Chapter 4 then discusses goal structures as performance frameworks, a very different yet complementary, and by no means incompatible, type of approach.

Program Logic

Developing useful measures of program performance requires a clear understanding of what a program does and the results it is intended to accomplish (Poister, 1978; Wholey, 1979; Broom, Harris, Jackson, & Marshall, 1998; Sowa, Selden, & Sandfort, 2004; McDavid & Hawthorn, 2006). Program logic models are schematic diagrams that represent the logic underlying a program's design, indicating how various components are expected to interact, the goods or services they produce, and how they generate the desired results—the logic by which program activities are expected to lead to targeted outcomes (Poister, 1978; Poister, McDavid & Magoun, 1979; Hatry, Van Houten, Plantz, & Greenway, 1996; Funnell & Rogers, 2011; Knowlton & Phillips, 2012). Clarifying desired outcomes and the underlying logic by which they are expected to be achieved is essential for effective performance management, and a good logic model can provide the scaffolding for building a performance measurement system (Frechtling, 2007). Once a logic model has been developed and adopted, the relevant performance measures can be identified systematically and confidently.

Program Logic Models

Public programs should be planned and managed with an eye toward specifying and achieving desirable results. They should be viewed as interventions involving service delivery or enforcement activity designed to address some problem, meet some need, or have a favorable impact on some unsatisfactory condition in a way that has been defined as serving the public interest. The positive impacts so generated constitute the program's intended results, which would justify support for the program in the first place. A program's intended results, or its outcomes, occur "out there" in the community, within a targeted area or target population, or across the nation or state or local jurisdiction generally, not inside the program itself or the agency or organizational unit that operates it. Obviously the intended results should be clearly understood and monitored on a regular basis. If a programmatic entity cannot articulate worthwhile results and provide evidence that programmatic activity is indeed producing them, continued support should be questioned at the very least.

Thus, any sound program design must be based on a set of assumptions regarding the services it provides, the clients it serves or the cases it

FIGURE 3.1 GENERIC PROGRAM LOGIC MODEL

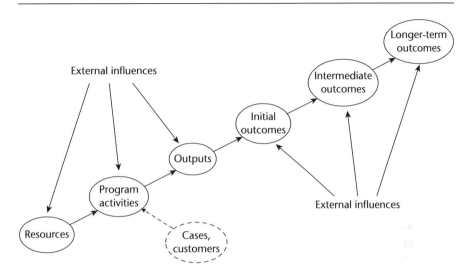

treats, its intended results, and the logic of how the use of resources in particular programmatic activities is expected to produce these results. This set of assumptions constitutes a theory of action or intervention logic that embodies a theory of change regarding the way programmatic processes bring about desired changes in individuals, groups, or communities that can be represented schematically by a logic model (Funnell & Rogers, 2011). Figure 3.1 shows a generic program logic model that can help clarify these assumptions for any public program. Such a model can be used as an organizing tool for identifying the critical variables in program design, the role each plays in the underlying logic, and the presumed relationships among them.

Resources are used to carry on program activities and provide services that produce immediate products, or outputs. These outputs are intended to lead to outcomes, which are the substantive changes, improvements, or benefits that are supposed to result from the program. Frequently these outcomes themselves occur in sequence, running from initial outcomes to intermediate and longer-term outcomes. Usually the logic underlying a program design is also predicated on a flow of customers who are served by a program or a set of cases the program deals with. In addition, it is important to recognize the external factors in a program's environment or operating context, which may influence its performance.

The sets of activities that make up the work of most public programs involve the provision of services or the enforcement of laws or regulations (or both). For example, the principal activities in a neighborhood health clinic might include conducting physical examinations and well-baby checks, giving inoculations, and prescribing treatments and medications for illnesses and chronic conditions; in the criminal investigations unit of a local police department, the principal activities would include examining crime scenes, interviewing witnesses, examining physical evidence, checking out leads, and gathering additional information. These programmatic activities and the outputs they produce need to be identified clearly, whether they are carried on by public sector employees working in the program or by private firms or nonprofit organizations that are contracted to carry out service delivery.

The principal resources that most public and nonprofit programs use are personnel, physical facilities, equipment, materials, and contract services. Personnel may include volunteers as well as employees, and sometimes it is helpful to break them down into occupational categories, tracking, for example, the numbers of uniformed patrol officers, detectives, crime lab personnel, and support staff in order to gauge labor productivity in a local police department.

In many public programs, especially those carried on by production-type agencies, the work performed and the results obtained apply to cases or groups of cases that come into the program or are treated by the program in some fashion. Frequently the cases are the program's primary customers (or consumers or clients). This is almost always true for human service and educational programs—patients treated in public hospitals, children served by a foster care program, clients aided in a counseling program, or students enrolled in a community college, for example—but customers are also often the principal cases in other types of programs, for instance, disabled persons using demand-responsive transportation services or the number of families living in dwelling units provided by a public housing authority.

However, with some programs, the most likely definition of cases may be something other than customers. For example, while the customers of a state highway maintenance program are individual motorists, it makes more sense to think of the cases to be processed as consisting of road miles or road segments to be maintained. Similarly, the implicit customer of the Keep Nebraska Beautiful program is the public at large, but the "cases" treated by this program consist of small, targeted geographical areas. While the cases processed by a state's driver's license permitting program are individual applicants, the customers, the cases processed by a state's vehicle registration program, are probably best defined as the vehicles rather than the customers who are registering them. Often a public or nonprofit program may define its cases in more than one way. For example, the US Internal Revenue Service may consider the individual customer as the case with respect to its tax preparation assistance function but focus on the tax return as the case in terms of its collections and auditing functions.

It is important to identify external influences in thinking about a program's logic because they may be critical in either facilitating or impeding success. Many of these external influences concern client characteristics or the magnitude or severity of need for the program, but they are by no means limited to that. Any factor or condition—physical, social, economic, financial, psychological, or cultural—that is likely to influence program performance and is largely beyond the control of the program or agency may be relevant to track as an external influence. For example, winter weather conditions may explain differences in the performance of a highway maintenance program from year to year, while differences in labor market conditions may explain differences in the effectiveness of similar job training programs in different localities, and variation in local industrial base, land use patterns, and commuting behavior are likely to influence the federal Environmental Protection Agency's success in enforcing clean air standards in different parts of the country. Such external factors are important to take into account in clarifying a program's underlying logic because they can be extremely helpful in interpreting the meaning of performance data.

Outputs versus Outcomes

The most important distinction to be made in identifying program logic is that between outputs and outcomes. Outputs represent what a program actually does and what it produces directly; outcomes are the results it generates. Operations managers appropriately focus on the production of high-quality outputs in an efficient manner, but managers who are concerned with overall performance must look beyond outputs to outcomes because they represent program effectiveness. In terms of program logic, outputs have little inherent value because they do not constitute direct benefits, but they are essential because they lead directly to these benefits or trigger the causal sequences of changes that lead to the desired results.

Outputs are best thought of as necessary but insufficient conditions for success. They are the immediate products or services produced by a program, and without an appropriate mix and quality of outputs, a program will not be able to generate its intended results. However, if the underlying program logic is flawed—if the assumptions of causal connections between outputs and results do not hold up in reality—the desired outcomes will not materialize, at least not as a result of the program. Usually the production of outputs is largely, although not exclusively, under the control of program managers, but outcomes tend to be influenced more strongly by a wider array of external factors beyond the program's control. Thus, the production of outputs is no guarantee that outcomes will result, and it is important therefore to measure outcomes directly in order to monitor program performance. Table 3.1 shows typical outputs and outcomes for a few selected public services.

Outputs often represent the amount of work performed or the volume of activity completed, such as hours patrolled by the police, miles of highway constructed, AIDS education seminars conducted or antibody tests given, or the number of vocational training classes conducted in a juvenile justice boot camp. Sometimes outputs are measured in terms of the number of clients or cases treated, for example, the number of crimes investigated or calls for service responded to by the police, the number of AIDS patients given treatment or counseling, or the number of youths discharged from juvenile boot camps.

Outcomes are the substantive results generated by producing these outputs. Criminal investigations and arrests do not really count for much— for instance, if the police are not able to solve the crimes they are working on, and reconstructed highway segments do not serve any particular public interest or create value if they do not result in improved flow of traffic and reduced travel times for the motorists using them. Similarly, AIDS-awareness seminars are not particularly worthwhile if they do not lead to decreases in the kinds of risky behavior—unprotected sex and use of dirty drug needles, for example—that spread the HIV virus. And training units and hours spent in after-care activity are not effective in attaining their rehabilitative purposes if the youths discharged from boot camps are not productively engaged in school or work and refraining from further criminal activity. Outcomes are the ultimate criteria for gauging program effectiveness, but as direct products of program activity, outputs are critical for achieving intended outcomes.

Given this careful distinction, however, it must be noted that the connections between outputs and outcomes are often more fluid than a simple dichotomy. It could be argued, for example, that arrests made by the police as the result of criminal investigations are really outcomes

TABLE 3.1 ILLUSTRATIONS OF OUTCOMES VERSUS OUTPUTS

Program or Activity	Outputs	Outcomes
Crime control	Hours of patrol conducted	Reduction in crimes committed
	Response to calls for service	Reduction in injuries and fatalities due to crimes
	Crimes investigated	
	Arrest made	Reduction in property damage or loss due to crime
	Crime solved	
Highway maintenance	Project designs completed	Improved traffic flow
	Highway miles constructed	Reduced travel times
	Highway miles reconstructed	
AIDS prevention and treatment	Seminars conducted	Increased awareness and knowledge regarding AIDS
	Brochures mailed	
	AIDS antibody tests given	Decrease in risky behavior
	Hot-line calls responded to	Decrease in incidence and prevalence of AIDS
	Group counseling sessions conducted	Reduction in AIDS-related fatalities
	AIDS patients treated	
	Number of referrals given to clients	Reduction in number of babies testing positively for HIV
Juvenile justice boot camps	Physical training units completed	Fewer legislation passed
	Educational units completed	Policy changes implemented
	Vocational training units completed	New programs authorized
		Changes in program strategy or design implemented
	Youths discharged	
	After-care activity hours conducted	Alternative service delivery arrangements implemented
Policy research, planning, and evaluation	Policy analyses completed	Proposed legislation passed
	"White papers" distributed	Policy changes implemented
	Policy briefings conducted	New programs authorized
	Program designed and revised	Changes in programs strategy or design implemented
	Needs assessment completed	
	New program plans developed	Alternative service delivery arrangements implemented
	Client surveys conducted	
	Program evaluations completed	

rather than outputs, although certainly not the ultimate outcome of their work. Similarly, it might make sense to think of services provided as outputs but to consider services consumed as outcomes. For example, the number of training programs offered might be considered as a program's principal output, while the number of participants completing these programs could be thought of as an outcome. The number of participants trained, however, is probably a better reflection of the amount of activity completed, or an output. Rather than a very strict, dichotomous distinction between outputs and outcomes, what is important is an identification of the real results targeted by a program and the sequence of accomplishments that must occur in order to achieve them. This might be thought of as a results chain—a sequence from outputs to impacts, or the logic of program activities, outputs, initial outcomes, intermediate outcomes, and longer-term outcomes, the format used in this book.

The distinction between outputs and outcomes may also vary depending on the perspective from which they are viewed. For a staff support function such as policy research, planning, and evaluation in a federal agency, for example, typical outputs might be policy analyses completed, program designs revised, needs assessments completed, and program evaluations conducted. In some cases, producing these outputs might be intended to lead to such outcomes as additional legislation passed or new programs authorized by the Congress. Whereas the implementation of policy changes, revised program strategies, or service delivery arrangements by the agency in response to recommendations from the policy research would constitute outputs for the agency as a whole, these same measures would constitute outcomes for the office of policy research, planning, and evaluation itself.

Diverse Logic Models

Outputs, outcomes, and other elements can be identified in logic models that may be as general or detailed, or as simple or complex, as needed. Although it is always a mistake to bend reality to fit a preconceived model, the kind of program logic models presented here are quite flexible and can be adjusted to represent any public or nonprofit program. For example, the set of program components to be included can range from only one to numerous activities, and the connections between outputs and desired outcomes may be very direct, or they can occur through numerous initial and intermediate results. Similarly, the strands of logic that connect

FIGURE 3.2 CRISIS STABILIZATION LOGIC MODEL

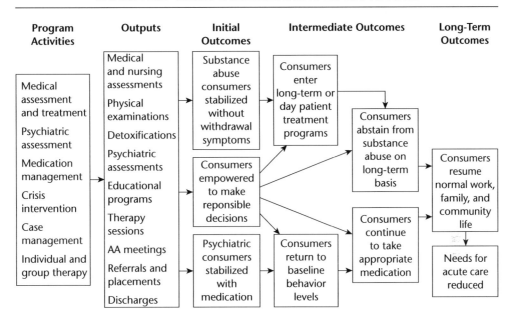

outputs to various outcomes can converge at different points and in different sequences along the way.

Although these models show the logic generally moving from left to right, they are not necessarily designed to represent the chronological order in which treatments are provided. These are logic models, not flow-charts that show the sequence in which individual cases move through a system.

A Crisis Stabilization Unit

Figure 3.2 shows a logic model for a two-county crisis stabilization unit in suburban Atlanta, Georgia. The mission of this program is to provide effective and safe stabilization to persons experiencing symptoms of decompensation due to psychiatric illnesses or substance abuse or dependence. The consumers treated by the program have subacute psychiatric diagnoses or a history of continuous substance abuse such that abrupt stoppage would cause physiological withdrawal. The principal resources of the unit are the facilities and supplies, along with medical, professional, and support staff. The services they provide include medical assessment and treatment, psychiatric assessment, medication management, crisis intervention, case management, and individual and group therapy.

The crisis stabilization unit produces a variety of outputs that reflect the work performed in providing services, such as medical assessments and nursing assessments conducted, physical examinations conducted, medical detoxifications completed, psychiatric assessments, education program modules, therapy sessions, Alcoholics Anonymous (AA) meetings, and referrals or placements. The initial outcomes produced by these service outputs are substance abuse consumers who have been stabilized through detoxification without physiological withdrawal symptoms and the number of psychiatric consumers who have been stabilized with medication. A complementary initial outcome is consumers who have been empowered through counseling, educational programs, and support groups to make more responsible decisions regarding their own behavior. For the substance abusers, the intermediate outcomes are that they enter appropriate long-term or day-patient treatment programs and continue to abstain from drugs and alcohol over the long run. For the psychiatric consumers, the intermediate outcomes are that after being discharged from the unit, they return to baseline or desired behavior levels and continue to take their appropriate medications. For both clientele groups, the intended longer-term outcomes are that they resume normal patterns of work, family, and community life and that all of this results in reduced needs for acute care for them.

A Vocational Rehabilitation Program

Figure 3.3 represents the logic underlying a vocational rehabilitation program provided by a state human services department. The clients of this program are individuals with disabilities due to birth defects, injuries, or progressive long-term illnesses that present special challenges in finding work and holding a job. The mission of the program is to help these clients prepare for resuming their occupations or learning new ones, securing suitable jobs, and remaining employed. To pursue this mission, the vocational rehabilitation agency provides a number of interdependent services, including counseling and guidance, occupational and related training, the provision of specialized equipment, employer development and job development, placement assistance, and on-the-job evaluations of clients' ability to do the required work.

The initial outcome of all this activity is that clients have developed the knowledge and skills needed to engage in occupations that are viable for them and that they apply for suitable jobs in the competitive marketplace or, in some cases, sheltered workshops. The intermediate outcome

FIGURE 3.3 VOCATIONAL REHABILITATION LOGIC MODEL

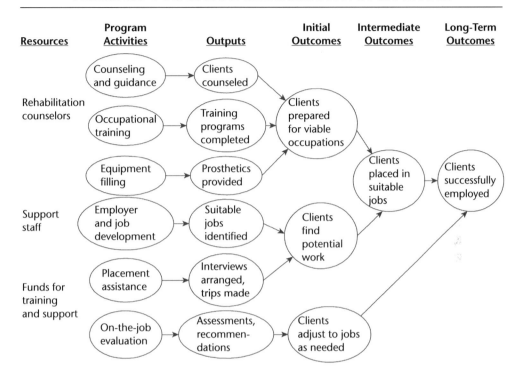

is that the clients are placed in suitable jobs. Once clients have secured suitable jobs, the program may provide on-the-job evaluations with recommendations to assist them in adjusting to new jobs. This is all aimed at helping clients to continue working in suitable jobs and being successfully employed over the long run. To the extent this longer-term outcome is achieved, the program's mission is being met effectively.

State Highway Safety Program: A Supraprogram Logic Model

Individual public programs often cluster into larger sets of related programs in which their results chains interact in pursuit of broader goals even though they are delivered separately by different agencies or organizational units. For example, figure 3.4 shows a logic model for a state government's highway safety program consisting of four major components: driver licensing, highway patrol, safety promotion, and traffic engineering. In some states, all four of these functions are the responsibility of a single agency, but that is often not the case. In Georgia, for instance, driver

FIGURE 3.4 STATE HIGHWAY PROGRAM LOGIC MODEL

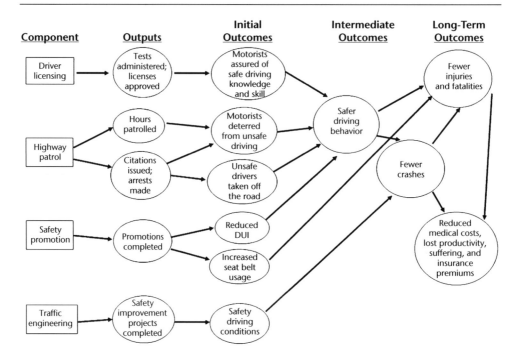

licensing is the responsibility of the Department of Driver Services, highway patrol is performed by the Georgia State Patrol, safety promotion efforts are led by the Governor's Office of Highway Safety, and traffic engineering is within the purview of the Georgia Department of Transportation.

However, since these four functions are collectively concerned with reducing highway crashes, injuries, and fatalities resulting from crashes and the cost and suffering that derives from them, a central executive agency such as a state's office of planning and budget might well benefit from monitoring their performance on a coordinated basis. While each of these agencies delivers its own outputs, which are expected to generate particular kinds of initial outcomes, the driver licensing, highway patrol, and safety promotion programs are all aimed at ensuring safe driving behavior as an intermediate outcome, and the safety promotion program is also expected to lead directly to fewer highway-related injuries and fatalities, while the traffic engineering program is intended to lead directly to the longer-term outcome of fewer highway crashes. The combined logic also holds that the first three programs will contribute indirectly to fewer crashes, and all four programs should lead to the longer-term outcome of reduced costs and suffering resulting from highway crashes. Tracking the performance of these four programs in concert as they form a larger system provides a more comprehensive picture of the effectiveness of a state's overall highway safety program.

The Sexually Transmitted Disease Prevention System

Traditionally sexually transmitted disease (STD) prevention programs in the United States operated through direct service delivery—screening, diagnosis, treatment, and partner services—provided by local STD clinics supported in part with funding from the US Centers for Disease Control (CDC) primarily through state health departments. A decade or so ago, however, as a result of environmental and program assessments, CDC staff became convinced that this approach was no longer adequate, due largely to increasingly fragmented health care delivery systems, the lack of coordination among related health programs at the local level, and the fact that the clinics did not have a strong track record in reaching some of the most critical target populations. Thus, they concluded that STD prevention programs needed to implement a broader range of strategies to leverage impact on a variety of other stakeholders, such as managed care organizations, private medical practices, schools, detention and corrections facilities, and community-based organizations in order to reach out to at-risk persons and effectively contain the spread of syphilis, gonorrhea, and chlamydia.

Figure 3.5 shows the logic model that was developed as the performance framework for the STD prevention system envisioned under this new paradigm. It is important to understand that this was an early attempt to model the comprehensive national STD prevention system rather than the CDC's STD prevention program itself. This model represents the logic by which a variety of system components bring about intermediate outcomes involving safer-sex behaviors, increased use of condoms, and decreased duration of STD infections, which are expected to lead to decreased exposure, incidence, and prevalence of the targeted STDs.

While these longer-term outcomes continued to be monitored in terms of incidence and prevalence rates, however, interest began to focus more on the earlier-stage outputs and immediate outcomes so that the CDC could begin to monitor the extent to which state and local STD prevention programs were having impacts on the larger system in productive ways. This would require local grantees to report STD prevention- and control-related activities on the part of schools, health networks, and even jails in addition to their own activities and outputs.

FIGURE 3.5 STD PREVENTION PROGRAM LOGIC MODEL

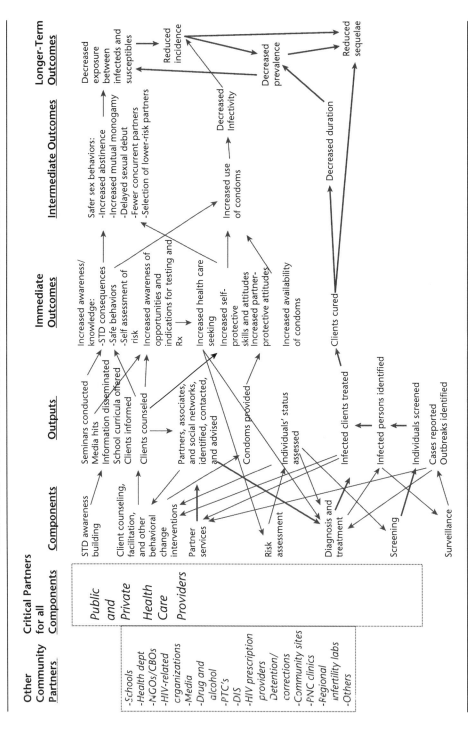

Note: NGO stands for nongovernmental organizations and CBO stands for community-based organizations.

Performance Measures

The purpose of developing a logic model is to clarify what goes into a program, identify its customers, pinpoint the services it provides, identify the immediate products or outputs it produces, and specify the outcomes it is supposed to generate. Once this logic has been articulated, in a narrative or in a schematic, or both, the most relevant measures of program performance can be identified on a systematic basis. Although they are often combined into different categories, for the most part the relevant types of performance measures are measures of outputs, efficiency and productivity, service quality, outcomes, cost-effectiveness, and customer satisfaction. One additional type of performance measure, system productivity indicators, can also be included in many measurement systems.

Depending on the purpose of a given performance measurement system and the level of detail on which the monitoring may focus, various of these types of performance measures will be of paramount importance, but it usually makes sense to consider all of them in designing a performance measurement system. For any given program, all of these types of performance measures can generally be derived directly from the logic model. In addition, other types of measures, in particular resources and workload measures, are often monitored on a regular basis in performance measurement systems, even though they are not usually considered to be performance measures in their own right. Beyond performance measures, external variables representing environmental or contextual factors, including needs indicators that are likely to influence programmatic results, might also be included in performance measurement systems.

Output Measures

Output measures are important because they represent the direct products of public agencies or programs. They often measure volumes of programmed activity, such as the number of training programs conducted by a job training program, the number of seminars presented by an AIDS prevention program, the miles of new four-lane highways constructed by a state transportation department, or the hours of routine patrol logged in by a local police department. Outputs are often measured in terms of the amount of work that is performed—for example, the number of detoxification procedures completed by a crisis stabilization unit, the number of job interviews arranged for clients of a vocational rehabilitation program, or the gallons of patching material used on roads by highway maintenance crews. Finally, output measures sometimes represent the number of cases that are dealt with by a program, such as the number of flight segments handled by the nation's air traffic control program, the number of AIDS clients who receive counseling, or the number of crimes investigated by the police.

Outputs are sometimes measured at different stages of the service delivery process, and we can think of outputs chains occurring in some programs. For instance, the outputs of crime investigation are usually specified as the number of initial responses to crimes reported, the number of crimes investigated, and the number of arrests made. Juvenile justice boot camps often measure the numbers of juveniles under their charge who complete various training modules and receive other services and the number of juveniles who are discharged from the camps, as well as the number of after-care visits or activities reported. All of these stages of outputs are relevant to track because they provide some indication of the amount of activity or work completed or the number of cases being treated in some way.

Efficiency and Productivity Measures

Efficiency measures focus on the operating efficiency of a program or organization, relating outputs to the resources used in producing them. They are most frequently operationalized as unit cost measures expressed as the ratio of outputs to the dollar cost of the collective resources consumed in producing them. Thus, the cost per crime investigated, the cost per highway project design completed, the cost per AIDS seminar conducted, the cost per ton of residential refuse collected, and the cost per training program completed are all standard efficiency measures. While the operating efficiency of the air traffic control program could be measured by the cost per flight segment handled, a measure of the efficiency of a state board of nursing's disciplinary program would be the cost per investigation completed.

It may be appropriate to track a variety of efficiency measures for a given program. For example, the cost per psychiatric assessment completed, the cost per detoxification procedure conducted, the cost per therapy session conducted, and the cost per support group meeting might all be relevant for a crisis stabilization unit if it has an activity-based accounting system that can track the actual costs for these separate activities. More general measures are often employed, such as the cost per highway lane mile maintained or the cost per case in a child support enforcement program, but they are really based more on workload than outputs. One particular efficiency measure that is often used along these lines is the per diem—the cost per client per day in such residential programs as hospitals, crisis stabilization units, juvenile detention centers, and group homes for mentally disabled persons operated by nonprofit agencies.

While operating efficiency is most commonly expressed by these unit cost measures, however, it is also measured in terms of cycle times, the average time required to produce a single unit of output. With respect to a driver licensing program, for example, the process for renewing licenses in a given drivers' licensing center might generate a renewed license every two minutes on average, while the average time required for a state board of nursing to complete an investigation regarding a reported violation of the authorized scope of practice for nurses licensed in a given state might be 168 days. Such time-based efficiency measures can also be expressed as the volume of output produced in a certain period of time, for example, the feet of guardrail installed per day by a highway maintenance program or the number of claims cleared per month by a disability adjudication process.

Productivity indicators are a special type of efficiency measure that focus on the rate of output production per some specific unit of resource, usually staff or employees. Since public service delivery tends to be labor intensive, labor productivity measures are prevalent in performance monitoring systems focusing on the production of outputs. To be meaningful, they also must be defined in terms of some particular unit of time. For example, the number of flight segments handled per air traffic controller per hour and the number of lane-miles of highway resurfaced per maintenance crew per day are typical measures of labor productivity, as is the number of nursing violation investigations completed per investigator per year.

In some cases, labor productivity ratios use the unit of measurement in both the numerator and denominator, for example, the number of task hours completed per production hour worked on a highway maintenance activity or the number of billable hours of work completed per production hour worked in a state government printing plant. Beyond labor productivity, in some cases the specific resource used as the basis for a productivity indicator may measure equipment rather than personnel, for example, the number of standard images printed per large press per hour in a government printing office or the number of revenue vehicle miles operated per month per bus in a public transit agency's fleet.

Staff-to-client ratios are sometimes loosely interpreted as productivity measures, but this may be misleading. For example, the number of in-house consumers per full-time staff member of a crisis stabilization unit may represent productivity because those consumers are all receiving treatment. However, the number of cases per adjuster in a state workers' compensation program does not really provide much information about the productivity of those employees because some or many of those clients or cases may generate very little, if any, activity. The number of clients per employee in a vocational rehabilitation program may not be particularly useful either, again because the services being provided vary so widely from one client to the next, but the number of clients counseled per vocational rehabilitation counselor would be more meaningful because it represents the amount of work performed per staff member.

Service Quality Measures

The concept of quality pertains most directly to service delivery processes and outputs because they define the service that is being provided. When we think about measuring outputs, we tend to think first of quantity—how much service is being provided—but it is equally important to examine the quality of outputs as well. However, this is not primarily a distinction between hard and soft measures. While service quality is usually assessed subjectively at an individual level, performance measurement systems track quality using more objective, quantitative data in the aggregate.

The most common dimensions of the quality of public and nonprofit services are turnaround time, accuracy, thoroughness, accessibility, convenience, courtesy, and safety. For example, people who are trying to renew their driver's license tend to be most concerned about the accessibility of the location where they do this, the convenience afforded in completing the process, the total time including waiting time that it takes to complete the transaction, and, of course, the accuracy of the paperwork that is processed (so that they won't have to return or repeat part of the process). In the Federal Aviation Administration's air traffic control program, the most important indicator of service quality is the number of controller errors (instances in which controllers allow pilots to breach minimum distances to be maintained between airplanes) per 1 million flight segments handled.

Frequently measures of service quality are based on standard operating procedures that are prescribed for service delivery processes. Quality ratings of highway maintenance crews, for instance, are usually defined by the extent to which the establishment of the work site, handling of traffic through or around the work site, and the actual work of patching potholes or resurfacing pavement comply with prescribed operating procedures for such jobs. Juvenile justice detention centers have operating procedures regarding such processes as safety inspections, fire prevention, key control, perimeter checks, the security of eating utensils, supervision, and the progressive use of physical force or chemical agents in order to ensure the security of the facility and the safety of the juveniles in their custody. Quality assurance ratings are really compliance measures, defined as the extent to which such processes are performed in compliance with prescribed procedures. Yet other quality indicators, such as the number of escapes from juvenile detention facilities or reported instances of child abuse, probably more meaningful in terms of overall program performance, are defined more directly in terms of desired outputs, juveniles detained safely and securely in this example.

Outcome Measures

It is fair to say that outcome measures constitute the most important category of performance measures because they represent the degree to which a program is producing its intended outcomes and achieving the desired results. These may relate to initial, intermediate, or longer-term outcomes. Outcome measures for the air traffic control program, for example, might include the number of near misses reported by pilots, the number of midair collisions, and the number of fatalities per 100 million revenue passenger–miles flown.

The most important outcome measures tie back to the basic purpose of a program. For example, the crisis stabilization unit exists to stabilize persons with psychiatric or drug-induced mental crises and help them modify behaviors in order to avoid falling into these same circumstances again. Thus, a key effectiveness measure might be the percentage of all initial admissions that constitute readmissions within thirty days. Similarly, the most important indicator of the effectiveness of a vocational rehabilitation program is probably the number or percentage of clients who have been successfully employed in the same job for six months. Along these same lines, the most relevant effectiveness measures for a juvenile detention center are probably the percentage of discharged youth who are attending school or engaged in gainful employment and the percentage who have not recidivated back into the criminal justice system within one year of having been discharged. Effectiveness measures for an AIDS prevention program would be likely to include morbidity and mortality rates for AIDS, along with the percentage of newborn babies who test positive for HIV.

Cost-Effectiveness Measures

Whereas indicators of operating efficiency are unit costs of producing outputs, cost-effectiveness measures relate cost to outcome measures. Thus, for the crisis stabilization unit, cost-effectiveness would be measured as the cost per stabilized consumer. For the vocational rehabilitation program, the most relevant indicators of cost-effectiveness would be the cost per client placed in suitable employment and the cost per client successfully employed for six months or more. The cost-effectiveness of criminal investigation activity would probably be measured as the cost per crime solved.

Effectiveness measures often become more esoteric and present more difficult methodological challenges in operationalizing indicators. For example, the cost-effectiveness of highway construction might well be conceptualized as the cost per person-hour of reduced travel time, while the most relevant cost-effectiveness indicator for an AIDS prevention program would probably be the cost per AIDS fatality avoided. Both of these make complete sense in terms of program logic, but they are difficult to operationalize.

Customer Satisfaction Measures

Measures of customer satisfaction are often closely related to service quality indicators, but the two are not identical and should be considered separate categories of performance measures. Similarly, customer satisfaction measures are often associated with effectiveness measures, but they provide a different perspective on overall program performance. For example, measures of customer satisfaction with a vocational rehabilitation program might be based on data from client evaluation forms asking how satisfied they were with training programs they participated in, counseling services they received, and assistance that was provided to them in finding a job. These all focus on program outputs. In addition, clients who have been placed in jobs might be surveyed after several months to assess their satisfaction with these jobs, focusing on program effectiveness. These customer satisfaction ratings may or may not square with more tangible measures of program outputs and effectiveness, but they do provide a complementary perspective.

One way of gauging customer satisfaction is to track complaints. For example, a public library system might monitor the number of complaints received from patrons per week in each branch library. Second, some public and nonprofit agencies use customer response cards to solicit immediate feedback regarding specific instances of service delivery. A government printing office, for instance, might track the percentage of its customers who rate their products as "good" or "excellent." Probably the most frequently used means of soliciting customer feedback is the customer survey, for example, the percentage of victims reporting that they were "satisfied" with the initial police response to their case. Similarly, a crisis stabilization unit might track the percentage of consumers rating their services as "good" or "excellent," while a highway maintenance operation might estimate the percentage of motorists who are "satisfied" or "very satisfied" with the condition of the roads they travel on.

System Productivity Measures

Although the term does not appear often in typologies of performance measures, another useful type of performance measure consists of system productivity measures. These measures examine the ratio of outcome measures to related output measures in order to gauge the effectiveness of a public agency or program in converting outputs to outcomes. For example, public transit agencies often monitor the number of passenger trips carried on the system, the principal outcome measure, per vehicle mile or vehicle hours operated, which are standard output measures. Along the same lines, police agencies can track the number of convictions obtained (outcome) to the number of arrests made or cases solved (output), and child support enforcement programs can measure the number of cases with support payment obligated per absentee parent located, while housing rehabilitation programs can monitor the number of dwelling units brought into compliance with codes per loan made under the program. In each of these cases, the system productivity measure provides a clear indication of the extent to which producing specified outputs leads to the accomplishment of desired outcomes.

Resource Measures

Two other types of indicators, resource and workload measures, are usually not thought of as performance measures in their own right, but they are often used in computing other performance measures and are sometimes used in conjunction with other performance measures. All the various types of resources supporting a program can be measured in their own natural measurement units—for example, number of teachers, number of school buildings or classrooms, number of computer work stations in a local school system—or they can be measured and aggregated in their common measurement unit, which is dollar cost. Although resource measures constitute investment at the front end rather than something produced by the program, when managerial objectives focus on improving the mix or quality of resources—maintaining a full complement of teachers, for instance, or increasing the percentage of teachers with a master's degree—then it may be appropriate to track resource measures as indicators of performance. However, the principal use of resource measures in tracking program performance is as a basis for computing efficiency measures, such as the cost per hour of classroom instruction, or cost-effectiveness measures, such as the cost per student graduated.

Workload Measures

Workload measures are often of great concern to managers because they represent the flow of cases into a system or numbers of customers who need to be served. When work standards are in place or average productivity rates have been established, workload measures can be defined to represent resource requirements or the backlog of work in a production system—for example, the number of production hours needed to complete all jobs in the queue in a government printing office or the number of crew-days required to complete all the resurfacing projects that would be needed to bring a city's streets up to serviceable standards. In some cases, when managerial objectives focus on keeping workloads within reasonable limits—not exceeding two workdays pending in a central office supply operation, for example, or keeping the workweeks pending within two weeks in a disability determination program, or reducing the number of cases pending in a large county's risk management program by closing more cases than are opened in each of the next six months—then workload measures may appropriately be viewed as performance measures.

External and Other Environmental Measures

In addition to actual performance measures, it is often helpful for performance monitoring systems to track other measures—variables external to a program itself—which are likely to influence programmatic outcomes and perhaps the production of outputs, efficiency, and service quality as well. For example, the principal outcomes of public transit systems have to do with ridership measured by such indicators as passenger trips carried per month, and ridership is expected to be influenced by such programmatic factors as the amount of transit service provided, the quality of that service, and the fares that are charged. However, other environmental factors, such as unemployment rates, automobile ownership, and the price of gasoline, are likely to exert strong influence on the ability of a transit system to attract ridership as well. Similarly, the success of a city's housing rehabilitation program in raising the percentage of dwelling units that meet decent, safe, and sanitary conditions may depend heavily on the quality of the existing housing stock, the percentage of absentee ownership, socioeconomic characteristics, percentage of vacant properties, the quality of neighborhood schools, and the extent of community cohesion in targeted areas.

In the real world, public and nonprofit programs are designed and delivered within the context of a constant cause system in which an often complex web of physical, social, economic, cultural, political, and interpersonal factors exerts strong causal influence on the kinds of problems that programs are intended to address and the outcomes they are intended to generate. Such programs operate in open systems within which these exogenous variables pertain to the public sector (e.g., other departments and related programs, elected officials, funding agencies) as well as society at large (McDavid & Hawthorn, 2005). While it may be helpful for program planners to first develop system dynamics models (Funnell & Rogers, 2011) of these causal systems and then identify likely intervention points and develop a logic for intervening in the system in order to improve outcome conditions, this is not necessary or particularly helpful for purposes of performance measurement and monitoring.

However, such external factors that are well beyond the control of the program may have an overwhelming influence on its ability to generate the desired kinds of outcomes. Thus, although these external factors do not constitute part of the program logic itself, logic models should not be developed in ignorance of these factors, and it can be very helpful to reference them in conjunction with logic models in order to provide an understanding of the context within which the program logic is expected to operate (Frechtling, 2007).

Given their importance in influencing the extent to which a program's logic is likely to function as anticipated, it can be extremely helpful to track these kinds of external nonprogrammatic factors along with the actual performance measures in order to help interpret and understand the meaning of performance data on a given program over time or data that are monitored to compare the performance of similar types of programs or organizations over time. Because these external factors can facilitate or constrain the performance of public programs and organizations, these kinds of contextual data can be essential for making sense of performance data, and thus it may be helpful to build the relevant environmental variables into monitoring systems along with the actual performance measures.

Needs Indicators

One special type of external variable that bears mention here is needs indicators, measures that represent the extent and characteristics of the need for a public program. While for a public transit agency a principal needs measure might be the percentage of the population in its service area that is transit dependent, needs indicators for a housing rehabilitation problem might be the percentage of dwelling units that are not in compliance with local building and sanitation codes or the percentage of households living in substandard dwelling units. Similarly, the need for an HIV/AIDS treatment program might be measured by the percentage of the population living with HIV or the percentage of new babies born with HIV. The need for a high school student retention program would likely be measured by the dropout rate before the end of the junior year in a local school district.

While such needs measures obviously play a crucial role in needs assessments and program planning efforts, they are germane to program evaluation and performance monitoring systems as well. Since needs indicators represent the kinds of problematic conditions that public programs are often designed to remediate, outcome measures often focus on the extent to which needs have been addressed. For example, one needs indicator for local police agencies is the number of personal and property crimes reported per 1,000 population each month. Principal outcome measures for police work include the percentage of crimes solved and the percentage of reported crimes for which a conviction is obtained. If police efforts are successful over time in both taking criminals out of the general population and deterring other potential perpetrators from committing crimes, we might well expect overall crime rates in the local community to decrease. Thus, one longer-term outcome might be measured as the percentage reduction in overall crime rates, the other side of the coin of the original needs indicator representing baseline crime rates. Tracking needs indicators in ongoing performance monitoring systems, then, can often provide a complementary indication of a program's overall effectiveness over time.

Integrated Sets of Performance Measures

When a good logic model has been developed for a public program, one can identify the kinds of measures that would be appropriate to include in a performance monitoring system directly from the model. It is important to understand that we are not referring to the actual performance indicators at this point; these will have to be operationalized in terms of data sources, observations, and definitions regarding what should count and what should not count, as discussed fully in chapter 4. However, when we are working with a good logic model, what we should try to measure—the products and services, knowledge, capabilities, behaviors and actions, conditions and results, and so forth that constitute performance—should become readily apparent. First, the outputs and the outcomes shown in the logic model translate directly into output and outcome measures. Productivity measures will be based on ratios of those outputs to various categories of resources going to the program, and efficiency measures will be based on ratios of those same outputs to the dollar value or time invested in producing them.

To identify the appropriate measures of service quality requires examining the outputs specified in the model and identifying the important dimensions of the quality of the outputs or the activities or processes associated with producing them. Customer satisfaction measures will focus on satisfaction with the service delivery processes that customers or clients have experienced, the outputs that have been produced, or the outcomes they have experienced. Cost-effectiveness measures will consist of ratios of the resulting outcomes to the dollar value of the resources invested in producing the outputs that have led to these outcomes.

Teen Mother Parenting Education Program

Figure 3.6 presents a logic model for a teen mother parenting education program operated by a nonprofit organization in a particular local area. The goals of the program are to help ensure that pregnant teenagers deliver healthy babies, that they are equipped to care for their babies, and that they don't have additional pregnancies until they are ready to care for additional babies. Service delivery consists of conducting classes on prenatal care and infant parenting, and the program's outputs could be measured in terms of the number of classes conducted or, more meaningfully, the number of pregnant teenagers completing the program.

The outcomes that the classes are intended to produce occur in three strands of logic. First, teens who complete the program will be knowledgeable about prenatal nutrition and healthy habits. This will lead to their following proper guidelines regarding nutrition and health, and this will lead to a higher probability of the desired outcome of delivering healthy babies. Second, as an initial outcome of the classes, these teens will also be more knowledgeable about the proper care, feeding, and interaction with their infants, which will lead to the intermediate outcome of their actually providing the same to their babies once they are born.

Then the delivery of healthy babies and assurance that they will be provided with proper care should result in these babies achieving appropriate twelve-month milestones regarding physical, verbal, and social development. The third strand of logic really leads to a different longer-term outcome: having completed the classes, these pregnant teenagers are also more knowledgeable about birth control options and parental responsibilities. This is supposed to lead to more responsible sexual behavior—abstinence or use of birth control methods—to ensure that they do not have additional pregnancies until their education is complete and they are married with adequate family resources in place to provide responsible parenting to additional children they might have.

Indicators in each of these categories can potentially be identified to measure the performance of most programs provided by governmental and nonprofit organizations. For example, table 3.2 illustrates the kind of performance measures that might be appropriate for monitoring the performance of the teen mother parenting education program. These measures are derived directly from the program logic model presented in

FIGURE 3.6 TEEN MOTHER PARENTING LOGIC MODEL

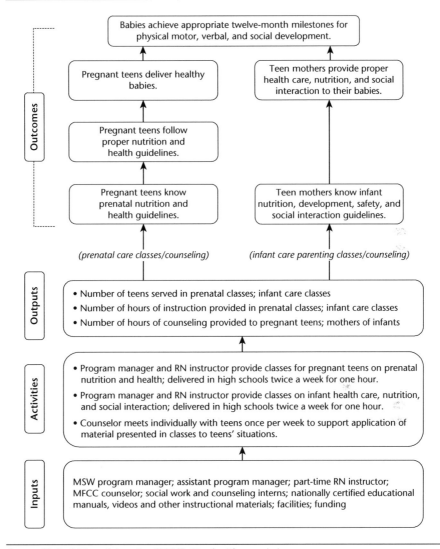

Source: United Way of America (2002). Used with permission.

TABLE 3.2 TEEN MOTHER PARENTING EDUCATION PERFORMANCE MEASURES

Outputs

Number of prenatal classes conducted

Hours of instruction in prenatal classes

Number of infant care classes conducted

Hours of instruction in infant care classes

Number of participants completing prenatal classes

Numbers of participants completing infant care classes

Hours of counseling provided to pregnant teens

Hours of counseling provided to mothers of infants

Operating Efficiency

Cost per course completed

Cost per instructional hour

Cost per pregnant teen completing the program

Cost per counseling hour

Labor Productivity

Number of pregnant teens completing program per staff-hour invested

Service Quality

Course evaluation ratings by participants

Effectiveness

Test scores regarding prenatal care and the care and feeding of and interaction with babies

Percentage of participants who eat at least four calcium servings and one serving of each of the other nutritional food groups daily

Percentage of participants who do not smoke

Percentage of participants who take a prenatal vitamin daily

Percentage of participants within proper ranges for prenatal weight gain

Percentage of newborn babies weighing at least 5.5 pounds and scoring 7 or above on the Apgar scale

Percentage of attendees observed to provide proper care and feeding of and interaction with babies

Percentage of attendees' babies clinically evaluated as achieving appropriate twelve-month milestones

Cost-Effectiveness

Cost per healthy baby achieving appropriate twelve-month milestones

Customer Satisfaction

Percentage of program completers reporting satisfaction with program after babies are born

figure 3.6. The program outputs are the number of courses conducted and the number of participants completing the program. Thus, operating efficiency would be measured by the cost per course conducted and the cost per participant completing the program, and labor productivity could be measured by the number of pregnant teens completing the program per staff-hour invested in its delivery. Service quality in this case might be measured by some professional assessment of the quality of the materials used in the course, teaching techniques employed, and the actual delivery of the course or, as suggested in table 3.2, we might rely on course evaluations from program participants.

Numerous outcome measures are shown because the program logic model shows three strands of results with multiple outcome stages in each. So the effectiveness measures range from scores on tests regarding the kind of knowledge the program is designed to impart, to the percentage of participants delivering healthy babies, the percentage of these babies achieving appropriate twelve-month developmental milestones, the percentage of these mothers subsequently reporting abstinence or the use of recommended birth control techniques, and the percentage of these teenage mothers who are high school graduates, married, and in no need of public assistance at the time of their next pregnancy. Cost-effectiveness measures might be defined by relating costs to any of these outcomes, but the most compelling ones might be the cost per healthy baby achieving appropriate twelve-month milestones and the cost per repeat premature pregnancy avoided. Finally, the most meaningful indicator of customer satisfaction might be the percentage of teens completing the program who report overall satisfaction with it at some time well after their babies have been born.

Canadian Pension Plan Disability Program

As a second example, consider the logic model proposed for the Canadian Pension Plan Disability (CPPD) Program shown in figure 3.7. The principal components of this entitlement program include outreach to potentially eligible recipients of the program, eligibility determination, client recourse system, case management, and workforce reintegration. The first four of these components feed into each other in a pipeline sequence leading to individuals who qualify for the disability benefits applying to the program, being found eligible for benefits, and receiving monthly benefit checks. Through periodic assessments of recipients' capabilities for reentering the workforce and the provision of vocational rehabilitation

FIGURE 3.7 CANADIAN PENSION PLAN DISABILITY LOGIC MODEL

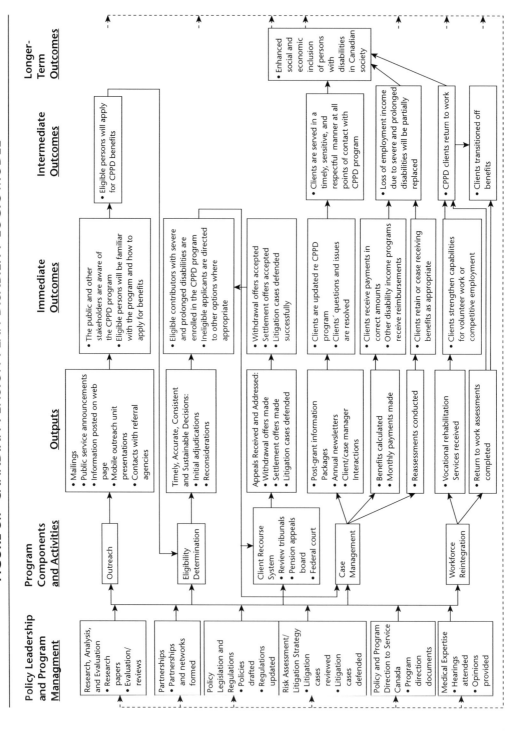

TABLE 3.3 PERFORMANCE MEASURES FOR THE CANADIAN PENSION PLAN DISABILITY PROGRAM WORKFORCE REINTEGRATION COMPONENT

Outputs	Number of clients receiving vocational rehabilitation services
	Number of return-to-work assessments completed
Operating efficiency	Cost per client in caseload
	Cost per return-to-work assessments completed
Immediate outcomes	Number of clients assessed as being ready to work
	Number of clients who have returned to work
	Number of clients who have left disability program benefits
	Percentage of clients who remain off benefits for six months or longer
	Percentage of clients who return to benefits using the fast track application process
Cost-effectiveness	Program cost per client who returns to work
	Program cost per client who leaves benefits
	Program cost per client who remains off benefits for six months or more
Longer-term outcomes—CPPD program	Percent of twenty-two- to sixty-four-year-old population receiving CPPD benefits
	Mean average benefit payout to recipients and families
	Percentage of total net income of recipients provided by CPPD
	Percentage of CPPD recipients who are benefiting from the disability tax credit
	Percentage of clients returning to work
Cost-effectiveness	Administrative cost per client receiving benefits
	Administrative cost per $100 of benefits received
	Operating cost per client receiving benefits

services, the fourth program component assists clients in reintegration into the workforce and leaving the benefit program when feasible.

Table 3.3 shows suggested performance measures running from outputs to intermediate outcomes for each of these program components, as well as measures relating to the longer-term outcome of enhanced social and economic inclusion of persons with disabilities in Canadian society. For each component of the CPPD program, a set of measures has been identified, including output and outcome measures, along with a mix of efficiency, labor productivity, service quality, and customer satisfaction measures in order to provide a balanced portrait of that component's performance. While the output measures and various stages of outcome measures are drawn directly from the logic model in figure 3.7, the efficiency and productivity measures are developed based on ratios of outputs to units of resources, and the service quality and customer satisfaction measures are intuited from the model by asking, "What are the most relevant quality dimensions of these outputs and the service delivery processes associated with them?" and, "What are the most important aspects of service delivery, outputs, and/or outcomes in terms of customer satisfaction?"

Developing Logic Models

Obviously a critical first step in developing performance measures for public and nonprofit programs is to identify what should be measured. The program logic models presented in this chapter encourage focusing on end results, the real outcomes that a program is supposed to generate, and the outputs or immediate products that must be produced in order to bring about those results. Developing such logic models helps to identify what is important to measure.

But how does one go about developing a logic model for a particular public or nonprofit program? Looking at formal statements of mission and, especially, goals and objectives is a good place to begin because they should articulate the kinds of outcomes that are expected to be produced. Since results-oriented management systems require performance measures that are directly tied to goals and objectives, this linkage is discussed in greater detail in chapter 4. Beyond goal statements regarding outcomes, the logic outlined by a program logic model is based on theory, experience, and research. Thus, reviewing relevant academic literature on intervention theories, program plans and other descriptions, and evaluation studies in particular substantive areas, along with engaging knowledgeable stakeholders in discussions regarding intervention strategies and program design, can help provide the kind of information needed to flesh out a logic model.

There is a wide variety of program logic models in terms of scope and complexity, level of detail, formatting, and strategies for articulating the flow of logic leading to outcomes that goes far beyond the scope of this book. The goal should always be to develop a coherent model that clearly communicates the logic by which programmatic activities are expected to lead to the intended outcomes. Some books that provide in-depth discussion of logic models and their development and serve as useful resources in this regard include McDavid and Hawthorn (2006), Frechtling (2007), Funnell and Rogers (2011), and Knowlton and Phillips (2012). In addition, the outcome indicators project has developed prototype logic models and illustrative sets of performance measures for fourteen specific program areas of interest to nonprofit organizations (www.urban.org/center/cnp/projects/outcomeindicators.cfm) and a report published by United Way of America (Hatry, Van Houten, Plantz, & Greenway, 1996) provides guidelines for developing performance frameworks and measures for nonprofit organizations. Selected tips for creating useful logic models culled from these sources include the following:

- State constructs in the model as simply and precisely as possible.
- Distinguish accurately between outputs and outcomes.
- Identify outcomes as intended results rather than specific measures.
- Focus on the key elements, and remove nonessential elements.
- Include interactions and feedback loops when appropriate, but avoid unnecessary arrows.
- Avoid dead-ends—elements that do not lead directly or indirectly to intended outcomes.
- Identify expected time frames for immediate, intermediate, and long-term outcomes to occur.
- Employ the appropriate level of granularity—the level of detail that will be most helpful given the purpose of the performance measurement system.
- Ensure readability, and avoid mysterious acronyms.

A backward-mapping approach beginning with identification of longer-term outcomes is often helpful in delineating the logic underlying program logic models, especially in program planning but also in performance measurement. With a clear understanding of what the desired longer-term outcomes are, you can ask, "What are the impediments to these outcomes occurring on their own, and what has to happen in order to generate these longer-term outcomes?" Answering these questions will help to identify the necessary initial and intermediate outcomes that must be generated. They in turn should tie directly to outputs being directly produced by the program. While beginning at the outset of the program logic by identifying activities and outputs and then identifying subsequent outcomes may be effective in developing a logic model, a backward-mapping approach may at least in some cases lead to a more appropriate logic model because it is rooted in the desired results from the outset. Combining the two approaches by beginning with outcomes but then working both "back and forth and up and down" through the various components is often a central part creating a sound logic model (Frechtling, 2007, 90).

Either way, developing a program logic model will usually be most successful when approached as a collaborative process (Funnel & Rogers, 2011). In addition to program managers, it often helps to engage employees, service delivery staff, consumers, agency clients, program advocates, governing board members, and other concerned parties in the process. While it may be very helpful for an analyst or program staff to sketch out an initial version of the model to get the process moving, it will usually be much more effective in the long run to involve other parties in fleshing it out, refining it, and moving toward a final product. Thus, developing a logic model may be an iterative process with a few rounds of review and revision. However, if consensus on the model can be built among these various stakeholders through such a process, the probability that the performance measures derived from the model will be broadly supported is greatly increased.

Whatever approach is used in a particular performance measurement effort, the cardinal rule should be never to bend reality to fit a preconceived model. What is important is to model the program or organization as it is or as it should be; the model should be thought of as a tool for understanding how the program is intended to operate. Fortunately, the program logic methodologies presented here are very flexible and should be adaptable to almost any programmatic or organizational setting. Once the model has been developed and a strong consensus has been built around it as an appropriate performance framework, it tends to become the arbiter of issues regarding what aspects of performance should be included in a monitoring system, and measures of outputs, quality, efficiency, productivity, effectiveness, cost-effectiveness, and customer satisfaction can be defined with confidence.

References

Broom, C., Harris, J., Jackson, M., & Marshall, M. (1998). *Performance measurement concepts and techniques.* Washington, DC: American Society for Public Administration/Center for Accountability and Performance.

Frechtling, J. A. (2007). *Logic modeling methods in program evaluation.* Hoboken, NJ: Wiley.

Funnell, S. C., & Rogers, P. J. (2011). *Purposeful program theory: Effective use of theories of change and logic models.* San Francisco: Jossey-Bass.

Hatry, H., Van Houten, T., Plantz, M. C., & Greenway, M. T. (1996). *Measuring program outcomes: A practical approach.* Alexandria, VA: United Way of America.

Knowlton, L. W., & Phillips, C. C. (2012). *The logic model guidebook: Better strategies for great results.* Thousand Oaks, CA: Sage.

McDavid, J. C., & Hawthorn, L.R.L. (2006). *Program evaluation and performance measurement: An introduction to practice.* Thousand Oaks, CA: Sage.

Poister, T. H. (1978). *Public program analysis: Applied research methods.* Baltimore, MD: University Park Press.

Poister, T. H., McDavid, J. C., & Magoun, A. H. (1979). *Applied program evaluation in local government.* Lexington, MA: Lexington Books.

Sowa, J. E., Selden, S. C., & Sandfort, J. R. (2004). No longer unmeasurable? A multi-dimensional integrated model of nonprofit organizational effectiveness. *Nonprofit and Voluntary Sector Quarterly, 33*(4), 711–728.

United Way of America. (2002). *Teen mother parenting education program logic model.* Unpublished chart.

Wholey, J. S. (1979). *Evaluation: Promise and performance.* Washington, DC: Urban Institute.

## CHAPTER FOUR

TARGETING RESULTS

Clarifying Goals and Objectives

What are goals, objectives, service standards, and targets? How should agency or program goals and objectives be stated in order to facilitate results-oriented management and performance measurement? How are goals and objectives related to performance indicators? This chapter discusses the kinds of goals and objectives used in public and nonprofit organizations; it also explores how performance measures are often derived from statements of goals and objectives and how sometimes the measures themselves are used to further specify goals statements.

Mission, Goals, and Objectives

Usually the most meaningful performance measures are derived from the mission, goals, objectives, and, sometimes, service standards that have been established for a particular program. This is because goals and objectives, and to a lesser extent mission and service standards, define the desired results to be produced by an agency or program. Clear goals and objectives are intended to improve organizational performance by focusing employees' energy and efforts on desired results (Locke & Latham, 1990). Thus, there is usually a direct connection between goals and objectives on the one hand and outcomes or effectiveness measures on the other. While it is often very useful to develop logic models to fully understand all the performance dimensions of a public or nonprofit program, depending on the purpose of the measurement system it is sometimes sufficient to clarify goals and objectives and then define performance measures to track their accomplishment.

It should be understood that there are no universal distinctions among these terms in the public management literature, and there is often considerable overlap among them, but the definitions we use in this book are workable and not severely incompatible with the distinctions others have made. *Mission* refers to the basic purpose of an organization or a program, its reason for being, and the general means through which it accomplishes that purpose. *Goals* are general statements about the results to be produced by the program, and *objectives* are more specific milestones to be achieved in order to accomplish the goals. Whereas goals are often formulated as very general, often timeless, sometimes idealized outcomes, objectives should be specified in more tangible terms.

US Department of Health and Human Services

The US Department of Health and Human Services (DHHS) is a good example of a large federal department that has gone through the process of clarifying its mission, goals, objectives, and performance measures in compliance with the Government Performance and Results Act (GPRA) of 1993 and the more recent GPRA Modernization Act of 2010. DHHS, the federal government's principal agency for protecting the health of Americans and providing essential human services, manages more than three hundred programs through eleven operating agencies and an extended network of state, local, and other grantees in a wide variety of areas, such as medical and social science research, food and drug safety, financial assistance and health care for low-income individuals, child support enforcement, maternal and infant health, substance abuse treatment and prevention, health insurance, and services for older Americans. The department's formal mission statement is, "To enhance the health and well-being of Americans by providing for effective health and human services and by fostering strong, sustained advances in the sciences underlying medicine, public health, and social services."

To pursue this mission, DHHS has identified the five following strategic goals, which are formulated in very broad statements:

Goal 1: Strengthen health care.

Goal 2: Advance scientific knowledge and innovation.

Goal 3: Advance the health, safety, and well-being of the American people.

Goal 4: Increase the efficiency, transparency and accountability of HHS programs.

Goal 5: Strengthen the nation's health and human services infrastructure and workforce.

For each of these strategic goals, DHHS (2012) has defined a number of supporting objectives that are somewhat more targeted and specific in terms of desired behaviors, conditions, or circumstances. With respect to goal 3, for example, to "advance the health, safety, and well-being of the American people," the following objectives have been set:

Objective 3.A: Promote the safety, well-being, resilience and healthy development of children and youth. (p. 50)

Objective 3.B: Promote economic and social well-being for individuals, families, and communities. (p. 54)

Objective 3.C: Improve the accessibility and quality of supportive services for people with disabilities and older adults. (p. 58)

Objective 3.D: Promote prevention and wellness. (p. 62)

Objective 3.E: Reduce the occurrence of infectious disease. (p. 67)

Objective 3.F: Protect Americans' health and safety during emergencies and foster resilience in response to emergencies. (p. 71)

As will be seen in subsequent chapters, performance measurement is often a process of sequential specification from very general goals to specific indicators. The challenge is to ensure that the operational indicators that measure particular kinds of results in fact represent the kinds of outcomes intended by the general goals. The six objectives supporting goal 3 are still quite general statements of intended accomplishments, but they are clearly more focused indications of intended results that are tied directly to the goals.

In the next step in the sequence, each objective is fleshed out with multiple performance measures, as illustrated in table 4.1 for objective 3.A, promoting the safety, well-being, resilience, and healthy development of children and youth. Data sources are provided for each of the seven

TABLE 4.1 GOALS, OBJECTIVES AND PERFORMANCE MEASURES: US DEPARTMENT OF HEALTH AND HUMAN SERVICES

Goal 3:   Advance the health, safety, and well-being of the American people.
Objective 3.A. Promote the safety, well-being, resilience and healthy development of children and youth.

Measures	Lead Agency	Data Source	2013 Target
For those children who had been in foster care less than 12 months, maintain the percentage that has no more than two placement settings	ACF	Adoption and Foster Care Reporting System	80%+
Of all children who exit foster care in less than 24 months, the percentage who exit to permanency (reunification, living with relative, guardianship or adoption)	ACF	Adoption and Foster Care Reporting System	92.5%+
Of all children who exit foster care after 24 or more months, the percentage who exit to permanency (reunification, living with relative, guardianship or adoption)	ACF	Adoption and Foster Care Reporting System	73.5%+
The percentage of youth living in safe and appropriate settings after exiting ACF-funded transitional living program (TLP) services	ACF	The Runaway and Homeless Youth Management Information System	86%+
The percentage of middle and high school students who report current substance abuse	SAMHSA	Grantees' Bi-Annual Reports	20%−
The percentage of children receiving trauma informed services showing clinically significant improvement	SAMHSA	NCTSI Cross-Site Evaluator, IFC Macro, Core Data Set	43%+
The number of antibiotic courses prescribed for ear infections in children under five years of age per 100 children	CDC	National Ambulatory Med Care Survey, and National Hospital Ambulatory Medical Care	49%−

Note: ACF: Administration for Children and Families; SAMHSA: Substance Abuse and Mental Health Services Administration; CDC: Centers for Disease Control and Prevention.

Source: US Department of Health and Human Services (2012).

measures, along with a level of performance on that measure targeted for the year 2013 and the operating agency charged with lead responsibility for attaining it. For example, one measure that reflects the well-being and healthy development of children is the percentage of children who had been in foster care less than twelve months who exited foster care into a permanent arrangement with relatives, guardians, or adoptive parents. The Administration for Children and Families has lead responsibility for performance in this area, and the data to operationalize this measure will be taken from the adoption and foster care reporting system, while the target on this measure for FY 2013 is 92.5 percent or higher.

Obviously each of these seven performance measures represents one slice, or dimension, of this particular objective, one perspective on what the results should look like. All seven indicators in this measure set are clearly aligned with the objective of promoting the safety, well-being, resilience, and healthy development of children and youth. Collectively this set of measures is intended to provide a balanced perspective on whether and the extent to which progress is made in accomplishing this objective over time.

Goals, Objectives, and Program Logic

While goals structures provide a different starting point as opposed to program logic models for identifying the aspects of performance that should be captured in a measurement system, the two are by no means incompatible. Indeed, in managing public and nonprofit programs, program managers and others frequently establish goals and objectives for their programs that are likely to focus on varying aspects of the program and its underlying logic. In general, managers are concerned with ensuring that programmatic activities are conducted efficiently and productively, that the quality of these activities and the outputs they produce are of high quality, that outputs are produced at the required levels, that the intended outcomes do in fact materialize, and that clients are satisfied with both the services they receive and the outcomes they experience. However, at any time, their goals and objectives are likely to focus in particular on those program components and performance criteria where improvement is most needed, and these focal points of interest are likely to change over time as conditions require.

As an example, consider a state government's vocational rehabilitation program (see the logic model in figure 3.3). Looking at the overall longer-term outcome, clients successfully employed, suppose that performance has been eroding in terms of appropriate fit between what clients have been prepared to do with the requirements of the jobs they are in, clients working productively in those jobs, clients remaining in those jobs for significant periods of time, clients' satisfaction with the jobs they are in, and employers' satisfaction with the clients' productivity and the quality of their work. Clearly, under these circumstances, management might establish a major goal of increasing the percentage of clients successfully employed on all the criteria noted.

Working back through the program logic, the data might indicate that the program is not doing a good job of preparing clients for viable occupations, an initial outcome in the logic model, and appropriate objectives might be set regarding better preparation of clients for such occupations, which might be different from the kinds of occupations the program has been focusing on. In turn, this might lead to a finding that the training programs conducted, a chief output of this program, and new objectives might well focus on strengthening those training programs. Alternatively, the program might be doing a good job of providing training programs and preparing clients for viable occupations, but the problem lies in the fact that staff has not been doing a good job of identifying good prospective jobs. Thus, clients often must settle for jobs that are not particularly well suited for them, and this is not working out well in the long run for either the clients or the employers. This would likely lead to new objectives to increase both the volume and quality of this particular output: suitable jobs identified. In addition, further investigation may find that staff are not producing useful on-the-job evaluations of clients in the initial jobs, allowing "misfits" to continue, and this might lead to clearer objectives regarding the production of more discerning assessments with more helpful recommendations, addressing another quality-of-output issue. The point here is that goals and objectives might well pertain to any or all of the elements in a program logic, and while they might shift over time as might a logic model itself, they often provide a good point of departure regarding those aspects of a program's performance that are important to measure.

"SMART" Objectives

It is often helpful for program objectives to specify milestones to be attained within certain time periods, but in practice, objective statements are often overly general, vague, and open-ended in terms of time. Poorly written objectives fail to convey any management commitment to achieve particular results, and they provide little guidance for defining meaningful measures to assess performance. However, specific goals tend to help focus energy and attention on producing desired results in specific amounts rather than being scattered across a range of necessary and unnecessary activities (Carroll & Tosi, 1973). Truly useful program objectives can be developed using the SMART convention, stating objectives that are Specific in terms of the results to be achieved: Measurable, Ambitious but Realistic, and Time-bound (Broom, Harris, Jackson, & Marshall, 1998). With respect to highway traffic safety programming, for example, the objective of reducing the reported number of crashes on the nation's highways to fewer than 3 per 100 million vehicle-miles driven and the number of highway accident fatalities down to no more than 10 per 100,000 US residents by the year 2020 would be a SMART objective.

SMART objectives clearly indicate the kind of result or improvement to be obtained within a specified time period. The measure to be used in determining whether an objective has been achieved at the end of that period should also be identified along with the SMART objective. For example, the measures to be used in conjunction with the highway safety objectives stated above will be the number of reported crashes per 100 million vehicle-miles operated and the number of highway accident–related fatalities per 100,000 US residents, both to be drawn from the Fatality Analysis Reporting System maintained by the National Highway and Transportation Administration. In addition, SMART objectives establish targets—levels on performance measures that programs or agencies have identified to be achieved within the specified time period. For the measure of reported crashes per 100 million vehicle miles traveled, the target identified above is 3 or lower, while the target for the number of highway accident fatalities per 100,000 population is 10 or lower.

Table 4.2 shows examples of possible SMART objectives for a variety of public and nonprofit programs. For example, a nonprofit firm providing residential services for persons with mental disabilities might target an average occupancy rate of 90 percent or higher in the facilities it operates, while a local police department might set an objective of reducing the number of reported burglaries within its jurisdiction by 10 percent next year as compared to the current year. Similarly, a local school system might aspire to achieve an 80 percent pass rate on a particular suite of standardized exams by the 2015–2016 school year, while a local Big Brothers/Big Sisters program might set an objective of increasing the number of youth

TABLE 4.2 SMART OBJECTIVES WITH TARGETS

Program	SMART Objective
Residential services for persons with mental disabilities	Increase the occupancy rate in community living arrangements to 90 percent by fiscal 2015
Local crime control	Reduce the number of reported burglaries by 10 percent next year compared to the current year
Big Brothers/Big Sisters	Increase by 20 percent over the next two years the number of youth who are active in mentoring relationships with adults who have completed the prescribed training
Public transit service	Increase revenue-generating passenger trips by 25 percent over the next five years
Vocational rehabilitation	Increase the number of clients placed in suitable jobs by an additional 800 placements next year over the current year
Public schools	Achieve an 80 percent pass rate on the Criterion-Referenced Competency Tests in reading, English, and math in all schools by 2016
Aviation safety	Reduce the number of dangerous incidents on airport runways to below 300 next year
Smoking cessation	Reduce the percentage of adults smoking cigarettes to 12 percent by the year 2020
Foster care	Increase the percentage of children exiting foster care in less than 24 months who exit into permanent living arrangements to 93 percent

who are active in mentoring relationships with adults who have completed prescribed training for this activity by 20 percent over the next two years.

The idea underlying SMART objectives is that the targets should be set at levels that are both ambitious and yet realistic. While some targets call for maintaining current or minimally improving performance levels, in the context of results-oriented management and the drive to improved performance, it is desirable to set targets that are relatively ambitious "stretch objectives" designed to challenge the program or organization to find ways to make meaningful improvement in performance. Very modest targets are not likely to encourage people to work harder and smarter to strengthen performance significantly. More ambitious targets, particularly when there is clearly strong commitment to them from higher levels of authority, can have a galvanizing effect on people and motivate program managers and employees to "stretch the envelope" in a quest to really make a difference.

Yet the targets established by SMART objectives must also be realistic and achievable in order to be productive. Overly aggressive targets that are out of reach or beyond the grasp of a program to achieve within the time period specified can be counterproductive because by definition, they amount to programming failure. Such targets are highly likely to backfire and create disincentives for working toward improved performance in the long run. Thus, finding a happy medium in establishing targets often requires careful assessment and sound judgment.

Performance Standards: Child Support Enforcement

The term *performance standard* is often used interchangeably with *targets*, particularly when they refer to outcomes and reflect performance expectations that are fairly constant over time. Consider the child support enforcement program operated by a state's department of human resources or social services. The mission of this program is to help families rise or remain out of poverty, and reduce their potential dependency on public assistance, through the systematic enforcement of noncustodial parents' responsibility to provide financial support for their children. Figure 4.1 presents the logic model for this program, working through three basic components designed to obligate support payments by absentee parents, collect payments that are obligated, and assist absentee parents, if necessary, to secure employment so that they are financially able to make support payments. The logic moves through locating absentee parents, establishing paternity when necessary, and obtaining court orders to obligate support payments, as well as helping absentee parents to earn wages, but the bottom line is collecting payments and disbursing them to custodial parents to ensure that children receive adequate financial support.

The following performance standards have been established for this program, each with clear targets:

1. Establishing paternity for at least 80 percent of the children in the program's caseload who were born out of wedlock
2. Obligating support payments for at least 50 percent of the total number of cases
3. Keeping the cases that are in arrears in making payments to less than 50 percent

FIGURE 4.1 CHILD SUPPORT ENFORCEMENT PROGRAM LOGIC MODEL

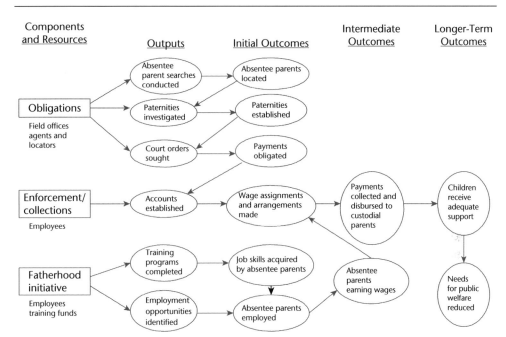

4. Collecting at least 40 percent of all the support that has been obligated

All four of these performance standards tie directly to initial, intermediate, or longer-term outcomes as specified in the program logic model. Although these standards might appear to be quite modest to the uninitiated, they might be considered to be fairly ambitious by this particular agency, given current performance levels and the difficulties in tracking down some absentee parents, establishing paternity, securing court orders, and collecting payments.

In any case, these standards, along with the program logic model, suggest that the following kinds of performance measures should be monitored over time:

Output measures
- Absentee parent searches conducted
- Paternity investigations completed
- Court orders sought

- Training programs completed
- Employment identified

Productivity measures
- Cost per noncustodial searches per locator
- Active cases maintained per agent
- Training programs conducted per training staff member

Efficiency measures
- Cost per paternity investigation completed
- Cost per account established
- Cost per noncustodial parent completing training program

Service quality and customer service measures
- The percentage of inquiries from custodial parents responded to within twenty-four hours

Outcome measures
- Percentage of children in caseload born out of wedlock with paternity established
- Percentage of noncustodial parents earning wages
- Percentage of cases in arrears
- Percentage of obligated support collected

Cost-effectiveness measures
- Cost per case of paternity established
- Cost per absentee parent employed through fatherhood initiative
- Total support collected per $1 on program expenditure

Customer/client satisfaction
- Percentage of custodial parents reporting they are satisfied with service received from their primary agents

The most salient output measures are the number of absentee parent searches conducted, the number of paternity investigations completed, and the number of court orders sought. The productivity measures are the number of noncustodial searches conducted per locator and the number of training programs conducted per training staff member, as well as the number of active cases maintained per child support enforcement agent, although the latter might well be considered to be more of a workload measure. The efficiency measures represent unit costs of such outputs as paternity investigations conducted, accounts established, and training programs completed. The one service quality indicator shown is actually a customer service indicator: the percentage of custodial parents who report being satisfied with the assistance they have received.

The most relevant outcome measures directly represent the performance standards shown earlier, including the percentage of caseload children born out of wedlock who have paternity established, the percentage with support payments obligated, the percentage of cases in arrears on making payments, and the percentage of all obligated support that is collected. The percentage of noncustodial parents who are earning wages tracks the effectiveness of the fatherhood initiative. Two of the cost-effectiveness measures, the cost per case of paternity established and the cost per absentee parent employed through fatherhood initiative, relate critical initial outcomes to the cost of realizing them. And since the bottom line in terms of outcomes is measured by the dollar value of support payments collected, the most comprehensive measure of cost-effectiveness is the value of total collections per one dollar in program expenditure. Depending on assessments of the actual performance of this program based on ongoing performance monitoring, the agency might well decide to set goals for improvement and possible SMART objectives as well on some or all of these kinds of indicators.

Setting Targets

Although many performance measurement systems establish SMART objectives with targets to be achieved on each indicator, other systems purposefully do not do so. Whether to set targets depends on the purpose of the measurement system and the management philosophy in the organization. For example, many state transportation departments have been in the forefront of the performance management movement (Transportation Research Board, 2001) and the majority of them incorporate targets in the measures they track.

In contrast, the New Mexico State Highway and Transportation Department took a different approach with respect to the approximately eighty indicators of performance in seventeen key result areas covered in its Compass system, which became the driving force of management and decision making in the department in the early part of the past decade (Poister, 2004). In keeping with the continuous improvement philosophy underlying the department's quality improvement program, from which the Compass evolved, the department preferred not to establish targets on these measures. This policy was based on the belief that targets can have ceiling effects and actually inhibit improvement rather than provide incentives to strengthen performance. Thus, the implicit objective is to continuously improve performance on these measures over time.

Nevertheless, the dominant approach in public and nonprofit organizations is to set targets and then measure performance in accomplishing them. How, then, are such targets established? How do managers arrive at targets of a 25 percent increase in transit ridership, a 10 percent decrease in burglaries, or a 20 percent increase in mentoring relationships with at-risk youth? There are at least five ways of approaching the issue:

1. *Past trends approach.* The most common approach is to look at current performance levels on the indicators of interest, along with the past trends leading up to these current levels, and then set targets that represent some reasonable degree of improvement over current performance. Current performance levels often provide an appropriate point of departure, but in a less-than-stellar agency, they may underrepresent the possibilities, so the question to ask is, "To what degree should we be able to improve above where we are now?"

2. *Forecasting approach.* Extrapolating on past trends, an agency might develop forecasting models for projecting future performance levels based on a continuation of past trends and assumptions regarding future values of key driving forces incorporated in the model, including both external, contextual factors and program delivery. The performance levels predicted by the model for future years, assuming a constant cause system, can then be used as a point of departure in setting targets representing incremental or perhaps more dramatic improvement in performance levels that the agency aspires to achieve going forward.

3. *Production function approach.* This approach analyzes the service delivery process, assesses the production possibilities, and determines what level of performance can reasonably be expected, given constraints on the system. The analysis, which might be performed for subunits and then rolled up to the agency or program as a whole, should take into account any changes in resource levels, intervention strategies, treatments, program design, service delivery arrangements, or operations that might be expected to have an impact on overall productivity. This production function approach works particularly well for setting output targets to be achieved by a production process. It may be less helpful in setting appropriate targets for real outcomes when precise relationships between outputs and outcomes are not clearly understood.

4. *Subunits approach.* This approach is based on analyses of differences in performance among organizational or programmatic subunits delivering the same set of services. Often there may be significant or even widespread variation in performance among regional or district offices delivering a state agency program or neighborhood units or policy precincts in a local government jurisdiction. Sometimes a "better than the best" strategy is used based on the philosophy that "if region

1 can produce results at the 95 percent level, we should be able to expect all our regions to perform at levels that equal or exceed that." This approach, however, may result in targets that are overly ambitious for some or many of these operating units. If the analysis is able to sort out the extent to which the leading performers are more successful because they are managing the program more effectively as opposed to simply because they are working in a more benign operating environment, the agency may be able to set differential targets for the subunits that are still ambitious but more realistic.

5. *Benchmarking approach.* Finally, setting appropriate targets may be informed by comparative performance data on other similar agencies or programs. Benchmarking performance against other entities, as discussed in chapter 14, can help identify norms for public service industries as well as star performers in the field, which can be helpful in setting targets for a particular program or agency. A program that finds itself performing considerably lower than other similar programs, for example, might first set targets for itself based on other programs that are somewhat higher in the rankings but not necessarily at the top, while an agency that is already in the top quartile might set targets that approximate the performance of the leading performers in the field. A major challenge in using the benchmarking approach is to find truly comparable programs or agencies in the first place, or to make adjustments for differences in operating conditions in interpreting the performance of other entities as the basis for setting targets for a particular program or agency.

Whichever approach is used in developing SMART objectives, the intent should be to set targets that are both ambitious and realistic. Thus, agencies might be well advised to set moderately challenging targets that will motivate managers and employees to find ways to improve performance but refrain from going over the top in setting targets that are unrealistically high, in which case they would be preordaining failure. Perhaps more important, as they set targets for moderate performance improvements and then attain those target levels, they can continue to set incrementally higher targets and ratchet up meaningful performance improvements over time. Again, target setting may be partially an analytical exercise, but to do it well also requires sound judgment of the possibilities and constraints involved.

Increasingly, public and nonprofit agencies are setting target levels for desirable outcomes identified through their strategic planning processes. Particularly when an agency has a wide variety of programs to manage, summarizing expected results and associated targets helps to provide a strategic view of its portfolio of activities. Focusing on five global results areas in its strategic planning process, the United Way of Metropolitan Atlanta established five major goals concerning healthy babies, access to primary health care, financial self-sufficiency, education, and homelessness for 2014 with targets identified for each as follows:

- Increase the number of babies that are born healthy by 10 percent.
- Reduce the number of preventable emergency room visits by eighty-four thousand.
- Improve the income and financial self-sufficiency of ninety-five thousand families.
- Increase the number of adults with college degrees or comparable credentialing by 5 percent.
- To reduce the homeless population by 4,700 individuals.

Setting these proportional targets was based in part on making incremental improvements in baseline conditions in these areas in addition to assessments of the extent to which the United Way would be able to mobilize community-wide resources to combat these problems. The United Way developed sets of strategies for accomplishing each of the five goals, along with both output and outcome measures to monitor progress in advancing the strategies and achieving the goals, as discussed further in chapter 8.

Service Standards

Complicating the lexicon surrounding goals, objectives, and targets is the term *standards*. The term *standards* is often used interchangeably with *targets*, but to some people, standards refer to more routine performance expectations that are fairly constant over time, whereas targets may be changed more frequently as actual and potential trends change over time. Performance standards, then, tend to relate to programmatic or agency outcomes, whereas service standards refer more often to service delivery processes.

Service standards are specific performance criteria intended to be attained on an ongoing basis. They usually refer to characteristics of the service delivery process, service quality, or productivity in producing outputs. In some cases, service standards are distinct from a program's objectives, but probably more often, service standards and objectives are synonymous or closely related. In any case, if there is not a clear sense about what a program's mission, goals, objectives, and perhaps service standards are, it is important to clarify them before attempting to identify meaningful measures of its performance.

The mission of a state government's office supply support service, for example, might be framed as meeting the needs of all state agencies, school districts, and local government jurisdictions for office supplies and other materials on a timely basis. At a particular point in time, its principal goals might be to improve service quality and maintain or increase its market share in a competitive business environment. A supporting objective of the latter goal might be to increase the number of customer orders coming in to the central supply warehouse by 10 percent over the next year. With respect to the goal concerned with "growing the business" further, the program may have established the following kinds of service standards:

- To deliver all shipments within three working days of receipt of orders
- To fill at least 95 percent of all orders completely in the first shipment (with no items on back order)
- To fill at least 99 percent of all orders correctly in the first shipment

A related productivity standard might be to ship twenty product lines per employee per hour.

These standards might be considered the objectives of the program, or there might be other objectives, such as increasing the percentage of customers indicating on response cards that they were satisfied with the service they received to 85 percent during the next year. Alternatively, if the program has only been achieving a "fill rate" of 80 percent, a key objective may be to raise it to 90 percent during the next year and achieve the standard of 95 percent by the following year. Understanding what a program is supposed to accomplish through clarifying mission, goals, objectives, service or performance standards, and targets, however they are configured, can help tremendously in identifying critical performance measures.

Table 4.3 illustrates service standards for a number of public services. Rather than setting performance targets regarding outcomes, these service standards all focus on service delivery, the production of outputs, service quality, or levels of service. For example, the sexually transmitted disease prevention program funded by the US Centers for Disease Control has a service standard that calls for interviewing partners

TABLE 4.3 ILLUSTRATIVE SERVICE STANDARDS

Program	Service Standard
Sexually transmitted disease control	Interview identified partners of clients with primary or secondary syphilis within 14 days
Highway resurfacing	Maintain National Highway System roads to below 120 on the International Roughness Index
Nursing regulation	Complete investigations of reported violations within 180 working days
Child support enforcement	Return telephone inquiries from custodial parents within 24 hours
Disability determination	Adjudicate all claims within 70 working days from receipt of a fully documented claim
Foster care	Limit the number of placements of children in their first year in foster care to no more than 2
Public transit service	All transit vehicles to arrive at designated bus stops within plus or minus 3 minutes of scheduled arrival times
Vocational rehabilitation	Complete an on-the-job evaluation within 4 weeks of clients beginning a new job
Driver licensing	Process license renewals within 20 minutes of when customers enter drivers' license centers

of individuals diagnosed with primary or secondary syphilis within four-teen days of the client's identification of these partners. Similarly, the disability adjudication process funded by the US Social Security Administration states that claims for disability benefits should be adjudicated within seventy working days of receiving a claim.

Some service standards focus on service quality rather than timeliness. For instance, a state highway maintenance program may set a standard for ride quality that calls for maintaining all of its roads on the National Highway System at a roughness level at or below 120 on the international roughness index, while a local public transit system may work hard to adhere to a service standard calling for buses to arrive at all regular bus stops within plus or minus three minutes of scheduled arrival times. Similarly, an after-care program run by a state's juvenile justice program may have a policy that caseworkers or counselors should have weekly face-to-face meetings with all juveniles discharged from juvenile boot camps during the first six months after the date of discharge, an output-oriented service standard.

Frequently public agencies establish targets for adherence to service standards, especially when they are failing to do so successfully, but are motivated to improve performance in those areas. For example, a state transportation department may have a service standard calling for highway capacity on major interregional corridors to be sufficient so that traffic can move at the posted speed limit, but its performance monitoring indicates that it is meeting this standard on only 55 percent of the mileage on those interregional roads. In an effort to improve its performance on this standard, it establishes a target that calls for increasing the percentage of that road mileage on which traffic does move at the posted speed limit up to 65 percent by the end of the following fiscal year and up to 75 percent over the next three fiscal years.

Consider a state juvenile justice after-care program whose performance monitoring reveals that only 40 percent of the juveniles discharged from boot camps within the past six months are being contacted at least once per week by program staff, the service standard that has been established for the program. This may lead the program to establish a target to the effect that at least 50 percent of juveniles who have been discharged from boot camp in the past six months will in fact be contacted by their case manager or other appropriate program staff weekly over the next fiscal year.

Programmatic versus Managerial Goals and Objectives

To be useful, performance measures should focus on whatever kinds of results managers want to accomplish. From a purist program evaluation–based perspective, appropriate measures are usually seen as focusing on programmatic goals and objectives, the real outcomes produced by programs and organizations out in the field. However, from a practical managerial perspective, performance measures focusing on implementation goals and the production of outputs are often equally important. Thus, public and nonprofit organizations often combine programmatic or outcome-based goals and objectives along with more managerial or output-based goals and objectives in the same management systems.

Both programmatic and managerial objectives should be stated as SMART objectives and tracked with appropriate performance measures. For example, the programmatic objectives of a community crime prevention program might be to reduce personal crimes by 20 percent and property crimes by 25 percent in one year, along with the goal of having at least 90 percent of all residents feeling safe and secure in their own neighborhoods. These outcomes could be monitored with basic reported crime statistics and an annual neighborhood-based survey. More managerial objectives might include the initial implementation of community policing activities within the first six months and the startup of at least twenty-five neighborhood watch groups within the first year. These outputs could be tracked through internal reporting systems.

All governmental jurisdictions maintain workers' compensation programs to ensure that employees who are injured in the course of their work are provided with appropriate medical treatment and, if necessary, rehabilitation services, time off from work, and other benefits as required by law. Figure 4.2 illustrates the underlying logic of a state government's workers' compensation program, which, in addition to claims processing, promotes safety in the workplace and emphasizes injured employees'

FIGURE 4.2 STATE WORKERS' COMPENSATION PROGRAM LOGIC MODEL

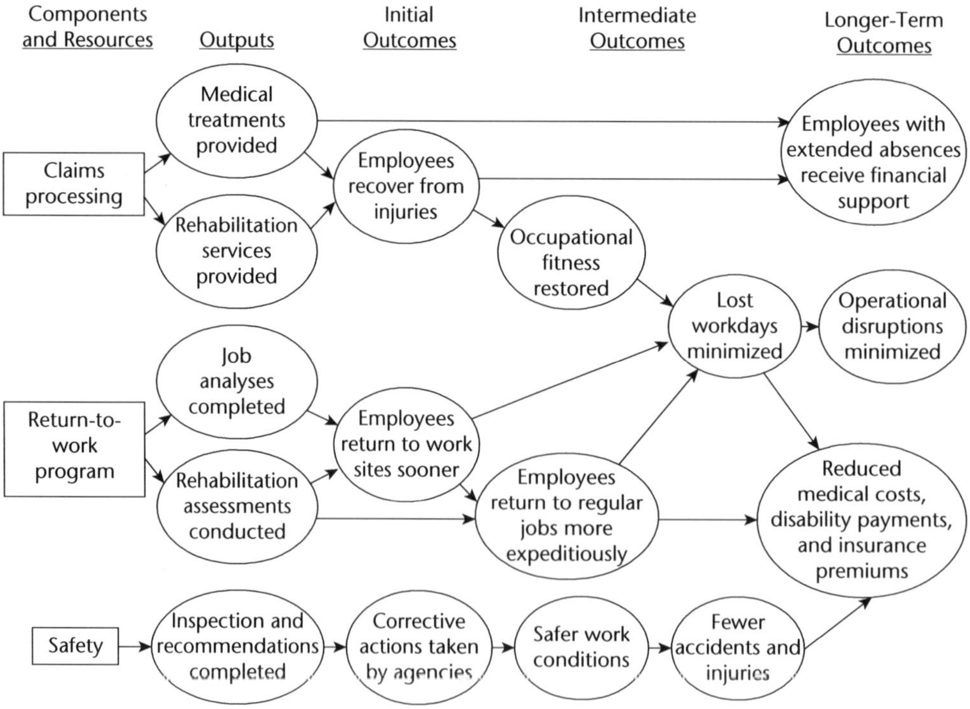

return to work as soon as practicable. From the state's point of view, the critical outcomes are that employees recover from their injuries and return to their work sites and regular jobs so that lost workdays and operational disruptions are minimized. From injured employees' perspective, the critical outcomes are not only that they recover from their injuries and return to work, but also that financial support is provided if extended or even permanent absences from work are necessary.

Table 4.4 shows the goals, service standards, and targets that have been developed for this program. Of particular interest here are the targets. Whereas the goals are appropriately more general and the service standards are routine in a way, the objectives call for specific changes in performance levels, for instance, to reduce the number of late claim filings (output quality) by 30 percent from the previous year or to reduce the total cost of workers' compensation claims (operating efficiency) by 15 percent from the previous year. One objective focuses on managing workload by closing at least as many claims each month as the number

TABLE 4.4 SERVICE STANDARDS AND MANAGEMENT OBJECTIVES: WORKERS COMPENSATION PROGRAM

Program Goals	Service Standards	Management Objectives
To promote safety programs in state government and assist state agencies in their efforts to prevent on-the-job employee injuries	To file WC-1 reports (first reports of injuries) for all lost time claims to the State Workers' Compensation Board within 21 days of the date the employer becomes aware of the injuries	To reduce the number of late WC-1 filings by 30 percent from last year
To provide for proper and timely processing of workers' compensation claims in order to ensure that injured employees receive appropriate medical treatments, rehabilitation services, and other benefits as required by law	To pay all workers' compensation lost time benefits that are approved within 21 days of the date the employer becomes aware of injuries	To close at least as many claims each month as the number of new cases created in order to maintain or improve on the current backlog of cases
To implement a return-to-work program in order to facilitate the return of injured employees to productive work in their agencies as practically possible	To pay all medical bills associated with workers' compensation claims within 60 days of receipt of acceptable invoices	To contract with a managed care organization in order to reduce the total cost of workers' compensation claims by 15 percent from last year
		To implement an aggressive return-to-work program in order to reduce lost time days by 15 percent annually

of new cases opened, while the last one focuses on a key measure of effectiveness, reducing the number of lost time days by at least 15 percent from last year through the implementation of an aggressive return to work program.

Given current performance levels in this particular agency, all four of these objectives are considered to be ambitious yet realistic, and they are all SMART objectives in terms of specifying the nature and magnitude of expected results within a particular time period. In addition, straightforward performance indicators can be readily operationalized for each of these objectives, along with the service standards, and collectively they will provide management with a clear picture of the overall performance of this workers' compensation program.

Public and Nonprofit Goal Structures

As indicated earlier in this chapter and as will be further discussed in chapter 8, public and nonprofit organizations frequently elaborate goal structures with lower-level goals supporting higher-level goals. For example, an agency might have identified strategic goals supported by programmatic goals, which in turn are linked to critical and secondary objectives. Alternatively, it may establish organization-wide goals that are linked through supporting division goals down through the structure to office goals, branch goals, section goals, and work unit goals and ultimately to goals for individual managers or employees to achieve. But the question still remains as to the substantive concerns these goal structures address.

Clearly one useful framework for identifying appropriate goals and objectives is the kind of program logic models and associated performance measures discussed in chapter 3. Public and nonprofit organizations frequently set goals for increasing or improving the quality of outputs produced by a particular program, and they also set goals focusing on increasing the volume of outcomes or altering characteristics of outcomes produced, as well as changing the mix of outcomes produced by a program. Similarly, goals might be established for improving the quality of products or services delivered by a program or increasing the efficiency and productivity of service delivery processes, and other goals might be established for increasing customer satisfaction with the services they receive from the program or the outcomes they experience as a result of participating in a program or receiving services from a program. In addition, goals might be defined in terms of the priority populations or target groups to be reached by the program.

However, performance management systems often focus on an organization's performance rather than that of particular operating programs. Some public organizations have full responsibility for a single program, while others, particularly larger department-level agencies, are responsible for multiple programs and services, and agencies may also share responsibility for some programs with other agencies. In any case, the goals that are important to an agency almost always include some that are directly related to programs, but the agencies are also likely to have other organizational or nonmission-oriented goals concerning development, management capacity, technology, external support, and so forth as well. In their book on the balanced scorecard as a framework for strategic planning, as discussed in chapter 8, Kaplan and Norton (1996) proposed that private firms should be establishing goals and attendant performance measures not only from the perspective of financial performance or the bottom line, but also goals with respect to customers, business processes, and learning and growth.

Many organizations in the public sector have developed their own balanced scorecards, and most adopt the same four perspectives—financial, customer, internal processes, and learning and growth—although they tend to identify the customer or citizen perspective as the most important goals and establish goals in the other three perspectives to support achievement of those customer- or citizen-oriented goals (Niven, 2003). In a similar vein, Boyne and Walker (2004) identified five "action areas" that constitute strategy content in the public sector—markets, services, revenues, internal organization, and external organization—and this model also provides a useful framework for goal setting in the public sector.

Similar kinds of performance frameworks have been developed for the nonprofit sector focusing on such perspectives as social mission achievement, program effectiveness, and participant-centered outcomes in addition to organization and management capacity and external support (Moore, 2003; Sowa, Selden, & Sandfort, 2004; Urban Institute, 2006). However, public and nonprofit organizations tend to differ significantly with respect to emphasis on goals and performance measures focusing on institutional support and revenues. While some public organizations such as toll roads, public utilities, and regulatory agencies earning revenue through fees collected often place substantial emphasis on goals and performance measures concerning revenues, particularly those that operate in competitive markets such as public transit agencies, in most public agencies financial resources are thought of as a given from dedicated revenue sources or budget allocations, falling on the input side of the performance framework rather than as results. Thus, as discussed in chapter 3, resource measures are typically used in computing efficiency, productivity, and cost-effectiveness measures but are not often considered as performance measures in their own right. However, as self-created entities rather than government agencies with semiguaranteed financial revenues, nonprofit organizations must of necessity secure their own revenue—from members or regular contributors, charitable donors, and government grants or contracts in addition to paying customers—in order to ensure their continued ability to pursue their social missions. Thus, institutional support, and especially revenue and resources, tend to figure much more prominently in the goals and performance measures set by nonprofit organizations as compared with public agencies.

Goals, Objectives, and Measures

Obviously managers need to forge close linkages between goals and objectives, on one hand, and performance measures, on the other. It is critical to monitor measures of performance in terms of accomplishing outcome-oriented, programmatic objectives, but often it is important to track measures focused on the achievement of more managerially oriented objectives as well. In some instances, goals and objectives are stated in terms of the general kinds of results intended to be produced by programmatic activity, and then performance indicators must be developed to track their achievement. In other cases, however, the objectives themselves are defined in terms of the measures that will be used to track results.

Sometimes performance standards or service standards are established and tracked independently, while at other times, objectives or targets are set in terms of improving performance on those standards. Although there is not one right way to do it, the bottom line for results-oriented managers is to clearly define intended results through some mix of goals, objectives, standards, and targets and then track performance measures that are as closely aligned as possible with these results.

References

Boyne, G. A., & Walker, R. M. (2004). Strategy content and public service organizations. *Journal of Public Administration Research & Theory, 14*(2), 231–252.

Broom, C., Harris, J., Jackson, M., & M. Marshall. (1998). *Performance measurement concepts and techniques.* Washington, DC: American Society for Public Administration/Center for Accountability and Performance.

Carroll, S. J., & Tosi, H. L. (1973). *Management by objectives: Applications and research.* New York: Macmillan.

Kaplan, R. S., & Norton, D. P. (1996). *The balanced scorecard: Translating strategy into action.* Cambridge, MA: Harvard University Press.

Locke, E. A., & Latham, G. P. (1990). *A theory of goal setting and task performance.* Englewood Cliffs, NJ: Prentice Hall.

Moore, M. H. (2003). *The public value scorecard: A rejoinder and an alternative to strategic performance measurement and management in non-profit organizations* (Working Paper 18). Cambridge, MA: Hauser Center for Nonprofit Organizations, Harvard University.

Niven, P. R. (2003). *Balanced scorecard step-by-step for government and nonprofit agencies.* Hoboken, NJ: Wiley.

Poister, T. H. (2004). *Strategic planning and decision making in state departments of transportation.* Washington, DC: Transportation Research Board.

Sowa, J. E., Selden, S. A., & Sandfort, J. R. (2004). No longer unmeasureable? A multidimensional integrated model of nonprofit organizational performance. *Nonprofit and Voluntary Sector Quarterly, 33*, 711–728.

Transportation Research Board. (2001). *Performance measures to improve transportation systems and agency operations: Conference proceedings.* Washington, DC: Transportation Research Board.

Urban Institute. (2006). *Building a common outcome framework to measure nonprofit performance.* Washington, DC: Urban Institute.

US Department of Health and Human Services. (2012). *Fiscal year 2013 annual performance report and performance plan.* http://www.hhs.gov/budget/performance-appendix-fy2013.pdf

CHAPTER FIVE

DEFINING PERFORMANCE INDICATORS

Once you have identified a program's intended outcomes and other performance criteria, how do you develop good measures of these things? What do useful performance indicators look like? And what are the characteristics of effective sets of performance measures? Where do you find the data to operationalize performance indicators? In order for monitoring systems to convey meaningful information about program performance, the measures used must be appropriate and meet the tests of sound measurement principles. This chapter begins to focus on the how of performance measurement: how to define measures of effectiveness, efficiency, productivity, quality, client satisfaction, and so forth that are valid, reliable, and truly useful.

Operational Indicators

In thinking about defining specific performance measures, we first have to make a distinction between the measures themselves and the operational indicators used to represent them. The measures of performance that are identified through program logic models or goal structures, or simply by decisions by managers or analysts or suggestions from other stakeholders, provide a general sense of what the measures will focus on but not precisely how they will be measured or observed or computed. Operational indicators redefine the measures in terms of the data sources that will be accessed, the observations that will be made, and criteria for what counts versus what does not count in operationalizing the measures so that they can be monitored over time. The term *metrics* is often used in the field of performance measurement to refer to the operational indicators that define the way a measure is specified or observed and the categories or units on the sale used to operationalize it.

Many, or at least most, performance measures—*variable names* in the language of statistical analysis—such as recidivism in juvenile justice programs, cycle time in an investigations process, or clients placed in employment situations by a job training program can be operationalized in multiple ways, which creates a need for clear definitions and rules regarding how a measure will be operationalized. Consider the performance measure commonly referred to as the student-faculty ratio in the field of higher education. What category of students should be included in the computation of this measure: full-time students only or part-time students as well, undergraduate or graduate students or both, students on campus or those taking courses online? What about students who are matriculating in an academic degree program but are not enrolled in any courses this particular semester? Similarly, what categories of faculty members should be included in the ratio: teaching faculty only, research faculty, part-time versus full-time faculty, visiting faculty, individuals with faculty status who are in administrative positions, or faculty members on leave this semester?

As another example, how do we specify a measure of crime rate as an outcome of a crime prevention program? Should it focus only on personal crimes or property crimes—or both? Should we use reported crime statistics, or should we conduct victimization surveys to compute crime rates? The alternative approaches to operationalizing either the student-faculty ratio or crime rates are likely to generate differing results and different impressions of what the performance of such programs actually looks like. Thus, it is critical to define operational indicators carefully and precisely in order to ensure that the various audiences for whom a measurement system is intended will have a clear understanding with respect to what is actually being measured in a given instance.

Before we discuss the challenges of measurement issues, it may be helpful to picture the numerical or statistical forms in which performance indicators can be specified. The most common of these statistical formats— raw numbers, averages, percentages, ratios, rates, and indexes—provide options for defining indicators that best represent the performance dimensions to be measured.

Raw Numbers

Although some authorities on the subject might disagree, raw numbers often provide the most straightforward portrayal of certain performance measures. For example, program outputs and output targets are usually specified in raw numbers, such as the miles of shoulders to be regraded by a county highway maintenance program, the number of books circulated by a public library system, or the number of claims to be cleared each month by a state government's disability determination unit. Beyond outputs, effectiveness measures often track program outcomes in the form of raw numbers. For instance, a local economic development agency may track the number of new jobs created in the county or the net gain or loss in jobs at the end of a year, and state environmental protection agencies monitor the number of ozone action alert days in their metropolitan areas.

Using raw numbers to measure outputs and outcomes has the advantage of portraying the actual scale of operations and impacts, and this is often what line managers are the most concerned with. In addition to programming and monitoring the number of vehicle-miles and vehicle-hours operated each month, for instance, a public transit system in a small urban area might set as a key marketing objective the attainment of a total ridership of more than 2 million passenger trips for the coming year. Although it might also be useful to measure the number of passenger trips per vehicle-mile or per vehicle-hour, the outcome measure of principal interest will be the raw number of passenger trips carried for the year. In fact, the transit manager might also examine the seasonal patterns over the past few years and then prorate the objective of 2 million passengers for the year into numerical ridership targets for each month. He or she would then track the number of passenger trips each month against those specific targets as the system's most direct outcome measure.

Averages

Sometimes statistical averages can be used to summarize performance data and provide a clearer picture than raw numbers would. In an effort to improve customer service, for example, a state department of motor vehicles might monitor the mean average number of days required to process vehicle registration renewals by mail; a local public school system may track the average staff development hours its teachers engage in. Similarly, one measure of the effectiveness of an employment services program might be the median weekly wages earned by former clients who have entered the workforce; a public university system might track the effectiveness of its recruiting efforts by monitoring the median verbal and mathematics SAT scores of each year's freshman class. Such averages are more readily interpreted because they express the measure on a "typical case" basis rather than in the aggregate.

Even the particular type average being employed could make a significant difference in the results generated, as well as the responses suggested by a performance measurement system. Suppose, for example, that the top priority in a state's transportation department is to improve ride quality on its highways and that the metric being used to track progress in this area is the median average score on an index of pavement roughness of all these roads, which is heavily skewed to the high side (with a low percentage of the roads showing very high roughness levels). If the district and area maintenance managers across the state are strongly incentivized to improve performance on this measure to the greatest extent possible, they might well focus on making fairly modest improvements on a large number of those road segments with current roughness scores that are slightly to somewhat higher than the median. If instead the operationalized indicator is specified as the mean average roughness score and there are strong incentives in place to improve performance on that measure, the maintenance managers would be much more likely to focus attention on making dramatic improvements in pavement smoothness on the relatively few roads that are in the high end of the skew of the distribution. This same scenario could well apply to heavily skewed distributions to the high side of a distribution of cycle time of investigations conducted by a regulatory agency or, in the reverse, to a distribution of standardized test scores in a local school district that is heavily skewed to the low side.

Percentages, Rates, and Ratios

Percentages, rates, and ratios are relational statistics that can often express performance measures in more meaningful context. Percentages can be especially useful in conveying the number of instances with desired outcomes, or "successes," as a share of a total number of cases—for example, the percentage of teen mothers in a parenting program who deliver healthy babies, the percentage of clients of a nonprofit agency working with persons with mental disabilities who are placed in competitive employment, and the percentage of youths discharged from juvenile justice programs who don't recidivate back into the criminal justice system within six months.

Percentages can often be more definitive performance measures than averages, particularly when service standards or performance targets have been established. For instance, tracking the average number of days required to process vehicle registration renewals by mail can be a useful measure of service quality, but it doesn't provide an indication of the number of customers who do, or do not, receive satisfactory turnaround time. If a standard is set, however, say to process vehicle renewals within three working days, then the percentage of renewals actually processed within three working days is a much more informative measure of performance.

Expressing performance measures as rates helps put performance in perspective by relating it to some contextual measure representing exposure or potential. For instance, a neighborhood watch program created to reduce crime in inner-city neighborhoods might track the raw numbers of personal and property crimes reported from one year to the next. However, to interpret crime trends in the context of population size, the national Uniform Crime Reporting System tracks these statistics in terms of the number of homicides, assaults, robberies, burglaries, automobile thefts, and so on reported per 1,000 residents in a local jurisdiction. Similarly, the effectiveness of a birth control program in an overpopulated country with an underdeveloped economy might be monitored in terms of the number of births recorded per 1,000 women of childbearing age. Accident rates are usually measured in terms of exposure factors, such as the number of highway traffic accidents per 100 million vehicle-miles operated or the number of commercial airliner collisions per 100 million passenger miles flown. In monitoring the adequacy of health care resources in local communities, the Federal Health Care Financing Administration looks at such measures as the number of physicians per 1,000 population, the number of hospitals per 100,000 population, and the number of hospital beds per 1,000 population. Tracking such measures as rates helps interpret performance in a meaningful context.

The use of ratios is prevalent in performance measurement systems because they too express some performance dimension relative to some particular base. In particular, ratios lend themselves to efficiency, productivity, and cost-effectiveness measures because they are all defined in terms of input-output relationships. Operating efficiency is usually measured in terms of unit costs—for example, the cost per vehicle-mile in a transit system, the cost per detoxification procedure completed in a crisis stabilization unit, the cost per course conducted by a teen parenting program, and the cost per investigation completed by the US Environmental Protection Agency. Similarly, productivity could be measured by such ratios as the tons of refuse collected per crew-day, the number of cases cleared per disability adjudicator, flight segments handled per air traffic controller, and the number of youths counseled per juvenile justice counselor. Cost-effectiveness measures are expressed in such ratios as the cost per client placed in competitive employment or the parenting program cost per healthy infant delivered.

Percentages, rates, and ratios are often preferred because they express some dimension of program performance within a relevant context. More important, however, they are useful because as relational measures, they standardize the measure in terms of some basic factor, which helps control for that factor in interpreting the results. As will be seen in chapter 6, standardizing performance measures by expressing them as percentages, rates, and ratios also helps afford valid comparisons of performance over time, across subgroups, or between a particular agency and other similar agencies.

Indexes

An index is a composite measure that is computed by combining multiple measures or constituent variables into a single summary measure. For example, one way the Federal Reserve Board monitors the effectiveness of its monetary policies in preventing excessive inflation is the consumer price index (CPI), the calculated cost of purchasing a standard set of household consumer items in various markets around the country. Because indexes are derived by combining other indicators, scores, or repeated measures into a new scale, some of them seem quite abstract, but ranges or categories are often defined to help interpret the practical meaning of different scale values. Researchers frequently develop and use indexes to measure multidimensional concepts such as psychological well-being or quality of life. Thus, they can be particularly useful for measuring outcomes in programmatic areas whose intended results are complex, as illustrated in table 5.1. However, they can also apply to service quality and customer satisfaction as well.

Indexes are used as performance measures in a variety of program areas. For instance, the air quality index (AQI) is the standardized measure

TABLE 5.1 ILLUSTRATIVE INDEXES FOR PERFORMANCE MANAGEMENT

Index	Domain/outcome	Source
Air Quality Index	Air quality	http://www.airnow.gov
Photometric Index	Litter	http://www.fs.fed.us
International Roughness Index	Highway ride quality	http://www.fhwa.dot.gov
Duke Activity Status Index	Individual functional capacity	www.cscr.org
Colorado Symptom Index	Psychological well-being	National Institutes of Health
Patient Health Questionnaire Mood Scale	Depression	www.sfaetc.ucsf.edu
Wisconsin Quality of Life Index	Quality of life	www.ncbi.nlm.nih.gov
Adaptive Behavior Scales	Mental health	

that state and local air pollution control programs use to monitor compliance with federal clean air standards and notify the public about levels of air pollution in their communities. State and local air monitoring stations and national air monitoring stations employ sensors that use ultraviolet, visible, or infrared light to measure concentrations of nitrogen dioxide, ground-level ozone, carbon monoxide, sulfur dioxide, and particulate matter in the air over a path of several meters up to several kilometers in length (Plaia & Ruggieri, 2011). In metropolitan areas, these measurements are taken daily and incorporated into formulas that are used to compute a value on the AQI that ranges from 0 for pristine air up to 500, which represents air pollution levels that would pose immediate danger to the public. For purposes of practical interpretation, the AQI is often broken down into five categories: good, unhealthy for sensitive groups, unhealthy, very unhealthy, and hazardous.

The Adaptive Behavior Scales (ABS) are standardized scales developed to assess the level of functioning of individuals with mental disabilities in two areas: personal independence and responsibility and social behaviors (Dixon, 2007). They are often used by public and nonprofit agencies working with people with mental disabilities to assess their needs and monitor the impact of various programs on clients' level of functioning. The overall scale consists of eighteen domains—for example, independent functioning, physical development, language development, self-direction, self-abusive behavior, and disturbing interpersonal behavior—which in turn have subdomains that are represented by a series of items. For example, one subdomain of the independent functioning domain concerns eating, and this is measured by four items

TABLE 5.2 DUKE ACTIVITY STATUS INDEX

	Activity	Yes	No
1	Can you take care of yourself (eating, dressing, bathing, or using the toilet)?	2.75	0
2	Can you walk indoors such as around your house?	1.75	0
3	Can you walk a block or two on level ground?	2.75	0
4	Can you climb a flight of stairs or walk up a hill?	5.50	0
5	Can you run a short distance?	8.00	0
6	Can you do light work around the house like dusting or washing dishes?	2.70	0
7	Can you do moderate work around the house like vacuuming sweeping floors or carrying in groceries?	3.50	0
8	Can you do moderate work around the house like scrubbing floors or lifting and moving heavy furniture?	8.00	0
9	Can you do yard work like raking leaves weeding or pushing a power mower?	4.50	0
10	Can you have sexual relations?	5.25	0
11	Can you participate in moderate recreational activities like golf, bowling, dancing, doubles tennis, or throwing a baseball or football?	6.00	0
12	Can you participate in strenuous sports like swimming, tennis, football, basketball, or skiing?	7.50	0

Note: The maximum value is 58.2, and the minimum value is 0. The test-retest reliability is .81.

focusing on the use of table utensils, eating in public, drinking, and table manners.

In human services programs, psychological scales are often used to assess client outcomes. For example, the Duke Activity Status Index is used to measure a client's functional capacity. It is based on answers given on a self-administered questionnaire containing twelve questions regarding an individual's ability to engage in or perform activities that are considered to be a normal part of daily living, as shown in table 5.2. The items are weighted according to the difficulty or energy required in each activity, and the responses are summed to an overall score that ranges from 0 to 58.2.

With respect to the statistical form of performance measures, indexes do not constitute a different type of statistical measure but rather are composite scales that represent the degree of some characteristic or condition. Thus, like other performance measures, they may be expressed as raw numbers, averages, or percentages. For example, a performance monitoring system might report the number of days with unhealthy air quality in

TABLE 5.3 ILLUSTRATIVE HIGHWAY MAINTENANCE PERFORMANCE MEASURES

Performance Indicator	Performance Dimension	Statistical Form
Gallons of patching material applied	Resource	Raw number
Lane-miles resurfaced	Output	Raw number
Cost per lane-mile resurfaced	Operating efficiency	Ratio
Miles of shoulders graded per crew-day	Productivity	Ratio
Task hours completed per production hour	Productivity	Ratio
Mean quality assurance score	Quality	Average
Percentage of roads in compliance with American Association of State Highway and Transportation Officials standards	Immediate outcome	Percentage
Average pavement quality index	Immediate outcome	Median
Percentage of motorists rating ride quality as satisfactory	Customer satisfaction	Percentage
Customer Service Index	Customer satisfaction	Raw number
Accidents per 100 million vehicle-miles with road condition as a contributing factor	Outcome	Rate

Source: Adapted from Poister (1997).

Atlanta or the percentage of clients of a nonprofit agency in New Jersey whose adaptive behavior is in the "moderately independent" range.

Mixed Measures

Many performance monitoring systems include a mix of measures expressed in the various forms we've discussed here. For example, table 5.3 illustrates a sample of conventional measures used in tracking the performance of highway maintenance programs. They include raw numbers of resource materials and outputs, ratios for efficiency and productivity indicators, mean average quality assurance scores, median pavement quality index scores, percentages of satisfactory roads and satisfied customers, and accident rates related to road conditions.

Identifying Possible Performance Indicators

While managers, analysts, and consultants involved in developing performance measurement systems often define indicators on their own, working directly from logic models or goal structures, there are often resources available that share information on measures used in a program area that might well provide a starting point for developing more customized indictors in a given instance. Such sources often provide information on the purpose and usefulness, and strengths and weaknesses, of these measures. Examples of these sources of measures that have been used and in some cases assessed include the following:

> *Health:* McDowell, *Measuring Health: A Guide to Rating Scales and Questionnaires* (2006)
>
> *Education:* Manno, Crittenden, Arkin, and Hassel, *A Road to Results: A Performance Measurement Guidebook for the Annie E. Casey Foundation's Educational Program* (2007)
>
> *Municipal services:* Ammons, *Municipal Benchmarks: Assessing Local Performance and Establishing Community Standards* (2012)
>
> *Transportation:* American Association of State Highway and Transportation Officials, *Strategic Performance Measures for State Departments of Transportation* (2003)

Sources

The data used in performance measurement systems come from a wide variety of sources, and this has implications regarding the cost and effort of data collection and processing, as well as quality and appropriateness. In some cases, appropriate data exist in files or systems that are used and maintained for other purposes. They can be extracted or used for performance monitoring as well, whereas the data for other measures will have to be collected specifically for the purpose of performance measurement.

With regard to the highway maintenance measures shown in table 5.3, information on the gallons of patching material applied may be readily available from the highway department's inventory control system, and data on the number of lane-miles resurfaced, the miles of shoulders graded, and the actual task and production hours taken to complete these activities may be recorded in its maintenance management system. The cost of this work is tracked in the department's activity-based accounting system. The quality assurance scores are generated by teams of inspectors who audit a sample of completed maintenance jobs to assess compliance with prescribed procedures. The pavement quality index and the percentage of roads in compliance with national American Association of State Highway and Transportation Officials (AASHTO) standards require a combination of mechanical measurements and physical inspection of highway condition and deficiencies. The percentage of motorists rating the roads as satisfactory may require a periodic mail-out survey of a sample of registered drivers. The accident rate data can probably be extracted from a data file on recorded traffic accidents maintained by the state police.

The categories of data shown in the following list are not intended to be exhaustive or mutually exclusive, but they do indicate major sources of performance data:

- Existing data compilations
- Clinical examinations
- Agency records
- Tests
- Administrative records
- Surveys
- Follow-up contacts
- Customer response cards
- Direct observation
- Specially designed instruments

Sometimes existing databases that are maintained by agencies for other purposes can meet selected performance measurement needs of particular programs. Many federal agencies maintain compilations of data on demographics, housing, crime, transportation, the economy, health, education, and the environment that may lend themselves to tracking the performance of a particular program. Many state government agencies and some nonprofit organizations maintain similar kinds of statistical databases, and a variety of ongoing social surveys and citizen polls also produce data that might be useful as performance measures.

Agency and Administrative Records

By far the most common source of performance data consists of agency records. Public and nonprofit agencies responsible for managing programs and delivering services tend to store transactional data that record the flow of cases through a program, the number of clients served, the number of projects completed, the number of services provided, treatment modules completed, staff-client interactions documented, referrals made, and so on. Much of this focuses on service delivery and outputs, but other transactional data maintained in agency records relate further down the output chain regarding the disposition of cases, results achieved, or numbers of complaints received, for instance. In addition to residing in management information systems, these kinds of data are also found in service requests, activity logs, case logs, production records, records of permits issued and revoked, complaint files, incident reports, claims processing systems, and treatment and follow-up records, among other sources.

Beyond working with transactional data relating specifically to particular programs, you can also tap administrative data concerning personnel and expenditures, for example, to operationalize performance data. In some cases, these administrative data may also be housed in the same programmatic agencies that are responsible for service delivery, but often they reside in central staff support units, such as personnel agencies, training divisions, budget offices, finance departments, accounting divisions, and planning and evaluation units. Sources of such administrative data might include time, attendance, and salary reports, as well as budget and accounting systems and financial, performance, and compliance audits.

Follow-Up Contacts

In some program areas where the outcomes are expected to materialize outside the agency and perhaps well after a program has been completed, it is necessary to make follow-up contacts with clients to track effectiveness. Often this can be accomplished through the context of follow-up services. For example, after juvenile offenders are released from boot camp programs operated by a state's department of juvenile justice, the department may also provide after-care services in which counselors work with these youths to help them readjust to their home or community settings; encourage them to engage seriously in school, work, or other wholesome activities; and try to help them stay away from further criminal activity. Through the follow-up contacts, the counselors keep track of the juveniles' status in terms of involvement in gainful activity versus recidivism.

Many kinds of human service programs—vocational rehabilitation and teen parenting education programs, for instance—use similar kinds of follow-up contacts with clients as a source of data on program outcomes. In other cases where follow-up contact is not part of usual programmatic activity, former clients can be contacted or surveyed by the mail, telephone, or personal visits expressly for the purpose of soliciting information for measures of service quality, customer satisfaction, and program effectiveness.

Direct Observation

Many times, measuring outcomes requires some type of direct observation, by means of mechanical instruments or personal inspections, in contexts other than follow-up client contacts. For example, state transportation departments use various kinds of mechanical and electronic equipment to measure the condition and surface quality of the highways they maintain, and environmental agencies use sophisticated measuring devices to monitor air quality and water quality. In other cases, trained observers armed with rating forms make direct physical inspections to obtain performance data. For instance, local public works departments sometimes use trained observers to assess the condition of city streets, sanitation departments may use trained observers to monitor the cleanliness of streets and alleys, and transit authorities often use them to check the on-time performance of the buses.

Clinical Examinations

Some performance monitoring data come from a particular kind of direct observation: clinical examinations. Physicians, psychiatrists, psychologists, occupational therapists, speech therapists, and other professionals may all be involved in conducting clinical examinations of program clients or other individuals on an ongoing basis, generating streams of data that might feed into performance measurement systems. For example, data from medical diagnoses or evaluations may be useful not only in tracking the performance of health care programs but also in monitoring the effectiveness of crisis stabilization units, teen parenting programs, vocational rehabilitation programs, disability programs, and workers' compensation return-to-work programs, among others. Similarly, data from psychological evaluations might be useful as performance measures in correctional facilities, drug and alcohol abuse programs, behavioral-shaping programs for persons with mental disabilities, and violence reduction programs in public schools.

Tests

Tests are instruments designed to measure individuals' knowledge in a certain area or their skill level in performing certain tasks. Obviously these are most relevant for educational programs, as local public schools routinely use classroom tests to gauge students' learning or scholastic achievement. In addition, some states use uniform "Regents"-type examinations, and a plethora of standardized exams that are on a widespread basis, which facilitate tracking educational performance on a local, state, or national level and allow individual schools or school districts to benchmark themselves against others or national trends. Beyond education programs, testing is used to obtain performance data in a wide variety of other kinds of training programs, generating measures ranging from the job skills of persons working in sheltered workshops to the flying skills of air force pilots and fitness ratings of police officers.

Surveys and Customer Response Cards

As will be discussed in chapter 13, public and nonprofit agencies also employ a wide range of personal interview, telephone, mail-out, and other self-administered surveys to generate performance data, most often focusing on feedback regarding service quality, program effectiveness, and customer satisfaction. In addition to surveys of clients and former clients are surveys of customers, service providers or contractors, other stakeholders, citizens or the public at large, and even agency employees. However, survey data are highly reactive, and great care is needed in the design and conduct of surveys to ensure high-quality, objective feedback.

One particular form of survey that is becoming more prevalent as a source of performance data is the customer response card. These are usually brief survey cards containing only a handful of straightforward questions that are given to customers at the point of service delivery, or shortly after, to monitor customers' satisfaction with the service they received in that particular instance. Such response cards might be given out, for example, to persons who just finished renewing their driver's license, individuals just about to be discharged from a crisis stabilization unit, child support enforcement clients who have just made a visit to their local office, or corporate representatives who have just attended a seminar about how their firms can do business with state government. These response cards not only serve to identify and, one hopes, resolve immediate service delivery problems but also generate data that in the aggregate can be useful in monitoring service quality and customer satisfaction with a program over time.

Specially Designed Measurement Tools

Although the vast majority of the measures used in performance monitoring systems come from the conventional sources we have already discussed, in some cases it is desirable or necessary to design special measurement instruments to gauge the effectiveness of a particular program. For example, the national Keep America Beautiful program and its state and local affiliates use the photometric index developed by the American Public Works Association to monitor volumes of litter in local communities. The photometric index is operationalized by taking color slides of a sample of ninety-six-square-foot sites in areas that are representative of the community in terms of income and land use. The specific kinds of sites include street curb fronts, sidewalks, vacant lots, parking lots, dumpster sites, loading docks, commercial storage areas, and possibly rural roads, beaches, and parks. There may be on the order of 120 such sites in the sample for one community, and the same sites are photographed each year.

The pictures are projected over a grid map, and the "littered" squares in each photograph are counted. The resulting photometric index value, which is computed as the number of littered squares per slide, is tracked each year as an indicator of the extent to which the program is having an impact in terms of reducing the accumulation of litter in each of these specific kinds of sites, as well as in the community at large. This measurement instrument, specially designed to monitor a principal intended outcome of the Keep America Beautiful program, is probably best categorized as a form of indirect observation.

Validity and Reliability

As we have seen, for some performance measures good data may be readily at hand, whereas other measures may require follow-up observation, surveys, or other specially designed data collection procedures. Although available data sources can obviously be advantageous in terms of time, effort, and cost, readily available data are not always good data—but they aren't always poor quality either. From a methodological point of view, good data are those with a high degree of validity and reliability—that is, they are unbiased indicators that are appropriate measures of performance and provide a reasonable level of consistency, precision, and statistical reliability. There are numerous good sources on the process of developing and testing measures from a methodological or research perspective, such as those by Shulz and Whitney (2005) and DeVellis (2012).

Reliability

Performance indicators are measures defined operationally in terms of how the measure is taken or the data are collected. For example, the operational indicator for the number of students entering a state's university system each year might be the number recorded as having enrolled in three or more classes for the first time during the preceding academic year by the registrar's office at each of the institutions in the system. Similarly, the operational indicator for the number of passengers carried by an urban transit system might be the number counted by automatic registering fare boxes; the percentage of customers who are satisfied with the state patrol's process for renewing drivers' licenses might be measured by the percentage who check off "satisfied" or "very satisfied" on response cards that are handed out to people as they complete the process.

The reliability of such performance indicators is a matter of how objective, precise, and dependable they are. Consistency over time is one aspect of reliability; if the same measuring instrument—for example, a survey, test, or other observation—is used on the same subject or subjects in the same way at different times, if the subject has really not changed on the dimension of interest over that period of time, the measurement should yield the same results in order to be considered reliable. To the extent that it produces different results, the indicator lacks precision, producing a range of estimates of the true value of the measure rather than a single value or only slight variation around it. For instance, if repeated queries to a university registrar's office asking how many students are enrolled in classes during the current semester yield a different number every time, the measure lacks consistency or dependability and thus is not very reliable. The range of responses might provide an indication of roughly how many students are enrolled in classes, but it certainly is not a precise indicator. With survey instruments and other kinds of indicators observed on a sample of cases, clients in a program, for example, test-retest reliability can be assessed by using the instrument at two points in time on the same sample and running a correlation between the two sets of data. The closer the correlation coefficient is to 1.0, the greater the reliability of the measure.

A lack of interrater reliability also presents problems in performance data. If a number of trained observers rating the condition of city streets look at the same section of street at the same time, using the same procedures, definitions, categories, and rating forms, yet the rating they come up with varies substantially from observer to observer, this measure of street condition clearly is not very reliable. Although the observers have been trained to use this instrument the same way, the actual ratings that result appear to be based more on the subjective impressions of the individual raters than on the objective application of the standard criteria. Such problems with interrater reliability can occur whenever the indicator is operationalized by different individuals observing cases and making judgments, as might the case, for instance, when housing inspectors determine the percentage of dwelling units that meet code requirements, when workers' compensation examiners determine the percentage of employees injured on the job who require longer-term medical benefits, or when staff psychologists rate the ability of mildly and moderately mentally disabled clients of a nonprofit agency to function at a higher level of independence. If they are not applying the measuring instrument, making observations, or counting things the same way, the data will lack interrater reliability.

Reliability problems may also occur when the performance data are reported from different sources or locations. For example, when the same indicators are reported regularly by various district offices, subordinate work units, or project sites, there may be differences in the way things are recorded that will cause reliability problems when the data are aggregated and reported out at the department or program level. As will be seen in chapter 14, the potential for this kind of reliability problem can be magnified geometrically when data on the same measures are reported by separate agencies or programs in a comparative measurement process to benchmark the performance of any one agencies against the field at large. If these agencies are operationalizing the indicators differently, even though they assume they are reporting on the same measures, the data lack reliability and comparisons are likely to be meaningless or misleading.

Finally, internal consistency reliability focuses on the extent to which each of the items in an index or scale correlates with the other items in the scale, which would be expected if the various items are measuring various dimensions of the overall core concept. A statistical test, Cronbach's alpha, can be used to measure the strength of the intercorrelations among all the items included in a measure; an alpha of .60 or higher is commonly considered acceptable.

From a measurement perspective, the perfect performance indicator may never exist because there is always the possibility of some error in the measurement process. To the extent that the error in a measure is random and unbiased in direction, this is a reliability problem. Although quality assurance processes need to be built into data processing procedures, there is always a chance of accidental errors in data reporting, coding, and tabulating, and this creates reliability problems. For example, state child support enforcement programs track the percentage of noncustodial parents who are delinquent in making obligated payments, and computing this percentage would seem to be a simple matter. At any given time, the parent is either up-to-date or delinquent in making these payments. However, the information on the thousands of cases recorded in the centralized database for this program pertaining to numbers of children in households, establishment of paternity, obligation of payments, and current status comes from local offices and a variety of other sources in piecemeal fashion. Although up-to-date accuracy is critical in maintaining these records, errors are made and slippage in reporting does occur, and the actual accounts are likely to be off the mark a little (or maybe a lot). Thus, in a system that tracks this indicator monthly, the computed percentage of delinquent parents may overstate the rate of delinquency some months and understate it other months. Although there is no systematic tendency to overrepresent or underrepresent the percentage of delinquent parents, this indicator will not be highly dependable or reliable.

Validity

Whereas reliability is a matter of objectivity and precision, the validity of a performance measure concerns its appropriateness, that is, the extent to which an indicator is directly related to and representative of the performance dimension of interest. If a proposed indicator is largely irrelevant or only tangentially related to the desired outcome of a particular program, then it will not provide a valid indication of that program's effectiveness. For example, scores on the verbal portion of the SATs have sometimes been used as a surrogate indicator of the writing ability of twelfth graders in public schools, but the focus of these tests is really on vocabulary and reading comprehension, which are relevant but only partially indicative of writing capabilities. In contrast, the more recently developed National Assessment of Educational Progress test in writing provides a much more direct indicator of students' ability to articulate points in writing and to write effective, fully developed responses to questions designed specifically to test their writing competence.

Consider the validity of unemployment statistics, for instance. The indicator of the unemployment rate in the United States reported by the Bureau of Labor Statistics each month is based on surveys of sixty thousand households concerning the employment status of household members over sixteen years of age. Those who indicate that they do not have jobs but have looked for work during the past four weeks are classified as being unemployed; those who indicate that they are working in full-time or part-time jobs are considered to be employed. The unemployment rate is computed as the number of those classified as unemployed taken as a percentage of the total household members considered to be in the labor force as represented by the number of employed plus unemployed individuals. The validity of this standard measure is often questioned, however, principally because it underestimates actual unemployment levels by not including unemployed individuals who have looked for work sometime in the past year but not in the past four weeks, or those who may be unemployed for much longer periods of time but have given up looking for work ("The Real Jobless Rate," 2009).

As another example, the aim of a metropolitan transit authority's welfare-to-work initiative might be to facilitate moving employable individuals from dependence on welfare to regular employment by providing access to work sites through additional transportation services. As possible measures of effectiveness, however, the estimated number of homeless individuals in the area would be largely irrelevant, and the total number of employed persons and the average median income in the metropolitan area are subject to whole hosts of factors and would be only marginally sensitive to the welfare-to-work initiative. More relevant measures might focus on the number of individuals reported by the welfare agency to have been moved off the welfare rolls, the number of "third-shift" positions reported as filled by manufacturing plants and other employers, or the number of passenger trips made on bus trips that have been instituted as part of the welfare-to-work initiative. However, each of these measures still falls short as an indicator of the number of individuals who were formerly without jobs and dependent on welfare who now have jobs by virtue of being able to get to and from work on the transit system.

Most proposed performance measures tend to be at least somewhat appropriate and relevant to the program being monitored, but the issue of validity often boils down to the extent to which they provide fair, unbiased indicators of the performance dimension of interest. Whereas reliability problems result from random error in the measurement process, validity problems arise when there is systematic bias in the measurement process, producing a systematic tendency to overestimate or to underestimate program performance. For instance, crime prevention programs may use officially reported crime rates as the principal outcome measure, but as is well known, many crimes are not reported to the police for a variety of reasons. Thus, these reported crime rates tend to underestimate the number of crimes committed in a given area during a particular time period. The percentage of total crimes reported as "solved" by a local police department would systematically overstate the effectiveness of the police if it includes cases that were initially recorded as crimes and subsequently determined not to constitute crimes but were still carried on the books labeled as "solved" crimes. An alternative would be to conduct victimization surveys to estimate the extent to which crimes occur, but for any number of reasons, respondents may not supply candid or accurate information, which could cause validity problems or reliability problems, or both.

Developing valid indicators of program effectiveness is often particularly challenging because the desired outcomes are somewhat diffuse, only tenuously connected to the program, or affected by numerous other factors beyond the program's control, or because they do not lend themselves to practical measurement. For example, a performance monitoring system for the US Diplomatic Service might track the use of resources, numbers of strategy sessions, numbers of contacts with representatives from other countries, numbers of agreements signed, and so on, but much of the work occurs informally and behind closed doors; progress is open to very subjective interpretation; and the real impact in terms of maintaining the peace or gaining strategic advantage is difficult to determine. Alternatively, consider the US Forest Service, for which the real impact of conservation measures and reforestation programs implemented now will not materialize until several decades into the future. In such cases, the most practical approach may be to rely primarily on output measures or to try to identify reasonable proximate measures, as discussed later in this chapter.

Even for public and nonprofit programs whose intended outcomes are a lot closer to being within reach, defining valid outcome indicators may still be difficult. For instance, a crisis stabilization unit may monitor the percentage of its consumers who complete treatment and are discharged but then turn up again as readmissions in the unit within thirty days. However, discharged consumers may move out of the area or turn up at some other facility with the same problems within thirty days, or they may become unstabilized with the same psychiatric or substance abuse problems they were experiencing before but simply not get needed help the next time around. Thus, the percentage of readmissions within thirty days would certainly be a relevant measure, but it is likely to be a biased indicator with a tendency to underestimate the percentage of discharged consumers who in fact do not remain stabilized for very long.

For many human service programs, it is difficult to follow clients after they leave the program, but that is often when the real outcomes occur. The crisis stabilization unit observes consumers only while they are actually short-term residents of the facility, and thus it cannot track whether they continue to take prescribed medications faithfully, begin to use drugs or alcohol again, or continue participating in long-term care programs. Appropriate measures of effectiveness are not difficult to define in this case, but operationalizing them through systematic client follow-up would require significant additional staff, time, and effort that is probably better invested in service delivery than in performance measurement.

As another example, a teen mother parenting program can track clients' participation in the training sessions, but it will have to stay in touch with all program completers in order to determine the percentage who deliver healthy babies, babies of normal birth weight, babies free from HIV, and so on. But what about the quality of parental care given during the first year of infants' lives? Consider the options for tracking the extent to which the teen mothers provide the kind of care for their babies that is imparted by the training program. Periodic telephone or mail-out surveys of the new mothers could be conducted, but in at least some cases, their responses are likely to be biased in terms of presenting a more favorable picture of reality. Alternatively, trained professionals could make periodic follow-up visits to the clients' homes, primarily to help the mothers with any problems they are experiencing. By talking with the mothers and observing the infants in their own households, they could also make assessments of the adequacy of care given. This would be feasible if the program design includes follow-up visits to provide further support, and it would probably provide a more satisfactory indicator even though some of the mothers might be on their best behavior during these short visits, possibly leading to more positive assessments that overstate the quality of care given to the infants on a regular basis.

Researchers and others are continually working to improve the kinds of indicators that are used in monitoring performance. For example, homelessness is a major concern in many urban areas in the United States, as well as many other countries, but it is difficult to compute with any assurance the percentage of homeless individuals in a local area who are being served to some degree by homeless shelters run by public or non-profit organizations, for instance, or even determine whether the number of homeless individuals has been increasing or decreasing over time. The various sources that might shed light on the number of homeless people living in a community are likely to count things differently; by the very nature of the problem, it may be difficult or impossible to find or identify many individuals who are homeless; and when homeless people are in fact interviewed, their memory of dates may be poor and fade as time from a period of homelessness passes. One response to this issue has been the development of the residential follow-back calendar to help subjects improve their recall of the number of days they have been homeless over the past year by (1) taking more time to remember, (2) decomposing a class of events into subclasses, (3) recalling events in reverse chronology, and (4) listing boundaries or landmarks to assist accurate recall (Tsemberis, McHog, Williams, Hanrahan, & Stefancic, 2007). This is a good example of the ongoing efforts to refine indicators in order to strengthen the validity of performance measures in many policy and program areas.

Bases of Validity

Although validity is partly a matter of subjective judgment, there are at least four bases on which to "validate" performance measures:

- Many indicators simply have *face validity*; they are clearly valid measures "on the face of it." For instance, the number of fares paid as recorded by registering fare boxes on its buses during a given month is obviously an appropriate measure of a local transit system's ridership for that month.
- *Consensual validity* is conferred on a performance measure when a number of experts and others working in the field develop an apparent consensus that it is appropriate. For instance, there is a consensus among managers of local government fleet maintenance operations that the percentage of vehicles that are available for use, on average, is

a valid indicator of their programs' effectiveness. Note that in both of these examples, there is clearly room for error. If some individuals board the buses and make transit trips without paying a fare, then that indicator systematically undercounts ridership; in the case of the fleet maintenance operations, some vehicles could be allowed to remain in service or go back into service when they have serious operating problems, in which case that indicator would overstate program effectiveness. However, it should be kept in mind that validity, like reliability, is still a matter of degree.

- *Content validity* refers to the extent to which the content of a test or measurement instrument reflects the domains or dimensions of the concept or constructs being measured. Since the intended outcomes of many public and nonprofit programs are multifaceted concepts, content validity is often of importance to performance measurement. A local nonprofit agency in the United States, for instance, may be providing services to recently arrived immigrant families to help them become more self-sufficient in terms of proficiency in speaking English, mastery of basic financial literacy, ability to get and hold jobs, ability to afford decent housing, and ability of their children to succeed in school. If a single overall measure is desired for tracking clients' overall progress in becoming self-sufficient, the index should include one or more elements that match each of these initial or intermediate outcomes.

- *Concurrent* or *correlational validity* occurs when some indicator that is being tested correlates well statistically with another indicator that is already considered to be a proven measure. For instance, the international roughness index (IRI) directly measures the smoothness of a highway's surface, but transportation departments feel comfortable using it as an indicator of overall ride quality because in panel studies conducted on a rigorous experimental basis, IRI values correlate highly with motorists' rating of ride quality based on their firsthand experience.

- *Predictive validity* is conferred on an indicator when values on that measure at present can be used to reliably predict some outcome in the future. For example, consider military bases whose principal mission is to train and otherwise prepare forces for combat readiness. Monitoring resources, activities, and outputs is fairly straightforward for these operations, but measuring combat readiness directly will be possible only when the forces they have trained become engaged in actual combat. However, if it has been determined, based on experience, that effectiveness ratings of troops' performance in simulated maneuvers have correlated strongly with their performance when they have subsequently been committed to combat, then these effectiveness ratings have predictive validity as an indicator of combat readiness.

Common Measurement Problems

In working through the challenge of defining useful operational indicators, system designers should always anticipate likely problems and try to avoid or circumvent them. Common problems that can jeopardize reliability or validity, or both, include noncomparable data, tenuously related proximate measures, tendencies to under- or overreport data, poor instrument design, observer bias, instrument decay, reactive measurement, nonresponse bias, and cheating.

Noncomparability of Data

Whenever data are entered into the system in a decentralized process, noncomparability of data is a possibility. Although uniform data collection procedures are prescribed, there is no automatic guarantee that they will be implemented exactly the same way from work station to work station or from site to site. This can be a problem within a single agency or program, as people responsible for data input from parallel offices, branches, or work units find their own ways to expedite the process in the press of heavy workloads, and they may end up counting things differently from one another. Thus, in a large agency with multiple data entry sites, care must be taken to ensure uniform data entry.

In large agencies delivering programs through a decentralized structure, for example, a state human services agency with 104 local offices, the central office may wish to track certain measures in order to compare the performance of local offices, or it may want to roll up the data to track performance on a statewide basis. Particularly if the local offices operate with a fair degree of autonomy, there may be significant inconsistencies in how the indicator is operationalized from one local office to the next. This could jeopardize the validity of comparisons among the local offices as well as the statewide data. The probability of noncomparable data is often greater in state and federal grant programs, when the data input is done by the individual grantees—local government agencies or nonprofit organizations—who, again, may set up somewhat different processes for doing so.

The problem of noncomparable data is often especially acute with respect to benchmarking efforts, in which a number of governmental jurisdictions or nonprofit agencies provide their own data to a central source (using uniform procedures, one hopes). There may be substantial discrepancies in the way they maintain their own data and enter them into the centralized system, thereby largely invalidating comparisons among them.

Tenuous Proximate Measures

When it is difficult to define direct indicators of program performance or is not practical to operationalize them, it is often possible to use proximate measures instead. Proximate measures are indicators that are thought to be approximately equivalent to more direct measures of performance. In effect, proximate measures are less direct indicators that are assumed to have some degree of correlational or predictive validity. For example, records of customer complaints are often used as an indicator of customer satisfaction with a particular program. Actually, customer complaints are an indicator of dissatisfaction, whereas customer satisfaction is usually thought of as a much broader concept. Nevertheless, in the absence of good customer feedback using surveys, response cards, or focus groups, data on complaints often fill in as proximate measures for customer satisfaction.

Similarly, the commonly stated purposes of local public transit systems are to meet the mobility needs of individuals who don't have access to private means of transportation and to reduce the use of private automobiles in cities by providing a competitive alternative. Transit systems rarely track measures of these intended outcomes directly. Instead, they monitor overall passenger trips as a proximate measure that they believe to be correlated with these outcomes.

Sometimes when it is difficult to obtain real measures of program effectiveness, monitoring systems rely on indicators of outputs or initial outcomes as proximate measures of longer-term outcomes. For example, a state department of administrative services may provide a number of support services, such as vehicle rentals, office supplies, and printing services to the other operating agencies of state government. The real impact of these services would be measured by the extent to which they enable these operating departments, their customers, to perform their functions more effectively and efficiently. However, the performance measures used by these other agencies are unlikely to be at all sensitive to the marginal contribution of the support services. Thus, the department of administrative services might well just monitor indicators of output and service quality on the assumption that if the line agencies are using these support services and are satisfied with them, then the services are in fact contributing to higher performance levels on the part of these other agencies.

Although proximate measures can often be useful, validity problems emerge when they are only tenuously related to the performance criteria of interest. Consider for a moment a municipal government's neighborhood revitalization program that is trying to encourage the construction of infill residential and small business developments in order to strengthen the economic viability of target areas within the city limits. The most direct indicator of the success of the program might be the number of such housing and small business units constructed in those areas, but a leading indicator that would be expected to point in that direction would be the number of units for which building permits have been issued. However, the building permits represent intentions rather than actions, and it may be that many of the construction plans for which permits have been sought are never realized. Thus, this proximate indicator would lead to biased counts that underrepresent the number of units actually constructed.

Underreporting or Overreporting

Whereas some measures are simply sloppy and overrepresent some cases while undercounting others, thereby eroding reliability, other performance indicators have a tendency to underreport or overreport on a systematic basis, creating validity problems. For instance, reported crime statistics tend to underestimate actual crimes committed because for various reasons, many crimes go unreported to the police. Periodic victimization surveys may provide more valid estimates of actual crimes committed, but they require considerable time, effort, and resources. Thus, the official reported crime statistics are often used as indicators of the effectiveness of crime prevention programs or police crime-solving activities even though they are known to underestimate actual crime rates. In part, this is workable because the reported crime statistics may be valid for tracking trends over time, say on a monthly basis, as long as the tendency for crimes to be reported or not reported is constant from month to month.

One critical concern of juvenile detention facilities is to eliminate, or at least minimize, instances of physical or sexual abuse of children in their custody by other detainees or by staff members. Thus, one performance measure that is important to them is the number of child abuse incidents occurring per month. But what would be the operationalized indicator for this measure? One possibility would be the number of such incidents reported each month, but this really represents the number of allegations of child abuse. Considering that some of these allegations may well be unfounded, this indicator would systematically tend to overestimate the real number of such incidents. A preferred indicator would probably be the number of child abuse incidents that are recorded on the basis of full investigations when such allegations are made. However, as is true of reported crime rates in general, this measure would underestimate the actual number of child abuse incidents if some victims of child abuse in these facilities are afraid to report them.

Poor Instrument Design

Sound design of measuring instruments is essential for effective performance measurement. This is particularly important with surveys of customers or other stakeholders; items that are unclear or that incorporate biases can lead to serious measurement problems. Often such surveys include questions that are vague, double-barreled, or ambiguous, and because respondents are likely to interpret them in different ways, the resulting data include a considerable amount of "noise" and thus are not very reliable.

A more serious problem arises when surveys include biased items—leading questions that, intentionally or not, prompt respondents to answer in a certain way. For example, an agency's ongoing customer satisfaction survey could include questions and response choices that are worded in such a way as almost to force respondents to give programs artificially high ratings. This would obviously overestimate customer satisfaction with this program and invalidate the survey data. These kinds of problems can also apply to other modes of performance measurement, such as trained observer ratings and other specially designed measurement tools. The important point here is that care should always be taken to design measurement instruments that are clear, unambiguous, and unbiased.

Observer Bias

Biased observers are another source of severe validity problems. Even with a good survey instrument, for instance, an interviewer who has some definite bias, either in favor of a program or opposed to it for some reason, can obviously bias the responses in that direction by introducing the survey, setting the overall tone, and asking the questions in a certain way. In the extreme, the performance data generated by the survey may actually represent the interviewer's biases more than they serve as a valid reflection of the views of the respondents.

Clearly the problem of observer bias is not limited to survey data. Many performance measures are operationalized through observer ratings, including inspection of physical conditions, observation of behavioral patterns, or quality assurance audits. In addition, performance data from clinical evaluations by physicians, psychologists, therapists, and other professionals can also be vulnerable to observer biases. To control for this possibility, careful training of interviewers and observers and emphasis on the need for fair, unbiased observation and assessment are essential.

Instrument Decay

In addition to sound instrument design, consistent application of the measure over time is critical to performance monitoring systems, precisely because they are intended to track key performance measures over time. If the instrument changes over time, it can be difficult to assess the extent to which trends in the data reflect real trends in performance versus changes in measurement procedures. For example, if a local police department begins to classify as crimes certain kinds of reported incidents that previously were not counted as crimes, then everything else being equal, reported crime rates will go up. These performance data could easily be interpreted as indicating that crime is on the rise in that area or that crime prevention programs are not working well there, when in reality the upward trend simply reflects a change in recording procedures.

Instrument decay refers to the erosion of integrity of a measure as a valid and reliable performance indicator over time. For instance, as part of a city sanitation department's quality control effort, it trains a few inspectors to conduct spot checks of neighborhoods where residential refuse collection crews have recently passed through to observe the amount of trash and litter that might have been left behind. At first the inspectors adhere closely to a regular schedule of visiting randomly selected neighborhoods and are quite conscientious about rating cleanliness according to prescribed guidelines, but after several months, they begin to slack off, stopping through neighborhoods on a hit-or-miss basis and making casual assessments that stray from the guidelines. Thus, the measure has decayed over this period and lost much of its reliability, and the data therefore are no longer meaningful.

Alternatively, a local transit system begins classifying certain kinds of transfers from one route to another as separate passenger trips, which was not done previously. Thus, its long-term trend lines show increasing numbers of passenger trips at this point, an invalid impression that is attributable only to a change in measurement procedures.

Instrument decay is a persistent problem in performance measurement, and it must be dealt with in two ways. First, when measurement procedures are intentionally changed, usually in an attempt to improve validity, it is important to document the change and note it in presentations of the data that incorporate periods before and after the change was instituted. Second, whether or not the definitions of measures are changed, it is important to maintain the integrity of the measures by ensuring close conformity with prescribed measurement procedures over time.

Reactive Measurement

Sometimes measurements can change because people involved in the process are affected by the program in some way or react somehow to the fact that the data are being monitored by someone else or used for some particular purpose. For instance, if a state government introduces a new scholarship program that ties awards to the grades students earn in high school, teachers might begin, consciously or unconsciously, to be more lenient in their grading. In effect, their standards for grading, or how they actually rate students' academic performance, change in reaction to the new scholarship program, but the resulting data would suggest that students are performing better in high school now than before, which may not be true.

Or consider an inner-city neighborhood that forms a neighborhood watch program in cooperation with the local police department, aimed at increasing personal safety and security, deterring crime, and helping the police solve crimes. As this program becomes more and more established, residents' attitudes toward both crime and the police change, and their propensity to report crimes to the police increases. This actually provides a more valid indicator of the actual crime level than used to be the case, but the data are likely to show increases in reported crimes even though this is simply an artifact of reactive measurement.

As illustrated by these two examples, reactive measurement may or may not have adverse impact, but it can weaken the validity of performance measures and create misleading impressions of comparisons over time. Thus, it makes sense to try to anticipate situations in which the measurement process itself might react to program stimuli and try to discern what the effect on the resulting performance data might be. Sometimes an analysis of other key measures that would not be reactive—such as SAT scores in the grade inflation example—or a comparison of trends in other cases not affected by the program, such as an analysis of reported crime statistics versus victimization survey data in neighborhoods with and without neighborhood watch programs, can help assess the likelihood of reactive measurement and its potential impact on performance data.

Nonresponse Bias

The quality of performance monitoring data is often called into question by virtue of being incomplete. Even with routine record-keeping systems and transactional databases, agencies often are unable for a variety of reasons to maintain up-to-date information on all cases all the time. So at any one time when the observations are being made or the data are being run, say, at the end of every month, there may be incomplete data in the records. If the missing data are purely a random phenomenon, this weakens the reliability of the data and can create problems of statistical instability. If, however, there is some systematic pattern of missing data—if, for instance, the database tends to have less complete information on the more problematic cases—this can inject a systematic bias into the data and erode the validity of the performance measure. Although the problem of nonresponse bias may technically be a sampling issue, its real impact is to introduce bias or distortion into performance measures.

Thus, in considering alternative performance indicators, it is a good idea to ascertain the basis on which the measure is drawn in order to assess whether missing data might create problems of validity or reliability. For example, almost all colleges and universities require applicants to submit SAT or ACT scores as part of the admissions process. Although the primary purpose of these test scores is to help in the selection process, average scores, or the midspread of these scores, can be used to compare the quality of applicants to that of different institutions or to track the proficiency of a particular university's freshmen class over several years.

However, SAT or ACT scores are also sometimes used as a proximate measure of the academic achievement of the students in individual high schools or school systems, and here there may be problems due to missing cases. Not all high school students take these tests, and those who do tend to be the better students; therefore, average SAT or ACT scores tend to overstate the academic proficiency of the student body as a whole. In fact, teachers and administrators can influence average SAT or ACT scores for their schools simply by encouraging some students to take the test and discouraging others. Thus, as an indicator of academic achievement for entire schools, SAT or ACT scores are much more questionable than, for example, standard exams mandated by the state for all students. When missing cases pose potential problems, it is important to interpret the data on the basis of the actual cases on which the data are drawn. Thus, average SAT scores can be taken as an indicator of the academic achievement of those students from a given high school who chose to take the exam.

When performance measures are derived from surveys, missing cases can result in flawed indicators due to possible nonresponse biases. Most surveys generate response rates well below 100 percent. If individuals who do respond to a survey tend to be those who are most interested in a program, for instance, or more involved with it, more familiar with its staff and services, more supportive of it, or more concerned with the future of the program one way or another, then their responses may not be very representative of what the overall data would look like if everyone had responded. The problem of nonresponse bias is even more notorious with respect to customer response card systems, in which some customers return cards frequently while others never respond. If customers who do turn in response cards tend to be a few active supporters, the resulting data will be artificially favorable, whereas if the only customers who return cards are those who have serious grievances with a program, the data will be skewed to highly negative ratings.

Nonresponse bias can be problematic when performance measures, especially effectiveness measures, come from follow-up contacts with former clients, whether through surveys, follow-up visits, or other direct contact. Especially with respect to human service programs, it is often difficult to remain in contact with all the individuals who have been served by a program or who completed treatment some time ago. And it may be the case that certain kinds of clients are much less likely to remain in contact. As would probably be the case with vocational rehabilitation programs, teen mother parenting programs, and especially crisis stabilization units, for example, the former clients who are the most difficult to track down are often those with the least positive outcomes, that is, those for whom the program may have been least effective. They may be the most likely ones to move from the area, drop out of sight, leave the system, or fall through the cracks. Obviously the nonresponse bias of data based on follow-up contacts that will necessarily exclude some of the most problematic clients could easily lead to overstating program performance. This is not to say that such indicators should not be included in performance monitoring systems—because often they are crucial indicators of long-term program effectiveness—but rather that care must be taken to interpret them within the confines of actual response rates.

Cheating

In addition to all the methodological issues that can compromise the quality of performance monitoring data, a common problem that can destroy validity and reliability is cheating. If performance measurement systems are indeed used effectively as a management tool, they carry consequences in terms of decisions regarding programs, people, resources, and strategies. Thus, managers at all levels of the organization want to "look good" in terms of the performance data. Suppose, for example, that air force bases whose function is training pilots to fly combat missions are evaluated in part by how close they come to hitting rather ambitious targets that have been set concerning the number of sorties flown by these pilots. The sorties are the principal output of these training operations, and there is a clear definition of what constitutes a completed sortie. If the base commanders are under heavy pressure to achieve these targets, however, and actual performance is lagging behind these objectives, they might begin to count all sorties as full sorties even though some of these have to be cut short for various reasons and are not completed. This tampering with the definition of a performance measure may seem to be a rather subtle distinction—and an easy one for the commanders to rationalize given the pressure to maintain high ratings—but it would represent willful misreporting to make a program appear to be more effective than it really is.

Performance measurement systems provide incentives for organizations and programs to perform at higher levels, and this is the core of the logic underlying the use of monitoring systems as performance management tools. Human nature being what it is, then, it is not surprising that people in public and nonprofit organizations are sometimes tempted to cheat—selectively reporting data, purposefully falsifying data, or otherwise "cooking the books" in order to present performance in a more favorable light. This kind of cheating is a real problem, and it must be dealt with directly and firmly. One strategy to ensure the quality of the data is to build sample audits into the overall design of the system, aimed at ensuring the accurate reporting and keeping the system honest.

In terms of the performance measures themselves, sometimes it is possible to use complementary measures that will help identify instances in which the data don't seem to add up, thus providing a check on cheating. In a state highway maintenance program, for instance, foremen inputting production data from the field might be tempted to misrepresent the level of output produced by their crews by overstating such indicators as the miles of road resurfaced, the miles of shoulders graded, or the feet of guardrail replaced. If these data are only marginally overstated, they will appear to be reasonable and will probably not be caught as errors. If, however, a separate system is used to report on inventory control and the use of resources, and these data are input by different individuals in a different part of the organization, then it may be possible to track these different indicators in tandem. Numbers that don't seem to match up would trigger a data audit to determine the reason for the apparent discrepancy. Such a safeguard might be an effective deterrent against cheating.

Selecting Indicators: Other Criteria for Performance Measures

While reliability and validity are the preeminent criteria of good measures from a research perspective, from the standpoint of managerial effectiveness, the measures used in performance monitoring systems should meet various other criteria as well:

- Meaningful and understandable
- Balanced and comprehensive
- Clear regarding preferred direction of movement
- Timely and actionable
- Resistant to goal displacement
- Cost-sensitive (not redundant)

Although some of these criteria apply in particular to each individual performance indicator, collectively they define the characteristics of effective sets of performance measures.

Meaningful Measures

Performance measures should be meaningful; that is, they should be directly related to the mission, goals, and intended results of a program, and they should represent performance dimensions that have been identified as part of the program logic. To be meaningful, performance measures should be important to managers, policymakers, employees, customers, or other stakeholders. Managers may be more concerned with productivity and program impact, policymakers may care more about efficiency and cost-effectiveness, and clients may be more directly concerned with service quality, but for a performance indicator to be meaningful, it must be important to at least one of these stakeholder groups. If no stakeholder is interested in a particular measure, then it cannot be particularly useful as part of a performance measurement system. Performance indicators must also be understandable to stakeholders. That is, the measures need to be presented in such a way as to explain clearly what they consist of and how they represent some aspect of performance.

Balanced and Comprehensive Measures

Within the scope and purpose of a given monitoring system, a set of performance measures should be balanced and comprehensive. A fully comprehensive measurement system should incorporate all the performance dimensions and types of measures discussed in chapter 3, including both outputs and outcomes and, if relevant, service quality and customer satisfaction in addition to efficiency and productivity. Even with systems that are more narrowly defined—focusing solely on strategic outcomes, for example, or, at the other extreme, focusing solely on operations—the measurement system should attempt to include indicators of every relevant aspect of performance. Perhaps most important, the monitoring system for a program with multiple goals should include a balanced set of effectiveness measures rather than emphasize some intended outcomes while ignoring others that may be just as important.

For example, the list that follows (from Bugler & Henry, 1998) shows a balanced set of performance indicators that are tracked to monitor the effectiveness of the State of Georgia's HOPE Scholarship program, which was initiated in 1994. HOPE pays the cost of full tuition for any institution in the university system of Georgia, plus one hundred dollars per semester for books, for any student who graduates from a high school in the state with a B average or higher as long as that student maintains a B average or higher while in college. It also reimburses Georgia students who attend private colleges in the state the equivalent of public school tuition as long as they meet the same requirements. The goals of the program, which is funded by revenue from the state lottery, are to motivate students to achieve better grades in high school, enable more high school graduates to go on to college, increase the number of minority students attending college, motivate more students from low-income families to attend college, encourage more Georgia high school graduates to attend colleges in Georgia rather than other states, and motivate college students in Georgia to perform better academically and remain in college through graduation. Collectively, the indicators shown here, which are tracked annually, provide a balanced portrait of the impact of the HOPE Scholarship program.

HOPE Scholarship Effectiveness Measures

- Number of HOPE Scholarship recipients
- Number of students entering Georgia institutions of higher education
- Percentage of high school students with a B or higher grade point average
- Percentage of HOPE recipients still in college one, two, and three years after entering
- Average grade point average and credit hours earned per year by HOPE recipients
- Percentage of initial recipients who retain the scholarship after one, two, and three years
- Number and percentage of entering freshmen who are African Americans
- Number of Pell Grant applications from Georgia
- Number of Georgia college students funded by Pell Grants
- Number of Georgia students attending selected colleges in other states

Measures with Clear Preferred Direction of Movement

In order for a performance indicator to be useful, there must be agreement on the preferred direction of movement on the scale. If an indicator of customer satisfaction, for example, is operationalized as the percentage of respondents to an annual survey who say they were satisfied or very satisfied with the service they have received from a particular agency, higher percentages are taken to represent stronger program performance, and managers will want to see this percentage increase from year to year.

Although it might seem that this should go without saying, the preferred direction of movement is not always so clear. For instance, such indicators as the student-faculty ratio or the average class size are sometimes used as proximate measures of the quality of instructional programs at public universities, on the theory that smaller classes offer greater opportunity for participation in class discussions and increased attention to the needs of individual students both in and out of class. On that score, then, the preferred direction of movement would be to smaller class sizes. College deans, however, often like to see classes filling up with more students in order to make more efficient use of faculty time and cover a higher percentage of operating costs. Thus, from a budgetary standpoint, larger class sizes might be preferred. Generally if agreement on targets and the preferred direction of movement cannot be reached in such ambiguous situations, then the proposed indicator should probably not be used.

Timely and Actionable Measures

To be useful, performance measures also should be timely and actionable. One of managers' most common complaints about performance measurement systems is that they do not report the data in a timely manner. When performance measures are designed to support a governmental unit's budgeting process, for instance, the performance data for the most recently completed fiscal year should be readily available when budget requests or proposals are being developed. In practice, however, sometimes the only available data pertain to two years earlier and are out-of-date as a basis for making decisions regarding the current allocation of resources. Performance data that are intended to be helpful to managers with responsibility for ongoing operations—such as highway maintenance work, central office supply, claims processing operations, or child support enforcement customer service—should probably be monitored more frequently, on a monthly or quarterly basis, in order to facilitate addressing operational problems more immediately. Although reporting frequency is really an issue of overall system design, as discussed in chapter 2, it also needs to be taken into account in the definition of the measures themselves.

To be actionable, the indicator must be tied to something within a program's sphere of influence—some criterion that the program or management can have an impact on. As long as performance measures are tied to appropriate goals and objectives, they are usually actionable, even though the program rarely has anything approaching total control over desired outcomes. For example, it is often an uphill struggle, but transit authorities can be held accountable for maintaining ridership, and juvenile detention centers can be expected to reduce recidivism rates. Thus, ridership and recidivism rates are actionable measures for these organizations.

In contrast, some proposed performance indicators may be well beyond the control of the program and thus not actionable. For instance, one way in which public hospitals track their performance is through surveys of patients who have been recently discharged, because they can provide useful feedback on the quality and responsiveness of the services they received. Suppose, however, that one particular item on such a survey refers to the availability of some specific service or treatment option. The responses to this item are consistently and almost universally negative, but the reason for this is that none of the insurance companies involved will cover this option, and thus it is beyond the control of the hospital. Because there is little or no chance of improving performance in this area, at least under the existing constraints, this measure cannot provide any new or useful feedback to hospital administrators.

Measures That Are Resistant to Goal Displacement

One of the most critical issues in the definition of performance measures concerns goal displacement, the tendency of managers and others to perform directly toward the indicators in ways that are detrimental to the real goals of the program or organization. For instance, if a local school system focuses too sharply on students' performance on certain standardized tests as a measure of academic achievement, teachers who are familiar with that particular testing strategy and format may be inclined to narrow the curriculum or teach to the test at the expense of promoting real learning in their classes. Furthermore, raising the stakes of such standardized testing may also lead to cheating on the part of administrators, teachers, and students; the exclusion of low-performing students from the testing; and encouraging low-performing students to drop out of school. Instead they should be working to increase student retention as well as address declines in teacher morale and a migration of good teachers from inner-city schools to more affluent suburban schools where stronger family and community support for education makes legitimate improvement in standardize test scores more readily achievable (Nichols & Berliner, 2007).

Similarly, it has been reported that in response to standards set by Great Britain's National Health Service to reduce hospital accident and emergency room waiting times, hospitals required patients to wait in ambulance queues outside hospital property until they were confident that patients could be seen within a four-hour period as specified by the standards. Furthermore, hospitals engaged in strategic cancellation of appointments with patients and delayed important follow-up appointments in order to meet waiting time targets in other areas, in some cases leading to severe negative impacts in patients' health status (Bevan & Hood, 2006).

Although performance measurement systems are intentionally designed to influence behavior in positive ways, when goal displacement occurs, it affects performance adversely. For example, a state transportation department that is trying to revitalize the productivity of its highway maintenance program may emphasize the number of lane-miles that are resurfaced each month as a key output indicator. If maintenance supervisors and foremen know that top management is focusing on this measure and tying rewards and penalties to it, they will naturally want to resurface as many lane-miles as possible, everything else being equal. This may produce the desired results, but if the maintenance crews are hard-pressed to achieve these output targets or are overzealous in trying to "look good" on this measure, they may engage in quick "dump-and-run" operations resulting in poor-quality resurfacing jobs that fail to improve ride quality appreciably and will have to be repeated on shorter-than-average cycle times. Or the maintenance managers might concentrate the resurfacing jobs on roads with lower traffic volumes where the work can be completed more easily and quickly, but this would have little impact on improving ride quality on the roads that are used most heavily by motorists. Or they could program extraordinary amounts of resurfacing work to the exclusion of other kinds of maintenance work, such as drainage improvements, which would have a long-term negative impact on overall highway condition. Thus, working to perform well on the specific resurfacing indicator could actually be counterproductive in terms of the more important goals of improving ride quality, placing a high priority on roads that are used the most heavily, and maintaining the overall condition of the roads in the long run.

Goal displacement most often arises from unbalanced performance measures, and it can usually be avoided by defining sets of indicators with balanced incentives that channel performance toward desired outcomes. For example, the desired outcome of a vocational rehabilitation program is to help clients prepare for and find satisfactory employment. A key performance measure here might be the percentage of clients exiting the program who are subsequently employed. This indicator certainly points in the right direction, but if it is the only measure of success, it could prompt staff to engage in practices that would maximize the percentage employed yet be counterproductive in the long run. They might push clients into the lowest-paying jobs or part-time jobs that are easy to get, at the expense of placing them in more satisfactory positions. They could also give top priority to placing clients who are already more marketable to gain quick successes at the expense of helping clients with severe disabilities, for whom it tends to be much more difficult to find jobs. However, it is not difficult to define additional indicators that would control for this kind of behavior—for example:

- The percentage of all employed clients who work thirty-five hours or more per week
- The percentage of all employed clients who are employed in competitive, self-employed, or business-enterprise-type employment
- The percentage of severely disabled clients who have achieved competitive, self-employed, or business-enterprise-type employment
- The percentage of all employed clients with earnings equal to or greater than the minimum wage
- The percentage of employed clients earning wages above the poverty level of $645 per month for a family of one

Tracking performance on such a set of outcome measures would not only provide a more complete picture of program effectiveness but also reduce the likelihood of goal displacement by restoring balance to the incentive structure. Because it would be in the agency's interest to perform well across the board on this mix of indicators, the agency would be much less inclined to place its clientele in less competitive jobs and fail to emphasize the needs of severely disabled clients.

Cost-Sensitive Performance Measures

The principle that performance measures should be cost-effective should go without saying, but it cannot be emphasized too strongly. Implementing measurement systems can entail considerable cost, especially in data collection and processing, and the results should be worthwhile. Some types of measures are more costly than others. For example, special-purpose surveys, inspections, and clinical evaluations tend to be more expensive than routinely recorded transactional data, but collecting even the more routine agency data can be time consuming and require considerable extra effort, especially if they must be input by dispersed staff out in the field and then be confirmed on a sample basis by a quality control unit.

Thus, collecting and processing performance data should be viewed as a purposeful investment that will provide useful information to managers and policymakers. Although it is obviously desirable to develop a balanced set of indicators to monitor a program's performance, sometimes there are trade-offs between quality and cost when the measures that are the most meaningful, or with the strongest validity and reliability, are also the most costly. Certainly care should be taken not to include overly redundant performance measures or fairly extraneous indicators that could be costly to obtain without adding much information about a program's performance. Ultimately, however, it usually comes down to making a judgment about the usefulness of proposed performance measures in relation to the cost, time, and effort expended in collecting them.

Systematic Assessment of Performance Measures

Given the numerous challenges in operationalizing useful performance measures, it often makes sense to approach the development of performance indicators as an iterative process moving from the initial definition of measures to a systematic assessment of these measures, which may lead in turn to refinements, exploration of alternative operational indicators, and so forth before selecting the measures to include in a monitoring system. At the core of this process, it may help to develop an initial set of indicators, consider them as potential measures, and then systematically assess the strengths and weaknesses of these candidate measures and move toward decisions regarding the selection of measures accordingly. Table 5.4 shows a template for guiding such an assessment for a set of performance measures pertaining to the Canadian Pension Plan Disability Program on a number of the measurement criteria discussed above. Recognizing that virtually no measure is perfect and that assessments of a measure's strengths and weaknesses are largely subjective and are likely to vary from individual to individual, using such a template to help guide a group of stakeholders who are likely to view the measures from different perspectives through such a process can be particularly helpful.

TABLE 5.4 CPPD PERFORMANCE INDICATORS ASSESSMENT: ELIGIBILITY DETERMINATION

Current Indicators	Proposed Indicator	Type of Indicator	Definition	Source of Data	Meaningful	Preferred Direction of Movement	Actionable	Target	Valid	Reliable	Resistant to Goal Displacement
# initial applications adjudicated		Output	# initial application decisions	RPDB With R7, this data will come from ERS—also calculated in WIID.	Yes	N/A	Yes	None	Very Strong	Very Strong	Yes
	Applications adjudicated per FTE adjudicator	Labor Productivity				Up	Yes				
	Expense per application adjudicated	Efficiency	Unit Cost per File	Data from Finance	Yes	Down	Yes	None. Needs to be developed	Strong	Questionable	Yes
Initial applications: Months of work on hand		Workload	Inventory divided by avg # of decisions for the past 3 months	RPDB With R7, this data will come from ERS—also calculated in WIID. (uses 1 month instead of 3 in the denominator)	Yes	Down. Keep below 3. However, a low number will indicate work can be moved to this area.	Yes	≤ 3.0 months	Strong (denominator based on previous months work which can vary)	Strong	Yes
Initial applications: % processed within 120 calendar days		Service Quality (Also Efficiency)	% of decisions made within 120 calendar days of receipt of completed application	RPDB With R7, this data will come from ERS.	Yes	Up	Yes	≥ 75%	Strong	Strong	No. Regions can pick and choose which files to do to meet target.
	Initial applications: Accuracy rate	Service Quality	To be developed	Yes		Up	Yes	≥ 95%			

Guidelines for Defining Performance Measures

Defining useful performance measures can be challenging. For some organizations and programs, it may be a straightforward process, but in other cases, the specification of good performance indicators may require substantial ingenuity and careful judgment in addition to sound logic. The following guidelines for defining useful performance indicators sum up much of the discussion in this chapter:

- Work directly from program logic models and clear statements of goals, objectives, and service standards to define performance indicators.
- Attempt to develop balanced sets of performance indicators, but avoid overly redundant or only tangentially related measures.
- Reject proposed indicators that will not be meaningful to managers, policymakers, and other relevant stakeholders.
- Wherever possible, define indicators that will have a high degree of face validity to intended users and external audiences.
- Examine the validity and reliability of proposed measures and, everything else being equal, select those that are the least problematic given their intended use.
- Use proximate measures where necessary, but avoid those that are only tenuously related to the performance criteria of interest.
- Try to anticipate problems of goal displacement and incorporate other indicators to counteract it as appropriate.
- Make judicious assessments of trade-offs between the quality of performance indicators versus the cost of collecting the data.
- Define measures for which clear data trails will be available in order to allow for effective quality assurance procedures.
- Provide clear definitions of data sources and data collection procedures to facilitate uniform reporting from decentralized sites.

References

American Association of State Highway and Transportation Officials. (2003). *Strategic performance measures for state departments of transportation: A handbook for CEOs and executives.* AASHTO.

Ammons, D. N. (2012). *Municipal benchmarks: Assessing local performance and establishing community standards* (3rd ed.). Armonk, NY: M.E. Sharpe.

Bevan, G., & Hood, C. (2006, February 18). Health policy: Have targets improved performance in the English NHS? *British Medical Journal,* 419–422.

Bugler, D. T., & Henry, G. T. (1998). *Evaluation of Georgia's HOPE scholarship program, impact on college attendance and performance.* Georgia Council for School Performance. http://www.arc.gsu.edu/csp/default.htm

DeVellis, R. F. (2012). *Scale development: Theory and applications.* Thousand Oaks, CA: Sage.

Dixon, D. R. (2007). Adaptive behavior scales. *International Review of Research in Mental Retardation, 34,* 99–140.

Manno, B. V., Crittenden, S., Arkin, M., & Hassel, B. C. (2007). *A road to results: A performance measurement guidebook for the Annie E. Casey Foundation's Education Program.* Baltimore, MD: Annie E. Casey Foundation.

McDowell, I. (2006). *Measuring health: A guide to rating scales and questionnaires* (3rd ed.). New York: Oxford University Press.

Nichols, S. L., & Berliner, D. C. (2007). *Collateral damage: How high-stakes testing corrupts America's schools.* Cambridge, MA: Harvard Education Press.

Plaia, A., & Ruggieri, M. (2011). *Air quality indices: A review. Reviews in Environmental Science and Bio/Technology, 10,* 165–179.

Poister, T. H. (1997). *Performance measurement in state departments of transportation.* Washington, DC: Transportation Research Board, National Research Council.

The real jobless rate: The government says unemployment is "down" to 10%, but better measures suggest things are worse. (2009, December 21). *Time,* 39.

Shulz, K. S., & Whitney, D. J. (2005). *Measurement theory in action: Case studies and Exercises.* Thousand Oaks, CA: Sage.

Tsemberis, S., McHog, G., Williams, V., Hanrahan, P., & Stefancic, A. (2007). Measuring homelessness and residential stability: The residential time-line follow-back inventory. *Journal of Community Psychology, 35*(1), 29–42.

## CHAPTER SIX

REPORTING PERFORMANCE DATA

How do you effectively communicate the results of performance measurement? Which formats are best for displaying different kinds of performance data? Are graphics always necessary when communicating performance results? Once performance data are collected and measures are computed, managers, staff, and analysts must decide on the most effective ways to communicate the results. This chapter addresses considerations that should be taken into account in the display of performance data and presents several examples of display formats.

Performance Data and Their Audience

Organizations implement measurement systems to monitor performance and communicate the results to managers, clients, governing bodies, and other stakeholders. The output of these systems, in fact, are focused on reporting results. To communicate performance effectively, managers and staff should take into account both the nature of the performance data and the needs of the audience for the data.

Nature of the Performance Data and Comparative Frameworks

A performance measurement system may include measures of resources, workload, outputs, outcomes, efficiency and productivity, quality, client satisfaction, and cost-effectiveness. Some of these measures may be expressed as raw numbers, others as averages, percentages, or rates or ratios. In some cases, indexes may have been created as summary variables to represent, for example, overall service quality or program effectiveness. The data may be collected weekly, monthly, quarterly, or annually. Furthermore, the scope of the measurement system may focus solely on a program or organization as a whole, or it may be designed to afford comparisons among various programmatic divisions or organizational units such as geographically dispersed regions or districts.

Whatever kinds of performance data are being monitored, it is important to keep in mind that the value of a given measure observed at one particular time is rarely useful. Rather, performance data are converted into performance information for reporting in some appropriate comparative framework. The principal types of comparisons are

- Over time
- Against targets
- Among operating units
- Compared with other programs
- Other breakouts

These kinds of comparisons are relevant with respect to the design of data displays that will convey performance information in meaningful ways. First, what is the time orientation of the data? It might be helpful to show the time series data for a measure over the past several weeks, months, or years up to the current or most recent observation in order to provide an indication of what the long-term trend has been and whether performance on the measure has been improving or worsening over that period. Second, when targets have been established for certain performance measures, as discussed in chapter 4, it might be important to report the actual level of performance on a given indicator versus the targeted level of performance to clarify the extent to which actual performance meets, exceeds, or falls short of the target. Third, when services are delivered to the public or clients on a decentralized basis, disaggregating the data down to the level of organizational units or geographic regions can be helpful in terms of assessing, in addition to long-term trends overall, the extent to which performance varies—for instance, from district to district or precinct to precinct—and identifying the leading performers as well as the units whose performance is more problematic. Fourth, when feasible, it can be very helpful to compare a program's or agency's performance with that of other similar kinds of programs or agencies. For example, a state office of child support enforcement might benefit from comparing its own performance with that of other state child support enforcement programs operating in similar environments. Finally, reporting other kinds of breakouts—breaking down standardized test scores across various racial/ethnic groups of students in a local public school system or comparing the number of personal injuries reported for different kinds of facilities or venues in a state park systems, for instance—may provide additional insight as to the incidence of possible performance problems beyond an indication of whether performance has been improving or declining on the whole.

In addition, those who are developing formats for reporting performance data should ask themselves whether there are any aspects of the data that require additional explanatory information. For example, have there been variations in the data over time that are important to highlight, or have there been unusual occurrences that have affected performance? If so, it may be useful to integrate a comment field in the presentation of performance results. This would allow for explanation or comment on the data that may not be readily apparent through presentation of the numbers or graphics alone. The answers to these questions will help guide the choice of display format.

Needs of the Audience

The better that system designers understand the information needs of their intended audiences, the more effectively they will be able to communicate performance results. The data should be displayed in a way that maximizes the audience's ability to quickly, easily, and accurately understand what the data represent. Managers and staff may accomplish this by communicating performance results in a way that is appropriate to the audience. Overall, the level of sophistication and interest of the audience must be considered. In some cases, the same data may be displayed differently for different groups. For example, it is likely that an audience internal to the organization or one very familiar with its activities are more likely to prefer and benefit from more detail and perhaps more breakdowns of the data, whereas the general public might be better served with a simple, easily understandable display of the performance data. Elected officials often prefer information that is brief and quickly understandable, whereas the media would prefer an easily understandable, attractive presentation of data. The audience may prefer to view only numerical performance results, or they may benefit from explanatory information to highlight different aspects of the performance data.

Reporting Formats

There are many alternatives to choose from in terms of formats for reporting performance information. The remainder of this chapter presents several alternative formats for displaying performance data results and discusses the appropriate uses and advantages of each. Examples range from tabular and graphical displays to scorecards and maps.

Although these examples are useful for illustrating a range of data display formats, it is important to note that there are myriad ways in which any of these formats can be adapted to suit the reporting needs of both the organization and the audience.

Basic Tables and Spreadsheets

Not all performance measurement systems involve elaborate databases. In fact, for some organizations, a performance data management system may simply involve detailed and well-organized tables or spreadsheets.

For example, the upper half of figure 6.1 illustrates a spreadsheet format presenting performance data for several functions such as construction management, contract administration, highway system condition, and plan delivery in the Ohio Department of Transportation (ODOT). Interestingly, performance on each of these functions is represented by an index computed with a number of more specific indicators, with each index ranging from 0 to 100 (representing top performance). In addition to the index value for each function, this report shows a composite index value covering all these functions, and it also breaks down these performance indexes for each of ODOT's twelve operating districts as well as for the department as a whole. In addition, this spreadsheet incorporates a "roll-up/drill down" feature (not shown) that allows viewers to quickly find supporting data for any elements of particular interest in the table. For instance, using the

FIGURE 6.1 OHIO DOT ORGANIZATIONAL PERFORMANCE INDEX EXECUTIVE SUMMARY

Organizational Performance Index: Executive Summary Reports
Index Summary

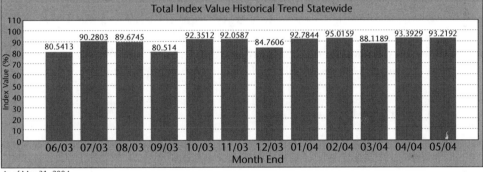

District	Total Index Value	Construction Management	Contract Administration	Equipment and Facilities	Finance	Information Technology	Plan Delivery	Quality and Human Resources	System Conditions
1	95.8333	83.3333	100.0	72.0238	100.0	88.8889	100.0	75.0	100.0
2	91.6667	79.1667	100.0	82.7381	100.0	100.0	50.0	87.5	95.0
3	97.9167	91.6667	100.0	85.119	100.0	100.0	80.0	93.75	91.6667
4	97.9167	91.6667	100.0	83.9286	100.0	100.0	95.0	68.75	100.0
5	100.0	91.6667	100.0	91.6667	100.0	100.0	95.0	93.75	100.0
6	100.0	83.3333	100.0	86.3095	100.0	88.8889	83.3333	93.75	93.3333
7	95.8333	91.6667	100.0	88.6905	100.0	100.0	65.0	87.5	100.0
8	100.0	91.6667	100.0	87.5	100.0	100.0	95.0	87.5	98.3333
9	89.5833	87.5	100.0	66.6667	100.0	100.0	50.0	75.0	100.0
10	95.8333	100.0	100.0	90.4762	100.0	100.0	90.0	56.25	93.3333
11	93.75	79.1667	100.0	95.8333	100.0	100.0	65.0	87.5	100.0
12	91.6667	79.1667	100.0	82.7381	100.0	100.0	70.0	81.25	93.3333
ODOT INDEX	93.2192	91.6667	100.0	90.4762	100.0	94.4444	83.3333	87.5	98.3333

Total Index Value Historical Trend Statewide

80.5413 | 90.2803 | 89.6745 | 80.514 | 92.3512 | 92.0587 | 84.7606 | 92.7844 | 95.0159 | 88.1189 | 93.3929 | 93.2192

Index Value (%)

Month End: 06/03 07/03 08/03 09/03 10/03 11/03 12/03 01/04 02/04 03/04 04/04 05/04

As of May 31, 2004

electronic version of the report, one could click on the index value of 83.3333 for the construction management function in district 1 and find the performance scores for that district on a number of subfunctions that make up that index, such as field supervision, on-time performance, cost control, and contractor evaluation.

Spreadsheet designs can also be useful for displaying performance data for different time periods, thereby allowing comparisons to be made by month, quarter, or year. In another example of a simple tabular design, the State of Texas provides reports in tabular format for all agencies as part of its annual performance measures report. Columns display not only performance data by quarters but also targeted performance levels for the year, year-to-date performance, and the percentage of the annual target that has been met to date. Stars are used to highlight measures for which the performance varies more than 5 percent from its targeted performance level. This can be a useful way to draw attention to an individual item.

Performance reports generated directly from a spreadsheet or database have the advantage of being convenient and easy to access for users. They are also economical to produce and allow rapid, regular updating. Once the spreadsheet is designed, it requires relatively little work to generate the report. As data are updated, the report can be generated for the next month very quickly. This sort of report is especially useful for performance items that need to be viewed regularly.

Tabular displays of performance data do not always provide the most desirable format for all audiences, however. Fairly dense spreadsheets such as the one in figure 6.1 tend to be best suited for audiences who are very familiar with the program activities detailed in the spreadsheet and wish to see detailed figures. For individuals who do not view the spreadsheet report on a regular basis, understanding the data may be very time consuming. Some individuals may be interested in only a few summary items, in which case graphical formats could be preferable.

Common Graphical Displays

Many software packages make it easy and quick to display data in a variety of graphical formats. Graphical displays of data have the advantage of quickly communicating performance results without requiring in-depth knowledge of the raw numbers. Graphics are especially useful for showing trends over time, or the relationship of different groups to one another. Perhaps most important, graphical displays allow information to be easily absorbed by a wide range of audiences. They have the advantage of easy readability for audiences who are intimidated by or uninterested in the actual numbers. Displaying performance data in any of these simple graphical formats is appropriate for dissemination to both internal groups and external stakeholders, such as policymakers or the media. The general public and even policymakers may be most interested in trends or comparisons of groups; these are easily communicated using graphical displays. Graphical displays can also be memorable; individuals may be more likely to remember a trend illustrated by a line graph or a relative comparison illustrated by a bar chart than the actual numbers.

Common graphical display formats are pie charts, bar charts, line graphs, and cluster charts. Simple bar charts are especially useful for displaying performance data. The lower half of figure 6.1 is a bar chart showing the statewide composite index value of the Ohio Department of Transportation's performance over a twelve-month period from June 2003 through May 2004. Curiously, the graph shows a drop in these overall scores every three months. While the composite scores consistently run in the low 90s in July, August, October, November, January, February, April, and May, they drop into the 80s—in three cases, the low or mid-80s—in September, December, March, and June of the year in question. If this finding is not already explained by some corresponding cyclical pattern in ODOT's operations, it would likely raise questions and prompt looking deeper in the data to determine the reasons that performance would drop below the average every three months like this.

Stacked bar charts can be used to report the frequency with which programs or agencies meet varying thresholds of performance targets. For example, figure 6.2 shows data monitored by the US Centers for Disease Control and Prevention (CDC) on the proportion of cases diagnosed with primary or secondary syphilis who are then interviewed by local sexually transmitted disease programs within the number of days targeted by CDC at three different levels. While the graph shows the proportion of cases interviewed within seven days, the principal target, it also shows the proportion interviewed within fourteen days, a fallback target, and then within thirty days, a further fallback target. Also of interest is the fact that figure 6.2 displays these performance data for each of the ten standard federal regions as well as for the nation as a whole, which from CDC's perspective constitutes comparisons among units, or internal benchmarking.

Bar graphs may also be constructed as cluster charts with individual bars for breaking out groups within the data to allow for comparisons across groups or clusters of cases. Figure 6.3, for example, reports statewide data on customer ratings of a driver's license renewal process solicited by the state's department of driver services over the course of fiscal year 2014. The ratings in the response cards were excellent, good, fair, and poor, and the results are broken down by two groups of customers: those who renewed their licenses in person in one of the driver service centers and those who completed the process online. As might be expected, the ratings differ substantially between the two service modalities. While a large majority, nearly 65 percent, of the online customers rated the

FIGURE 6.2 PROPORTION OF PRIMARY OR SECONDARY SYPHILIS CASES INTERVIEWED WITHIN SEVEN, FOURTEEN, AND THIRTY DAYS MEDIAN PROPORTION FOR US AND HEALTH AND HUMAN SERVICES REGIONS

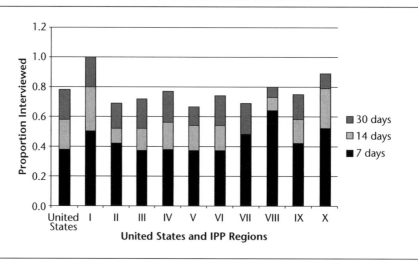

Source: US CDC, Division of Sexually Transmitted Disease (2004).

service as good or excellent, a majority of those who renewed their licenses in person rated the service as only fair or poor. Overall, then, just under half of all the customers who filled out the customer response cards gave the service a positive rating, while slightly more than half gave it a negative rating.

Line graphs are most typically used to chart performance trends over time. For example, figure 6.4 shows annual revenue ridership totals, which represents a bottom-line outcome measure in the local public transit industry in the United States, for the Metropolitan Atlanta Rapid Transit Authority (MARTA) from 2002 to 2011. These data are further broken down by MARTA's rail system and its bus system. Ridership on the two systems tracked each other very closely from 2002 through 2006, declining precipitously from around 80 million revenue passengers in 2003 and then leveling off at around 70 million through 2006. However, while ridership on the bus system continued to hover around the 70 million mark through 2008 and then increased somewhat in 2009 before dropping to fewer than 65 million passenger trips by 2011, the number of revenue passengers on

FIGURE 6.3 CUSTOMER RATINGS OF DRIVER LICENSE RENEWAL PROCESS, FISCAL YEAR 2014

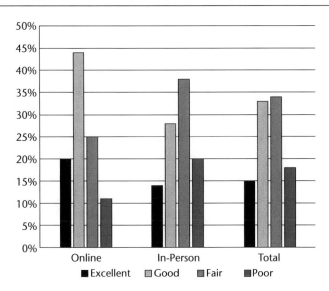

FIGURE 6.4 MARTA REVENUE PASSENGERS, 2002–2011

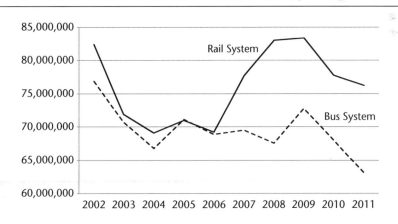

FIGURE 6.5 ON-TIME AND ON-BUDGET COMPLETION OF HIGHWAY CONSTRUCTION PROJECTS AT THE VIRGINIA DEPARTMENT OF TRANSPORTATION, FISCAL YEAR 2002 RESULTS

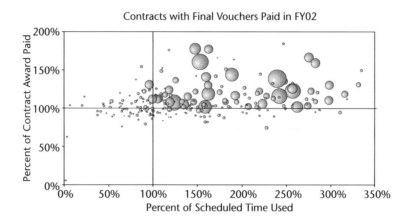

MARTA's rail system turned the corner in 2007 and then rose up to more than 80 million passenger trips in 2008 and 2099 before dropping down somewhat above the 75 million mark in 2010 and 2011. Line graphs like this one can paint a vivid picture of an agency's performance over time, and in this case the old adage that a picture can tell the story of a thousand words is clearly true.

Bubble graphs can be very useful for reporting data on two indicators of performance simultaneously on a set of cases broken down by service delivery venues, organizational units, and geographic areas or, projects, while taking into account some other dimension of these cases. The upper half in figure 6.5, for example, is a bubble chart showing on-time performance and on-budget performance for all highway construction projects completed in fiscal 2002 by the Virginia Department of Transportation (VDOT). Each bubble in the chart represents one of these completed projects.

The reference line at 100 percent on the horizontal axis represents the point at which projects have come in on precisely the number of days they were programmed to take. Projects to the right of the reference line were late in reaching completion; for example, projects plotted at 200 percent required twice as many days to reach completion than the number of days programmed. Similarly, the reference line at 100 percent on the vertical axis represents projects that were brought in exactly on budget, costing neither more nor less than the amount specified in the contract between VDOT and the highway contractors that actually build these projects. The bubbles above this reference line are projects whose actual cost exceeded VDOT's projected costs, and projects plotted below the reference line came in under budget.

In this case, the bubble size represents the size of the completed highway project, as represented by their dollar value as a surrogate measure of the magnitude of the work required to build it. As is evident from the bubble chart in the upper half of figure 6.5, the majority of projects completed by VDOT in 2002 took longer than programmed, many significantly longer, and a majority of these projects came in over budget as well. Most of the larger projects completed by VDOT in 2002 especially were both over time and over budget, many dramatically so. With a few exceptions, the only projects that were completed on time or on budget (or both) were very small projects. This state of affairs signaled an urgent need at VDOT to improve the performance of its highway construction program, and that became the department's top priority.

Improving performance on these criteria is represented by moving projects down and to the left in these graphs. The bubble chart in the lower half of figure 6.5 shows the same performance data for VDOT highway projects completed in 2002. Clearly VDOT's performance improved dramatically over the intervening six years, with the majority of projects having been completed in less time than programmed or under budget, or both, and with a few exceptions, most of those projects that failed to come in on time and on budget were within 25 percent of their targets rather than up to three times their planned completion time and two times their allotted budgets.

Such bubble charts offer great potential for reporting performance data in a compelling manner whenever the data are being used to assess the performance of multiple programs, projects, organizational units, or grantees, for example, and the two key performance indicators are measured on interval scales. The following applications might be interesting and meaningful ones:

- An international development program wishes to assess the performance of all projects it has funded that are meeting both numerical output targets and outcomes, with the size of each bubble representing the number of people affected by each funded project.
- A state transportation department wishes to track the performance of each of its local area highway maintenance operations on measures

of pavement condition as measured on the international roughness index and customer satisfaction with ride quality as measured by a customer satisfaction index computed with survey data, with the size of each bubble representing the number of lane miles of state highway that each highway maintenance operation is responsible for.

• A national association of state boards of nursing wishes to monitor the performance of each member board in terms of both cycle time in processing applications for nursing licenses and cycle time in completing investigations of reported practice violations, with the size of the bubble representing the number of nurses within the purview of each state board of nursing.

Scorecards and Dashboards

Graphical displays of data such as those described in the preceding section are common and familiar to many stakeholder groups. It is useful to display data using a scale and a graphic that the audience readily understands. For audiences that might be intimidated by even simple bar or pie charts, the creative use of pictorial items from everyday life makes the data display more accessible and less threatening. For example, figure 6.6 shows the use of a thermometer to illustrate the overall quality of care for a public hospital as solicited in brief interviews with recent patients. Using the thermometer, "hotter" is better in terms of quality, whereas "cooler" implies poorer-quality care. In this example, a number of comparative items are also displayed on the thermometer, such as the benchmark goal level, the system mean for twenty hospitals, and the low score from the survey results. It is a nonthreatening, efficient way to show not only the performance results but also their relationship to other key figures. The patient feedback shown in the thermometer is also displayed in tabular format, along with ratings from other dimensions, including overall nursing and overall physician quality, willingness to return, willingness to recommend, and helpfulness of visit. Other data useful to the audience are also shown in a bar graph (reasons for visits to the health care center) to add an additional level of respondent information to the report.

In another example, figure 6.7 illustrates a dashboard display with an automotive flavor to convey performance results for a department of juvenile justice. In this example, both the current status of certain performance items, represented by the arrows, as well as target levels, shown with solid lines, are displayed on each gauge. For example, the actual

FIGURE 6.6 EXAMPLE OF A CREATIVE GRAPHICAL DISPLAY: HOSPITAL PATIENT FEEDBACK

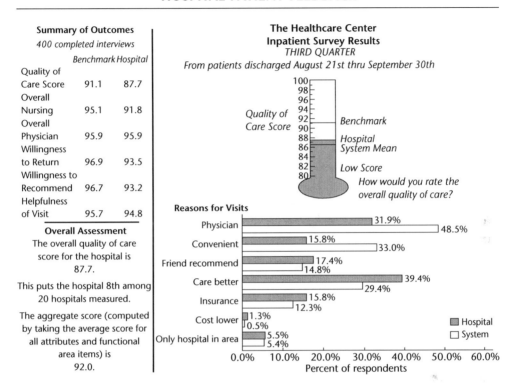

Summary of Outcomes

400 completed interviews

	Benchmark	Hospital
Quality of Care Score	91.1	87.7
Overall Nursing	95.1	91.8
Overall Physician	95.9	95.9
Willingness to Return	96.9	93.5
Willingness to Recommend	96.7	93.2
Helpfulness of Visit	95.7	94.8

Overall Assessment

The overall quality of care score for the hospital is 87.7.

This puts the hospital 8th among 20 hospitals measured.

The aggregate score (computed by taking the average score for all attributes and functional area items) is 92.0.

The Healthcare Center Inpatient Survey Results
THIRD QUARTER
From patients discharged August 21st thru September 30th

Quality of Care Score — 100, 98, 96, 94, 92, 90, 88, 86, 84, 82, 80

Benchmark
Hospital System Mean
Low Score

How would you rate the overall quality of care?

Reasons for Visits

Reason	Hospital	System
Physician	31.9%	48.5%
Convenient	15.8%	33.0%
Friend recommend	17.4%	14.8%
Care better	39.4%	29.4%
Insurance	15.8%	12.3%
Cost lower	1.3%	0.5%
Only hospital in area	5.5%	5.4%

Percent of respondents — 0.0% 10.0% 20.0% 30.0% 40.0% 50.0% 60.0%

■ Hospital □ System

number of escapes is above the target level, as are cases of reported abuse, whereas the recidivism rate of discharged juveniles is lower than the target. Here, the arrow on the dashboard is implied to be moving in an upward direction. Below the dashboards, "traffic signals" (best displayed in color) are used to indicate how well a number of ongoing operations are moving along. Red is used to indicate a problem for an individual item, yellow to indicate a warning, and green to indicate that the item is within an acceptable range, or cruising. This pictorial example allows users to quickly scan the display and see where trouble spots may be.

The terms *scorecard* and *dashboard* are not used consistently in the field of public management, and they are often used interchangeably. Typically, however, they are meant to refer to formats for displaying performance information that can be taken in and understood at a glance. Figure 6.8 shows the dashboard provided by the US Patent Office, which indicates

FIGURE 6.7 EXAMPLE OF A PICTORIAL DISPLAY: DASHBOARD

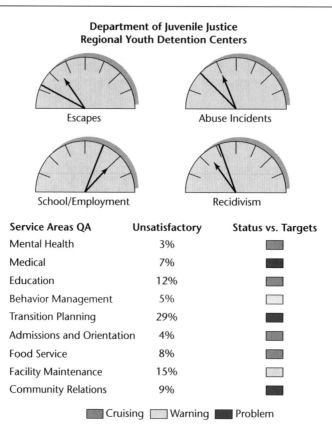

**Department of Juvenile Justice
Regional Youth Detention Centers**

Service Areas QA	Unsatisfactory	Status vs. Targets
Mental Health	3%	
Medical	7%	
Education	12%	
Behavior Management	5%	
Transition Planning	29%	
Admissions and Orientation	4%	
Food Service	8%	
Facility Maintenance	15%	
Community Relations	9%	

■ Cruising ☐ Warning ■ Problem

the status of the office's operations on eight key performance indicators and is posted and updated monthly online. As rendered in black and white in this book, it is impossible to see the distinct colorations surrounding the dials that represent various gradations in performance levels, which presumably are meaningful to managers who are responsible for various aspects of the patent office's operations.

Figure 6.9 shows part of a municipal police department's scorecard. It shows performance data on numerous measures of performance related to three different goals that focus on reducing Part 1 crimes, improving clearance rates, and hiring and developing police officers. In the column on the left the arrows indicate at a glance whether performance at this point has improved (up arrows) or declined (down arrows) since the previous reporting period. Of particular interest in this scorecard is

FIGURE 6.8 US PATENT OFFICE DASHBOARD (IN PROGRESS)

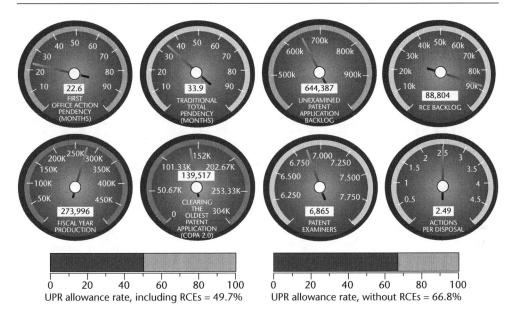

the reporting of data on actual performance as well as targets, and also showing the variance between the two. For example, while the target crime rate for homicides was 9.2 reported homicides per 100,000 population, the actual reported data indicate 9.3 homicides per 100,000 population. Thus, the actual homicide rate slightly exceeded the target by 1.09 percent, indicating that actual performance failed to meet the target by that margin.

Maps

There is a wide range of options to choose from in pictorial graphical displays. For example, with programs or organizations that serve broad geographical areas, it is sometimes desirable to map the variation across subareas in order to facilitate comparisons among them and identify where the higher-performing and lower-performing programs or districts are. The creative use of mapping can be particularly useful in displaying performance results when spatial variation in outputs and outcomes is of interest. With advances in geographic information systems (GIS), maps can be increasingly integrated in performance reporting. For example, the upper half of figure 6.10 displays ratings of local

FIGURE 6.9 MUNICIPAL POLICE DEPARTMENT SCORECARD

Reduce Crime

		Measures	Actual	Target	Meeting Target	Variance Percentage
↑		Crime—Homicide	9.30	9.20	No	1.09
↓		Crime—Rape	10.00	16.70	Yes	−40.12
↓		Crime—Robbery	243.00	253.00	Yes	−3.95
↑		Crime—Aggravated Assault	334.00	326.00	No	2.45
↑		Crime—Burglary	858.00	519.00	No	65.32
↑		Crime—Larceny	1,701.00	1,436.00	No	18.45
↑		Crime—Auto Theft	548.00	438.00	No	24.94
↑		Crime	3,702.00	3,110.00	No	19.03

Improve Clearance Rate of Crimes

		Measures	Actual	Target	Meeting Target	Variance Percentage
↑		Crime Clearance Rates—Homicide	81.7%	67.0%	Yes	21.9
↑		Crime Clearance Rates—Rape	64.7%	49.0%	Yes	32.0
↓		Crime Clearance Rates—Robbery	21.9%	31.0%	No	−29.4
↑		Crime Clearance Rates—Aggravated Assault	61.2%	56.0%	Yes	9.3
↓		Crime Clearance Rates—Burglary	9.9%	15.0%	No	−34.0
↑		Crime Clearance Rates—Larceny	20.3%	19.0%	Yes	6.8
↓		Crime Clearance Rates—Auto Theft	10.3%	14.0%	No	−26.4

Hire and Develop High-Quality Police Staff

		Measures	Actual	Target	Meeting Target	Variance Percentage
↓		Recruit Officers	4	20	No	−80
↓		Specialized Training	9,172	12,780	No	−28
↓		Employee Attrition Rate	13.0	6.8	No	91.2
↓		Percent of Budget Position Filled—Sworn	95%	100%	No	5
↓		Percent of Budget Filled—Civilian	92%	100%	No	8
↓		Percent Current on Preventative Maintenance Vehicles	73%	100%	No	−27

FIGURE 6.10 RATINGS OF PUBLIC SCHOOL SYSTEMS AND LOCAL SCHOOLS, SAN FRANCISCO METROPOLITAN AREA

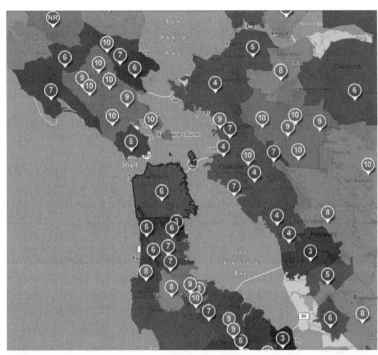

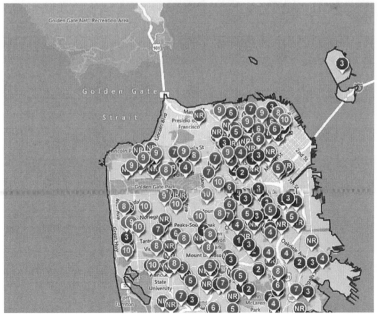

public school systems in the San Francisco metropolitan area based on average scores on standardized tests used in California. As posted online, the small circles on the map use the conventional green—yellow—red color scheme to represent individual schools that fall in the upper, middle, and lower tiers, respectively. More specifically, the numbers inside the circles indicate which decile each school system falls into. For instance, a school represented with a 1 ranks above the lowest 10 percent of all the school districts in the state, while a system represented by a 6 scored higher than 60 percent of the schools, and a school district with a rating of 9 ranked higher than 90 percent of all school systems in the state. The map in the lower half of figure 6.10 focuses solely on the City of San Francisco, where each circle represents an individual elementary, middle, or high school, using the same color coding and numbers as in the upper half of the figure. Users can also call up comparisons of these ratings by grade and by student groups defined by such variables as gender, ethnicity, and special student status within each school.

Maps can be especially useful for presenting performance information whenever service delivery is decentralized geographically. For example, the New York City Police Department's CompStat system tracks the incidence of crimes and maps this information by the five boroughs and fifty-nine community districts, as well as block by block, on a real-time basis, and it also provides longitudinal comparisons by comparing these maps over time. The City of Baltimore maps the spatial distribution of the occurrence of such problems as cases of lead paint flaking. Many state transportation departments display performance data regarding road condition, safety hazards, and construction projects on maps at the district and county level, and a state's child support enforcement agency might well map the variation in payment delinquency across all of its local offices where enforcement activities are actually carried out.

Overall, creative graphical and pictorial displays can be especially useful for communicating with the media, in press releases, and in annual reports or news briefs read by a variety of audiences. Organizations should choose pictorial displays that make sense to their audience and are appropriate for the services they provide. Like other graphical displays, the results can be memorable to some individuals who are not likely to recall the precise numbers. However, unlike the simpler graphical displays discussed earlier, displays such as these do require some expertise in graphics and may not be easily generated by all staff. More specialized software or graphical design may be required.

Conclusion

The output of a performance measurement system is generally a performance report of one form or another, and the data are frequently posted online as well as documented in hard-copy reports. Public and nonprofit organizations are often interested in demonstrating their performance to a variety of stakeholders, and they need to keep in mind that the overall utility of a performance measurement system resides in large part in the accessibility and understandability of its results, that is, how quickly, easily, and accurately the intended audiences are able to understand and absorb the performance reporting. In deciding the best way to communicate their organization's performance results, managers and staff need to consider not only the nature of the data to be presented but also the information needs and interests of their audiences for the information. Because these interests may well vary significantly by stakeholder group—for instance, managers, employers, partners, customers, governing bodies, and funding agencies—it often makes sense to report the same data in different formats to different audiences.

With these differences in mind, organizations should be creative in designing reports, and they need not feel restricted to the easiest, most common display formats. Using a mix of display formats may also be useful, with many performance reports employing a combination of tables, bar graphs, line graphs, maps, and perhaps other pictorial displays to present their performance information effectively. The choices of display formats must also be guided by the level of measurement used in each indicator—nominal, ordinal, and interval—and the comparative frameworks within which the data are to be presented, including comparisons over time, against targets, across operating units or other breakdowns, and against other similar programs or agencies.

Finally, to be creative in developing reporting formats, organizations need to be familiar with and take advantage of software technologies. The range of display options continues to increase as advances in software technology greatly improve the ease and accessibility of different display formats for even relatively unsophisticated computer users. As the production values continue to improve and the variety of formats continues to expand, however, and as the software becomes steadily more user friendly and more easily accessible, however, there is a temptation sometimes to focus more on the appearance of the report than the substance. The principal criterion in designing performance reports is not glitzy formats but rather a mix of formats that converts the data to information effectively, making the most appropriate comparisons, and presents the performance information in the most meaningful and compelling manner possible.

## CHAPTER SEVEN

ANALYZING PERFORMANCE INFORMATION

W hen a governmental or nonprofit agency has developed a set of performance indicators and implemented a system for tracking them on
a regular basis, what kind of analysis can help make effective use of the
performance data? What kinds of comparisons are most appropriate for
converting data into information and interpreting the results in a meaningful way? Using a local public transit system and a state child support
enforcement office as illustrations, this chapter presents the four principal
ways of analyzing the data generated by performance monitoring systems
so as to assess how well or poorly a program is actually performing: over
time, against targets, among subunits, and against external benchmarks.

Public Transit System Performance

While performance data often convey meaning to public managers and
service delivery employees at face value, systematic analysis of the data can
be used to convert data to information that provides greater understanding
of how well a program or agency is performing and sometimes offers
insights as to what factors are facilitating or hindering performance
improvement (Newcomer, 2010). Ammons (2008) points out that while
more advanced statistical models can sometimes be helpful in this regard,

it is often the case that simple descriptive statistics such as means, ranges, standard deviations, and percentages are all that is required to summarize the data and provide a portrait of what performance looks like in the aggregate at a particular point in time. Furthermore, he shows how breaking the data down for simple comparisons and relating one performance measure to others can help analyze staffing patterns, the demand for services, workload and production capacity, and the costs of operating programs and capital projects. Hatry (2006) focuses more on outcomes and analyzing change in outcomes over time, examining clusters of outcomes, and relating outcome data back to output data and other performance measures.

Figure 7.1 presents a basic model of the logic underlying a conventional public transit system consisting of a primary service delivery component and two support components: maintenance and planning and marketing. Inputs into the system are such resources as employees, vehicles, facilities, equipment, and materials, which can be measured in their

FIGURE 7.1 LOCAL TRANSIT SYSTEM LOGIC MODEL

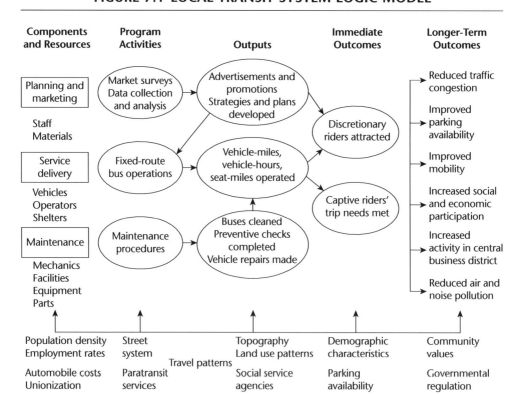

individual units or summarized as dollar costs. The program itself is a production process in which policy, design, and operational parameters such as marketing strategies, routes and schedules, fare structure, and preventive maintenance procedures determine exactly how these resources are converted into outputs.

The principal outputs of a transit system are vehicle-miles and vehicle-hours operated, measures of the amount of service provided to the community. Another output measure, seat-miles of service provided, represents the system's capacity. It is at the output stage of the transit system logic that interdependencies among the program components begin to appear. For example, the maintenance outputs—buses cleaned, preventive maintenance checks conducted, and repairs completed—contribute to both the ability to produce the service outputs—vehicle-hours and miles operated—as well as the quality of these outputs. Similarly, some of the planning and marketing outputs, such as strategies and plans, feed directly into the service components.

Although various policy objectives are often assigned to public transit, its overall objective may best be summarized as providing affordable mobility. Thus, the immediate outcomes are usually seen as meeting the travel needs of so-called captive riders, those who don't have alternative means of transportation available, and attracting discretionary riders to the system. Over the long run, increased mobility and transit ridership can also contribute to broader impacts relating to other community goals, such as more widespread participation in social and economic activities, increased activity in the central business district, reduced traffic congestion, improved parking availability, and even reduced air and noise pollution. The model also recognizes numerous environmental variables ranging from demographics and employment rates to topography, land use patterns, and travel patterns that can facilitate or impede system performance.

Exhibit 7.1 lists a number of performance measures that are commonly used by transit managers, governing boards, and funding agencies, grouped by performance dimension and relating directly to the program logic model. First, total expense is included in the list because managerial performance is often keyed in part to cost-containment objectives. Similarly, the standard outputs, such as vehicle-miles and vehicle-hours, are basic operational elements that are often included in monitoring systems as scale factors. Measures of various aspects of the quality of service, such as the percentage of bus trips that are operated on time according to published schedules or the percentage of passenger trips requiring transfers, reflect on how satisfactory the service is from the customers' point of view.

EXHIBIT 7.1 TRANSIT SYSTEM PERFORMANCE MEASURES

Resources and outputs
  Total expense
  Vehicle-hours
  Vehicle-miles
  Seat-miles

Labor productivity
  Vehicle-hours per employee
  Vehicle-hours per operator
  Vehicle-miles per maintenance
  employee

Vehicle productivity
  Vehicle-miles per vehicle
  Vehicle-hours per vehicle

Efficiency
  Expense per vehicle-mile
  Expense per vehicle-hour
  Variable cost per vehicle-mile
  Variable cost per vehicle-hour

Service quality
  Percent on-time trips
  Percent transfers
  Accidents per 100,000 vehicle-miles
  Service interruptions per 100,000 vehicle-miles

Service consumption
  Passenger trips
  Annual rides per capita revenue
  Revenue per passenger trip

Utilization
  Passenger trips per vehicle-hour
  Passenger trips per vehicle-mile
  Passenger miles per seat-mile
  Revenue per vehicle-hour

Cost-effectiveness
  Cost per passenger trip
  Percent cost recovery (revenue/expense)
  Deficit
  Net cost per passenger trip

Following the logic model in figure 7.1, the effectiveness of public transit systems is usually measured in terms of ridership. This is measured most directly by the number of passenger trips made on the system, but for comparative purposes, the annual rides per capita in the service area might also be of interest. Service consumption may also be measured by the amount of revenue generated by the system as well as by the revenue per passenger trip, as at least a partial reflection of the value of the benefit patrons receive. The overall productivity of a transit system can be viewed in terms of utilization rates, that is, the extent to which it is used relative to the amount of service provided. Thus, the number of passenger trips per vehicle-hour and passenger trips per vehicle-mile are often tracked, as well as passenger miles traveled per seat-mile provided, which is the percentage of capacity that is used. In addition, the ability of a transit system to generate revenue in relation to the amount of service provided is represented by the measure of revenue per vehicle-hour.

Labor productivity indicators relate outputs to the employees contributing to the production of those outputs. Because wear and tear on the vehicles is reflected more accurately by vehicle-miles rather than vehicle-hours, vehicle-miles operated per maintenance employee is an appropriate indicator of labor productivity for the maintenance program, whereas the vehicle-hours generated per vehicle operator better represent the labor productivity of the service component. Vehicle productivity can be measured by either vehicle-hours or vehicle-miles operated per active vehicle in the fleet. Operating efficiency is measured by the unit costs of producing the outputs, such as the expense per vehicle-hour and the cost per vehicle-mile.

Finally, cost-effectiveness indicators relate the immediate or longer-term outcomes generated by a program to the cost of the resources going into it, most directly the cost per passenger trip. Although few public transit systems, if any, are expected to finance themselves fully from earned revenue, in the business enterprise sense of the bottom line, cost-effectiveness is expressed in terms of the relation of revenue to expense or the percentage cost recovery. The operating deficit incurred and the net cost per passenger trip are other frequently used indicators of cost-effectiveness.

Trends over Time

Because performance monitoring systems track selected indicators of program performance at regular intervals over time, the data naturally accumulate in time series databases that lend themselves most readily to gauging trends and making comparisons over time. For example, figure 7.2

FIGURE 7.2 RVT RIDERSHIP, FISCAL YEAR 2008–2012

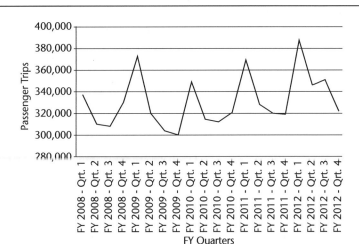

Source: River Valley Transit. Used with permission.

shows quarterly ridership data from fiscal year 2008 through fiscal year 2012 on the public transit system operated by River Valley Transit (RVT) in Williamsport, Pennsylvania. It is immediately evident that ridership on RVT is marked by significant seasonal variation, as is the case with many other public transit systems. The number of passengers peaks during the first quarter each year due to the substantial additional ridership generated by the Little League World Series, which is played in Williamsport in August each year. Ridership then drops down to more normal levels in the second quarter (fall) and tends to decline somewhat further in the third quarter (winter) when cold weather tends to decrease bus patronage somewhat. Second, with respect to long-term trends, after appearing to having decreased somewhat from FY 2009 to 2010, it has climbed noticeably from FY 2010 through 2012.

More important, looking at changes in total ridership over time, the number of passengers carried on the RVT system may appear to have declined somewhat between FY 2009 and FY 2010, but ridership grew noticeably from FY 2010 to FY 2012, still following a very regular pattern of seasonal variation. While RVT's average ridership in a quarter seems to be somewhere in the vicinity of 340,000 passengers per month, it varies from a low of a little more than 300,000 to a little over 380,000 passengers. Because maintaining or increasing ridership is so essential to transit system viability, this long-term view provides a relevant strategic context.

However, although these trends provide an indication of the direction in which RVT's overall ridership has been headed over the long run, the sharp fluctuations toward the latter portion of the series also raise questions about the most current status of ridership on the system. Thus, a more precise reading of the most recent period might be more important from a managerial perspective.

Table 7.1 shows the same ridership data, broken down by regular revenue passengers versus trips made by senior citizens during the "free fare" period paid for by the Commonwealth of Pennsylvania, for the four quarters of FY 2012. Because transit ridership is characterized by considerable seasonal variation, as is the case with outcomes in other program and policy areas as well, the most relevant comparison over time is not of the current quarter against the immediately preceding quarter but rather against the same quarter in the preceding year.

Senior citizen ridership, which constitutes nearly 20 percent of RVT's annual ridership, is fairly stable over the four quarters of the fiscal year, steady in the range of 53,000 to 57,000 per quarter. However, the number of trips made by regular revenue passengers varies much more substan-

TABLE 7.1 RVT RIDERSHIP BY QUARTER

Passengers	First Quarter 2012	Second Quarter 2012	Third Quarter 2012	Fourth Quarter 2012	FY 2012 Four— Quarter Totals
Revenue passenger	329,606	291,372	297,759	264,970	1,183,707
Prior year	310,699	274,538	274,796	265,863	1,125,896
Gain or loss	18,907	16,834	23,963	(893)	57,811
Senior citizens	57,511	54,879	53,120	57,261	222,771
Prior year	58,035	53,175	45,371	53,444	210,025
Gain or loss	(524)	1,704	7,749	3,817	12,746
Total passengers	387,117	346,251	350,879	322,231	1,406,478
Prior year	368,734	327,713	320,167	319,307	1,335,921
Gain or loss	18,383	18,538	30,712	2,924	70,557

Source: River Valley Transit. Used with permission.

tially, from a high of 329,606 in the first quarter to a low of 264,970 in the fourth quarter. Table 7.1 also compares these ridership levels with the same data for the preceding year, FY 2011. The number of regular revenue passengers in FY 2012 exceeded that number in FY 2011 for the first three quarters of the year, but then dropped off slightly in the fourth quarter, on balance showing a gain of some 57,000 for the year as a whole. Conversely, the number of senior citizen trips in the first quarter of FY 2012 was slightly less than in FY 2011, but senior citizen ridership in FY 2012 exceeded that in FY 2011 during the second, third, and fourth quarters, resulting in an increase in senior citizen ridership of nearly 13,000 trips for the year as a whole. Overall, then, RVT's total ridership increased from 1,335,921 in FY 2011 to 1,406,478 ion FY 2012 for a gain of 5.3v percent.

Comparisons against Standards and Other Agencies' Performance

Monitoring systems often measure actual performance against program objectives, service standards, or budgetary targets in order to gauge the extent to which programs are meeting explicit expectations. For example, RVT has defined a set of twenty-nine standards relating to labor productivity, operating efficiency, service quality, utilization, and cost-effectiveness, and it assesses actual performance against these standards annually. A selected set of these standards is shown in table 7.2, along with RVT's actual performance on these criteria for fiscal year 2011, the most recent year for which the comparison data are available. Where the data are available, statewide averages for the other small and medium-sized transit

TABLE 7.2 RIVER VALLEY TRANSIT PERFORMANCE STANDARDS

	RVT Standard	RVT Actual	Average Statewide Class 3 Systems
Productivity Standards			
Vehicle-miles per employee	>15,000	17,867.3	12,862.2
Vehicle-miles per operator	>22,000	23,823.0	17,877.2
Vehicle-miles per maintenance employee	>80,000	122,518.3	93,553.0
Vehicle-hours per vehicle	>2,000	2,513.7	1,859.8
Vehicle-miles per vehicle	>28,000	38,983.1	24,400.5
Efficiency Standards			
Expense per vehicle-mile	<$10.53	$6.44	$9.58
Expense per vehicle-hour	<$147.44	$99.92	$134.04
Service Quality Standards			
Percentage of trips +−5 minutes			
Nonpeak periods	>95%	97.9%	NA
Peak periods	>90%	93.3%	NA
Percentage of transfers	<10%	3.9%	NA
Collision accidents per 100,000 vehicle-miles	<3.0	2.02	NA
Vehicle-miles between road calls	>4,000	7,247	NA
Vehicle-miles between service interruptions	>25,000	27,808	NA
Utilization Standards			
Annual rides per capita	NA	20.2	12.9
Passenger trips per vehicle-mile	>1.8	1.6	2.8
Passenger trips per vehicle-hour	>24	25.4	38.2
Passenger-miles per vehicle-mile	>5.0	8.2	10.1
Cost-Effectiveness			
Cost per passenger trips	<$3.85	$3.93	$4.09
Revenue per passenger trip	>$0.78	$0.62	$0.73
Net cost per passenger trip	>$3.07	$3.31	$3.36
Percentage cost recovery	20%	$15.7%	20.9%

Source: River Valley Transit. Used with permission.

systems in Pennsylvania (in such urban areas as Allentown, Reading, Harrisburg, Johnstown, Lancaster, Altoona, Erie, Wilkes-Barre, Scranton, State College, and York) are also shown as a basis of comparison. For example, one RVT standard calls for operating 15,000 or more vehicle-miles per employee. In fiscal 2011 it actually exceeded this standard by some 2,867 vehicle-miles per employee and also substantially exceeded the statewide average of 12,862.

RVT has set a standard of operating 95 percent of all bus trips within plus-or-minus five minutes of scheduled times during nonpeak periods and 90 percent during peak periods, and according to sample check data, it exceeded both in fiscal 2011. It also outperformed the service quality standards concerning safety and service interruptions due to mechanical failures. With a transfer ratio of only 3.9 percent, RVT's was far superior than its standard of 10 percent or fewer passenger trips requiring transfers.

The internal operating efficiency standards are interesting in part because they are based after the fact on the other comparable systems in the state. In order to take inflating costs in the transit industry in general into account, RVT has established standards for expense per vehicle-mile and expense per vehicle-hour that do not exceed statewide averages by more than 10 percent. In both cases, in fact, RVT registered substantially lower unit costs than the statewide averages on both these standards.

Regarding utilization standards, which really represent the broader conception of overall system productivity, the annual transit rides per capita in the service area is an indicator of the extent to which the community uses the transit system. This measure reflects directly on the quality of transit service and the effectiveness of efforts to market this service to the community. While it does not have a specific standard regarding the number of passenger trips per capita, in fiscal 2012 RVT carried slightly more than twenty trips per capita, exceeding the statewide average by a considerable margin. Looking at passenger trips per vehicle-mile and trips per vehicle-hour operated as well as passenger-miles per vehicle-mile, however, RVT fell behind the statewide averages, although it exceeded its own standard on the latter two of these standards,

Finally, with respect to cost-effectiveness, on the one hand, RVT's actual cost per passenger trip slightly exceeded its standard of $3.85, although it was a little lower than the statewide average on this marker. On the other hand, its revenue per passenger for the year was below expectations, resulting in a cost recovery factor of just 15.7 percent as compared with its standard of 20 percent.

FIGURE 7.3 RVT RIDERSHIP BY ROUTE, FISCAL YEAR 2012

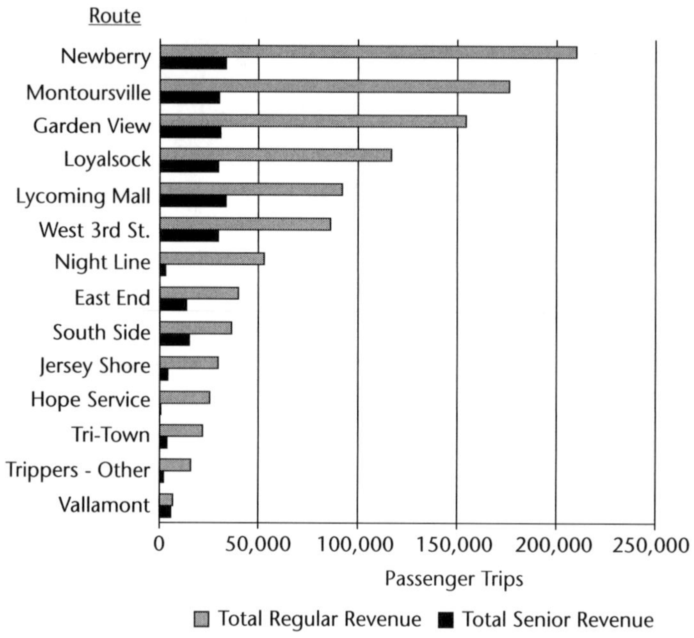

Route

Total Regular Revenue   ■ Total Senior Revenue

Source: River Valley Transit. Used with permission.

Analytics: Route Analysis

Most public transit agencies compare performance indicators across the various bus routes or rail lines they operate in order to distinguish between the stronger- and weaker-performing parts of the system. For example, RVT monitors the level of ridership on its various routes on a weekly basis, and this helps inform short-term adjustments and longer-term revision of its route structure and operating schedules. Figure 7.3 shows regular revenue passengers and free fare senior citizen passenger trips made on each route in fiscal 2012. Clearly, the Newberry, Montoursville, Garden View, and Loyalsock routes are the backbone of the system, carrying almost two-thirds of all passenger trips made on RVT. These are followed by the Lycoming Mall and West 3rd Street routes, which together with the top four routes carry more than 80 percent of all trips on the system. The remaining routes are smaller neighborhood routes or specialty routes that carry fewer passenger trips. Free-fare senior citizen ridership is spread fairly consistently over these routes with a few exceptions. The Hope Service and Trippers routes primarily serve work-related trips so fewer trips are made by senior citizens on these routes, while the Vallamont Route terminates at the Williamsport Home, an independent living center that generates most of the trip making on this route.

Analysts often dig deeper into performance by computing ratios of other indicators of relationships among different types of performance measures. For example, the ratio of passenger trips taken to vehicle-miles operated and the ratio of the number of passenger-miles traveled per vehicle-mile traveled are both system productivity measures, indicating the rate at which outputs are converted to outcomes. *Analytics* is a term that is sometimes used to refer to the more extensive use of data, statistical analysis, and explanatory and predictive models to inform fact-based decision making and improve performance (IBM Center for the Business of Government, 2012). In some cases, those models incorporate environmental variables external to the program or agency in models that are built to explain the variation in results. For instance, in order to understand how its programmatic parameters influence outcomes, RVT annually updates a multiple regression model using monthly time series data to determine the extent to which the number of days the system operates, the number of vehicle-miles of service provided, and the cost of a day pass—the most typical fare paid on that system—influence the number of passenger trips taken on the bus system. The model also incorporates as additional control variables measures of two external variables—the price of gasoline (representing the cost of the most likely alternative means of transportation) and the local area unemployment rate. In the model developed over the period from 2007 to 2011, the regression coefficients indicated the following, controlling for sequential months:

- An increase of 1 percentage point in the local unemployment rate leads to a decrease of 1,422.7 passenger trips.
- An increase of one cent in the price of a gallon of gasoline is associated with 190.8 additional passenger trips.
- One additional vehicle mile operated is associated with 3.7 additional passenger trips.
- One more cent in the price of a day pass is associated with a decrease of 295.7 passenger trips.

These kinds of ratios can be valuable in estimating the ridership response to changes in policy, operations, or service delivery plans in any programmatic area.

While RVT's overall cost recovery factor is 15.7 percent, it also tracks its variable cost recovery factor, the portion of variable costs recovered through earned revenue, on an annual basis as well. To do this, cost functions that are driven by vehicle-hours operated, such as operators' wages, supervisors' salaries, and fringe benefits for those classes of employees, are divided by the number of vehicle-hours operated, while other cost functions such as maintenance-related salary and wages, fuel and lubricants, tires and inner tubes, and liability insurance costs are divided by the number of vehicle hours operated during a fiscal year. These cost factors—in fiscal 2012, $46.01 per vehicle-hour and $1.81 per vehicle-mile—are multiplied by the total numbers of vehicle-hours and vehicle-miles, respectively, operated on each individual route to estimate the variable cost of providing transit service on a route-by-route basis.

These estimates are shown in table 7.3. Overall, RVT recovers 25 percent of its variable cost through earned revenue, but that varies widely from route to route. While the Newberry and Downtown Connector routes

TABLE 7.3 ESTIMATED VARIABLE COST RECOVERY PER ROUTE, CALENDAR 2012

Route	Estimated Variable Cost*	Fare Box Revenue	Net Cost	Percent Variable Cost Recovery
Newberry	$ 406,319	$ 174,531	$ 231,788	42.95%
Montoursville	444,760	142,196	302,564	31.97%
Garden View	390,065	142,398	247,667	36.51%
Loyalsock	384,150	116,050	268,100	30.21%
Vallamont	51,983	13,570	38,413	26.10%
West Third Street	311,968	100,763	211,205	32.30%
South Side	219,555	52,443	167,112	23.89%
East Side	243,689	50,248	193,441	20.62%
Super Nightline East	93,947	17,949	75,998	19.11%
Super Nightline West	75,246	12,401	62,844	16.48%
Lycoming Mall	296,860	68,851	228,009	23.19%
Downtown Connector	20,731	8,852	11,879	42.70%
Tri-Town Connector	267,467	19,772	247,695	7.39%
Hope Fixed Route	268,298	22,791	245,507	8.49%
Jersey Shore	310,681	26,175	284,506	8.43%
Trippers	91,042	5,643	85,399	6.20%
Totals	**$ 3,876,761**	**$ 974,633**	**$ 2,902,127**	**25.14%**

Note: *Estimated variable cost = ($46.01 × vehicle-hours) + ($1.81 × vehicle-miles)
Source: River Valley Transit. Used with permission.

recover 42 percent in revenue, at the other end of the spectrum, the Tri-Town and Jersey Shore routes, the Trippers, and the Hope Fixed Route service all had variable cost recovery factors under 10 percent. Not surprisingly, the workhorse routes such as Newberry, Montoursville, Garden View, and Loyalsock all recover more than 30 percent of their estimated variable costs through the fare box because they have high load factors. Other routes at the low end of variable-cost recovery, such as the Jersey Shore and Tri-Town routes, are rural routes with longer trips and lower load factors, leading to their low variable-cost recovery factors. In a period of great fiscal austerity they might well be more likely candidates for service cutbacks or incremental fare increases in order to strengthen RVT's overall cost recovery.

Sampling and Statistical Reliability

When we consider the analysis of performance data, the issue of statistical reliability is sometimes a concern. More often than not, the data monitored by performance measurement systems are population data; that is, they are based on data for all relevant cases. Thus, assuming that the data are recorded accurately, entered the same way by all units in a decentralized reporting process, and entered into the software system correctly, reliability is not an issue. For example, data on vehicle-miles operated and passenger trips carried on a public transit system are readily available from onboard mechanical counters. However, sometimes data are reported on a sample basis. For example, the number of passenger-miles traveled on a transit system might be counted using a simple random sample of bus trips operated, or customer feedback might be solicited through surveys of a sample of passengers once each year. Sampling is used to save time, money, and effort in data collection, but with sampling, there is always the possibility of error. When performance data are collected on a sample basis, therefore, the sample size should be large enough to provide an adequate level of statistical reliability, with a practically significant degree of precision at the 90, 95, or 99 percent confidence level. Reports of performance data collected on a random sample basis should state their level of statistical reliability.

For example, as part of its grants management process, the Federal Transit Administration (FTA) requires local transit agencies to report on the number of passenger-miles traveled on their systems as an outcome measure. As these systems continue to acquire and deploy more sophisticated passenger counting and scanning technology, monitoring the total passenger-miles traveled should become a simple matter. At this point, this is a laborious process in which trained observers ride buses and count the number of passengers boarding and alighting at each stop on a route. Those data are then fed into computer programs to determine the number of passengers riding the bus on a given route segment, multiply that number by the length of that segment in miles (or fractions of miles), and then adding up those passenger miles across all the segments of that route for that particular bus trip.

Clearly the cost of physically monitoring all trips on all bus routes would require efforts that would be all out of proportion with the benefit of having those data. Thus, the FTA requires small bus systems to report data on passenger-miles traveled on their systems only every three years and to base those numbers on relatively small sample estimates. The regulations require use of simple random samples or their equivalent that are sufficiently large to provide estimates in the form of 95 percent confidence intervals that have a level of precision that is within plus or minus 10 percent of the sample means. In fiscal year 2011, for instance, RVT sampled 645 bus trips over the course of the year and recorded a mean average of 91.26 passenger-miles per bus trip with a standard deviation of 92.21, signifying wide variation in load factors. These data produced a 95 percent confidence interval from 84.13 to 98.39, which is plus or minus 7.8 percent and thus well within the FTA requirements. Given that 67,638 bus trips were operated during the fiscal year, the sample estimate of the passenger-miles traveled on the RVT system that year was somewhere in the range of 5,690,385 and 6,654,490. In common parlance, based on that relatively small sample of fewer than 1 percent of all bus trips operated, one could be 95 percent certain that the total number of passenger trips carried on the system was somewhere in that range.

Effectiveness of a Child Support Enforcement Program

As a second example of how to analyze performance data, consider a state's child support enforcement program, whose objectives are to establish paternity of absentee parents, obligate child support payments from absentee parents, collect those payments, and disburse them to custodial parents for use in supporting the welfare of the children in question. Operating through forty-two local offices clustered in six regions around the state, the program has established targets on a set of performance measures that are monitored monthly and aggregated for quarterly review

TABLE 7.4 STATE CHILD ENFORCEMENT PROGRAM RESULTS, FIRST QUARTER 2012

Performance Measures	Performance Results	Performance Targets
Percentage of children in caseload born out of wedlock with paternity established	74.10	>80
Percentage of total cases with support payments obligated	47.70	>50
Percentage of cases in arrears	49.90	<50
Percentage of obligated support collected	37.80	>40
Percentage of clients satisfied	49.80	>55
Total collections per $1 expenditure	$1.13	>$1.30

sessions conducted by central office staff along with regional and local office directors. (See figure 4.1 in chapter 4 for logic model underlying this program.)

Table 7.4 shows performance data on selected measures for the first quarter of fiscal year 2012. At that point, the percentage of children born out of wedlock for whom paternity had been established stood at 74.1 percent, which fell short of the target of 80 percent on that measure. Similarly, the percentage of cases (each child covered by this system constitutes a case) for whom support payments had been obligated was 47.7 percent, which was also lower than the corresponding target of 50 percent or higher. However, the percentage of cases that were in arrears in making those payments was 49.9 percent, which was right at the target of 50 percent or lower. However, only 37.8 percent of the obligated support was collected during that quarter, which fell somewhat short of the target of 40 percent or more being collected. While almost half of the custodial parents responding to a survey conducted by the program indicated that they were satisfied with the service they experienced, that fell short of its target of 55 percent or more as well. Finally, the total amount of child support collected by the program in relation to total operating cost that quarter was $1.13, which also fell short of its target of $1.30 or more. Thus, for the most part, the program fell short of its targets for that quarter.

Table 7.5 shows these same data broken down by the six regions, along with two indicators representing external conditions that might be expected to influence the program's performance: the unemployment rate and the percentage of absentee parents who were working and earning wages during that quarter. At 8.4 percent, the unemployment rate was

TABLE 7.5 SELECTED PERFORMANCE MEASURES BY REGION (IN PERCENTAGES)

Region	Unemployed	Wages	Arrears	Collected	Satisfied
1 Mean	8.375	63.250	44.250	40.125	70.6250
N	8	8	8	8	8
2 Mean	11.857	58.286	53.714	37.286	64.0000
N	7	7	7	7	7
3 Mean	11.429	59.429	52.000	38.571	69.7143
N	7	7	7	7	7
4 Mean	15.286	50.714	61.571	30.000	53.2857
N	7	7	7	7	7
5 Mean	12.000	57.500	47.667	37.167	57.1667
N	6	6	6	6	6
6 Mean	12.714	65.714	40.429	43.286	72.2857
N	7	7	7	7	7
Total mean	11.857	59.286	49.857	37.810	64.8333
N	42	42	42	42	42

lowest in region 1, while at the high end, it was over 15 percent in region 4. Not surprisingly, the percentage of absentee parents who were earning wages was relatively high at 63.2 percent in region 1 and lowest in region 4, with only 50.7 percent earning wages. The payments-in-arrears measure was lowest in regions 6 and 1 and the highest by far in region 4, and the percentage payments collected was lowest in region 4 and highest in regions 6 and 1. Thus, the percentage custodial parents who were satisfied with the program was highest in regions 6 and 1, at 72.2 percent and 70.6 percent, respectively, and lowest in region 4 at 53.3 percent. Regions 2, 3, and 5 tended to be near the midpoint on all six of these performance measures, and performance on collections, delinquency, and client satisfaction clearly seemed to be influenced significantly by the variation in economic condition such as unemployment rate and the percentage absentee parents who were earning wages.

Looking at long-term trends in these indicators may also help in understanding what is going on with respect to this program. Figure 7.4 shows the long-term trends in six of these indicators from fiscal 2006 through the first quarter of fiscal 2012. Two reference lines help to interpret the data in the figure; the vertical line at the second quarter of fiscal 2008 denotes a major streamlining of operations in the program's local

FIGURE 7.4 CHILD SUPPORT ENFORCEMENT PERFORMANCE, 2006–2012

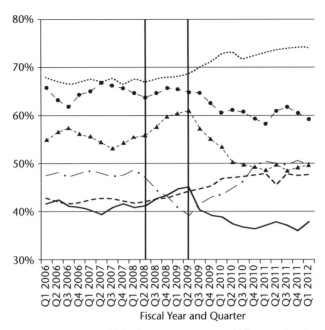

offices, which was designed to free up agents' time to do more fieldwork, and the reference line at the second quarter of FY 2009 represents the onset of economic stagnation as a result of the national economic recession that was then taking hold.

The data show that performance on all of these indicators began registering for three or four quarters following the streamlining initiative that was completed in early 2008, suggesting that it had a beneficial effect in terms of increasing paternity establishment payment obligations and payment collections, decreasing payments in arrears, and thus increasing customer satisfaction. However, after the onset of the Great Recession, establishing paternity and obligating payments continued to rise, payments in arrears reversed itself and began to rise again, and obligations

FIGURE 7.5 PERCENTAGE OF CASES IN ARREARS BY UNEMPLOYMENT RATE FIRST QUARTER, FISCAL YEAR 2012

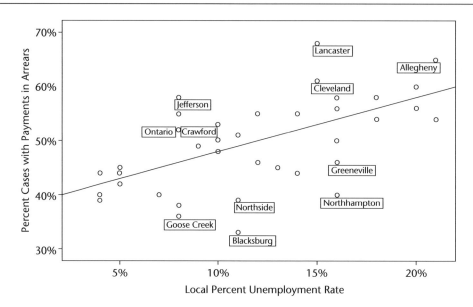

collected turned downward, as did customer satisfaction. Thus, the immediate outcomes most under the influence of the program's operation itself, paternity establishment and payment obligations, began to improve after the streamlining initiative was completed and continued to improve even after the recession took hold. However, the intermediate outcomes regarding payments in arrears and percentage obligated payments collected, along with overall custodial parent satisfaction, after beginning to improve as a result of the process reengineering effort then worsened steadily again after the recession led to difficulties regarding unemployment and the percentage of absentee parents earning wages.

Clearly the unemployment rate and percentage of absentee parents earning wages in this state have a significant impact on its ability to provide effective child support enforcement. Thus, figure 7.5 shows one performance indicator, the percentage of cases with payments in arrears, for each of the program's forty-two local offices plotted over the unemployment rate, which ranged from less than 5 percent to more than 20 percent in the first quarter of fiscal 2012. This figure, which shows a strong positive relationship between these two measures, facilitates internal benchmarking among the local offices on the payments-in-arrears indicator because it compares their performance in terms of cases with payments in arrears while controlling for the unemployment rate in their local areas. Local offices well above the regression line—especially the Ontario, Jefferson, Crawford, Cleveland, Lancaster, and Allegheny offices—reported noticeably higher percentages of cases with payments in arrears than would be expected based on the relationship between payments in arrears and the local unemployment rate. Local offices well below the regression line, most notably the Goose Creek, Blacksburg, Northside, Northhampton, and Greeneville offices, reported significantly lower percentages of cases with payments in arrears than would be expected based on their local unemployment rates. Follow-up investigation would be required to determine whether and the extent to which these leading-edge offices are performing better than others because they are managed more effectively or use more effective practices as opposed to the possibility that they are operating in more benign local environments in terms of other factors that go beyond the effect of unemployment rates.

Conclusion

Whether they are based on full population or sample data, performance measures are meaningless on their own without some context to help interpret what they actually show about program performance. Is performance improving or declining? Are we meeting specified standards and achieving our objectives? Are some parts of the operation—different field offices, organizational units, or various other system components, for example—performing better than others? How do we stack up against other similar agencies or programs? These are the relevant questions, and they are addressed by comparing the data generated by performance measurement systems over time against established targets, across subunits, or against external benchmarks.

Yet we must acknowledge three points to help qualify this analysis of performance data. First, we need to recognize that the kinds of comparisons illustrated in this chapter constitute only a surface-level analysis of program performance. Observing a set of indicators at periodic intervals over time provides performance data that are descriptive in nature but not rigorously evaluative. When the data generated by ongoing performance monitoring systems show, for instance, that a program's intended outcomes are increasing, that can be taken as a matter of fact, but the data rarely prove that the program itself causally produced these beneficial results. Rather, we typically assume that the cause-and-effect relationships reflected in the program logic model are valid, and when the performance data show an increase in program output and a commensurate increase in effectiveness, for example, we conclude that the program is effective. As a practical matter, this often makes sense, but when we are less certain about the causal connections in the logic underlying a program, these assumptions need to be tested with more intensive analysis using experimental or nonexperimental designs before we can have faith in what the performance measures seem to be saying about program effectiveness. This is the function of intensive program evaluations rather than more descriptive performance measurement systems.

Second, external forces often exert heavy influence on the results of ongoing performance measurement systems, and these should be taken into account in examining the data generated by performance measurement systems. With respect to public transit systems, for instance, not only unemployment rates and the price of gasoline but many other external factors, such as population density, automobile ownership rates, and socioeconomic patterns, are likely to wield heavy influence over the viability and performance of a local public transit agency.

The point is that any number of external factors that are far beyond a program's control may exert strong influence over its performance. These factors should be identified as part of the process of building a logic model, and they should be tracked at least in some informal way so as to shed additional light on the practical meaning of performance data. As discussed in chapter 6, many performance measurement reporting formats contain comment fields for just this purpose.

Third, we should always keep in mind that performance measures tend to raise more questions than they answer (Behn, 2003). Beyond describing current performance and how it has trended over time, we can sometimes analyze relationships among various performance measures, and in some cases we can also drill down to obtain more detailed information on an agency's or program's performance. However, while we can see what performance looks like, we often need to go beyond the data generated by ongoing performance monitoring systems to learn more about the whys and wherefores of program performance, assess causal relationships, and identify the drivers that can facilitate or hinder performance improvement. Thus, in addition to undertaking in-depth program evaluations at times, the issues raised by performance measurement may lead agencies to undertake (1) analyses of contract and grants management processes; (2) quality, productivity, and process improvement efforts; (3) cost or cost function, cost-effectiveness, or even benefit-cost analyses; or

(4) management analyses focusing on staffing patterns or service delivery systems and so forth.

As long as we keep these three caveats in mind concerning the essentially descriptive nature of performance monitoring data and the often overwhelming influence of external variables on performance, we can often use the kind of data produced by performance measurement systems to analyze program performance within reasonable bounds. This analysis comes from (1) making the kinds of comparisons discussed in this chapter, (2) developing a composite picture of performance by examining these kinds of comparisons and their interrelationships on a whole set of balanced indicators, and (3) keeping track of influential environmental conditions and external variables that might help us interpret trends in performance.

References

Ammons, D. N. (2008). Analyzing performance data. In P. de Lancer Julnes, F. S. Berry, M. P. Aristiqueta, & K. G. Yang (Eds.), *International handbook of practice-based performance management.* Thousand Oaks, CA: Sage.

Behn, R. D. (2003). Why measure performance? Different purposes require different measures. *Public Administration Review, 63,* 586–606.

Hatry, H. P. (2006). *Performance measurement: Getting results* (2nd ed.). Washington, DC: Urban Institute Press.

IBM Center for the Business of Government & Partnership for Public Service. (2012). *From data to decisions II: Building an analytical culture.* Washington, DC: Author.

Newcomer, K. E. (2010). Using statistics in evaluation. In J. S. Wholey, H. P. Hatry, & K. E. Newcomer (Eds.), *Handbook of practical program evaluation* (3rd ed.). San Francisco: Jossey-Bass.

PART THREE

STRATEGIC APPLICATIONS OF PERFORMANCE MANAGEMENT PRINCIPLES

Performance management systems serve a variety of purposes in public and nonprofit agencies. Whereas some performance measurement processes are stand-alone reporting systems, most are designed specifically to support other important management and decision-making processes. Although the approach to developing measurement systems discussed throughout this book is appropriate for all types of applications, part 3 discusses seven principal types of applications that are of strategic value to many public and nonprofit agencies.

Chapter 8 discusses the critical role that performance measures play in successful strategic planning efforts; it focuses on the need to track progress in implementing strategic objectives and accomplishing strategic goals and objectives. Chapter 9 discusses approaches to using performance measures to inform budgeting processes, focusing on both advantages and limitations. Chapter 10 examines the role of performance measures in performance management systems designed to direct and control the work of organizational units, individual employees, and programs. Chapter 11 addresses performance-based approaches to managing grants and contracts, and chapter 12 looks at the use of performance measures in process improvement efforts aimed at improving service quality and productivity. Then chapter 13 discusses processes for soliciting feedback from customers and other stakeholders that can be helpful to improving program or agency performance. Finally, chapter 14 focuses on the use of comparative performance measures to benchmark program or organizational performance against other agencies or programs. Emphasized throughout this part of the book is the notion that performance measurement systems developed to support these different applications tend to vary systematically in terms of the kinds of measures used, level of aggregation, and reporting frequencies, as well as other design features.

## CHAPTER EIGHT

USING PERFORMANCE MEASURES TO SUPPORT STRATEGIC PLANNING AND MANAGEMENT

Why are performance measurement systems essential for supporting public and nonprofit agencies' strategic planning and management processes? Clearly strategic management requires good information on performance, but what kinds of performance indicators are most useful in strategic planning and management, and how can they be used most advantageously to strengthen strategic management and decision making? This chapter provides an overview of the processes of strategic planning and management, defines the role of performance measurement in these processes, and discusses the development and use of measurement systems, including the balanced scorecard, to support them.

Strategic Planning and Management

The terms *strategic planning* and *strategic management* are often used interchangeably, but in fact they are not the same thing. Strategic planning is the process of clarifying mission and vision, defining major goals and objectives, and developing long-term strategies for moving an organization into the future in a purposeful way and ensuring a high level of performance in the long run. Strategic management is the "reasonable integration of strategic planning and implementation across an organization (or other entity) in an ongoing way to enhance the fulfill-ment of mission, meeting of mandates, continuous learning, and sus-tained creation of public value" (Bryson, 2011, p. 25). It includes both the strategic planning process and the actual focusing of organizational activi-ties around the implementation of the developed plan. Implementation of the developed plan requires the organization to conduct activities such as performance-based budgeting, performance measurement, and performance management in a holistic manner that complements the strategic plan.

Strategic planning has been defined as a "deliberative, disciplined approach to producing fundamental decisions and actions that shape and guide what an organization (or other entity) is, what it does, and why" (Bryson, 2011, pp. 7–8). It blends futuristic thinking, objective analysis, and subjective evaluation of goals and priorities to chart future courses of action. In contrast to more closed-system traditional long-range or program planning processes, strategic planning is a big picture approach that

- Is concerned with identifying and responding to the most fundamen-tal issues facing an organization in terms of long-term viability and performance
- Addresses the subjective question of basic purposes and the often com-peting values that influence mission, vision, and strategies
- Emphasizes the importance of external trends and forces as they are likely to affect the organization and its mission
- Attempts to be politically realistic by taking into account the needs, concerns, and preferences of internal and, especially, external stakeholders
- Relies heavily on the active involvement of senior-level managers and sometimes elected officials or governing boards, assisted by staff support where needed
- Requires key participants to confront candidly the most critical issues facing an organization or program in order to build commitment to plans
- Is action oriented and stresses the importance of developing plans for implementing strategies
- Focuses on implementing decisions now so as to position the organiza-tion favorably in the future (Poister & Streib, 1999).

Whereas strategic planning is typically undertaken to create or update an organization's strategic agenda, strategic management is the more comprehensive management process that integrates all major activities and functions and directs them toward advancing that strategic agenda (Vinzant & Vinzant, 1996; Poister & Streib, 1999). It is concerned with strengthening the long-term viability and effectiveness of public and non-profit organizations in terms of both substantive policy and management capacity. Strategic management integrates all other management processes to provide a coherent and effective approach to establishing, attaining, monitoring, and updating an agency's strategic objectives. Indeed, a thorough strategic management system "embraces the entire set of managerial decisions and actions that determine the long-run performance of an organization" (Koteen, 1989, p. 8). Indeed, Poister (2010) emphasizes the critical importance of tying strategic planning closely to performance management processes in order to institutionalize an effective strategic management process. The importance of doing so is underscored by research using survey data from more than three hundred nonprofit social service organizations in the United States that found a positive relationship between the range of performance measures they used, for example, workload and output measures, efficiency measures, outcome measures, customer satisfaction measures, and external benchmarks, and their effectiveness in making strategic decisions (LeRoux & Wright, 2010).

A strategically aligned and managed public or nonprofit organization is one in which budgeting, performance measurement, human resource development, program management, and all other management processes are guided by a strategic agenda that has been developed with buy-in from key actors and communicated widely among external constituencies as well as internally. Strategic management is concerned with implementing strategies and measuring performance as well as monitoring trends and identifying emerging issues that might require strategic responses. Thus, the strategic management process as illustrated in figure 8.1 places heavy emphasis on implementation as well as planning. For strategic plans to be effective, they must drive decisions and actions downward and throughout the agency. This includes ensuring that other kinds of plans, such as division plans, business plans, work plans, and plans for programs and projects, are developed within the framework and in support of the overall strategic plan. It also requires the fleshing out to the extent necessary and implementation of strategic initiatives to carry strategy forward, as well as managing and making decisions on a day-to-day basis in ways to further the organization's strategic agenda. To ensure that strategic plans will indeed become the driving force behind operating-level decisions and activities throughout the organization, strategic managers

FIGURE 8.1 THE STRATEGIC MANAGEMENT PROCESS

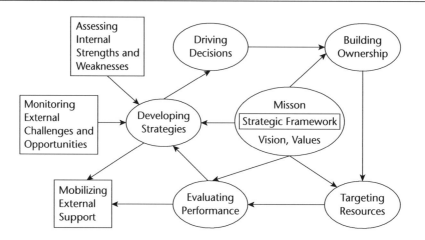

Source: Poister and Van Slyke (2002). Used with permission.

must build ownership of strategic goals and initiatives on the part of managers and employees, develop processes for targeting resources to fund strategic initiatives, monitor and evaluate performance in implementing strategies and generating the desired outcomes, and building external support where needed to move the strategic agenda forward (Poister & Van Slyke, 2002).

Implementation of strategic plans requires the commitment of the resources. As indicated in figure 8.1, some types of performance-based or performance-informed budgeting system in which funds can be tied to particular programs, projects, or activities and related to planned outputs and impacts can facilitate the allocation of resources so as to maximize their impact in advancing the strategic agenda. Such a budgeting process, as discussed in chapter 9, can ensure that specific strategic initiatives are adequately funded and provide incentives for supporting the strategic agenda wherever possible. Some public agencies require that budget proposals, as well as work programs from operating units working their way up to the executive level for approval, provide convincing support that the resources being requested will be used in ways that help advance overall strategic plans.

A good example of such an integrated system of the various components constituting strategic management is provided by the Pennsylvania Department of Transportation (PennDOT), a leader in this area among both Pennsylvania state agencies and state transportation departments generally during the administration of Governor Tom Ridge from 1994 to 2002 (Poister, Margolis, & Zimmerman, 2004). PennDOT conducted an elaborate strategic planning process beginning with extensive engagement of external stakeholders to help develop strategic goals and objectives, and then moved through a process of developing strategic initiatives and action plans by teams made up of individuals at various levels in the organization who were particularly well positioned or qualified to flesh out this process. Then the department used all possible ways to implement these plans and advance the overall strategic agenda through its business planning, budgeting, performance measurement, communications, and employee development and recognition processes to achieve an omnidirectional alignment of decisions and actions designed to move PennDOT very deliberately in the desired future directions.

Strategic Planning

Although every strategic planning effort is likely to be unique in some respects, most incorporate a basic set of common elements. Figure 8.2 shows a conventional process that reflects the way many public and nonprofit organizations go about strategic planning. Strategic planning is a ten-step process with some variations in the order (Bryson, 2011; Poister, 2003; Koteen, 1989):

1. *Agreement on a strategic planning process.* The first step of the strategic planning process requires that an individual or group of individuals formulate a plan. During this stage, an agreement must be negotiated between internal and external stakeholders that specify how the process will be conducted, including topics such as outreach, purpose, goals, deliverables, participant roles, and time lines.

2. *Clarification of organizational mandates.* The strategic planning team focuses on gaining a greater understanding of the formal and informal mandates that authorize or constrain the organization in order to provide an accurate interpretation of the entity's scope.

3. *Organizational mission and values.* Clarifying the organizational mission and values allows the participants of the strategic planning process to focus their attention on developing a plan that aims to accomplish the purpose of the organization in a way that upholds its values. Whereas the US Department of Transportation example found in this chapter begins its strategic plan with the mission, other organizations, as we will

FIGURE 8.2 CONVENTIONAL ITERATIVE STRATEGIC PLANNING PROCESS

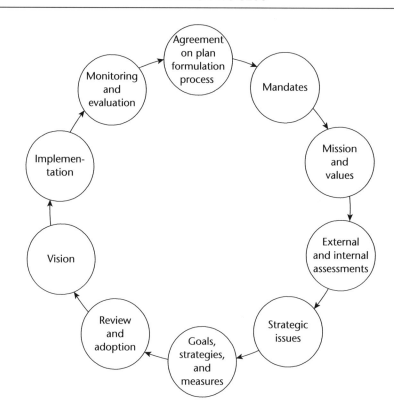

see in the State of Virginia example, prefer to begin the strategic planning process with the vision. In other words, some organizations start with their preferred future (or vision) while others begin with their statement of purpose (or mission).

4. *Assessment of external and internal environments.* This stage is primarily completed by conducting an internal strength and weaknesses and external opportunities and challenges (otherwise known as SWOC or SWOT analysis when the challenges are changed to threats) analysis. Conducting a SWOC analysis is a necessity in the strategic planning process because organizations do not exist in a vacuum; their activities are heavily influenced by internal and external forces. Internal analysis consists primarily of identifying and analyzing major strengths and weaknesses of the

organization or program. These strengths and weaknesses, which in conjunction with external threats and opportunities are critical for identifying strategic issues, may relate to aspects of performance, such as resource availability, management capacity, employee skills and morale, technology use, and external relations, as well as quality, productivity, service delivery, program effectiveness, and customer satisfaction. Strategic issues may arise from problems in any of these areas, but in most public and nonprofit service industries, issues of quality, productivity, program effectiveness, and client satisfaction are of critical importance. Thus, performance measures that track performance in terms of this bottom line of service delivery are often crucial for successful strategic planning.

5. *Identification of strategic issues facing an organization.* Strategic issues are the "fundamental policy questions or critical challenges affecting the organization's mandates, mission and values, product or service level mix, clients, users or payers, costs, financing, organization, or management" (Bryson, 2011, p. 55). The three-part statement for strategic issues is a problem statement in the form of a question, the factors leading to this challenge being categorized as a strategic issue, and the consequences that will result if the problem is not solved. Goals and objectives may be developed at this stage.

6. *Developing strategies and measures to manage the issues.* Once strategic issues are identified, action strategies must be developed to solve them. There are numerous approaches to strategy development; Bryson (2011, pp. 60–61) generally recommends two: a "five-part strategy development process" and "action-oriented strategy mapping." During the five-part process, an organization will identify methods to solve the issue, specify barriers that exist in the resolution of the problem, engage in the development of proposals that incorporate the previous two steps, and implement the selected proposal after a detailed action plan for the next year is agreed on. Action-oriented strategy mapping focuses on specifying causal relationships between different prospective options to address the issue. Basically, a mapping framework, similar to the logic models discussed in this book, is developed that depicts the theory, or "if this policy is pursued then this result will occur." This step will be useful for developing performance measures. A strategy must be technically and administratively feasible, acceptable to key stakeholders, fit with the culture of the organization, and be results focused to succeed.

7. *Review and adoption of the strategies and plan.* Proposed strategies are reviewed and approved by the decision makers of the organization. It is

important to monitor the opinions of key stakeholders during this period and to gain the support of key players in the organization for the plan.

8. *Establishing an organizational vision or preferred future.* If not already done so as discussed in step 3 of this process, members of the strategic planning committee must develop a vision that represents their desired future. While vision statements can come in many forms, they should be inspiring, achievable, concise, and clear; strive for improvement; and be consistent with the values of the organization.

9. *Implementation process.* This requires the creation of an action plan that specifies the roles of organizational subunits and members, goals, objectives, tasks, time lines, required resources, communication procedures, a method for evaluation and modification, and accountability measures. During this stage it is necessary to budget resources, both financial and personnel, in a manner that will ensure the future success of the strategic plan.

10. *Monitoring and evaluation.* Finally, the strategic plan should be evaluated along with the process that was used to develop it. Unsuccessful strategies should be replaced, and successful strategies must be examined to see if they are still relevant. The planning process must also be examined so that the next version of the plan can be improved.

This process ultimately incorporates both short-term and long-term goals into a document that will focus all of the organization's efforts behind a limited number of high-priority strategic issues that align with its mission. If done properly, strategic planning can lead to positive outcomes such as "the promotion of strategic thinking, acting, and learning…improved decision-making…enhanced organizational effectiveness [and] legitimacy…enhanced effectiveness of broader societal systems… and directly benefit the people involved [through increased] human, social, political, and intellectual capital" (Bryson, 2011, pp. 16–17). For example, using information gathered during an internal analysis, the American Red Cross uses its Field Operations Consolidated Information System (FOCIS) to track a set of performance measures concerning the delivery of "must" services (e.g., emergency communication, international tracing, multifamily disaster operations, and disaster education) and a variety of other "should" and "may" services, along with data on staff, volunteers, and financial resources. The data input is submitted electronically by the 990 local chapters of the Red Cross. Then a FOCIS report that tracks all these measures over the most recent five-year period is produced for each local chapter, each state, multistate regions, and the nation. In addition, for each of the measures, the report benchmarks a given state or local program against a reference group of other comparable geographical areas selected on the basis of similar demographics. These FOCIS data are used by management and governing boards at several levels in the Red Cross structure in planning, evaluation, and resource allocation.

Strategic Management

Strategic management systems need to incorporate strategic planning, performance-based budgeting, performance management processes, and performance measurement systems and tie them together in a coherent manner. Performance measures play a critical role in both performance-based budgeting systems and performance-based processes for managing organizations and employees, as will be discussed in chapters 9 and 10, respectively. However, whereas budgeting and performance management are essential for implementing strategic initiatives effectively, the performance measurement component of the strategic management process shown in figure 8.1 is concerned with tracking and evaluating the success of these initiatives. That is, performance measures are essential for monitoring progress in implementing strategic initiatives and assessing their effectiveness in producing the desired results.

These strategic initiatives often focus on service delivery, but they may also involve any other aspect of the organization's operations or management, as indicated by the strategic management model presented in figure 8.3. At its core are the values that are most important to the agency, its mission and the communities or constituencies it serves, and a vision of what the agency will be in the future. Around the outer ring of the model are a number of management responsibilities (intended to be illustrative rather than exhaustive) that must be coordinated in terms of their strategic implications. As indicated in figure 8.3, there are two-directional relationships between all these elements and the values, mission, and vision that drive the strategic management process. The model is best thought of as a constellation of key management functions orbiting around the core values, mission, and vision of any public or nonprofit organization, and the force that keeps them in orbit consists of the strategies that are formulated, implemented, and evaluated on an ongoing basis pursuant to the agency's values, mission, and vision.

FIGURE 8.3 STRATEGIC MANAGEMENT MODEL

Source: Poister and Streib (1999). Used with permission.

Strategic Performance Measures

In contrast to program planning, project planning, or operations planning, strategic planning in the public and nonprofit sectors tends to take a global perspective, consider long-term implications, and focus on the organization as a whole, or at least major components or major programs. Thus, the kinds of performance measurement systems that tend to be the most appropriate for supporting strategic planning and management efforts are those that portray the big picture using macrolevel indicators that track performance in the aggregate and relating to the whole organization or major units rather than to detailed operating data broken down by numerous subunits. Strategic performance indicators also tend to be observed over longer time frames, more commonly providing annual or possibly semiannual or quarterly data rather than more detailed daily, weekly, or monthly data.

At a community level, strategic performance measures are likely to be global measures focusing on individuals, families, or households in the local area. For example, the United Way of Metropolitan Atlanta estimates that some 634,800 families in the area are not financially self-sufficient, and one of its strategic goals is to help 15 percent or more of them (approximately 95,000) become financially self-sufficient over the next two years. To achieve this goal, the organization has identified a number of strategies focusing on workforce development, income supports, savings and assets, and affordable housing. With respect to workforce development, for instance, United Way tracks the number and percentage of individuals in the target population who complete transitional employment programs as an initial outcome indicator, the number and percentage of those who are employed in unsubsidized employment within thirty days after completing such programs and an intermediate indicator, and the number and percentage of individuals who have been employed for ninety days or more. Similarly, focusing on the target of creating a pathway out of homelessness for more than 4,700 homeless individuals in the Atlanta area, United Way monitors the number and percentage of homeless individuals who have been placed in a "program bed" and completed an individual service plan as an initial outcome indicator, the number and percentage of individuals in the target population who have maintained safe and stable housing for ninety days or more as an intermediate outcome indicator, and the number and percentage of those who have successfully graduated from transitional housing or who live in permanent housing for one year or longer as a long-term indicator of the effectiveness of that particular goal.

Virginia Performs: Using Vision to Develop Goals, Objectives, and Measures

The Council on Virginia's Future, a planning advisory council established in 2004 by the state government, developed a statewide performance measurement program in 2007. The program, Virginia Performs, is guided by the vision to create a state that is defined by "responsible economic growth, an enviable quality of life, good government, and a well-educated citizenry prepared to lead successful lives and to be engaged in shaping the future of the Commonwealth" (Council on Virginia's Future, 2013a). The system was developed to ensure that the services provided by the state were working to accomplish seven long-term goals falling under the categories of economy; education; health and family; natural, historic, and cultural resources; public safety; transportation; and government and citizens. These seven goals are determined by the Council on Virginia's Future and the state's leadership and then delegated to the responsible state agencies to fulfill through their key objectives and measures. The

FIGURE 8.4 VIRGINIA PERFORMS FRAMEWORK

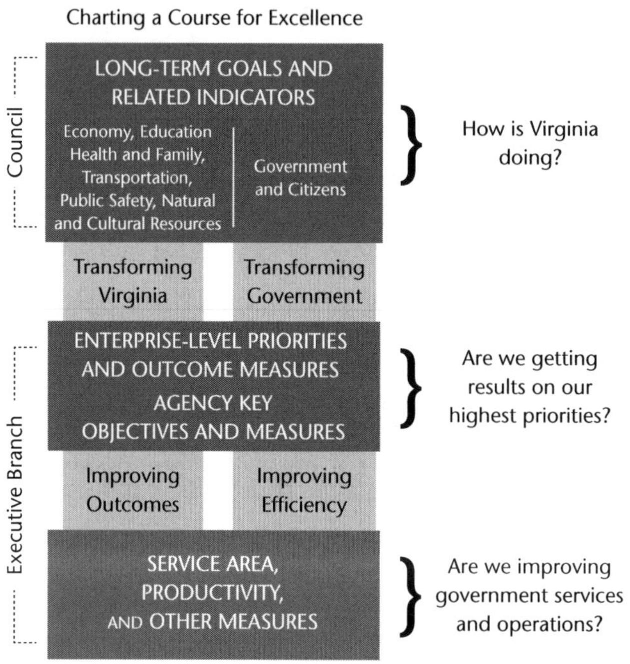

Charting a Course for Excellence

Source: Council on Virginia's Future (2013a). http://vaperforms.virginia.gov/extras/about.php. Used with permission.

agency performance measures are focused on examining internal efficiency and service outcomes. This framework is depicted in figure 8.4.

Agency-Based Strategic Goals

At the agency level, it is essential to define and monitor performance indicators that are tied directly to missions and strategies in order to be sure that programs are on track. Some organizations prefer to start their strategic planning process with vision instead of mission as in the State of Virginia example in figure 8.4. Public and nonprofit agencies are increasingly concerned with monitoring their performance in light of their mission or vision, and the linkages usually run through goals and objectives. When an organization has a clear understanding of the goals to support the mission, and of what more operational objectives need to be accomplished in order to reach the goals, then it can determine how to measure the success of particular programmatic activities and be confident that the performance indicators are consistent with its mission.

For example, the long-term goal related to the strategic issue of education is to "elevate the educational preparedness and attainment of [Virginia's] citizens" (Council on Virginia's Future, 2013b). The measures that are used to determine the state's progress on accomplishing this goal include school readiness, third-grade reading levels, fourth-grade reading and math levels, high school graduation rate, high school dropout rate, college graduation rate, and educational attainment. Each of these indicators is measured quantitatively and compared with previous years and accomplishments in other states across the nation. A select group of agency key objectives that fall under the education long-term goals and influence the specified education indicators include

- Increase the number of at-risk four-year-olds served by preschool initiatives
- Increase third-grade reading proficiency
- Provide quality education for children with sensory impairments
- Increase high school graduation rates and decrease dropout rates
- Increase the college and career readiness of high school students
- Increase enrollment in GED and postsecondary degree programs
- Enhance higher education access and affordability

Each of these objectives is then measured with corresponding performance indicators at the agency level to determine the effectiveness of the services provided. In other words, agency objectives and performance measures are derived from the indicators used to determine the state's quality of education, aligned with the corresponding long-term goal, developed from the state's vision for the future.

The information collected by this program is readily accessible to the public. For example, individuals who are interested in examining a brief overview of the state's performance in each of the seven long-term goal categories can view a performance scorecard. This scorecard includes each of the seven long-term goal categories, the primary measures that are being analyzed by the state, their performance trend, and the state's role in influencing each measure. When viewing the online version of the performance scorecard, individuals may select a measure to gain a better understanding of its definition, Virginia's performance in this category compared to other states, and the corresponding agency level measures. (See figure 8.5 for the Virginia Performs scorecard.) In addition to the

FIGURE 8.5 VIRGINIA PERFORMS PERFORMANCE SCORECARD

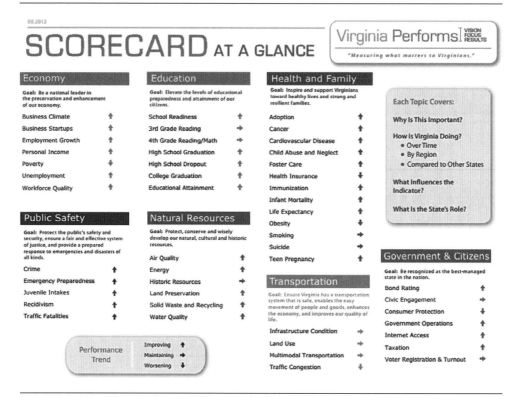

Source: Council on Virginia's Future (2013a). Used with permission.

scorecard, the website includes an explanation of why the measure is important; for example, school readiness is explained along with why it is important and the state's role in helping families (see http://vaperforms.virginia.gov/indicators/education/schoolReadiness.php). These explanations have been found to be crucial to the public understanding the role of government in addressing the issue and legislators willingness to pay for the data collection and the overall long-term survival of comprehensive performance management systems (Aristigueta, 2000).

Outcome and Output Measures

Because strategic planning is concerned with maintaining and improving organizational effectiveness, it is not surprising that often the most important performance measures used in the strategic management process are outcome indicators. These indicators are most often designed to track the effectiveness of services delivered, but they may also focus on other aspects of performance, such as the effectiveness of a change in organizational structure in improving customer relations, the performance of a training program in terms of strengthening employees' skills, or the impact of a public relations initiative on positive coverage by the media.

Some of the broadest strategic planning efforts undertaken in the United States are statewide planning processes like Virginia Performs. Strategic planning in the public and nonprofit sectors tends to focus on producing or improving programmatic outcomes. Thus, the performance measures used in strategic management systems often constitute direct effectiveness measures—for example, academic proficiency achieved or gainful employment resulting from education programs, or indicators of reduced travel times or decreased highway accident fatalities in the case of transportation programs.

However, because strategic plans are concerned with bringing about change in what public and nonprofit organizations actually do or how they go about providing service, strategic managers may need to rely heavily on output measures, in addition to outcome measures, to determine whether their organizations are implementing their strategic initiatives effectively. Indeed, output indicators often serve as proximate measures of outcomes, but they can also be critical indicators of success in their own right, particularly in the earlier stages of implementing strategic initiatives.

Performance measurement needs to be a critical element of both strategic planning and the overall strategic management process. Although current measurement systems are likely to serve the purpose of many strategic planning exercises, effective strategic management often requires new or revised systems to track particular indicators that are tailored to the specific strategic initiatives being implemented and monitored.

Focus on Output Measures: Library of Virginia

Output measures are part of the program logic and serve as proximate outcomes in situations where outcome measures would be too costly or difficult to obtain. They provide information on the provision and use of resources but fail to give an accurate representation of the actual results of the program. The Library of Virginia, whose mission is to "acquire, preserve, and promote access to unique collections of Virginia's history and culture and advance the development of library and records management

FIGURE 8.6 BALANCED SCORECARD

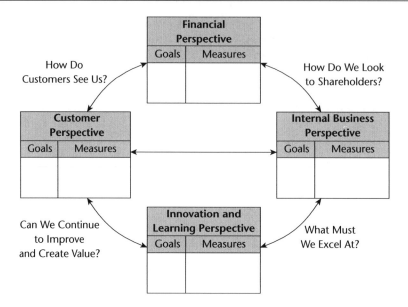

Source: Reprinted by permission of *Harvard Business Review,* figure entitled The Balanced Score-card Links Performance Measures. From "The Balanced Scorecard: Measures That Drive Performance," by R. S. Kaplan and D. P. Norton, *Harvard Business Review,* Jan./Feb. 1992. Copyright © 1992 by the Harvard Business School Publishing Corporation; all rights reserved. Kaplan and Norton (1992), p. 72.

services statewide," uses only output measures to determine its performance (Council on Virginia's Future, 2013b). The full list of performance measures, along with their corresponding objectives, is in figure 8.6.

The Library of Virginia uses output measures because its primary mission is to acquire and then promote access to information (see table 8.1). Objectives such as the provision of information can be measured through outputs such as the amount of materials circulated and participation in library programs. While outcome measures such as information learned could theoretically be used, they would be too costly to obtain, particularly for an organization that provides a service that is primarily demand driven. If the library were to begin to use performance measures that were considered to be too intrusive by patrons, visits to their facilities could decrease. It would also be difficult to develop a strong causal relationship between the services provided by the Library of Virginia and information obtained because a variety of

TABLE 8.1 OUTPUT PERFORMANCE MEASURES AND OBJECTIVES USED BY THE LIBRARY OF VIRGINIA

Measure	Objective
Number of contacts with state and local records officers	Increase the number of direct contacts with state and local records officers and coordinators to enhance the effectiveness of Virginia's records management program
Number of items of library archival records processed	Expand public access to the library's archival resources of Virginia's state government, circuit courts, private papers, counties, and cities
Number of attendees at lectures, symposia, and other programs for the public	Disseminate to the widest possible audience information about Virginia history and culture
Number of items from the library's collections served to users, in print, archival, microform, or electronic format	Expand access to archival resources and information services to state and local government agencies, historical and family history researchers, and the public
Number of items/pages in the library's collections preserved through microfilming and digitization	Conserve and reformat a wide variety of manuscript, newspaper, and other fragile collections
Number of active circuit court projects funded by the grant program	Preserve and protect circuit court records through the Circuit Courts Records Preservation grant project
Number of articles viewed, downloaded or printed from the Find It Virginia databases	Provide information to all Virginians effectively and efficiently through the strengthening of library resources
Number of participants in summer reading program	Provide information to all Virginians effectively and efficiently through the strengthening of library resources
Number of participants in winter reading program	Provide information to all Virginians effectively and efficiently through the strengthening of library resources
Circulation of children's library materials	Provide information to all Virginians effectively and efficiently through the strengthening of library resources
Number of professional contacts, site visits, and workshop attendees with the public libraries of the commonwealth	Provide assistance, counsel, and staff development to Virginia's public libraries to foster quality library service to all residents
Number of new bibliographic records added to the library's online collections catalogue	Increase access to library resources for the commonwealth's citizens, public libraries, and state and local governments through the effective use of acquisition, distribution, and cataloging
Circulation of library materials	Improve the quality of information resources and library services in Virginia's public libraries through the state aid program
Attendance at library programs	Improve the quality of information resources and library services in Virginia's public libraries through the state aid program
Unit cost of educational programming for K–12 students	Disseminate to the widest possible audience information about Virginia history and culture

Source: Council on Virginia's Future (2013b). Used with permission.

other variables, particularly the education system, can influence the accumulation of knowledge.

Focus on Outcome Measures: US Department of Transportation

The US Department of Transportation mission is to "serve the United States by ensuring a fast, safe, efficient, accessible and convenient transportation system that meets our vital national interests and enhances the quality of life of the American people, today and into the future" (http://www.dot.gov/mission/about-us). This department focuses on achieving its mission by pursuing objectives that fall under five strategic issues: safety, state of good repair, economic competitiveness, and environmental sustainability. Performance of the first strategic issue, safety, is almost exclusively measured by outcome measures. Examples of outcome measures that are used to determine the effectiveness of the Department of Transportation's programs that fall under the category of safety include these:

- Roadway fatality rate per 100 million vehicle-miles traveled (VMT)
- Passenger vehicle occupant fatality rate per 100 million VMT
- Large truck and bus fatality rate per 100 million VMT
- Number of fatal general aviation accidents per 100,000 flight hours
- Hazardous materials incidents involving death or major injury

The full list of performance measures that the department uses to determine progress toward the strategic issue of safety is in table 8.2. The department then uses the performance measure results to determine budget priorities, engage in rulemaking, focus in on areas for further research, and provide information to the public.

Balanced Scorecard Models

One useful framework that emphasizes the linkage between strategic objectives and performance measures is the balanced scorecard model developed by Kaplan and Norton (1996). Designed originally for private sector applications, this model was based on the premise that corporations need to look beyond such traditional financial measures as return on investment, profit and loss, and cash flow to gain a balanced picture

TABLE 8.2 PERFORMANCE MEASURES USED BY US DEPARTMENT OF TRANSPORTATION TO DETERMINE SAFETY

Performance Measure	2007	2008	2009	2010	2011	Target 2012	Actual 2012	Met or Not Met
Roadway fatality rate per 100 million vehicle-miles traveled (VMT).	1.36	1.26	1.15	1.11	1.10*	1.05	TBD^	Met (2011)*
Passenger vehicle occupant fatality rate per 100 million VMT.	1.08	0.97	0.89	0.84	0.83–0.89*	0.85	0.83–0.89*	TBD
Motorcyclist rider fatality rate per 100,000 motorcycle registrations.	72.48	68.52	56.36	54.82	56–58*	63	56–58*	TBD
Nonoccupant (pedestrian and bicycle) fatality rate per 100 million VMT.	0.18	0.18	0.17	0.17	0.16–0.17*	0.16	0.16–0.17*	TBD
Large truck and bus fatality rate per 100 million total VMT.	0.169	0.153 (r)	0.122 (r)	0.133	0.136*	0.117	0.110–0.127*	TBD
Number of commercial air earner fatalities per 100 million persons onboard.	NA	0.4	6.7	0.3	0.0*	7.6	0.0*	Met*
Number of fatal general aviation accidents per 100,000 flight hours.	NA	NA	1.17	1.10	1.13*	1.07	1.10*	Not Met*

TABLE 8.2 (CONTINUED)

Performance Measure	2007	2008	2009	2010	2011	Target 2012	Actual 2012	Met or Not Met
Category A&B runway incursions per million operations.	0.393	0.427	0.227	0.117	0.138	0.395	0.356	Met
Pipeline incidents involving death or major injury.	45	39	48	38	36	43	32*	Met*
Hazardous materials incidents involving death or major injury.	36	24	29	23	33	34	26*	Met*
Transit fatalities per 100 million passenger-miles traveled. (r)	NA	NA	NA	0.533	0.535	0.543	TBD#	Met (2011)
Rail-related accidents and incidents per million train-miles.	17.298	16.906	16.885	16.664	15.991	16.300	14.557*	Met*
Cumulative number of states and localities that adopt roadway designs that accommodate all road users (complete streets).	NA	NA	15	22	26	26	27	Met

Note: (r): revised performance measure; *based on preliminary results; ^December 2013 actual; #September 2013 actual.

of performance. As shown in figure 8.6, the balanced scorecard incorporates four perspectives: the customer perspective, the internal business perspective, the innovation and learning perspective, and the financial perspective. Corporate entities establish goals in each of these domains and then define measures to track their performance against these goals.

The kinds of measures used to track performance from the customer perspective include market share of products or services sold, on-time delivery, rankings by key accounts, and customer satisfaction indexes. Measures pertaining to the innovation and learning perspective focus on the development and sales of new products and services, as well as on employee attitudes, capabilities, and involvement. The internal business perspective tends to emphasize such elements as engineering efficiency and unit costs, actual production versus business plans, rework, safety incidents, and project management. All of these measures obviously have been used by business firms in the past, but the contribution of the balanced scorecard model is to encourage managers to consider these four perspectives as a comprehensive package.

For the service-oriented public and nonprofit sectors, objectives for the customer section of the balanced scorecard are particularly important and must address the critical questions of who our target customers, clients, and stakeholders are and, "What is our value proposition in serving them? (Niven, 2008, p. 17). In the private sector, these typically focus on one of three values: operational excellence, product leadership, or customer intimacy. These translate nicely to the public and nonprofit sectors when we decipher what these represent:

- Organizations that embody operational excellence tend to focus on convenience and accessibility, while those that focus on product leadership strive to continuously offer the best and most innovative products.
- Customer intimacy-centric organizations focus on developing a relationship with the individuals they serve and aim toward creating an atmosphere that epitomizes customer service.

Focusing objectives around one of these values allows public and nonprofit organizations to specialize in their approach to how they interact with customers, clients, and stakeholders.

Objectives for the internal processes section should also focus on improving services provided, or those things at which the organization must excel in order to add value to those it serves (Niven, 2008). In other words, the focused processes should be the ones that have a direct impact on the quality of services that customers receive.

The focus of the financial section objectives is on making sure that services are provided in a cost-effective manner by obtaining additional revenue streams, minimizing costs, and ensuring that assets are used in an effective and efficient manner. Typically objectives in the employee learning and growth section of the balanced scorecard focus on filling skill gaps that exist between the internal processes and customer sections of the strategy map. For example, organizations may find that they need to focus on training employees in areas that will allow them to successfully complete the objectives that link the internal processes and customer sections of the strategy map.

Balanced scorecards have gained greater appreciation and are viewed as a tool that links performance measures and strategy in a way that can communicate how an organization will fulfill its mission and achieve strategic objectives for both internal and external stakeholders. The balanced scorecard has three primary purposes: serving as a communication tool, a visual for strategic management, and a measurement system.

Due to the accessible nature of the balanced scorecard, it can serve as an effective tool to communicate the key strategic objectives that an organization is pursuing, along with the performance measures used to determine success to stakeholders. Strategy maps are an effective tool that can depict the primary objectives that must be accomplished in each of the sections of the scorecard for the goals of the organization to be accomplished.

Strategy Maps

Kaplan and Norton (2004) developed strategy maps after the balanced scorecard as a blueprint for describing, measuring, and aligning an organization's focus. Organizations find the strategy map useful as a communication tool and in constructing the balanced scorecard, as we will see in the Kenya Red Cross example.

Once objectives are determined through the strategy map, measures are selected to coincide with them. The map helps to make areas of alignment and misalignments more visible (Bryson, Eden, & Ackermann, 2014). These measures, the coinciding objectives, and the initiatives that are implemented to accomplish these objectives are what make up the balanced scorecard.

After the balanced scorecard is created, it becomes an integral part of a strategic management system by providing stakeholders with a concise vision for the overall strategy of the organization. This concise vision creates an environment where all members have a clear understanding of their role in the organization and of how their actions may lead to its long-term success. This tool is also useful in allocating resources in the budgeting process, and it provides a focus for training initiatives (Niven, 2008).

Use of the Balanced Scorecard in Kenya Red Cross

The balanced scorecard developed by Kenya Red Cross with the assistance of the Balanced Scorecard Institute has been of great assistance in focusing their efforts on accomplishing objectives that directly impact their mission. Arthur Omolo (2010), the chief financial officer and strategy champion of the organization, explained how the development process "revolutionized the strategic thinking at Kenya Red Cross" (p. 1). During this process, the Kenya Red Cross began to gain a better understanding of strategic objectives and to create the value proposition "always there." This better understanding of the strategy process manifested itself in improved strategic linkages between programs, increased clarity in objectives, and the inaugural use of performance measures and targets (Omolo, 2010). Figure 8.7 provides a brief overview of the mission, vision, core values, strategic themes, and value proposition of the organization. Each

FIGURE 8.7 KENYA RED CROSS MISSION, VISION, AND CORE VALUES OVERVIEW

Mission, Vision, Core Values, and Beneficiary Value Proposition	
MISSION: Our mission is to work with vigour and compassion through our networks and with communities to prevent and alleviate human suffering and save lives of the most vulnerable	**CORE VALUES:** • Commitment • Accountability • Service to Humanity • Trust
VISION: Our vision is to be the most effective, trusted and self-sustaining humanitarian organisation in Kenya	**BENEFICIARY VALUE PROPOSITION:** "Always There!"

Strategic Themes		
Operational Excellence Result: Timely and appropriate services competitively delivered with the involvement of the community	**Investing in Our People** Result: Highly skilled and motivated staff and volunteers chose to work for the society	**Building a Strong National Society** Result: Resilient communities served by a sustainable national society that has strong partnerships and is supported by appropriate legal framework

Strategy Map

Source: Kenya Red Cross Society (n.d.). http://balancedscorecard.org/Portals/0/PDF/KenyaRed%20 CrossScorecardPoster.pdf. Used with permission.

FIGURE 8.8 KENYA'S RED CROSS STRATEGY MAP

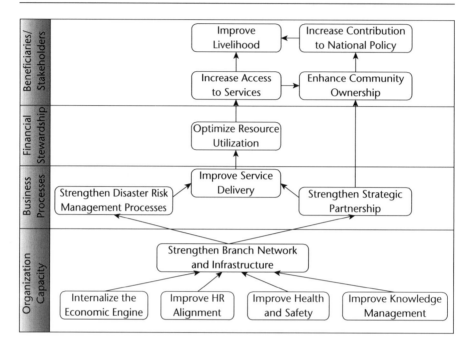

Source: Balanced Scorecard Institute (www.balancedscorecard.org) and Balanced Scorecard Eastern Africa. Used with permission. http://balancedscorecard.org/Portals/0/PDF/KenyaRed% 20CrossScorecardPoster.pdf

of these components led to the development of the strategy map (figure 8.8). Once the strategy map was completed, performance measures were developed to coincide with their respective objectives (table 8.3).

The brief overview of the mission, vision, core values, strategic themes, and value proposition for beneficiaries of the organization is useful because it provides individuals with an understanding of the goals that the Kenya Red Cross will pursue and strategies that it will use to achieve them. A quick glance at these graphic displays can provide a great deal of information to both internal and external stakeholders, and it unites all levels of the organization around a common culture.

The strategy map for this organization was developed under the premise that organization capacity would lead to improved business practices. Once business practices were improved, financial stewardship could be achieved, which in turn would lead to improved outcomes for

TABLE 8.3 KENYA RED CROSS SCORECARD

Objectives	Performance Measures	Targets	Initiatives
PERSPECTIVE: Beneficiary/Stakeholder			
Improved livelihoods	• Model households (households that meet minimum standards)	50%	• Strengthen the integrated approach to programming
	• Reduction on relief aid in target communities	20%	• Strengthen food security program
	• Lives saved during emergencies	100%	• Build skills and resources on search and rescue
Increase contribution to national policy	• KRCS components (structure, programming, disaster, emblem) supported by legal framework	100%	• Establish and implement a system for identifying and participating in national policy development
	• Appropriate national policies contributed to	75%	• Develop and implement a brand management strategy
	• Projects aligned to appropriate national policy	100%	
Enhance community ownership	• Average age of projects running after completion	10 yrs	• Establish and implement a community capacity building and leadership development program
	• Contribution to project budget by community (time, funds)	20%	
	• Projects replicated by community and partners	TBD	
Increase access to services	• KRCS services within the standard distance	95%	• Develop a policy on services to be delivered to beneficiaries and stakeholders
	• Beneficiaries reached (out of the most vulnerable)	TBD	
	• Information available to stakeholders	75%	• Develop and implement communication strategy
PERSPECTIVE: Financial Stewardship			
Optimize resource utilization	• Percentage of core cost to total cost	30%	• Establish and implement an ISO
	• Cost per beneficiary	TBD	• Strengthen the system for capturing and reporting costs per beneficiary

Source: Balanced Scorecard Institute (www.balancedscorecard.org) and Balanced Scorecard Eastern Africa. Used with permission. http://balancedscorecard.org/Portals/0/PDF/KenyaRed%20CrossScorecardPoster.pdf

beneficiaries and stakeholders. Notice in figure 8.8 the strategy map portrayal of how improved organizational capacity through alignment will eventually lead to improved access to services and livelihood for beneficiaries.

The scorecard provides information pertaining to objectives, their coinciding performance measures and targets, and the assigned initiatives. Most important, the scorecard becomes a tool for accountability to stakeholders.

Use of the Balanced Scorecard: City of Charlotte, North Carolina

For quite some time, the City of Charlotte, North Carolina, has been on the leading edge among local governments in terms of developing its capacity for results-oriented management through Management by Objectives (MBO), program budgeting, performance measurement, and other similar approaches. In 1995, Charlotte began experimenting with the balanced scorecard method as a comprehensive approach to strategic planning and performance measurement. This effort began with the city council's identifying seven broad, overarching goals it wanted to establish as top-level priorities for the city as a whole.

Because the council's priorities—including reducing crime, strengthening neighborhoods, promoting safe and convenient transportation, and promoting economic opportunities—all target substantive outcomes intended to benefit the general public, they were adopted as representing the customer perspective, as shown in figure 8.9. With the help of other top city officials, the council then identified goals regarding financial accountability, internal processes, and organizational learning and growth. The priorities from the other perspectives—expanding noncity funding, improving productivity, and closing the skills gap, for example—are seen not only as important in their own right but as strategies for accomplishing the customer-oriented priorities that represent the real bottom line in this plan.

Performance measures have been established for each of the council's customer-oriented priorities. For the goal of strengthening neighborhoods, for instance, the city council identified the following indicators: (1) change in the proportion of owner-occupied housing units in target neighborhoods, (2) the number of businesses created or retained in targeted business corridors, (3) employment rates in targeted neighborhoods, and (4) Part 1 and Part 2 crime rates per 1,000 population in these

FIGURE 8.9 CITY STRATEGY AND BALANCED SCORECARD: CHARLOTTE, NORTH CAROLINA

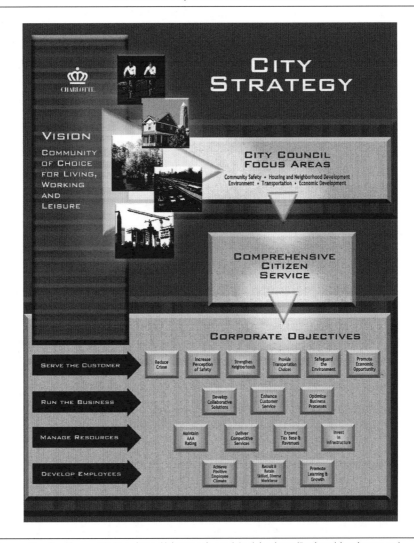

Source: Used with permission. http://charmeck.org/city/charlotte/Budget/development/
Documents/City%20strategy%20visual%20Charlotte.pdf

neighborhoods. Various city departments and programs will have to focus resources and activities on the goal of strengthening these neighborhoods in order to bring about improvement on these indicators.

The actual development of performance measures to support the balanced scorecard was piloted by the Charlotte Department of Transportation (CDOT), which at that time had responsibility for both city streets and the public transit system. Thus, CDOT has established a set of objectives from each of the four perspectives, although they have not yet been defined and formatted as SMART objectives. For each objective, CDOT defined at least one lead measure and one lag measure, as shown in table 8.4. The lead measures represent performance dimensions that must be achieved in order to achieve the objectives; the lag measures represent the broader impact of attaining the objective. CDOT defines operational indicators and collects data for each of the performance measures on a regular basis.

Balanced Scorecard and Logic Models

The balanced scorecard has been adopted in both public and nonprofit agencies because it serves as a straightforward and comprehensive framework for strategic planning and performance measurement. Whereas the kinds of measures that end up being incorporated for the most part are the same kinds of indicators presented earlier in this chapter—with the addition of internally oriented measures representing such aspects as employee development and satisfaction, use of technology, and management capacity—the balanced scorecard encourages taking a holistic view. The model is by no means incompatible with the program logic models emphasized in chapter 3 and used throughout this book. The real difference is that the balanced scorecard is a framework for measuring organizational performance, whereas the program logic model focuses on program performance.

Thus, whereas the purpose of a performance measurement system is to track the performance of specific operating programs, as is the case under the federal Government Performance and Results Act (GPRA) of 1993, GPRA Modernization Act of 2010, and similar legislation in many states, the program logic model provides an essential methodology for determining the important dimensions of performance to measure. However, where large, multifunctional public or nonprofit agencies wish to monitor their overall performance, the balanced scorecard can be very useful. Of course, even with a balanced scorecard framework, an agency

TABLE 8.4 OBJECTIVES AND MEASURES: CHARLOTTE DEPARTMENT OF TRANSPORTATION

Perspective	Objective	Lead Measures	Lag Measures
Customer	C-1 Maintain the transportation system C-2 Operate the transportation system C-3 Develop the transportation system C-4 Determine the optimal system design C-5 Improve service quality	C-1 Repair Response: repair response action C-1 Travel Speed: average travel speed by facility and selected location C-2 Commute Time: average commute time on selected roads C-2 On-Time Buses: public transit on-time C-3 Programs Introduced: newly introduced programs, pilots, or program specifications C-5 Responsiveness: % of citizen complaints and requests resolved at the CDOT level	C-1 High Quality Streets: condition of lane miles $\geq$90 rating C-2 Safety: citywide accident rate; no. of high-accident locations C-3 Basic Mobility: availability of public transport C-4 Plan Progress: % complete on 2015 Transportation Plan
Financial	F-1 Expand noncity funding F-2 Maximize benefit/cost	F-2 Costs: costs compared to other municipalities and private sector competition	F-1 Funding Leverage: dollar value from noncity sources F-1 New Funding Sources: dollar value from sources not previously available
Internal Process	I-1 Gain infrastructure capacity I-2 Secure funding/service partners I-3 Improve productivity I-4 Increase positive contacts with community	I-1 Capital Investment: $ allocated to capital projects in targeted areas I-2 Leverage Funding/Service Partners: new funding/resource partners identified I-3 Cost per Unit: cost per unit I-3 Competitive Sourcing: % of budget bid I-3 Problem Identification: source and action I-4 Customer Communications: no., type, frequency	I-1 Capacity Ratios: incremental capacity built vs. required by 2015 Plan I-2 No. of Partners: number of partners I-3 Street Maintenance Cost: cost/passenger I-4 Customer Surveys: survey results concerning service quality
Learning	L-1 Enhance automated information systems L-2 Enhance "field" technology L-3 Close the skills gap L-4 Empower employees	L-1 IT Infrastructure: complete relational database across CDOT L-3 Skills Identified: key skills identified in strategic functions L-4 Employee Climate Survey: results of employee survey	L-1 Information Access: strategic information available vs. user requirements L-2 Information Tools: strategic tools available vs. user requirements L-3 Skills Transfer: skill evidence in task or job performance L-4 Employee Goal Alignment: training/career development alliance with mission

Source: Charlotte Department of Transportation, City of Charlotte, North Carolina. Used with permission.

will want to track programmatic effectiveness, and a program logic model will be helpful in providing understanding to the sequence of events or program hypothesis and ensuring that the agency is focusing on the most relevant outputs and outcomes.

Performance Measurement and Strategic Management

Increasingly, public and nonprofit organizations are developing strategic plans and disciplining their management processes to ensure organizational follow-through in implementing strategic initiatives and accomplishing strategic objectives (Poister, 2010). Adhering to the principle that what gets measured gets done, these agencies define measures of success for each strategic goal or objective in order to focus attention on these top management priorities and to track progress in achieving results in strategic focus areas. Therefore, the measurement systems that are developed to support strategic planning efforts:

- Tend to focus on a mix of output and outcome measures that are of fundamental importance to the organization
- Emphasize global measures that pertain to the organization as a whole, although they may consist of roll-ups from decentralized divisions and units
- Employ measured scales on some indicators but may also include nominal measures and more qualitative indicators
- Often establish target levels on indicators of key results and then track actual performance against these targets
- Sometimes cascade performance measures down to major divisions and other organizational units to track strategic results at those levels, particularly in the case of multimission, multifunctional, or highly decentralized agencies

Thus, performance measures are critical elements of the strategic management process designed to create, implement, and evaluate strategic agendas. In larger, more complex agencies, an essential linkage in this process is to tie divisions' business plans or annual operating plans to the overall strategic plan and then, on a shorter time frame, monitor performance measures that are directly tied to the overall indicators of strategic results. In addition, there are two important tools for drilling strategic plans down into organizations and making sure that they are given priority at the operating level: the budgeting process and the performance management process, the latter for ensuring that individual-level work objectives are responsive to the agency's overall strategic objectives. Performance measures are indispensable elements in both of these processes, as will be discussed in chapters 9 and 10, respectively.

References

Aristigueta, M. P. (2000). The rise and fall of the Florida benchmarks. In A. Neely (Ed.), *Performance measurement: Past, present, and future* (pp. 16–23). Cambridge, UK: Fieldfare Publications.

Bryson, J. M. (2011). *Strategic planning for public and nonprofit organizations* (4th ed.). San Francisco: Jossey-Bass.

Bryson, J. M., Eden, C., & Ackermann, F. (2014). *Visual strategy: A workbook for strategy mapping in public and nonprofit organizations.* San Francisco: Jossey-Bass.

Council on Virginia's Future. (2013a). *About Virginia performs.* http://vaperforms .virginia.gov/extras/about.php

Council on Virginia's Future. (2013b). *Virginia Performs goals: Selected agency key objectives at a glance.* http://vaperforms.virginia.gov/extras/keyObjectives.php#key

Kaplan, R. S., & Norton, D. P. (1992). The balanced scorecard: Measures that drive performance. *Harvard Business Review,* Jan./Feb., 72.

Kaplan, R. S., & Norton, D. P. (1996). *The balanced scorecard: Translating strategy into action.* Cambridge, MA: Harvard College.

Kaplan, R. S., & Norton, D. P. (2004). *Strategy maps: Converting intangible assets into tangible outcomes.* Boston: Harvard Business Press Books.

Kenya Red Cross Society. (n.d.). http://balancedscorecard.org/Portals/0/PDF/ KenyaRed%20CrossScorecardPoster.pdf

Koteen, J. (1989). *Strategic management in public and nonprofit organizations: Thinking and acting strategically on public concerns.* New York: Praeger.

LeRoux, K., & Wright, N. (2010). Does performance measurement improve strategic decision-making? Findings from a National Survey of Nonprofit Social Service agencies. *Nonprofit and Voluntary Sector Quarterly, 39*(4), 571–587.

Niven, P. R. (2008). *Balanced scorecard step-by-step for government and nonprofit agencies.* Hoboken, NJ: Wiley.

Omolo, A. (2010, December 9). *Our experience with the balanced scorecard strategy development process.* Balanced Scorecard Institute. http://balancedscorecard.org/ Portals/0/PDF/KenyaRedCrossBSC.pdf

Poister, T. H. (2003). *Measuring performance in public and nonprofit organizations.* San Francisco: Jossey-Bass.

Poister, T. H. (2010). The future of strategic planning in the public sector: Linking strategic management and performance. *Public Administration Review, 70,* 246–254.

Poister, T. H., Margolis, D.L., & Zimmerman, D. E. (2004). Strategic management at the Pennsylvania Department of Transportation: A results-driven approach. *Transportation Research Record, 1885*, 56–64.

Poister, T. H., & Streib, G. (1999). Performance measurement in municipal government: Assessing the state of the practice. *Public Administration Review, 59*(4), 325–335.

Poister, T. H., & Van Slyke, D. M. (2002). Strategic management innovations in state transportation departments. *Public Performance and Management Review, 26*(1), 58–74.

Vinzant, D. H., & Vinzant, J. C. (1996). Strategy and organizational capacity: Finding a fit. *Public Productivity and Management Review, 20*(2), 139–157.

## CHAPTER NINE

PERFORMANCE-INFORMED BUDGETING

How has the budget process—one of the most systematic and essential components of public management—been influenced by the performance movement? How is performance information used in allocating budgetary resources? How do managers utilize performance information in the budget process relative to other information sources in budgetary decision making? In this chapter we explore the concept, development, and practice of performance budgeting. The idea of performance budgeting is not a new one, having a basis in the budgetary reform efforts of the mid-twentieth century. Such reforms sought to decouple the budget decision-making process from incrementalism, depoliticize it by making the process more objective, and tie budgetary allocations to performance to incentivize increased effectiveness or efficiency. These reforms took place alongside a broader movement to rationalize government in general (Stone, 2002). Performance-based budgeting (performance budgeting, for short) was swept into practice on the coattails of this movement. Breul (2007) concludes that PBB is the next logical step in the implementation of results-oriented government. Today performance information has been incorporated into the budget process to varying degrees at the federal, state, and local levels around the globe. Furthermore, what PBB promises in theory is better conceptualized as performance-informed budgeting in practice (Ho, 2011; Joyce, 2003). This chapter offers a review of the concept, a brief review of its historical development and implementation, and guidelines for incorporating performance information into the budget process or better integrating budgeting and performance management.

Performance in Public Budgeting: Conceptual Understanding

This book is about the application of performance information to public and nonprofit management to improve governance. This goal is accomplished by increasing efficiency, effectiveness, and accountability for results, which ultimately leads to adoption of best practices and selection of alternatives that are most cost-effective. This chapter in particular concentrates on the application of performance information to the budget process. The use of performance information in this context, whether at the local, state, or national level, and whether in public or nonprofit organizations, has come to be known as performance-based budgeting (PBB). The list of relevant terminology can be expanded to include any of the following: performance budgeting, performance management, results-based budgeting, zero base budgeting, performance-informed budgets or evidence-based decision making (Pattison, 2012). Each of these emphasizes the use of performance information in the budget process.

In a purely rational sense, the expectation of PBB is that budget allocations will be made according to performance, with strong performance rewarded with increased budgets and with weak performance punished by budget reductions. But public policy, and consequently public budgeting, is imperfectly rational, characterized by incomplete information, satisficing, and other symptoms of bounded rationality (Simon, 1978). Moreover, it is a subjective process. Recent research has revealed the extent to which different individuals can examine the same program and come to different conclusions about performance (Moynihan, 2006).

Traditionally public budgeting processes have been centralized and independent. They are core government functions, without which government would cease to operate. Performance management has developed only in the last few decades, making sufficient headway to become familiar in federal, state, and local government management repertoires. While performance management has become a valuable tool to ensure accountability, it is not always centralized and is often viewed as an ancillary management tool not core to government functionality. The idea of PBB hinges on the integration of these two independent processes to bring about stronger results and better budget decisions. Let's consider a description of PBB that helps to explain how it works in practice:

> "Performance budgeting" is a process for budget preparation and adoption that emphasizes performance management, allowing decisions about allocation of resources to be made in part on the efficiency and the effectiveness of service delivery. Performance management occurs when department heads and program managers use data derived from performance measurement systems to support decisions related to planning, organizing, staffing, developing, coordinating, budgeting, reporting, and evaluating—the core functions of management. Performance budgeting occurs when department heads and program managers use performance data to support and justify budget requests during the annual budget preparation process. (Rivenbark, 2004, p. 28)

A 2010 report by the National Performance Management Advisory Commission distinguishes performance budgeting from traditional budgeting as follows:

> Performance budgeting begins where the strategic plan and/or operational plan ends, using the objectives and strategies from the planning process as the basis for developing a spending plan. The primary purpose of performance budgeting is to allocate funds to activities, programs, and services in a manner most likely to achieve desired results. A performance approach to budgeting emphasizes accountability for outcomes (that is, what constituents need and expect from their government), whereas line-item budgeting focuses on accountability for spending from legally authorized accounts. (National Performance Management Advisory Commission, 2010, p. 25)

The report goes on to explain that simply including performance measures in the traditional line item budget does not constitute performance budgeting. Rather, the approach requires a shift in thinking about budgeting from inputs to outputs and outcomes as the object of accountability, an integration of budgeting and strategic planning to focus on long-term results, and greater attention to needs of residents and businesses (National Performance Management Advisory Commission, 2010).

Kelly and Rivenbark (2003) describe performance budgeting as the integration of the components of performance management—planning, performance measurement, benchmarking, and evaluation—into the framework of state and local government budgeting. In other words, performance budgeting is not a stand-alone technique but rather an extension of the traditional budget process that combines financial and operational accountability. Thinking about Key's (1940) question, PBB answers the question, "Did allocating x dollars to activity A accomplish what we intended?" and, "If not, should we adjust the allocation to activity A?" (Rivenbark, 2004, p. 27). In essence, we are looking at the effectiveness of past budget decisions (with respect to exacerbating certain public problems) in the context of decisions about the allocation of future resources.

Like so much of performance measurement and management, the depth of attention to effectiveness can and does vary significantly. PBB moves the focus of budgeting away from inputs and activities, characterized by the traditional line item, and begins to examine the true question of budgeting: What did we get for what we spent? This can be assessed simply in terms of outputs, or in more complex ways, such as efficiency, outcomes or impacts, and cost-effectiveness. A sophisticated performance measurement or management system is required to make similarly sophisticated budget decisions. As Moynihan (2008) has declared in the performance management doctrine, the best approaches are those that examine outcomes rather than outputs and those that reserve decision-making discretion at lower levels. This naturally pits financial objectives (characterized by control) against substantive objectives that are better characterized by responsiveness (Koppell, 2005). The purpose of budgeting is not one-dimensional but rather serves different purposes to different principals. For example, legislators use budgeting to allocate resources, whereas executives use the budget process to exert better control on agencies. Within agencies, the budget process may offer guidance to implementation.

The focus on performance and effectiveness as important dimensions of accountability is a significant step in public budgeting, but other factors influence budget decisions too. The use of performance information alone to make budgetary decisions fails to incorporate changes in the environment, such as changing levels of particular problems. One would not logically reward a program with a larger budget for high performance if that performance had eliminated the problem altogether, for example. This explains why agency missions begin to adapt over time. As one problem is removed, the agency must convince policymakers of additional needs to which their attention may turn. So if an environmental agency is tasked with preventing the extinction of a species and the population of that species rebounds, the agency may adapt by attending to other species or to preserving and protecting its habitat to prevent the conditions under which extinction might occur for the original species.

Budgeting is, at its core, a political process, characterized by interests, advocacy coalitions, and parties vying for allocation of resources toward their preferred programs and away from competing alternatives. It is important to keep this in mind because the name *PBB* connotes a degree of rationality that does not exist in practice. Rather, we should expect, as Moynihan (2008) suggests, that performance information be considered alongside other information in the decision-making process.

As Ho (2011) describes it, "Modern conceptions of PBB have mostly abandoned any traditional notions that appropriation amounts should be solely based on performance" (p. 393). He continues to explain that performance-informed budgeting is an "approach in which performance information is presented to policy makers throughout the budgetary process for informational purposes to aid decision-making" but with "no expectation of a clear and strong linkage of performance measurement to final budgetary amounts" (p. 393). Performance-informed budgeting, or performance-oriented budgeting, better characterizes reality because the terms imply that performance influences budgeting but is not the sole source of information. So while Ho (2011) and others (Joyce, 2003, for example) suggest that performance-informed budgeting better represents reality, the term *PBB* continues to dominate the literature, and it is the primary term we use here.

Potential Benefits of Performance-Informed Budgeting

Aside from the quest for greater rationality and accountability in the budgeting process, which might be considered ends in themselves, various authors have ascribed various potential benefits associated with the use of performance-informed budgeting under its various names. Table 9.1 provides a glimpse at some of the potential benefits that have been identified.

We see here that the incorporation of performance information into the budgeting process has a number of identifiable benefits. The potential alignment of performance goals with expenditures is one of the most significant benefits from a strategic management perspective. It also highlights the program logic by clearly elucidating the relationship between resources and performance. Unit cost data or cost-effectiveness data

TABLE 9.1 BENEFITS OF PERFORMANCE-INFORMED BUDGETING

Kelly and Rivenbark (2003)

Align service priorities and spending

Adds an information dimension to budget deliberations

Motivates employees and managers by recording progress toward goals

Signal to citizens that providers of public services are interested in improving quality

Mercer (2003)

Diagnostic tool to understand the relationship between resources and performance

Helps to justify budget requests through transparency about performance

Serves as the foundation for a comprehensive performance management system

Provides comparative unit costs that can feed benchmarking or best practices analysis

Young (2003)

Provides accountability to the public

Leads to improvement in program design

Helps agencies to link their daily activities to overall governmental outcomes

Aligns spending with established goals

Provides a comparison of cost-effectiveness among programs

developed for the budget process can be used for comparative purposes to identify best practices or for other forms of program learning such as benchmarking. This knowledge can lead to changes in program design. Of course, centralized budget systems often form the backbone of integrated organizational performance management systems due to the capacity available in the budget office, but also because of the cyclical regularity of the budget process.

Historical Development and the Current State of Performance-Informed Budgeting

The idea to use performance information to guide budget decisions has been alive and growing for decades (Ho, 2011; Grizzle, 1987). The first Hoover Commission recommended the use of performance budgeting in 1949; Congress responded by requiring its use by the military (Lee, Johnson, & Joyce, 2008). In 1950 the passage of the Budget Accounting and Procedures Act extended its use to the entire federal government (Lee et al., 2008). The goal of these efforts was to bring more program information into the budget decision-making process. There is little evidence that performance budgeting ever became the basis on which budget decisions were made in federal, state, or local governments, but the effort's enduring contribution is in the incorporation of greater program and performance information in budget documents (Lee et al., 2008). It is important to clarify that performance budgeting differs from performance-based budgeting; whereas the former focuses on workload or activity, the latter emphasizes results or outcomes.

Numerous federal budget reform efforts—and such reforms often originate at the federal level due to the magnitude of the budget—have come and gone since the 1960s. Each sought to use some aspect of performance information to guide budget allocations. In particular, efficiency is often a goal, and one cannot measure efficiency without first measuring outputs—the most rudimentary performance indicator. Planning-programming-budgeting in the 1960s was a federal initiative that sought to make program budget decisions on the basis of performance information. Zero-based budgeting was a related federal effort in the 1970s that forced agencies and programs to justify their budget allocations anew in each cycle. This effort sought to break with the incremental inertia of budgets, but it ultimately failed because the rational requirements necessitated more information collection, analysis, and interpretation than boundedly rational policymakers could muster. The next decade heralded the Management by Objectives movement, which set performance targets as the basis of budgeting.

The academic literature has drawn attention to the potential of PBB for better linking resource allocation to performance, but it has also raised numerous questions about the extent to which performance information actually influences budget decisions. Thomas Lauth (1987) even suggested that the idea that political elites would make resource allocation decisions based solely on productivity information is politically naive. Ho (2011) suggests that the budget process may become a battleground for competing interests based on values, political considerations, and gaming and that policy goals may not be equivalent to outcomes in the performance sense.

A number of authors, most writing in the pre-Government-Performance-and-Results-Act (GPRA) period, have expressed concern about how relevant and useful performance information could be in what has traditionally been a very political budget process (Caiden, 1998; Joyce, 2008; O'Toole & Marshall, 1987; Schick, 1990). Some studies go so far as to suggest that even when performance budgeting obtains support from political principals, its long-term success will be jeopardized by changes in administration and legislative turnover as newly elected leaders seek to emphasize their own projects and policies (Grizzle & Pettijohn, 2002; Wellman & VanLandingham, 2008). In spite of these criticisms, the Pew Center on the States (2009) suggests that states that use performance budgeting create a foundation for a better economic and fiscal future. By using PBB, states can make smarter spending decisions in boom years and informed budget cuts in periods of fiscal stress.

A number of studies have examined the extent to which PBB has been adopted, implemented, and effective at achieving various purposes. The major natural divisions in the literature seem to organize around the level of government—national or state and local—and the purpose of the article, whether prescriptive, descriptive, or analytical.

At the municipal level, for example, Poister and Streib (2005) surveyed local governments, finding that only about 44 percent used strategic planning, and fewer than half of those (48 percent) reported that performance information played an important role in determining resource allocations. Rivenbark and Kelly (2006) found that municipalities of all sizes are building capacity for performance budgeting by adopting performance measurement systems and augmenting their budget processes with performance results. Wang (2000) examined the use of performance information in budgets at the county level, finding that governments are using performance measurement in a wide range of budgeting areas, but that users are experiencing technical obstacles in conducting performance analysis and obtaining support from legislatures and citizens. Wang concludes that analytical competence and political support increase the use of performance measurement in budgeting at the county level.

More recent research has extended into local government budgeting from a more analytical perspective, helping to build theory in the area. Ho and Ni (2005) find that the largest 480 cities in the United States have made progress in developing outcome-oriented performance measures. They find as well that the choice of performance measures varies according to the type of municipal services and is affected by the level of professionalism in city management. In an in-depth study of Indianapolis, Ho (2011) found that the application of performance measurement is positively related to intradepartmental program budget changes, that is, movement of funds across programs within departments. Since these changes are predominantly the purview of managers and not policymakers, the finding suggests that PBB can improve local budget outcomes despite severe political constraints.

Looking at performance budgeting across states, we find the same breadth in the focus of academic inquiry. For example, Jordan and Hackbart (1999) survey state budget officers to examine states' organization, fiscal, and political capacity to implement performance budgeting. Melkers and Willoughby (2001) conducted a similar survey of legislative and executive budgeters from the fifty states and found that implementation of PBB systems is proceeding slowly; one of the greatest problems in the slow take-up is different perceptions of use and success among budget players across branches of government. Lu (2007) suggests that to succeed in performance-informed budgeting, agencies need improved managerial capacity to use performance information and improve measurement quality.

Hou, Lunsford, Sides, and Jones (2011) examine state use of PBB across three time periods to gain some sense of the effect of fiscal stress on the use of performance budgeting. They analyzed state-level PBB according to four elements: (1) the development of performance measures, (2) its applicability to budgeting and management processes, (3) its utility across the business cycle, and (4) its usefulness for budget players. They find PBB functions more effective for executive management purposes than for legislative purposes. Perhaps more important, states more heavily use PBB during strong economic times than times of fiscal stress; fiscal stress typically reduces the availability of incentives that could be used to reward strong performance.

A small but growing literature explores the implementation of performance budgeting in the international context as well (Lee & Wang, 2009; Martí, 2013; Sterck & Scheers, 2006; Mascarenhas, 1996).

These studies enlighten us on the extent to which performance budgeting has been able to penetrate traditional government budget processes, the conditions under which it is most effective, and the obstacles and pitfalls that have been encountered along the way. But the academic literature is typically concerned with theoretical questions more so than practical questions of application. The next section of the chapter investigates the current use of performance budgeting in state and local government and provides examples of current practice across several functional areas and governments. By looking at the unique application of performance budgeting across these practical examples, it is possible to appreciate the variation in implementation that exists as a result of governments developing and implementing performance budgeting systems that are appropriate for their political, social, and economic environments.

Current Practice

As Jennings and Hall (2012) have noted, "The press for greater rationality and professionalism in government has not been uniform, varying over time and across jurisdictions" (p. 248). This observation extends to performance measurement and performance budgeting as well. These particular management reforms have been diffused gradually from place to place rather than adopted uniformly. This section of the chapter examines a series of specific examples that characterize the current state of performance-informed budgeting in the United States.

One of the longest-standing state-level performance-informed budgeting systems was developed in Pennsylvania in 1968. The system mirrored the federal program of the same name adopted by the Department of Defense earlier in the decade. The program continues to be used after nearly fifty years, though not without evolutionary modification (Sallack & Allen, 1987). From the performance management perspective, one shift that should be of concern is that away from impacts and toward outputs as the object of budgetary performance assessments. But as Sallack and Allen note, the program cannot be judged a failure simply on those grounds. Essentially, the "Budget Code requires that all programs appearing in the budget have a stated objective describing the desired results and that all programs have a group of measures that quantify program performance in terms of results obtained" (www.portal.pa.state.us/portal/server.pt/document/1089182/budgetprocess_pdf, 5).

"While South Dakota is just beginning to explore performance management at the state level, Maryland has embraced the practice for nearly two decades. In 1997, then-Gov. Parris Glendening appointed an interagency steering committee, which developed a strategic planning and performance measurement approach to management and budget called Managing for Results" (Burnett, 2013). Maryland today has a systematic and fully integrated budget and management approach that incorporates strategic planning and performance measurement into the budget process. As of 2012, forty states had adopted laws mandating the use of some form of performance budgeting, including Michigan, Iowa, Texas, and North Carolina (Lu & Willoughby, 2012).

Let's consider a few examples from the states. Georgia has arrived at performance budgeting relatively recently. It adopted a statewide performance budgeting system that mandates submission of performance information from agencies and programs during the regular budget process:

> For the FY 2014 budget cycle, [Office of Planning and Budget] asked agencies to submit workload, efficiency and outcome measures for each program that delivers services. Agencies identified and reported actual performance data for FY 2009–2012. Measuring performance in these three areas will help state decision makers and agency stakeholders understand how efficiently programs are operated, how well the customers are served and whether programs are achieving their intended outcomes. (Governor's Office of Planning and Budget, 2014)

The process is facilitated by a one-page introduction to performance measures (http://opb.georgia.gov/sites/opb.georgia.gov/files/imported/vgn/images/portal/cit_1210/52/0/162878016Basic%20Measures%203-23-2010.pdf) to assist agencies in compiling the required performance information. Table 9.2 presents an example of the performance measures for one agency program, the Department of Agriculture's Consumer Protection division. Here we find key elements of performance information for the division, including quantitative values for each measure as well as a comparison over time to establish performance trends. Missing, though, is budget information against which performance may be based.

Another relative newcomer to the performance budgeting movement is Nevada, where PBB started during the preparation of the fiscal year 2012/2013 budget. Nevada uses performance budgeting to clearly specify goals by core government function and to link those functional goals to the governor's priorities. Figure 9.1 presents the goals, benchmarks, and gubernatorial priorities for one core government function, business and development services, for the 2014–2015 fiscal year. In this example, the performance budgeting effort is strategically oriented, concentrating on goals and benchmarks of success to guide action. According to the Nevada Budget Division's website:

> Priorities and Performance Based Budgeting (PPBB) is the process of identifying and prioritizing the Governor's vision as it relates to the state's core functions, their costs and delivering effective and efficient outcomes. This includes improved transparency to decision makers and the public; improved methods of measuring what the state does and

TABLE 9.2 PERFORMANCE MEASURES: GEORGIA DEPARTMENT OF AGRICULTURE CONSUMER PROTECTION DIVISION

Program Performance Measures	FY 2010 Actual	FY 2011 Actual	FY 2012 Actual	FY 2013 Actual
Number of establishments inspected	149,503.00	143,345.00	141,485.00	74,325.00
Number of violative samples from regulated food products	142.00	154.00	130.00	350.00
Percentage of companion animal establishments inspected for regulatory compliance	58.00%	60.00%	61.00%	100.00%
Percentage of establishments out of compliance warranting follow-up inspection	8.00%	13.00%	11.97%	11.90%
Percentage of food establishments inspected for regulatory compliance	NA	90.00%	87.00%	92.70%
Percentage of fuel establishments inspected for regulatory compliance (based on an eighteen-month inspection cycle)	76.00%	64.00%	70.00%	71.30%
Percentage of inspections completed	61.40%	60.40%	75.75%	99.00%
Percentage of noncompliant establishments found to be compliant at follow-up inspection	NA	NA	92.01%	92.00%

Source: Governor's Office of Planning and Budget, Performance Measure Report FY 2015, http://opb.georgia.gov/sites/opb.georgia.gov/files/related_files/site_page/FY15%20Performance%20Measure%20Report%20FINAL.pdf.

whether agencies are making a difference; linking activities of government to achievement of objectives; and providing a platform for improvement in funding and budgeting decisions. The goal is to answer the question, *"Why is our state spending money the way it is?"* (Nevada Budget Division, 2014)

In the governor's budget, which weighs in at over thirty-four hundred pages, budget information is organized by agency, then by division. Within

FIGURE 9.1 STATE OF NEVADA PRIORITIES AND PERFORMANCE-BASED BUDGETING

State of Nevada
Priorities and Performance Based Budgeting
Fiscal Years 2014 and 2015

Business Development and Services

Description and Purpose Programs and services that help to diversify and strengthen Nevada's economic foundation and future growth by ensuring appropriate and balanced regulation to cultivate industry, instill consumer confidence, and guide the responsible conduct of business activities.

	Economic Diversification — Diversify Nevada's economic base	Regulations — Create a regulatory environment that fosters economic growth	Compliance — Ensure regulated entities/ programs comply with applicable laws and regulations	Customer Service — Provide efficient, timely and responsive service to industry and members of the public and facilitate the resolution of disputes	Global Exports — Increase opportunities for industries to be successful and grow global exports of goods and services from Nevada	Tax Collection — Ensure the accurate and timely collection of taxes and fees	Consumer Education — Safeguard the public interest by educating consumers about their rights, responsibilities and opportunities	Economic Vibrancy — Position Nevada as a vibrant and appealing state that offers residents and visitors unique tourism and cultural experiences
Objective								
Benchmark	New Industry Sector Growth — Share of employment outside of Nevada's traditional industries (outside of mining, construction, hotels, gaming, or recreation...)	US Chamber State Rankings — Rank of a state's attractiveness as a place to start or expand a small business	Compliance Corrections — Percent of recommended corrective actions implemented	Call Wait Time — Percent of calls answered as quickly as agency standards require	Economic Growth — Growth rate of state economy (gross state product)	Revenue Collection — Percent of taxes/fees collected within the appropriate statutory or regulatory timeframes	Public Information Materials — Percent of business development and services agencies reviewing and revising public information materials annually	Visitor Volume — Number of visitor to Nevada
Benchmark	Employment Growth — Percent increase in businesses employing Nevadans	National Regulatory Flexibility Ranking — Assesses the flexibility and responsiveness of the State's regulatory systems	Compliance Resolution — Percent of initiated investigations, audits and cases successfully resolved in the favor of the regulatory agency	Compliance Resolution — Percent of cases and complaints resolved within the appropriate statutory or regulatory time frames	Export Increase — Percent increase in exports		Social Media — Percent of business development and services agencies participating in social media activities	Attraction Attendance — Attendance at Nevada State Museums And State Parks
Benchmark	Job Sector Growth — Percent increase in annual job growth in targeted economic sectors		Compliance Timeliness — Percent of investigations initiated and/or concluded within the appropriate statutory, regulatory, or agency time frames	Department of Motor Vehicles (DMV) Wait Time — Percent of DMV customers reaching a technician in 30 minutes or less	Export Growth — Growth in number of Nevada businesses exporting		Training and Outreach — Percent of business development and services agencies conducting training and/or consumer outreach activities	Tourism — Increase overnight visitation
Governor's Priorities	Sustainable and growing economy; safe and livable communities	Sustainable and growing economy	Sustainable and growing economy; safe and livable communities	Sustainable and growing economy	Sustainable and growing economy	Sustainable and growing economy	Sustainable and growing economy	Sustainable and growing economy

Common Objectives for all Admin and Other Support Services – Fiscal, Personnel and Payroll, Information Technology, and General Administration
Core Functions:

Pass Through - Payments made from one state executive account to another state executive budget account.

Other – Activities that do not align with any objective within any of the eight core functions.

each division, goals and targets are introduced, followed by performance targets for each activity. Following the performance information, financial information is presented by division and activity. Figure 9.2 presents an excerpt from the Nevada Department of Agriculture for two activities: Administration and Food and Nutrition Management.

Texas, which has been engaged in performance budgeting for more than two decades, has a more detailed, rigorous, and systematic process in use (Kamensky, 2013). Its system is top down and centralized. It begins with the governor's strategic plan that guides the budget proposal; the legislature then adopts a biennial budget that includes specific performance levels tied to the strategic plan. Agencies in the state, of which there are about two hundred, then prepare individual five-year strategic plans that are used to develop agency budget proposals. These agency proposals are organized around goals, each of which has identified strategies, outputs, and outcomes, followed by targets for each performance measure. Of course, these proposals also include information that is associated with traditional budget requests, such as the number of employees, finance methods, line item or objects of expense, and a capital budget.

The performance management process in Texas consists of three components: strategic planning, performance budgeting, and performance monitoring (Texas State Auditor, 2012). The performance budgeting component of the process is described as follows:

> The General Appropriations Act and the agency's operating budgets comprise the performance budgeting component of the SPPB System. The General Appropriations Act makes a biennial appropriation of resources and establishes performance targets based on the legislature's funding priorities. An agency's operating budget provides a more detailed and updated allocation of those resources and projected performance for each fiscal year. (Texas State Auditor 2012, p. 3)

The Texas approach identifies five criteria for an effective performance management system (Texas State Auditor 2012, p. 10):

- Results oriented: focuses primarily on outcomes and outputs
- Selective: concentrates on the most important indicators of performance
- Useful: provides information of value to the agency and decision-makers
- Accessible: provides periodic information about results
- Reliable: provides accurate, consistent information over time

FIGURE 9.2 PERFORMANCE BUDGET EXCERPT: NEVADA DEPARTMENT OF AGRICULTURE, 2014–2015 BUDGET

Activity: Administration

The Administration program provides leadership, sets policy, and establishes direction for the department and divisions. Administrative staff are responsible for providing enforcement and regulation of agricultural industries as well as protecting the state's investment infrastructure. Additionally, staff work with various communities, state and federal agencies, organizations, and the Board of Agriculture to increase agriculture as an industry and stimulate agriculture activity. Agency leadership provides overall supervision of administrative, fiscal, budget, and technical activities of the division and programs administered by the department.

Performance Measures

1. Customers Satisfied

	2012	2013	2014	2015
Type:	New	Projected	Projected	Projected
Percent:		74.82%	79.79%	85.11%

2. Population title

	2012	2013	2014	2015
Type:	New	Projected	Projected	Projected
Amount:		282	282	282

3. Value of Services and Commodities

	2012	2013	2014	2015
Type:	New	Projected	Projected	Projected
Dollars:		5,300,000,000	5,406,000,000	5,514,120,000

Resources

Funding		FY 2014	FY 2015
General Fund	$	21,907	21,729
	FTE	0.00	0.00
Transfers	$	2,446,602	2,524,479
	FTE	17.00	17.00
Other	$	15,891	15,891
	FTE	0.00	0.00
TOTAL	$	2,484,400	2,562,099
	FTE	17.00	17.00

Objectives	FY 2014	FY 2015
Wellness (Health Services)	621,100	640,525
Protect Resources (Resource Management)	621,100	640,525
Effective and Efficient Public Safety (Public Safety)	621,100	640,525
Compliance (Business Development and Services)	621,100	640,525

Activity: Food and Nutrition Management

This activity permits, certifies, and regulates dairies and nutritional elements.

Performance Measures

1. Students Participating in National School Lunch Program

	2012	2013	2014	2015
Type:	New	Projected	Projected	Projected
Percent:		55.70%	61.2%	64.5%

2. Students Participating in School Breakfast Program

	2012	2013	2014	2015
Type:	New	Projected	Projected	Projected
Percent:		29.3%	36.20%	40.10%

Resources

Funding		FY 2014	FY 2015
General Fund	$	106,934	106,934
	FTE	0.00	0.00
Federal Fund	$	131,753,915	131,639,346
	FTE	28.50	28.50
Other	$	12,248,896	14,466,627
	FTE	10.00	10.00
TOTAL	$	144,109,745	146,212,907
	FTE	38.50	38.50

Objectives	FY 2014	FY 2015
Wellness (Health Services)	36,027,436	36,553,227
Protect Resources (Resource Management)	36,027,436	36,553,227
Economic Diversification (Business Development and Services)	36,027,436	36,553,227
Compliance (Business Development and Services)	36,027,436	36,553,227

These criteria set the bar for agencies in the development and selection of performance measures that will be used for internal management but also in the budget process. In that performance targets are established for selected goals in the approved budget, quality measures and targets help to ensure strategic action on the part of agencies in daily actions. The report goes on to define quality measures (Texas State Auditor, 2012, p. 11):

- Responsive: reflect changes in levels of performance
- Valid: capture the information intended
- Cost-effective: justify the cost of collecting and retaining data
- Comprehensive coverage: incorporate significant aspects of agency operations
- Relevant: logically and directly relate to agency goals, objectives, strategies, and functions

The role of the auditor in the Texas approach lends significant legitimacy to the performance budgeting process. Consider the ramifications of poor performance measures or performance results based on faulty data; in order for performance management to function properly, the results must be valid and reliable. When management decisions are based on faulty information, the resulting decisions may not bring about the desired effect and may actually result in performance declines. The same principle applies to performance budgeting. When budget decisions are made using performance data, the resulting funding allocation represents assumptions that those data are accurate. If they are not accurate representations of reality, that is, they are not valid, the allocation of public resources to programs will not reflect the intentions of policymakers to reward high-performing programs and punish low-performing programs. Moreover, agencies may be able to game the system by falsifying data, creaming, or other measurement techniques to disguise the reality of their performance and give them an unwarranted advantage in the budget allocation. Agency performance is assessed quarterly by the agencies in Texas and reported to both the Legislative Budget Board and the Governor's Office of Budget, Planning, and Policy.

The auditor's office in Texas plays a central role in performance budgeting by auditing not only agency financial information but also performance measurement. Performance auditing is a contingent feature that strengthens the effectiveness of performance budgeting efforts. The auditor provides a lengthy guide to the performance budgeting process in Texas (sixty-four pages in the most recent iteration) to assist agencies in the process. (The guide to performance management in Texas is available on the state auditor's website: http://www.sao.state.tx.us/reports/main/12-333.pdf.) The report identifies criteria that determine when an agency is selected for audit using a risk assessment approach (Texas State Auditor, 2012, p. 22):

- Substantial changes in organizational structure or personnel
- Expressions of concern by legislators
- Patterns of unexpected performance
- Dollars appropriated to an agency
- Indications from previous audits that an agency has potential performance measure control weaknesses
- Frequency with which an agency's performance measures have been reviewed

If the process works as intended, and performance measures are used in making budget decisions, what options do the governor and legislature have to reward or punish agency performance results? The auditor's report identifies a series of potential incentives and disincentives (Texas State Auditor, 2012, p. 20):

Positive Incentives or Rewards

- Increased funding
- Exemption from reporting requirements
- Increased funding transferability
- Formalized recognition or accolade
- Awards or bonuses
- Expanded responsibility
- Expanded contracting authority

Negative Incentives or Redirection

- Evaluation of outcome variances for remedial plan
- Reduction of funding
- Elimination of funding
- Restriction of funding
- Withholding of funding
- Reduction of funding transferability
- Transfer of functional responsibility to another entity
- Recommendation for placement in conservatorship

- Direction that a management audit be conducted
- Direction that other remedial or corrective action plans be implemented

Now that we have reflected on the key components of the Texas process, it is useful to examine the result of that process. Texas issues a biennial budget, appropriating over $200 billion in total. Texas is a large state, and it is an understatement to say that the budget process is complex and requires significant capacity. The budget bill for the 2014–2015 biennium is nearly one thousand pages in length. The budget for the Department of Public Safety offers a good example of the resulting performance budget (figure 9.3). We see that there are three major divisions in the budget document. First, in the section labeled "items of appropriation," funds are allocated according to specific goals and further allocated among specific strategies. So for the first goal, Combat Crime and Terrorism, funds are divided across eight specific strategies: organized crime, criminal interdiction, border security, local border security, counterterrorism, intelligence, security programs, and special investigations.

The second part of the document provides traditional budget information according to objects of expenditure. Here we find the informational allocation of funds according to the traditional budget categories of salaries, benefits, travel, and so on. This traditional information is helpful because it provides insight into the approach the agency is using to accomplish its goals. For example, is it relying heavily on personnel or contractors? Does it require significant investments in capital and equipment—fixed costs—or maintenance and variable costs? It is also necessary for agency managers to keep tabs on the use of state funds during implementation.

The third section of the document expounds on the performance measures to be used in assessing the agency's performance for each of the identified goals and strategies. Here, specific levels are provided as performance targets in each fiscal year of the biennium. So for the first goal, Combat Crime and Terrorism, performance in reaching the goal will be assessed according to the Annual Texas Index Crime Rate, with a goal of maintaining a rate no higher than 3,880. Each strategy then offers specific targets. For organized crime, the number of arrests is targeted for three specific crimes individually: narcotics violations, motor vehicle theft, and other arrests outside these two categories. Similar targets are established for each goal and strategy in this and every other state agency.

FIGURE 9.3 TEXAS DEPARTMENT OF PUBLIC SAFETY, FISCAL YEAR 2014–2015 BUDGET

	For the Years Ending	
	August 31, 2014	August 31, 2015
Method of Financing		
General Revenue Fund[2]	$ 228,886,728	$ 358,474,924
Federal Funds	630,516,641	541,928,578
Other Funds		
Interagency Contracts - Criminal Justice Grants	5,933,431	5,933,431
State Highway Road No. 005[2]	475,232,387	373,385,121
Appropriated Receipts	23,923,922	23,923,922
Interagency Contracts	11,846,417	11,846,417
Bond Proceeds - General Obligation Bonds[3]	24,429,860	UB
Subtotal, Other Funds	$ 541,366,010	$ 329,083,891
Total, Method of Financing	$ 1,400,769,379	$ 1,279,492,393
Other Direct and Indirect Costs Appropriated Elsewhere in this Act	$ 1,465,285	$ 1,555,903
This bill pattern represents an estimated 100% of this agency's estimated total available funds for the biennium		
Number of Full-Time-Equivalents (FTE):	9,165.3	9,165.3
Schedule of Exempt Positions:		
Director. Group 6	$183,498	$183,498
Items of Appropriation:		
A. Goal: COMBAT CRIME AND TERRORISM		
A.1.1. Strategy: ORGANIZED CRIME	$ 58,654,629	$ 58,462,322
A.1.2. Strategy: CRIMINAL INTERACTION	$ 12,810,743	$ 12,833,289
A.1.3. Strategy: SCREEN SECURITY	$ 16,975,803	$ 18,497,676
A.1.4. Strategy: LOCAL BORDER SECURITY	$ 23,670,383	$ 23,564,486
A.2.1. Strategy: COUNTERTERRORISM	$ 534,072	$ 534,090
A.2.2. Strategy: INTELLIGENCE	$ 6,307,787	$ 6,307,787
A.2.3. Strategy: SECURITY PROGRAMS	$ 19,777,053	$ 19,779,609
A.3.1. Strategy: SPECIAL INVESTIGATIONS	$ 21,871,507	$ 21,791,999
Total, Goal A: COMBAT CRIME AND TERRORISM	$ 160,601,977	$ 161,771,258
B. Goal: ENHANCE PUBLIC SAFETY		
B.1.1. Strategy: TRAFFIC ENFORCEMENT	$ 167,781,021	$ 165,128,815
B.1.2. Strategy: COMMERCIAL VEHICLE ENFORCEMENT	$ 59,090,877	$ 59,515,094
B.2.1. Strategy: PUBLIC SAFETY COMMUNICATIONS	$ 15,872,072	$ 15,878,879
Total, Goal B: ENHANCE PUBLIC SAFETY	$ 242,743,970	$ 240,522,758
C. Goal: EMERGENCY MANAGEMENT		
C.1.1. Strategy: EMERGENCY PREPAREDNESS	$ 101,336,070	$ 63,387,932
Emergency Management Training and Preparedness.		
C.1.2. Strategy: RESPONSE COORDINATION	$ 5,838,821	$ 5,620,240
Emergency and Disaster Response Coordination.		
C.1.3. Strategy: RECOVERY AND MITIGATION	$ 490,848,003	$ 440,306,161
Disaster Recovery and Hazard Mitigation.		
C.1.4. Strategy: STATE OPERATIONS CENTER	$ 5,516,614	$ 5,518,876
Total, Goal C: EMERGENCY MANAGEMENT	$ 603,539,513	$ 515,333,209
D. Goal: REGULATORY SERVICES		
D.1.1. Strategy: CRIME LABORATORY SERVICES	$ 38,565,057	$ 36,305,662
D.1.2. Strategy: CRIME RECORDS SERVICES	$ 36,178,403	$ 36,077,752
D.1.3. Strategy: VICTIM SERVICES	$ 839,703	$ 839,820
D.2.1. Strategy: DRIVER LICENSE SERVICES	$ 22,863,799	$ 22,087,237
D.2.2. Strategy: DRIVING AND MOTOR VEHICLE SAFETY	$ 100,455,751	$ 96,943,197
D.3.1. Strategy: REGULATORY SERVICES ISSUANCE	$ 9,652,655	$ 9,662,655
D.3.2. Strategy: REGULATORY SERVICES COMPLIANCE	$ 15,809,472	$ 15,377,902
D.3.3. Strategy: REGULATORY SERVICES MODERNIZATION	$ 4,956,882	$ 4,966,893
Total, Goal D: REGULATORY SERVICES	$ 229,371,322	$ 229,664,118

FIGURE 9.3 (CONTINUED)

E. Goal: AGENCY SERVICES AND SUPPORT		
E.1.1. Strategy: HEADQUARTERS ADMINISTRATION	$ 17,199,221	$ 17,132,414
E.1.2. Strategy: REGIONAL ADMINISTRATION	$ 12,611,853	$ 12,615,146
E.1.3. Strategy: INFORMATION TECHNOLOGY	$ 55,959,400	$ 55,583,098
E.1.4. Strategy: FINANCIAL MANAGEMENT	$ 5,710,427	$ 5,310,498
E.1.5. Strategy: HUMAN CAPITAL MANAGEMENT	$ 2,192,285	$ 2,192,555
E.1.6. Strategy: TRAINING ACADEMY AND DEVELOPMENT	$ 13,401,142	$ 13,405,784
E.1.7. Strategy: FLEET OPERATIONS	$ 2,357,303	$ 2,367,845
E.1.8. Strategy: FACILITIES MANAGEMENT	$ 55,070,566	$ 29,887,680
Total, Goal E: AGENCY SERVICES AND SUPPORT	$ 164,512,192	$ 139,201,020
Grand Total: DEPARTMENT OF PUBLIC SAFETY	$ 1,400,769,379	$ 1,279,492,393
Object-of-Expense Informational Listing:		
Salaries and Wages	$ 488,032,412	$ 488,404,898
Other Personnel Costs	17,991,214	18,005,205
Professional Fees and Services	37,720,540	37,621,650
Fuels and Lubricants	28,111,944	27,190,028
Consumable Supplies	8,940,926	9,760,131
Utilities	18,214,041	18,185,364
Travel	8,932,399	8,569,107
Rent - Building	7,708,279	7,705,279
Rent - Machine and Other	1,761,155	1,761,155
Other Operating Expenses	94,919,641	95,520,352
Grants	582,334,800	495,232,312
Capital Expenditures	206,052,065	69,832,882
Total, Object-of-Expense Informational Listing:	$ 1,400,769,379	$ 1,279,492,393
Estimated Allocations for Employee Benefits and Debt Service Appropriations Made Elsewhere in this Act:		
Employee Benefits		
Retirement	$ 26,939,940	$ 32,577,542
Group Insurance	93,550,281	102,270,002
Social Security	35,403,983	37,213,535
Benefits Replacement	1,795,702	1,678,981
Subtotal, Employee Benefits	$ 157,759,905	$ 123,740,060
Debt Service		
TRFA GO Bond Debt Service	$ 21,366,802	$ 24,317,531
Lease Payments	136,873	136,126
Subtotal, Debt Service	$ 21,503,675	$ 24,853,657
Total, Estimated Allocations for Employee Benefits and Debt Service Appropriations Made Elsewhere in This Act	$ 179,263,581	$ 198,593,717

1. **Performance Measure Targets:** The following is a listing of the key performance target levels for the Department of Public Safety. It is the intent of the Legislature that appropriations made by this Act be utilized in the most efficient and effective manner possible to achieve the intended mission of the Department of Public Safety. In order to achieve the objectives and service standards established by this Act. The Department of Public Safety shall make every effort to attain the following designated key performance target levels associated with each item of appropriation.

	2014	2015
A. Goal: COMBAT CRIME AND TERRORISM		
Outcome (Results/Impact):		
Annual Texas Index Crime Rate	3,880	3,880
A.1.1. Strategy: ORGANIZED CRIME		
Output (volume):		
Number of Arrests for Narcotics Violations	1,500	1,500
Number of Arrests for Motor Vehicle Theft	300	300
Number of CID Arrests not Narcotics/Vehicle Theft	2,000	2,000
A.1.4. Strategy: LOCAL SOCIETY SECURITY		
Explanatory:		
Amount of Funds Provided for Local Border Security Operations	8,694,876	8,694,876

FIGURE 9.3 (CONTINUED)

A.3.1. Strategy: SPECIAL INVESTIGATIONS		
Output (volume):		
Number of Arrests by Texas Rangers	1,880	1,880
B. Goal: ENHANCE PUBLIC SAFETY		
Outcome (Resulted Impact):		
Annual Texas Highway Traffic Death Rate	1	1
B.1.1. Strategy: TRAFFIC ENFORCEMENT		
Output (volume):		
Number of Highway Patrol Service Hours on Routine Patrol	2,242,000	2,242,000
Number of Traffic Law Violator Contacts	3,400,000	3,400,000
B.1.2. Strategy: COMMERCIAL VEHICLE ENFORCEMENT		
Output (volume):		
# of Commercial Vehicle Enforcement Hours on Routine Patrol	907,000	907,000
Efficiencies:		
Number of Commercial Vehicle Traffic Law Violator Contacts	1,500,000	1,500,000
C. Goal: EMERGENCY MANAGEMENT		
Outcome (Resulted/Impact):		
Number of Public Entities with Open Disaster Security Grants	1,346	1,346
C.1.2. Strategy: RESPONSE COORDINATION		
Output (volume):		
Number of Emergency Incidents Coordinated	5,294	5,294
C.1.3. Strategy: RECOVERY AND MITIGATION		
Efficiencies:		
% of the State Population Covered by Hazard Mitigation Plans	78%	80%
D. Goal: REGULATORY SERVICES		
Outcome (Results/Impact):		
% Driver License ID Applications Completed within 45 Minutes	76%	77%
Concealed Handguns Percentage of Original Licenses Issued within 60 Days	100%	100%
Concealed Handguns Percentage of Renewed Licenses Issued within 40 Days	100%	100%
D.1.1. Strategy: CRIME LABORATORY SERVICES		
Output (volume):		
Number of Breath Alcohol Tests Supervised	47,000	47,000
Number of Drug Cases Completed	42,000	42,000
Number of Offender DNA Profiles Completed	65,000	65,000
Efficiencies:		
Average Cost of Supervising a Breath Alcohol Test	80	80
D.2.1. Strategy: DRIVER LICENSE SERVICES		
Output (volume):		
Number of Total Examinations Administered	4,900,000	4,900,000
D.3.1. Strategy: REGULATORY SERVICES ISSUANCE		
Output (volume):		
Concealed Handguns, Number of Original AND Renewal Handguns Licenses Issued	199,443	219,443
D.3.2. Strategy: REGULATORY SERVICES COMPLIANCE		
Output (volume):		
Regulatory Services Division. Number of Criminal Investigations Resolved	60	60
Controlled Substance. Number of Controlled Substance Prescriptions Reported	45,500,000	45,750,000

FIGURE 9.4 VIRGINIA PERFORMS: DEPARTMENT OF ENVIRONMENTAL QUALITY

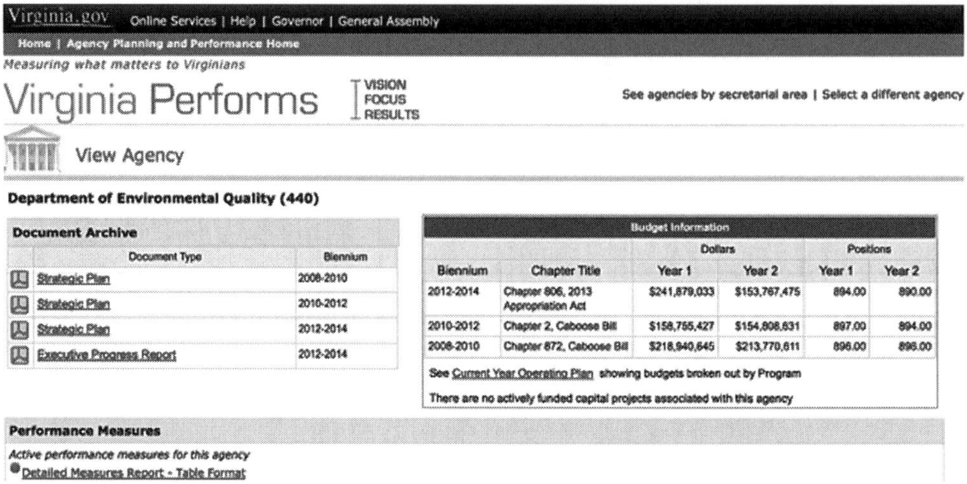

With respect to reporting performance budget information, Virginia has made strides in and is well ahead of most other states. Through an integrated web-based platform, Virginia Performs, the state's performance information is readily available (http://vaperforms.virginia.gov/), including budget information, which is clearly and concisely reported to the public by key functional areas (see https://solutions.virginia.gov/pbreports/rdPage.aspx?rdReport=vp_AgencyList). The information is conveniently displayed on maps using breakouts at the regional and county level as well to reveal performance variation within the state (http://vaperforms.virginia.gov/extras/maps.php). The data are further presented alongside strategic planning and budget information to reveal the connection between the three components. Figure 9.4 offers an example for one agency, the Virginia Department of Environmental Quality.

These state-level examples characterize what is going on across the nation in terms of performance budgeting in practice. Similar systems have been implemented at the local level in cities and counties. We briefly consider two examples. The City of Livingston, Montana, is a recent arrival on the performance budgeting scene. Its FY 2012 budget represents the result of five years of performance budgeting practice. As the city sees it, "Performance budgeting involves a shift away from a debate by the City

Commissioners of what is going to be purchased toward a debate regarding what is going to be accomplished" (City of Livingston, 2013, p. A2). At this point, each department has "identified performance objectives, identified and tracked workload indicators, and has established quantifiable performance measures" (p. A2).

The City of Livingston budget document, organized by department, first presents the program description and goals. This is followed by a traditional object code budget, budget highlights, staffing data, and projected versus actual performance and workload indicators. Figure 9.5 presents Livingston's FY 2014 budget information for the city police department.

The second city budget example comes from Albuquerque, New Mexico, which has embraced performance management and performance budgeting along with it. The city budget process encourages public participation in budget meetings. The process consists of two amalgamated components. The city describes the process as follows:

> The City's budget is formulated in two parts—a financial plan and a performance plan. The financial plan is organized by fund, department, and program strategy. Funds are groupings of related accounts that are used to maintain control over resources that have been segregated for specific activities. The performance plan is organized by Goal, desired community condition, and program strategy. These goals are adopted by the Mayor and City Council every 5 years, after significant community input. A goal is a long term result that is further defined by desired community conditions that would exist if the goal were achieved. Desired Conditions are the focus of indicators of progress, formulated and published every two years by a citizen commission, the Indicators Progress Commission. (City of Albuquerque, 2014)

In this fashion, the city draws on strategic planning to guide action and determine appropriate goals, strategies, and performance measures.

The examples we have provided from performance budget documents have reflected specific substantive programs offered by functional agencies. The excerpt from the most recent Albuquerque budget represents an administrative office—that of the city clerk—to show how performance budgeting applies equally to administrative services as well as functional programs. Figure 9.6 provides this example. Figure 9.6 follows the standard agency format found throughout the city budget document, beginning with a description of the agency and its services, followed by a

FIGURE 9.5 CITY OF LIVINGSTON 2014 POLICE DEPARTMENT PERFORMANCE BUDGET

Program Description

The police department budget unit accounts for costs associated with providing all law enforcement services for the City of Livingston, as well as community programs such as a School Resource Officer. The police department utilizes both patrol and investigative divisions to detect, prevent, and suppress crime and to enforce state criminal and traffic laws, and local ordinances.

Goals & Objectives

- Detection and prevention of criminal activity.

- Proactive enforcement of criminal laws.

- Investigation of crimes.

- Apprehension of criminal offenders.

- Participation in court proceedings.

- Assistance to those who cannot care for themselves or who are in danger of physical harm.

- Proactive enforcement of traffic laws.

- Resolution of day-to-day conflicts among citizens.

- Respond to calls for service from the public.

- Provide public education in areas of crime prevention.

- Preserve public safety and enhance security within the community.

- Be committed and dedicated to providing the highest level of service to all the citizens of our community.

- Partner with the community to address common problems and public safety needs.

- Continue to work with partner law enforcement agencies to include local, State and Federal agencies to improve information sharing and strengthen the working partnerships.

FIGURE 9.5 (CONTINUED)

Department Summary

Budget by Object of Expenditure Category	Actual FY 2011	Actual FY 2012	Budget FY 2013	Recommended FY 2014	Increase (Decrease)	Percent Change
Salaries & Wages	$ 750,523	$ 761,055	$ 767,106	$ 760,173	$ (6,933)	-1%
Operating & Maintenance	86,302	76,729	88,840	92,240	3,400	4%
Capital Outlay	27,436	12,229	114,590	119,694	5,104	4%
Debt Service	-	-	-	-	-	
Transfers Out	-	-	-	-	-	
Total	**$ 864,261**	**$ 850,013**	**$ 970,536**	**$ 972,107**	**$ 1,571**	**0%**

Division Summary

Division	Actual FY 2011	Actual FY 2012	Budget FY 2013	Recommended FY 2014	Increase (Decrease)	Percent Change
Operating Accounts	$ 113,738	$ 88,958	$ 203,430	$ 211,934	8,504	4%
Police Officers	729,266	739,721	745,415	760,173	14,758	2%
Parking Attendant	21,257	21,334	21,691	-	(21,691)	-100%
Debt Service Payments	-	-	-	-	-	
					-	
					-	
					-	
Total	**$ 864,261**	**$ 850,013**	**$ 970,536**	**$ 972,107**	**$ 1,571**	**0%**

FIGURE 9.5 (CONTINUED)

2014 Budget Highlights

Personnel Services

- The 0.6 Parking Enforcement Officer position has been eliminated
- A school resource officer is continued in the budget. One-half of the officer is paid by the school district

Capital Outlay
- The budget includes:
  - Two new vehicles are scheduled to be replaced in FY 2014.
  - The second of a three year software replacement program. FY 2014 includes $59,169 in software expenses.

Staffing Summary

Title	Actual FY 2011	Actual FY 2012	Budgeted FY 2013	Recommended FY 2014
Chief of Police	1.00	1.00	1.00	1.00
Assistant Chief of Police	1.00	1.00	1.00	1.00
Investigator/Patrol Officer III	1.00	1.00	1.00	1.00
Investigator/Patrol Officer II	-	1.00	1.00	1.00
Sergeant	3.00	3.00	3.00	3.00
Patrol Officer III	2.00	1.00	1.00	2.00
Patrol Officer II	1.00	2.00	2.00	1.00
Patrol Officer I	2.00	4.00	4.00	3.00
Patrol Officer I/SRO	-	-	-	1.00
Probationary Patrol Officer	3.00	-	-	-
Parking Enforcement Officer	0.60	0.60	0.60	-
Total	**14.60**	**14.60**	**14.60**	**14.00**

FIGURE 9.5 (CONTINUED)

Performance Measures

Measure	Actual FY 2011	Actual FY 2012	Projected FY 2013	Budgeted FY 2014
1. Customer Satisfaction Surveys - Our goal is to achieve a favorable (3 or higher) across all areas of the survey. The survey will be from those who have received a traffic citation.	4.8	4.7	4.5	4.5
2. Complaints against Officers as to Complaints Sustained as to Officer assigned calls (shown in ratio)	0:0:6335	6:5:6500	3:0:6600	0:0:6500

Workload Indicators

Measure	Actual FY 2011	Actual FY 2012	Projected FY 2013	Budgeted FY 2014
1. Calls per Officer	528	480	600	550
2. Arrests (Adult and Juvenile)	507	525	479	500
3. Citations Issued	555	500	883	800
4. Warnings Issued	348	300	405	400
5. Accidents Investigated	168	170	181	175

FIGURE 9.6 CITY OF ALBUQUERQUE OFFICE OF THE CITY CLERK FY 2014 BUDGET

OFFICE OF THE CITY CLERK

The Office of the City Clerk maintains all official records for the City of Albuquerque, conducts municipal elections, accepts bids from the general public, as well as accepts service of process for summons, subpoenas and tort claims on behalf of the City of Albuquerque. The Office of Administrative Hearings now a part of the Office of the City Clerk, is responsible for conducting all hearings specifically assigned to it by a City of Albuquerque ordinance, including vehicle seizures, animal appeals, handicap parking and personnel matters. The office also staffs the Zoning Hearing Examiner for the Planning Department. The City Clerk is also the direct supervisor of the Albuquerque Records Center where records are scanned, processed, stored and disposed of at the end of the retention periods.

Operating Fund Expenditures by Category ($000's)	FY12 ACTUAL EXPENSES	FY13 ORIGINAL BUDGET	FY13 REVISED BUDGET	FY13 EST. ACT. EXPENSES	FY14 APPROVED BUDGET	CURRENT YR/ PRIOR YR CHG
PERSONNEL	759	666	666	661	1,279	618
OPERATING	657	106	106	632	791	159
CAPITAL	0	0	0	0	0	0
TRANSFERS	349	21	21	21	45	24
GRANTS/PROJECTS	0	0	0	0	0	0
TOTAL	1,765	793	793	1,315	2,115	800
TOTAL FULL-TIME POSITIONS	11	11	11	11	16	5

BUDGET HIGHLIGHTS

The approved FY/14 General Fund budget for the Office of the City Clerk is $2.1 million, an overall increase of 166.7% above the FY/13 original budget. The increase is due to the transfer of the administrative hearing office from the Chief Administrative Officer department for $486 thousand and includes the transfer of five positions. This move will provide direct oversight of the administrative hearing office, and by being at Plaza del Sol, easier access for the public which coincides with the City's one stop shop philosophy.

Technical adjustments in FY/14 include changes in the way health benefits are funded from rate based to actual for health, dental and vision. This change resulted in an actual increase of four thousand dollars with an overall net increase of $49 thousand for the cost of health care and other employee benefits. Internal service costs associated with risk, fleet and communications decreased by $35 thousand. Also, one-time funding of $42 thousand for temporary staff is deleted in FY/14.

Included in the FY/14 approved budget is funding of $903 thousand for the 2013 Municipal Election in October. This includes an increase of four early voting sites to accommodate the increased popularity of early voting in Albuquerque in recent elections. This will aid in reducing election day wait times. Funding will provide at least one additional voting system per polling place in order to process voters more efficiently and reduce wait times, and adds two poll workers per site to accommodate the higher volume of voters being processed. Also included in the FY/14 budget is a reduction of six thousand dollars in repairs and maintenance in an effort to produce savings for the General Fund.

The Open and Ethical Elections Fund closed at the end of FY/12 and moved to a Trust and Agency Fund. It will continue to be administered by the Office of the City Clerk and provide public funding of elections as a means for candidates to run for Mayor or City Council without large donor contributions. It also insures citizens that the election process is fair, responsible, and ethical.

($000's)	FY12 ACTUAL EXPENSES	FY13 ORIGINAL BUDGET	FY13 REVISED BUDGET	FY13 EST. ACT. EXPENSES	FY14 APPROVED BUDGET	CURRENT YR/ PRIOR YR CHG
PROGRAM STRATEGY SUMMARY BY FUND:						
GENERAL FUND - 110						
CC Office of the City Clerk	1,433	793	793	1,315	1,682	367
CC Administrative Hearing Office	0	0	0	0	433	433
TOTAL GENERAL FUND - 110	1,433	793	793	1,315	2,115	800
OPEN & ETHICAL ELECTIONS PROJECT FUND 232						
City Clerk Projects	332	0	0	0	0	0
TOTAL APPROPRIATIONS	1,765	793	793	1,315	2,115	800
Intradepartmental Adjustments	0	0	0	0	0	0
NET APPROPRIATIONS	1,765	793	793	1,315	2,115	800

FIGURE 9.6 (CONTINUED)

OFFICE OF THE CITY CLERK

PERFORMANCE MEASURES

GOAL 7: COMMUNITY AND CULTURAL ENGAGEMENT - Residents are fully and effectively engaged in the life and decisions of the community to promote and enhance our pride, cultural values, and resources and ensure that Albuquerque's community institutions are effective, accountable, and responsive.

PROGRAM STRATEGY

CITY CLERK - Provide custodial and administrative functions for the City by meeting the requirements of federal, state, and local laws governing the custody and preservation of all City records, administration of the Inspection of Public Records Act, conducting municipal elections, support and staff the City's Board of Ethics.

Measure	Actual FY/11	Actual FY/12	Approved FY/13	Actual FY/13	Approved FY/14
DESIRED COMMUNITY CONDITION - Residents actively participate in civic and public affairs					
# of registered voters in City of Albuquerque	-	334,415	385,000	363,000	360,000
# of votes cast in Regular Municipal Election	-	38,850	n/a	n/a	40,000
# of Petitions process (verified and rejected)	4,003		20,000	62,540	10,000
# of Poll Workers hired and trained	3	188	n/a	5	400
# of Poll sites operated	-	49	n/a	n/a	62
Funds provided to participating candidates	$134,000	$0	$1,400,000	$701,928	$3,200
# of qualifying contributions and signatures processed	1,876	-	21,350	9,347	3,200
# of applicant candidates for public financing	4	-	10	10	6
# of Measure Finance Committees registered	1	-	3	2	10
# of Complaints and Petitions managed for Board of Ethics	1	4	1	1	10
# of records scanned, indexed and dedicated to system	345,415	366,909	260,000	435,416	350,000
# of boxes received and stored	1,040	1,129	625	1,700	1,500
# of public records inspections performed	1,200	1,370	1,300	2,100	3,000
# of trained in open records and inspections	-	179	125	300	200
# of 311 requests processed	30	1,309	1,300	453	1,000
# of research requests performed	850	610	800	335	800
# individuals trained in Open Meetings Act	-	-	125	100	120
# of legislation processed and published	184	189	225	115	200
# of contracts and EC's published	1,131	1,097	1,500	1,135	2,000
# of City liens processed	11,085	7,408	10,000	7,200	10,000
# of votes cast in Personnel Board Election	-	365	365	-	-
# of records with signature attested	447	327	500	310	500

GOAL 8: GOVERNMENTAL EXCELLENCE AND EFFECTIVENESS - Ensure that all existing communities are adequately and efficiently served with well planned, coordinated, and maintained infrastructure. Ensure that new development is efficiently integrated into existing infrastructures and that the costs are balanced with the revenues generated.

PROGRAM STRATEGY

ADMINISTRATIVE HEARING OFFICE - Conduct Quasi-Judicial Administrative Hearings before an impartial hearings officer, so that participants are assured of a hearing that complies with the due process of law, expeditious findings of facts and conclusions of law with final determinations.

Measure	Actual FY/11	Actual FY/12	Approved FY/13	Actual FY/13	Approved FY/14
DESIRED COMMUNITY CONDITION - Government protects the civil and constitutional rights of citizens					
Labor Board Hearings				14	30
Personnel Appeal Hearings				23	45
Animal Appeal Hearings				42	50
Section 8 Housing Appeals				10	15
Solid Waste Appeals				11	15
False Alarm Appeals				3	3
Abandoned Vehicle Appeal Hearing Request				10	12
Vehicle Seizures Hearings				1,325	1,500
Disabled Parking				1,065	1,500
ZHE Special Exception Request				492	525

FIGURE 9.6 (CONTINUED)

OFFICE OF THE CITY CLERK

PRIOR YEAR ACCOMPLISHMENTS

➢ Administered two special elections, requiring the processing of 36,859 petition signatures, including the city's first mail-in election in a decade which resulted in a higher voter turnout than the 2011 election. Total number of votes cast was 269,555.

➢ Trained city employees and board members in the inspection of public records act and the open meetings act in order to keep them in compliance with the laws.

➢ Legislation for 2002 – 2004 have been bound and stored with the record books. Legislation for 2005 – 2007 will be sent to be bound. 2008 and 2009 will be sent to the Records Center to be scanned into Filenet.

traditional object code budget, a year-over-year comparison, and then detailed performance information organized around city-level goals, strategies, and performance measures compared over time. Accomplishments from the previous year are highlighted.

Recently efforts to incorporate performance information into state and local budget processes have begun to assume different names or take narrower approaches. Two examples stand out. In the first example, Oregon has adopted a legislative mandate that agencies spend program budgets primarily on evidence-based practices. In the more recent example, the Pew-MacArthur Results First Initiative seeks to use cost-effectiveness analysis to guide state budget decisions. We consider each in turn.

Oregon has a legislative mandate that emphasizes performance evidence in the selection of agency programs. Oregon became the first state to legislatively mandate agency use of evidence-based practices. Senate bill 267 (ORS 182.525) was passed in 2008, requiring the expenditure of agency program budgets on only evidence-based programs. The requirement for covered agencies was incrementally increased over three biennial budgets from 25 percent in 2007 to 50 percent in 2009 and to the permanent 75 percent in 2011. (The statute is provided in the box for review.) This statute, unfortunately, leaves too much to the imagination. It fails to express a clear definition of what constitutes evidence, stating only that "evidence-based program means a program that: (a) Incorporates significant and relevant practices based on scientifically based research; and (b) Is cost effective" (http://www.oregonlaws.org/ors/182.515). The law is more specific about what constitutes scientifically based research:

> Scientifically based research means research that obtains reliable and valid knowledge by:
>
> (a) Employing systematic, empirical methods that draw on observation or experiment;
> (b) Involving rigorous data analyses that are adequate to test the stated hypotheses and justify the general conclusions drawn; and
> (c) Relying on measurements or observational methods that provide reliable and valid data across evaluators and observers, across multiple measurements and observations and across studies by the same or different investigators.

At issue here is that this definition is subject to interpretation. It could incorporate experimental designs, quasi-experimental studies, or other techniques. More important, the law fails to recognize that there are varied standards of evidence across fields of practice (Jennings & Hall, 2012). This means that the ultimate evidentiary requirements would vary across agencies by necessity. Nonetheless, it is a symbolic gesture that has had some profound substantive impacts on agency programming choices, and it is a clear example of early efforts to create accountability by using only programs with evidence of effectiveness. One of the principal criticisms of mandates of this nature is the potential that they might stifle experimentation and innovation. A second criticism is the failure to accommodate context in such decisions. Adopting a policy, program, or practice that works must take into account the particular contextual differences from place to place that may exacerbate, moderate, or eliminate the practice's effect.

One of the more interesting examples of attempts at state-level performance budgeting is driven by a collaborative between the Pew Charitable Trusts and the MacArthur Foundation. The Pew-MacArthur Results First Initiative reflects a cost-benefit approach to decision making with a flavor of evidence-based practice. Originally developed in Washington State by the Washington State Institute for Public Policy, this approach has been used there for over fifteen years. Using cost-benefit analysis, the program aims to help states invest in programs and policies that have been proven to work. Importantly, the collaborative approaches willing states with a wealth of expertise and technical capacity to facilitate the process. The approach consists of five straightforward steps: (1) Pew provides a national database of evidence on program effectiveness; (2) to this, states add their own state-specific population and cost data; (3) the model

Oregon Revised Statutes 182.525: Mandatory Expenditures for Evidence-Based Programs

(1) An agency as defined in ORS 182.515 (Definitions for ORS 182.515 and 182.525) shall spend at least 75 percent of state moneys that the agency receives for programs on evidence-based programs.

(2) The agency shall submit a biennial report containing:

    (a) An assessment of each program on which the agency expends funds, including but not limited to whether the program is an evidence-based program;

    (b) The percentage of state moneys the agency receives for programs that is being expended on evidence-based programs;

    (c) The percentage of federal and other moneys the agency receives for programs that is being expended on evidence-based programs; and

    (d) A description of the efforts the agency is making to meet the requirement of subsection (1) of this section.

(3) The agency shall submit the report required by subsection (2) of this section no later than September 30 of each even-numbered year to the interim legislative committee dealing with judicial matters.

(4) If an agency, in any biennium, spends more than 25 percent of the state moneys that the agency receives for programs on programs that are not evidence based, the Legislative Assembly shall consider the agency's failure to meet the requirement of subsection (1) of this section in making appropriations to the agency for the following biennium.

(5) The agency may adopt rules necessary to carry out the provisions of this section, including but not limited to rules defining a reasonable period of time for purposes of determining cost effectiveness. [2003 c.669 sec. 7; 2005 c.22 sec. 128; 2005 c.503 sec. 13]

Source: http://www.oregonlaws.org/ors/182.525.

computes the long-term costs and benefits of the program; (4) programs are ranked according to their return on investment; and (5) the resulting information is considered by policymakers during the budget process (Pew-MacArthur Results First Initiative, 2013).

Results First is currently working with thirteen states (Connecticut, Iowa, Idaho, Illinois, Kansas, Massachusetts, Mississippi, New Mexico, New York, Oregon, Rhode Island, Texas, and Vermont), and the list is expanding as willing states with sufficient capacity join the initiative (Pew-MacArthur Results First Initiative, 2014a). States are selected according to several criteria, including commitment to making evidence-based policy decisions, the ability to provide the data necessary to run the cost-benefit model, and a willingness to dedicate resources (including staff with data, statistical analysis and fiscal analysis skills) to the endeavor (Pew-MacArthur Results First Initiative, 2014b). Once these criteria have been met, Results First staff conduct conference calls and site visits to ensure the state is a suitable candidate. Once a state is accepted, Results First staff then become integrally engaged in the initiative, providing capacity through planning, organizing, and implementing to effort.

Effectiveness

Periods of increasing revenue offer potential to use performance information, but even when it is collected, it is seldom used during periods of economic decline. This is quite a paradox in that it is customarily periods of declining revenues that lead to calls for budget reforms. According to the National Association of State Budget Officers, states were rarely able to use their performance information because cuts have to be made quickly when revenue declines; this time pressure precludes analysis of performance information and data (Pattison, 2012). But once adopted, performance budgeting does seem to have some impact. In a state-level study, Lu and Willoughby (2012) discovered three clear advantages to the use of performance budgets: (1) states with longer histories of performance budgeting had greater liquidity, (2) laws in place longer periods of time reduce expenditures per capita, and (3) stronger performance budgeting requirements led to lower long-term financial liability. In other words, stronger performance budgeting requirements that have been in place longer seem to improve state fiscal health, controlling for other social, political, and economic factors.

Guidelines for Implementing Performance-Informed Budgeting

The key elements of performance budgeting consist of a strategic planning process to clarify goals and objectives, performance measurement, reporting of performance information, and a linkage of performance reports to the budget process. Such systems may also incorporate elements of evidence-based practice or benchmarking as well. These components can vary according to the design of the system with respect to its centralization or decentralization, the type of performance information used, the weight given to performance in the allocation process and so on. Most federal and state performance budgeting systems are centralized. Office of Management and Budget and state budget offices manage the process and establish its parameters. This has advantages and disadvantages.

Among the advantages are the significant capacity these offices have for regulating, controlling, and corralling agencies into annual budget requests. They are also able to impose a uniform system that generates equivalent information across agency and program types. This makes for a more uniform system of comparison across programs that often resemble differences akin to those found between apples and oranges. For example, the funding process might be biased if agency-generated performance reports were based on outputs for some agencies, efficiency for others, and cost-effectiveness for others still. And finally, the weight of these central agency requirements is met with responsiveness from line agencies as a result of their close proximity to the governor or president.

The disadvantages of such a centralized process include the potential for a lack of agency buy-in. When we think about the purpose of the performance measurement process for central budget agencies and for line agencies, there is potential for divergence. On the one hand, the value of performance measurement for line agencies rests more in the potential to improve service quality and to make management decisions throughout implementation. On the other hand, the purpose for budget agencies in the lead may be to exert political control over those agencies to ensure that line agency efforts are constrained to the narrow definition embodied by the performance objectives that are established and make informed allocation of resources across programs.

The greatest challenge to implementing a performance budgeting system in smaller governments is tied to capacity. At the agency level, capacity is required to organize the process and collect and provide data to policymakers. At the central level, in the mayor's or county executive's office, capacity is required to organize the parameters of the process, provide technical assistance to agencies, collect and aggregate performance information, and provide reports to legislative and executive policymakers. It will probably be necessary to provide training and technical assistance to agency managers in identifying performance indicators and collecting performance information. Smaller governments are often more politicized and less professionalized than their larger counterparts, so they may have fewer employees, and those employees are likely to have lower educational attainment. Moreover, they are likely to be laggards in the adoption of government reforms, so in the evolution of performance measurement, they may opt toward measuring outputs rather than outcomes or impacts. Good budget decisions, like program management decisions, depend on the validity and reliability of the information collected. For there to be a positive experience with performance budgeting, good performance information must be produced and interpreted properly.

Planning

Planning for performance budgeting occurs at two levels. First, the process itself must be planned. Decisions must be made about what information will be required, how it will be collected, and how it will be managed. Specific roles will need to be defined at both the central level, usually the budget office, and the agency level. Clear responsibility for the work must be delegated. Planning from this perspective consists of developing a consistent framework that applies to all agencies equally to ensure that the resource allocation is equitable. A fair process should generate fair results. The second part of planning is strategic planning at the agency level, typically constrained by guidance from the budget office. Here we are talking about identifying clear goals and objectives against which performance will be assessed at the conclusion of the budgetary cycle, usually the fiscal year.

The substance of these goals and objectives will obviously vary from agency to agency (e.g., the public value created by a police department differs considerable from a road or sanitation department). But the format needs to be consistent, which is where centralized guidance comes into play. If the police department picked measures that are outputs—such as arrests made—while the road department picked measures that are outcomes—such as reduction in accidents—then the budget decision would likely be biased in favor of the more sophisticated measures. Moreover, there is a range of possible measures that could be considered, such as efficiency, cost effectiveness, or customer satisfaction. If different agencies are producing measures that are not comparable side by side, then it becomes difficult to allocate resources equitably.

Measurement

With respect to measurement, it is essential that data are collected in a uniform manner. This means that the instrumentation used to collect data should be consistent across agencies to allow direct comparison. Agencies should not be left to design their own performance reports because those differences may introduce confusion and bias into the process. Proper measurement also requires consideration of the same time period; agencies should be reporting on performance during the same window.

In measurement, we may also seek to analyze data and convert them into information, giving those data meaning in the process. This may be done through a comparison against targets, over past years' performance, or across particular divisions or population groups. Another approach to analysis is benchmarking, whereby we compare our performance—and change in performance—against that of our peer group. In a centralized process, the city or county would need to select the peer group in advance, and it would not likely vary from agency to agency but rather be a group of the city's or county's peers. This opens a window into agencies' relative performance compared to others facing similar situations.

Reporting

Performance reports out of agencies should be consistent to allow direct comparison across programs and agencies. These reports should be timely and should be aggregated in by the central budget office for compilation and analysis. The more important step comes in reporting program and agency performance to policymakers and executives as part of the information packet preceding the budget process. The performance management doctrine (Moynihan, 2008) calls for the use of performance information to make it meaningful in improving agency outcomes and public policy decisions. Performance information must be presented in a usable fashion so that policymakers will have a grounded and informed basis on which to make funding allocation choices. This characterizes the substantive use of performance information in budgeting. And finally, reports to the public should offer performance information to substantiate the budget choices made. There are less desirable approaches to performance budgeting that pursue only symbolic goals. Such approaches simply collect and report performance information without making use of it in the decision process.

Consider transparency as the primary objective of reporting. If performance information is reported to the public, but it is not demonstrated how that performance information is connected to the budget process, then accountability is called into question. Transparency can be defined as the ability to access information that reveals how government carried out its business or made its decisions.

Verification

It is simply not sufficient to allow agencies to develop performance measures and report performance information. If that information is to be used in making management and budget decisions, steps must be taken to authenticate the validity of the data—that is, to hold the agency accountable for producing accurate and actionable data. One of the greatest criticisms of performance budgeting is its susceptibility to fraud or abuse. According to Smith (1999), PBB is more vulnerable to threats from fraud, falsification, and misrepresentation than were previous budgeting systems. This vulnerability grows from complexity, dependence on performance data, and year-to-year changes in strategic focus. This may be achieved through the auditing function, as it is in Texas, whereby performance data are verified in the same manner that financial data would be audited. The result is a determination of whether the performance data present an accurate picture of reality, and the threat of audit and the resulting repercussions helps to moderate perverse incentives and keep agencies honest.

Linkage to Budget Decision Process

Finally, PBB systems require a direct linkage to the budget system. Think about the many iterations through which performance information may be integrated into public management. Performance *measurement* is the act of assessing program or agency performance and reporting it to internal or external users. It is primarily a mechanism for holding the agency accountable to political principals and citizen stakeholders. Performance *management* is the use of performance information to strategically inform agency decisions during implementation but also in program and policy choices. Performance management emphasizes the use of performance information to improve performance. Both of these can operate independent of the budget process, and many have for some time.

There is reason to believe that agency-driven performance measurement efforts might bias the budget allocation by drawing in resources for agencies that report performance information because they appear more accountable than agencies that do not. If all agencies in a city were required by legislative or executive mandate to engage in performance measurement, this would contribute to agency control but would not necessarily contribute to the budget process. Decision makers might use such information informally or not at all. Formalizing performance measurement and reporting as part of the budget process does not ensure that allocation decisions will be made using this objective information, but it increases the likelihood that the information will influence funding determinations. As we have already discussed, strong performance is insufficient alone to determine an agency's funding. Rather, performance information must be considered in concert with need, the extent of the problem, external influences, and so on. Integrating performance information into agency budget requests does, however, add objectivity to the process by framing the decision around the lens of performance and accountability.

Standards and criteria must be laid out in formal terms in advance. The format of agency budget requests should conform to a consistent rubric, and the format of performance information should be made to conform to specific guidelines that include the type of performance measure (e.g., cost-effectiveness). Agencies should be evaluated on as level a playing field as possible, recognizing that the measures will by necessity vary for agencies of different types, such as those engaged in activities with a longer time horizon.

Other Considerations

Kamensky (2013) summarizes four recommendations for implementing performance budgeting:

1. Don't separate budget and finance systems from the strategic goals of political leaders. Such systems need to be tied to the overall strategies for the city.

2. Use analytics and evidence-based approaches to inform budgeting priorities. This helps target resources to the underlying cause of a problem rather than its symptoms.
3. Budgets should be organized around the outcomes or initiatives in the strategic plan, not around the traditional agencies and programs. This means a departure from line-item budgeting toward budgeting around priorities that may cross traditional boundaries.
4. Create a budget and finance structure that can accommodate such flexibility.

Conclusion

Over the course of the past two decades, tremendous strides have been made in the use of performance information in public program management. Most notably, federal and state governments have developed and institutionalized systems that require agencies or programs to undertake strategic planning to determine clear goals, measure performance with respect to those goals, and incorporate performance information across agencies and programs in the budget process so as to allow performance information to influence the allocation of scarce public resources. Many large city and county governments have also sought to balance incremental pressures with the more rational approach of performance-informed budgeting when they have sufficient capacity to do so. In the end, performance information represents only one of numerous types of information that the complex budgetary process seeks to assimilate into a meaningful and effective distribution of resources across deserving problems and needs. Paramount to this process is the highly political nature of budgeting and the control that is seemingly sacrificed by basing decisions on objective information. This may lead policymakers to be reluctant to make decisions purely on the basis of performance information.

Evidence of widespread use and potential benefits notwithstanding, there are concerns about performance-informed budgeting as well. As we have pointed out, a number of authors (Joyce, 2003; Ho, 2011) have challenged the use of the term *performance-based budgeting*, preferring instead the more accurately descriptive *performance-informed budgeting*. Some writers conclude that PBB should be viewed not as a replacement for traditional budgeting, but rather as an extension of traditional line-item budgeting (Cook & Lawrie, 2007). This is a more accurate depiction of reality; budget decisions are made in the same way they always have been, revolving around line items. But the discourse about budgets today is now influenced—at least symbolically—by discussions about goals and objectives, past performance, and levels of need. In other words, the language of performance measurement has made its way into the budget process, and budget decisions are now often made with performance as one relevant dimension. Performance-informed budgeting is a useful framework in that it encourages agencies to focus on what they should be doing and on delivering services in the most efficient and effective manner. Emphasizing outcomes in discussions about resources and inputs is a healthy perspective in the budget process even if decisions are ultimately guided more by ideology and incrementalism.

As time continues, capacity will be developed to better use rational performance information, as well as evidence of program effectiveness, in making budget and program decisions in more and more governments and nonprofit organizations. Standardized approaches will emerge, and capacity will be developed, enabling smaller and smaller governments to benefit from these approaches. The opportunity for adopting new performance budgeting practices seems to be during times of expanding economies and budgets rather than retractions (Hou et al., 2011), however, so caution should be exercised in the decision to implement budgeting reforms during periods of fiscal stress or decline. Performance budgeting has been shown to be difficult to carry out during such times. The use of performance information in budgeting may also grow as alternative terminologies and approaches are adopted that offer the same benefits under different nomenclature. Rational approaches to management and policymaking, such as evidence-based practice, focus attention on choosing and funding programs with evidence of effectiveness. Although it is not performance budgeting, performance information is used, and it presumably affects budget decisions that result from the process. The approach offers the appearance—and, when used correctly, substance—of added accountability while not so blatantly making policy and budget choices performance-determined.

References

Breul, J. D. (2007). GPRA—A foundation for performance budgeting. *Public Performance and Management Review, 30*(3), 312–331.

Burnett, J. (2013, November–December). Eye on the prize: States looking at goals, outcomes for budget decisions. *Capitol Ideas*. Lexington, KY: Council of State Governments. http://www.csg.org/pubs/capitolideas/2013_mar_apr/performancebasedbudgeting.aspx

Caiden, N. (1998). Public service professionalism for performance measurement and evaluation. *Public Budgeting and Finance, 18*(2), 35–52.

City of Albuquerque, New Mexico. (2014). *Budget.* http://www.cabq.gov/dfa/budget

City of Livingston, Montana. (2013). *City of Livingston, MT final budget: Fiscal year 2013–2104.* http://www.livingstonmontana.org/living/docs/FY14_Performance_Budget.pdf

Cook, T., & Lawrie, J. (2007). *Performance-based budgeting for North Carolina public transportation systems: Final report.* Raleigh: Institute for Transportation Research and Education, North Carolina State University.

Governor's Office of Planning and Budget. (2014). *Agency performance measures.* http://opb.georgia.gov/agency-performance-measures

Grizzle, G. A. (1987). Linking performance to funding decisions: What is the budgeter's roles? *Public Productivity Review, 10*(3), 33–44.

Grizzle, G. A., & Pettijohn, C. D. (2002). Implementing performance-based budgeting: A system-dynamics perspective. *Public Administration Review, 62*(1), 51–62.

Ho, A. T. (2011). PBB in American local governments: It's more than a management tool. *Public Administration Review, 71*(3), 391–401.

Ho, A. T., & Ni, A. Y. (2005). Have cities shifted to outcome-oriented performance reporting? A content analysis of city budgets. *Public Budgeting and Finance, 25*(2), 61–83.

Hou, Y, Lunsford, R. S., Sides, K. C., & Jones, K. A. (2011). State performance-based budgeting in boom and bust years: An analytical framework and survey of the states. *Public Administration Review, 71*(3), 370–388.

Jennings, E. T., & Hall, J. L. (2012). Evidence-based practice and the use of information in state agency decision making. *Journal of Public Administration Research and Theory, 22*(2), 245–266.

Jordan, M. M., & Hackbart, M. M. (1999). Performance budgeting and performance funding in the states: A state's assessment. *Public Budgeting and Finance, 19*(1), 68–88.

Joyce, P. G. (2003). *Linking performance and budgeting: Opportunities in the federal budget process.* Washington, DC: IBM Center for the Business of Government.

Joyce, P. G. (2008). Does more (or even better) information lead to better budgeting? A new perspective. *Journal of Policy Analysis and Management, 27*(4), 945–975.

Kamensky, J. M. (2013). *Performance budgeting: Texas style.* IBM Center for Business in Government. http://www.businessofgovernment.org/blog/business-government/performance-budgeting-texas-style

Kelly, J. M., & Rivenbark, W. C. (2003). *Performance budgeting for state and local government.* Armonk, NY: M. E. Sharpe.

Key, V. O. (1940). The lack of a budgetary theory. *American Political Science Review, 34*(6), 1137–1144.

Koppell, J. G. S. (2005). Pathologies of accountability: ICANN and the challenge of "multiple accountabilities disorder." *Public Administration Review, 65*(1), 94–108.

Lauth, T. (1987). Budgeting and productivity in state government: Not integrated but friendly. *Public Productivity Review, 10*(3), 21–32.

Lee, J., & Wang, X. (2009). Assessing the impact of performance-based budgeting: A comparative analysis across the United States, Taiwan, and China. *Public Administration Review, 69,* S60–S66.

Lee, R. D., Johnson, R., & Joyce, P. (2008). *Public budgeting systems.* Sudbury, MA: Jones & Bartlett.

Lu, Y. (2007). Performance budgeting: The perspective of state agencies. *Public Budgeting & Finance, 27*(4), 1–17.

Lu, Y., & Willoughby, K. (2012). Performance budgeting in the states: An assessment. *Viewpoints.* Washington, DC: IBM Center for the Business of Government. http://www.businessofgovernment.org/sites/default/files/Viewpoints_Lu.pdf

Martí, C. (2013). Performance budgeting and accrual budgeting. *Public Performance and Management Review, 37*(1), 33–58.

Mascarenhas, R. C. (1996). Searching for efficiency in the public sector: Interim evaluation of performance budgeting in New Zealand. *Public Budgeting and Finance, 16*(3), 13–27.

Melkers, J. E., & Willoughby, K. G. (2001). Budgeters' views of state performance-budgeting systems: Distinctions across branches. *Public Administration Review, 61*(1), 54–64.

Mercer, J. (2003). *Cascade performance budgeting: A guide to an effective system for integrating budget and performance information and for linking long-term goals to day-to-day activities.* John Mercer. http://strategisys.com/library/cascade_pb.pdf

Moynihan, D. P. (2006). What do we talk about when we talk about performance? Dialogue theory and performance budgeting. *Journal of Public Administration Research and Theory, 16*(2), 151–168.

Moynihan, D. P. (2008). *The dynamics of performance management: Constructing information and reform.* Washington, DC: Georgetown University Press.

National Performance Management Advisory Commission. (2010). *A performance management framework for state and local government: From measurement and reporting to managing and improving.* Chicago: Author. http://www.gfoa.org/downloads/APerformanceManagementFramework.pdf

Nevada Budget Division. (2014). *Priorities and performance based budget.* http://budget.nv.gov/PPBB/

O'Toole, D. E., & Marshall, J. (1987). Budgeting practices in local government: The state of the art. *Government Finance Review, 3*(5), 11–16.

Pattison, S. D. (2012, March 1). *Performance information: Impacts on state budgets and government management.* National Association of State Budget Officers. http://www.nasbo.org/budget-blog/performance-information-%E2%80%93-impacts-state-budgets-and-government-management

Pew Center on the States. (2009). *Trade-off time: How four states continue to deliver.* Washington DC: Pew Charitable Trusts.

Pew-MacArthur Results First Initiative. (2013, December 17). *The Pew-MacArthur Results first approach: Five simple steps to evidence-based decision making.* http://www.pewtrusts.org/our_work_detail.aspx?id=328599

Pew-MacArthur Results First Initiative. (2014a). *Results First in your state.* http://www.pewstates.org/uploadedFiles/PCS_Assets/2013/Results%20First%20In%20Your%20State%20brief.pdf

Pew-MacArthur Results First Initiative. (2014b). *State work.* http://www.pewstates.org/ projects/pew-macarthur-results-first-initiative-328069/state-work

Poister, T. H., & Streib, G. (2005). Elements of strategic planning and management in municipal government: Status after two decades. *Public Administration Review, 65*(1), 45–56.

Rivenbark, W. C. (2004). Defining performance budgeting for local government. *Popular Government, 69*(2), 27–36. http://ncinfo.iog.unc.edu/pubs/electronicversions/pg/ pgwin04/article3.pdf

Rivenbark, W. C., & Kelly, J. M. (2006). Performance budgeting in municipal government. *Public Performance and Management Review, 30*(1), 35–46.

Sallack, D., & Allen, D. N. (1987). From impact to output: Pennsylvania's Planning-Programming Budgeting System in transition. *Public Budgeting and Finance, 7*(1), 38–50.

Schick, A. (1990). Budgeting for results: Recent developments in five industrialized countries. *Public Administration Review, 50*(1), 26–34.

Simon, H. A. (1978). Rationality as process and as product of thought. *American Economic Review, 68*(2), 1–16.

Smith, J. F. (1999). The benefits and threats of PBB: An assessment of modern reform. *Public Budgeting and Finance, 19*(3), 3–15.

Sterck, M., & Scheers, B. (2006). Trends in performance budgeting in seven OECD countries. *Public Performance & Management Review, 30*(1), 47–72.

Stone, D. (2002). *Policy paradox: The art of political decision-making* (Rev. ed.). New York: Norton.

Texas State Auditor. (2012, March). *Guide to performance measure management: 2012 edition.* Austin: Texas State Auditor. http://www.sao.state.tx.us/reports/main/ 12-333.pdf

Wang, X. (2000). Performance measurement in budgeting: a study of county governments. *Public Budgeting and Finance, 20*(3), 102–118.

Wellman, M., & VanLandingham, G. (2008). Performance-based budgeting in Florida: Great expectations, more limited reality. In P. de Lancer Julnes, F. S. Berry, M. P. Aristigueta, & K. Yang (Eds.), *International handbook of practice-based performance management* (pp. 321–340). Thousand Oaks, CA: Sage.

Young, R. D. (2003, January). *Performance-based budget systems.* Los Angeles: USC Institute for Public Service and Policy Research, Public Policy and Practice.

CHAPTER TEN

MANAGING EMPLOYEES, PROGRAMS, AND ORGANIZATIONAL UNITS

How can you ensure that managers and employees focus their attention on strategic goals and objectives and that top management's priorities are driven down through the management layers to the workforce at the operating level? To what extent can you use performance measures to help direct and control the work of people in the agency so as to channel their energy and efforts toward accomplishing important organizational goals? What tools or approaches can facilitate strategic management of programs with an eye toward performance? What kinds of performance management systems are used in public and nonprofit organizations, and what kinds of performance measures can support them?

Organizational performance and management constitutes a holistic approach that requires a degree of aggregation. In practice, though, organizations consist of various parts and components. These may be structural divisions, such as organizational departments or agencies, or programmatic divisions that require the cascading of measures. *Cascading* means translating the organization-wide measures to the program level, support units or departments, and then to teams or individuals. Cascading should result in alignment across all levels of the organization. The organization alignment should be clearly visible through linking strategic goals, performance measures, and initiatives. Scorecards, discussed in chapter 8 of this book, are used to improve accountability through objective and performance measure ownership, and desired employee behaviors are incentivized with recognition and rewards. Alignment of performance measurement among these various levels, as well as linkages among them throughout the measurement process, will strengthen organizational integration and support stronger overall performance.

The performance of the organization as a whole depends on the performance of each individual, each program, and each operational division. Disaggregating performance management to these levels can be challenging. This chapter examines the use of performance measurement in an organization's most important components: its human resources, programs, and the strategic management of organizational divisions.

Performance Management Systems

In order for an agency to function effectively, managers, employees, programs, and organizational units must direct their work toward meeting targets and accomplishing objectives that are consistent with higher-level goals and objectives, top management priorities, strategic initiatives, and the agency's mission. This can be accomplished by setting more specific goals and objectives, developing operational plans and providing the wherewithal, monitoring progress and evaluating results, and taking appropriate follow-up actions that are aligned with overall organizational goals. In chapter 1, we presented a performance management framework that includes strategic planning, budgeting, management (or implementation) and evaluation, all supported by performance measurement. All of the organization's endeavors should be guided by the strategic plan, or more specifically by the strategic goals and objectives identified in that plan.

The term *performance management* refers to large-scale processes for managing the work of people and organizational units so as to maximize their effectiveness and improve organizational performance. In chapter 1, we indicated that performance management refers to the strategic daily use of performance information by managers to correct problems before they manifest in performance deficiencies. The principal role of a performance management system is to collect performance data across the organization (including all programs and divisions), and analyze and report these data, thereby ensuring that they reach users with discretion to act at key decision junctures to maintain the organization's alignment with its strategic imperatives.

Various approaches are available to facilitate performance management within the organization, whether a public agency, a local government, or a nonprofit organization. We explore a few such systems in this chapter to provide the flavor of current practice and to highlight some of the challenges posed by implementing such systems. Systems of this nature are constantly evolving, so our review is a cross-sectional snapshot of the current state of practice.

In the way of organization-wide, systematic approaches, the most common examples are Management by Objectives types of systems, which are focused directly on individual managers and employees, as well as large-scale government-wide or department-wide programs such as CompStat in New York City and CitiStat-type programs such as in Baltimore and other midsized US cities. At the federal level, we find the Program Assessment Rating Tool used by Office of Management and Budget during the George W. Bush administration to offer one systematic approach to monitoring performance, comparing performance across units, and directing performance information into the decision process via budget proposals. (Since we discuss this program in chapter 1, we do not repeat it here.) Performance monitoring systems, which focus more generally on programs or organizations, are also considered to be performance management systems (Swiss, 1991), though they are the least sophisticated of the group.

In addition to these centralized and integrated systems, there are other approaches and tools available to managers that have influenced the quest for improved performance in policymaking, planning, and implementation. Two such tools introduced in this chapter are evidence-based practice and program evaluation.

We now turn our attention to a variety of systems that facilitate the integration of performance management with the day-to-day management of personnel, programs, and organizational units. The chapter begins by introducing and comparing Management by Objectives (MBO) and performance monitoring systems as approaches to encouraging a strategic performance orientation throughout the organization.

Management by Objectives

MBO systems have been used in the private sector for over fifty years as a way of clarifying expectations for individuals' work and evaluating their performance accordingly. Peter Drucker believed that the system was useful in the private sector but would lack success in the public sector. Others, such as Joseph Wholey, disagreed and extended the model's use to the public sector by incorporating information sharing with stakeholders (Aristigueta, 2002).

MBO was introduced in the federal government by the Nixon administration and has become widespread in state and local government over the past four decades (Poister and Streib, 1995). Generally it has been found to be effective in boosting employee productivity and channeling individual efforts toward the achievement of organizational goals because it is based on three essential elements of sound personnel management: goal setting, participative decision making, and objective feedback (Rodgers & Hunter, 1992). Although the term *Management by Objectives* has not been in vogue for quite some time, MBO-type systems are in fact prevalent in the public sector, usually under other names.

MBO systems are tied to personnel appraisal processes and thus usually operate on annual cycles, although in some cases they may operate on a six-month or quarterly basis. In theory, at least, the process has four steps:

1. In negotiation with their supervisors, individual managers or employees set personal-level objectives in order to clarify shared expectations regarding their performance for the next year.
2. Subordinates and their supervisors develop action plans to identify a workable approach to achieving each of these objectives. At the same time, supervisors commit the necessary resources to ensure that these plans can be implemented.
3. Supervisors and subordinates monitor progress toward implementing plans and realizing objectives on an ongoing basis, and midcourse adjustments in strategy, resources, implementation procedures, or even the objectives themselves are made if necessary.
4. At the end of the year, the supervisor conducts the individual's annual performance appraisal, based at least in part on the accomplishment of the specified objectives. Salary increases and other decisions follow from this, and individual development plans may also be devised, if necessary.

Thus, the MBO process is designed to clarify organizational expectations for individuals' performance, motivate them to work toward accomplishing appropriate objectives, and enable them to do so effectively. For an example, we can look at an action plan developed for a deputy manager in a medium-sized local jurisdiction aimed at increasing traffic safety on city streets. The plan is associated with the following MBO objective: "To reduce the number of vehicular accidents on city streets by a minimum of 15 percent below 2015 levels, at no increase in departmental operating budgets." (Note that the objective is stated as a SMART objective, as discussed in chapter 4.) The following list, adapted from Morrisey (1976), outlines the action plan, which serves as a blueprint for undertaking a project aimed at achieving the stated objective:

Sample Action Plan

1. Determine the locations of highest incidence, and select those with the highest potential for improvement.
2. Set up an ad hoc committee (to include representatives of local citizens, traffic engineers, city planning staff, and police officers) to analyze and recommend alternative corrective actions, including education, increased surveillance, traffic control equipment, and possible rerouting of traffic.
3. Establish an information-motivation plan for police officers.
4. Inform the city council, city manager, other related departments, and the media about plans and progress.
5. Test the proposed plan in selected locations.
6. Implement the plan on a citywide basis.
7. Establish a monitoring system.
8. Evaluate initial results and modify implementation the plan accordingly after three months.

For this effort to be successful, it will be the responsibility of the city manager, the direct supervisor, to ensure the requisite resources in terms of cooperation from the participating departments.

Performance measures play a role at two stages in this MBO example. First, the action plan calls for establishing a monitoring system and using the data to evaluate initial results after three months. This monitoring system, which in all likelihood will draw on existing traffic enforcement reporting systems, will also be used after the close of the year to determine whether the expected 15 percent reduction in vehicular accidents has been accomplished. These data may be broken out by various types of accidents (e.g., single vehicle, multiple vehicle, vehicle-pedestrian) to gain a clearer understanding of the impact of this MBO initiative.

Alternatively, breaking the accident data out by contributing factors—such as mechanical failures, driver impairment, road conditions, or weather conditions—would probably be useful in targeting strategies as well as tracking results. In addition, depending on the kinds of interventions developed in this project, it may be helpful to track measures regarding patrol hours, traffic citations, seat belt checks, safety courses, traffic engineering projects, and so forth to provide further insight into the success or failure of this initiative. Thus, performance measurement plays an integral role in the MBO process.

There are several concerns with using a system like this to link individual performance to organizational goals. Let's consider a couple of the primary criticisms. First, employees will be reluctant to have their compensation tied to organizational or program performance when they perceive that such performance is beyond their control or influence. In the example, for example, driver actions and behavior is the direct cause of the accidents, and some traffic enforcement officers may have difficulty accepting responsibility for actions they do not directly control.

Some organizational goals may be subject to environmental factors beyond the control of any individual or the entire organization. For example, a major ice storm might strike with little warning, stranding motorists and leading to a considerable increase in accidents. To the extent weather patterns vary from year to year or quarter to quarter, the data may make it appear that performance was bad. In these cases, it will be necessary to construct a measurement system that controls for adverse events, perhaps by eliminating them from the performance score, or by indexing performance against that of neighboring cities to eliminate the performance reduction attributable to the adverse event. There are also low-incidence events that make MBO challenging. If we look to the field of public health, for example, one goal might be to prevent disease outbreaks. Such outbreaks are rare, and the likelihood that they would strike a given state or county in a given year are extremely low. Again, the agency takes responsibility for public health, but employees do not directly control the processes that lead to the outbreak, such as food contamination at its source in another state.

Bernard Marr (2009) indicates that implementing pay-for-performance systems in government, the public sector, and nonprofit organizations may be difficult or impossible. He also cautions that most systems that purport to reward individual-level performance actually measure completion of tasks without assessing the quality of that performance or whether it facilitated organizational performance. It may not be a good idea to base individual rewards on organizational performance for these reasons, but also because during years of fiscal cutback or restraint, there is little to no reward to allocate across employees.

Overall, MBO offers the potential to link organizational goals to individual evaluation. It is best to be able to identify individual-level performance objectives that logically map to the overall organization-level objectives. When that is done, individuals are able to take ownership of their actions as well as organizational performance. Care should be taken to develop systems that are fair, and it is essential that input from employees and managers forms the basis of a dialogue about what will be measured, how, and when, as well as how measures will translate into individual recognition, rewards, or penalties (when necessary).

Performance Monitoring Systems

At one level, performance monitoring is what this whole book is about: tracking key sets of performance measures over time to gauge progress and evaluate the results of public and nonprofit programs and activities. More specifically, performance monitoring systems constitute performance management systems designed to direct and control organizational entities, again by clarifying expectations and evaluating results based on agreed-on objective measures. Unlike MBO systems, performance monitoring systems do not focus so directly on the performance of individual managers and employees.

Although both MBO and performance monitoring systems seek to enhance performance through establishing clear goals and objective feedback, there are some key differences between these two approaches, as summarized in table 10.1 (adapted from Swiss, 1991).

The most crucial difference between these systems is in their respective focus: whereas MBO systems focus attention directly on the performance of individual managers and employees, performance monitoring systems formally address the performance of programs or organizational units. Thus, MBO is a much more personalized process, bringing incentives to bear directly on individuals, whereas with performance monitoring processes, the incentives tend to be spread more diffusely over organizational entities. In terms of the overall management framework, MBO systems are usually rooted in personnel systems, whereas performance monitoring is usually carried out as part of strategic management, program management, or operations management. And these systems are often centralized in agencies such as the Office of Management and Budget (OMB) at the federal level, or state budget offices.

TABLE 10.1 KEY CHARACTERISTICS OF PURE MBO AND PERFORMANCE MONITORING SYSTEMS

Dimension	MBO Systems	Performance Monitoring Systems
Principal Focus	Individual managers and employees	Programs or organizational units
Orientation	Usually projects	Ongoing programs or continuing operations
Goal Setting	Face-to-face negotiations	Often unilateral, based on past performance
Performance Measures	Outputs and immediate outcomes, along with quality and productivity	Outcomes emphasized, along with quality and customer service
Changes in Measures	Frequent changes as objectives change	Usually continuing measures with only rare changes
Data Collection and Monitoring	Done by individual managers; reviewed with supervisors	Done by staff and distributed in regular reports

Based on the principle of participative goal setting, MBO objectives are usually negotiated in face-to-face meetings between pairs of supervisors and subordinates, often cascading from the executive level down to first-line supervisors, whereas higher-level management may set targets for performance monitoring systems unilaterally. In addition, whereas performance monitoring systems are usually oriented to ongoing programs, service delivery, or operations, MBO systems often focus on a changing mix of projects or specific one-time initiatives. Thus, MBO and performance monitoring represent two different approaches to performance management. It should be understood, however, that such pure versions of these systems are not always found in practice and that elements of these two approaches are often combined in hybrid systems.

Measures for Performance Management Systems

Measurement is a particularly interesting phenomenon with respect to the concept of performance management because the measures are intended to have an impact on behavior and results. Although researchers are usually interested in nonreactive measures, performance measures have a more overt purpose in monitoring systems. Performance measures are designed to track performance, and in performance management systems, they are used to provide feedback on performance in real time. For both

MBO and performance monitoring systems, this feedback—usually in conjunction with targets or specific objectives—is designed to focus managers' and employees' efforts and to motivate them to work "harder and smarter" to accomplish organizational objectives. These systems are predicated on the idea that people's intentions, decisions, behavior, and performance will be influenced by the performance data and how they are used.

Both approaches are usually considered to be outcome oriented, but because MBO systems are so directly focused on the job performance of individuals, they often emphasize output measures as opposed to true effectiveness measures. Managers in public and nonprofit organizations often resist the idea of being held personally accountable for real outcomes because they have relatively little control over them. Thus, MBO systems often use output measures, and perhaps some immediate outcome measures, along with quality indicators and productivity measures over which managers typically have more control. Performance monitoring systems, in contrast, because they are less personalized, often emphasize real outcomes along with efficiency, productivity, and quality indicators and, especially, measures of customer satisfaction.

One basic difference between these two approaches to measurement is that because MBO systems are often project oriented, with a varying mix of initiatives in the pipeline at any one time, the measures used to evaluate a manager's performance tend to change frequently over time. In contrast, performance monitoring systems tend to focus on ongoing programs, service delivery systems, and operations, and therefore the measures used to track performance are fairly constant, allowing trend analysis over time. Finally, the measures used to assess individuals' performance in MBO systems are usually observed or collected by those individuals themselves and reported to their supervisors for the purpose of performance appraisal, whereas performance monitoring data are usually collected by other staff who are assigned to maintain the system and report out the data.

MBO Measures

The measures used to evaluate performance in MBO systems address different kinds of issues because those systems often specify a variety of objectives. During any given MBO cycle, an individual manager is likely to be working on a mix of objectives, some of which may well call for improving the performance of ongoing programs or operations, and in fact the appropriate measures for these kinds of objectives may well be supplied by ongoing performance monitoring systems. In addition, though, managers often specify objectives that focus on problem solving, troubleshooting particular issues, implementing new projects, undertaking special initiatives, or engaging in self-development activities intended to strengthen work-related knowledge and skills. For the most part, the measures defined to evaluate performance on these kinds of objectives will be substantively different from those tracking ongoing programs or activities, and they are likely to be shorter-term indicators that will be replaced by others in subsequent MBO cycles.

In some cases, MBO systems focus largely on ongoing responsibilities and employ continuous measures to track the performance of individual managers. For example, table 10.2 shows the first page of numerous specific objectives established for one fiscal year for the commander of the Planning and Research Bureau of the Phoenix, Arizona, police department. The objectives are clustered in different areas of responsibility and are weighted by their relative importance. This example is also notable for its specification of maximum attainment, target levels, and minimum acceptable levels of performance. With respect to the first objective, regarding the processing of certain statistical reports, for instance, the target level is to process 95 percent of these reports before the deadline, the minimum level is set at 90 percent, and the maximum is 100 percent.

Most of the measures in this particular example are expressed as percentages or raw numbers. They are fairly typical performance indicators calibrated in scale variables that can be evaluated against target levels, and most of them can probably be tracked as going up or down over time because they concern ongoing responsibilities of this particular officer. However, one of these objectives, concerning the administration of an internal employee survey within the department, sets alternative dates as targets, and the indicator is operationalized as a discrete measure of whether a given target date is attained. It is also interesting to note that all the objectives in this example relate to outputs or quality indicators, not to outcomes or effectiveness measures.

Individual and Programmatic Performance Management

Performance measures are often essential to the effectiveness of performance management systems designed to direct and control the work of

TABLE 10.2 PERFORMANCE ACHIEVEMENT PROGRAM: CITY OF PHOENIX

PERFORMANCE ACHIEVEMENT PROGRAM PERFORMANCE PROGRAM _____ FY

Signature of Employee | Signature of Supervisor

1995/96		Planning and Research Bureau Commander	06/09/95
FY	Name	Position	Date

Responsibilities	Priority	Results	Observable Standards Min./Target/Max.	Weight	Responsible Person
Basic Police Services	21	1A. Percentage of requests for statistical reports received from and processed for line bureaus and precincts before deadline	90/95/100	5	Sergeants Henderson and Pitzer
		1B. Number of police facility inspections to identify problems that could reduce the building's life expectancy	2/4/64	4	Mr. Brueggeman
		1C. Percentage of on-site inspections during significant repairs or possible disruptive construction projects (power test)	90/95/100	5	Mr. Brueggeman
		1D. Percentage of timely notifications issued to the user bureau of an upcoming warranty expiration	90/98/100	4	Mr. Brueggeman
		1E. Number of facilities examined for major improvements or renovations; plan assistance for the improvement (example: academy range)	2/3/4	3	Mr. Brueggeman
Employee Safety, Morale, Effectiveness	12	2A. To receive feedback as to bureau service levels, meet with users _____ times	3/5/7	3	Commander Buchanan
		2B. Administer internal bureau Employee Morale/ Satisfaction Survey by _____	06-01/05-01/04-01		Sergeant Henderson
		2C. Conduct _____ quality circle meetings within the bureau involving representation from all employee levels to improve bureau operations	4/5/6	4	Sergeant Fisher

Source: City of Phoenix (2001). Reprinted with permission.

people in an organization and to focus their attention and efforts on higher-level goals and objectives. Governmental and nonprofit agencies use both MBO-type performance management systems and performance monitoring systems to do this. Monitoring systems are essentially measurement systems that focus on the performance of agencies, divisions, work units, or programs, whereas MBO-type systems focus on the performance of individual managers and, in some cases, individual employees. MBO systems often make use of data drawn from performance monitoring systems, but they may also use a number of other discrete one-time indicators of success that are not monitored on an ongoing basis.

Because MBO systems set up personal-level goals for individuals, managers and staff working in these systems often tend to resist including real outcome measures because the outcomes may be largely beyond their control. Because managers are generally considered to have more control over the quantity and quality of services produced, as well as over internal operating efficiency and productivity, MBO systems often emphasize measures of output, efficiency, quality, and productivity more than outcome measures. Because performance monitoring systems are less personalized, they are more likely to emphasize true effectiveness measures.

MBO systems and performance monitoring systems are both intended to have a direct impact on the performance of managers, employees, organizational divisions, and work units. However, for this to work in practice, the performance measures must be perceived as legitimate. This means that to some degree at least, managers and employees need to understand the measures, agree that they are appropriate, and have confidence in the reliability of the performance data that will be used to assess their performance. Thus, building ownership of the measures through participation in the process of designing them, or "selling" them in a convincing manner after the fact, is of critical importance. It is also essential that the integrity of the data be maintained so that participants in the process know that the results are fair.

Individual Targets and Actual Performance: Community Disaster Education Program

Some MBO-type performance management systems prorate targets over the course of a year and then track progress on a quarterly or monthly basis. For example, local chapters of the American Red Cross conduct community disaster education (CDE) programs through arrangements with public and private schools in their service areas, primarily using volunteer instructors. In one local chapter, which uses an MBO approach, the director of this program has a number of individual objectives she is expected to achieve during the fiscal year, including such items as the following:

- Launch professional development training for teachers in CDE.
- Institute Red Cross safe-schools training packages in schools.
- Initiate a new CDE training program, and recruit five volunteer instructors.
- Upgrade the CDE curriculum.
- Launch the Masters of Disaster curriculum kits.
- Train twenty-two thousand youth in CDE.
- Continue to develop and implement program outcome measures.

Most of these objectives are stated in general terms, and there is not a clear indication of precisely what will constitute success in accomplishing them. Only two of them have established target levels, but others could be reformulated as SMART (specific, measurable, ambitious, realistic, and time-bound) objectives. Performance on others will be determined based on periodic reviews of progress in activity intended to realize the objectives; in the director's annual performance evaluation, judgments will have to be made by her supervisor regarding whether she accomplished certain of these objectives. Thus, it is not surprising that one of the director's objectives is to "continue to develop and implement program outcome measures."

In contrast, the objective to train twenty-two thousand youth in CDE programs can be monitored directly. As shown in figure 10.1, the overall number of youth targeted to receive this training has been prorated over the course of the twelve-month fiscal year, based in part on seasonal patterns in this activity in prior years, as well as on the director's understanding of the feasibility of training particular numbers of youth in different months. Thus, this outcome measure can be tracked on a monthly basis and compared against the monthly targets in order to track her progress in reaching the target. Although the director has fallen slightly short of the targets in November and December, overall she is running slightly ahead of the targets over the first eight months of the fiscal year. However, the targets for March through June appear to be quite ambitious, so it remains to be seen whether the overall target of twenty-two thousand youth trained will be met by the end of the fiscal year.

FIGURE 10.1 NUMBER OF YOUTH TRAINED IN COMMUNITY DISASTER EDUCATION PROGRAMS

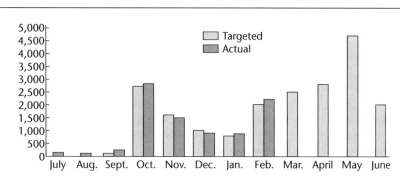

Measures for Monitoring Systems

For the most part, performance monitoring systems track measures that pertain to ongoing programs, service delivery systems, and activities at regular intervals of time. Whereas MBO systems often include a mix of continuous measures along with discrete indicators of one-time efforts (e.g., the satisfactory completion of a particular project), performance monitoring systems focus exclusively on measures of recurring phenomena, such as the number of lane-miles of highway resurfaced per week or the percentage of clients placed in competitive employment each month. Whereas MBO-type performance management systems typically draw on information from performance measurement systems as well as a number of other sources, performance monitoring systems actually constitute measurement systems.

For example, cities like Phoenix use monitoring systems to track the performance of each operating department and major program: community and economic development, fire protection, housing, human services, parks and recreation, police, and public transit—on a variety of indicators on a monthly basis. Each month, the performance data are presented in the City Manager's Executive Report, which states the overall goal of each department, identifies the key services provided, and affords data on a variety of performance indicators, most often displayed graphically and emphasizing comparisons over time.

Figure 10.2 presents excerpts of the performance data for Phoenix's neighborhood services program, taken from a sample edition of the City

FIGURE 10.2 NEIGHBORHOOD SERVICES PROGRAM: CITY OF PHOENIX

Neighborhood Services

Program Goal

To preserve and improve the physical, social, and economic health of Phoenix neighborhoods, support neighborhood self-reliance, and enhance the quality of life of residents through community-based problem-solving, neighborhood-oriented services, and public/private cooperation.

Key Services

Neighborhood Preservation/Code Enforcement, Housing Rehabilitation, Lead Hazard Control Program, Historic Preservation, Neighborhood Coordination, Community Development Block Grant Program, Graffiti Abatement, Neighborhood Fight Back Program, Neighborhood Economic Development, Neighborhood Initiative Area/Redevelopment Area Plan Implementation.

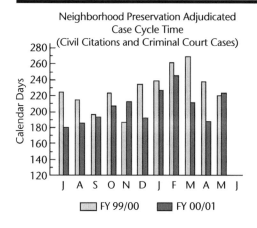

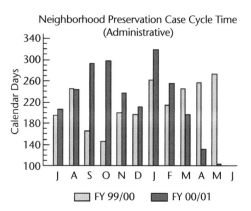

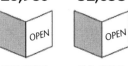

Cases Opened and Closed

1999-00 (Year-to-Date)	2000-01 (Year-to-Date)
26,986	32,658
OPEN	OPEN
27,311	30,823
CLOSED	CLOSED

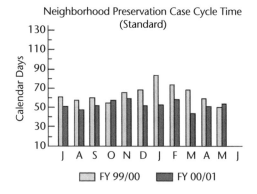

FIGURE 10.2 (CONTINUED)

Neighborhood Services — continued

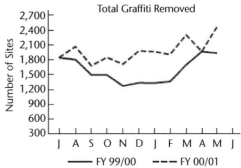

Total Graffiti Removed

— FY 99/00   - - - FY 00/01

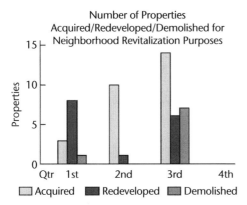

Number of Properties Acquired/Redeveloped/Demolished for Neighborhood Revitalization Purposes

☐ Acquired   ■ Redeveloped   ▨ Demolished

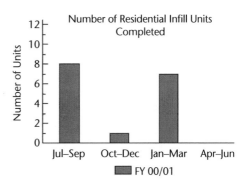

Number of Residential Infill Units Completed

■ FY 00/01

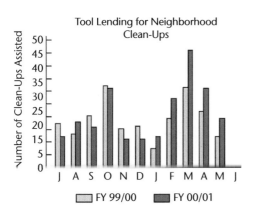

Tool Lending for Neighborhood Clean-Ups

☐ FY 99/00   ■ FY 00/01

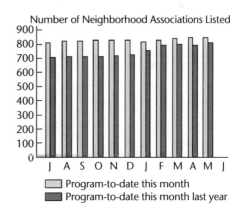

Number of Neighborhood Associations Listed

☐ Program-to-date this month
■ Program-to-date this month last year

FIGURE 10.2 (CONTINUED)

Neighborhood Services — continued

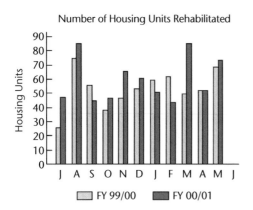

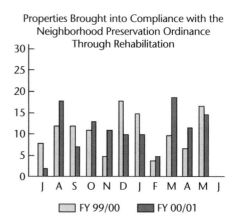

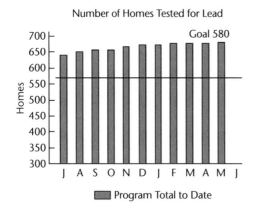

Manager's Executive Report. All of these measures are presented on a rolling twelve-month basis (with May therefore the most recent month with data available); the report also shows data from the previous year to provide more of a baseline and to facilitate comparing the current month's performance against the same month in the prior year, which is particularly relevant for measures that exhibit significant seasonal variation, such as the number of neighborhood cleanup efforts assisted.

As we might expect, many of these indicators tracked on a monthly basis are output measures, such as the number of residential infill units completed or the number of properties acquired, redeveloped, or demolished for revitalization purposes. Others focus on service quality, such as the cycle time for adjudicating or administering neighborhood preservation cases in terms of average calendar days. A couple of outcome measures are also incorporated into this portion of the report. For instance, whereas the number of housing units rehabilitated is an output measure, the number of properties brought into compliance with the neighborhood preservation ordinance is an outcome indicator. Similarly, whereas the number of homes tested for lead is an output indicator, the number of homes with lead hazards that were remediated is a measure of outcome.

Performance Monitoring: The Compass

Many public agencies use performance monitoring systems as management tools. The Compass system of the New Mexico State Highway and Transportation Department (NMSH&TD) constitutes a prototypical case in point. The Compass incorporates seventeen customer-focused results, and there is at least one performance measure for each result, with a total of eighty-three measures at present. Whenever possible, the measures have been chosen on the basis of available data in order to minimize the additional burden of data collection as well as to facilitate the analysis of trends back over time with archival data. However, as weaknesses in some of the indicators have become apparent, the measures have been revised to be more useful.

The seventeen results tracked by the Compass range from a stable contract letting schedule, adequate funding and prudent management of resources, and timely completion of projects, through smooth roads, access to divided highways, and safe transportation systems, to less traffic congestion and air pollution, increased transportation alternatives, and economic benefits to the state. Each result has an assigned "result driver," a higher-level manager who is responsible for managing that function and improving performance in that area. Each individual performance measure also has a measurement driver, assisted in some cases by a measurement team, who is responsible for maintaining the integrity of the data.

The Compass was initiated in 1996, and for four years, it constituted the department's strategic agenda. NMSH&TD has since developed a formal strategic plan; the bureaus and other operating units develop supportive action plans, all tied to Compass results and measures. However, the top management team still considers the Compass the main driving force in the department. Thus, a group of one hundred or so departmental managers—the executive team, division directors, district engineers, and middle-management "trailblazers"—meet quarterly to review the Compass. They conduct a detailed analysis of all eighty-three performance measures to assess how well each area is performing, identify problems and emerging issues, and discuss how to improve performance in various areas. NMSH&TD officials credit their use of the performance measures monitored by the Compass with significant improvements in traffic safety and decreases in traffic congestion and deficient highways over the past five years.

Compstat, CitiStat, and Similar Performance Management Systems

There has been a growing trend among local governments to pay closer attention to performance at the department, unit, or program level. New York City Police commissioner William J. Bratton adopted CompStat (Comparative Statistics) as a department-wide accountability system to monitor, map, and measure crime at the precinct level to identify particular problems; weekly meetings between police department executives and precinct commanders provide forums in which problems are discussed and strategies and approaches to problem solving are presented and adopted. Table 10.3 offers an excerpt from a weekly citywide CompStat report that reveals crimes by type and trends over time. Precinct-level reports offer similar comparisons.

Variations of the CompStat system have been replicated by other New York City departments, as well as departments in other governmental units around the world. Importantly, these systems seek to integrate the broad strategy of an entire organization with the individual units that comprise it. They are effective because they orient management functions around strategic performance goals and focus management attention on spots where performance is falling behind in key performance measures. The system relies heavily on current and reliable performance data to shape daily decisions.

One particularly fascinating model that mirrors the CompStat approach is the City of Seoul, Korea, OASIS system (oasis.seoul.go.kr). OASIS was adopted by the Seoul Metropolitan Government during the administration of former Mayor Oh Se-hoon. OASIS combines e-government, citizen participation, analysis, and action through a multitiered approach intended to garner improved performance through citizen trust in government and increased satisfaction and quality of life. Although it is not

TABLE 10.3 EXCERPT FROM WEEKLY NEW YORK CITY COMPSTAT REPORT, MARCH 16, 2014

Crime Complaints

	Week to Date			28 Day			Year to Date*			2 Year	13 Year	21 Year
	2014	2013	%Chg	2014	2013	%Chg	2014	2013	%Chg	%Chg	%Chg (2001)	%Chg (1993)
Murder	7	4	75.0	13	22	−40.9	53	62	−14.5	−32.1	−61.0	−86.6
Rape	25	37	−32.4	93	122	−23.8	254	285	−10.9	−11.8	−27.6	−58.7
Robbery	238	297	−19.9	1,050	1,133	−7.3	3,243	3,526	−8.0	−15.6	−40.0	−81.3
FeL Assault	327	363	−9.9	1,316	1,303	1.0	3,693	3,516	5.0	7.7	−13.5	−47.7
Burglary	287	306	−6.2	1,154	1,187	−2.8	3,283	3,391	−3.2	−11.3	−50.0	−83.7
Gr. Larceny	751	756	−0.7	2,944	3,034	−3.0	8,006	8,274	−3.2	0.3	−10.7	−48.1
G.L.A.	129	106	21.7	509	435	17.0	1,372	1,229	11.6	−4.8	−76.7	−94.0
TOTAL	*1,764*	*1,869*	*−5.62*	*7,079*	*7,236*	*−2.17*	*19,904*	*20,283*	*−1.87*	*−4.12*	*−36.96*	*−76.31*
Transit	30	41	−26.8	149	154	−3.2	471	509	−7.5	−19.2	−38.4	***.*
Housing	78	92	−15.2	340	317	7.3	946	899	5.2	6.5	−18.3	***.*
Petit Larceny	1,440	1,495	−3.7	5,652	5,719	−1.2	15,143	15,300	−1.0	−4.7	***.*	***.*
Misd. Assault	856	808	5.9	3,258	3,062	6.4	8,249	8,130	1.5	−6.1	***.*	***.*
Misd. Sex Crimes	57	64	−10.9	193	191	1.0	500	520	−3.8	−11.8	***.*	***.*
Shooting Vic.	38	16	137.5	76	60	26.7	191	203	−5.9	−28.2	−33.4	−82.4
Shooting Inc.	31	15	106.7	65	53	22.6	169	176	−4.0	−24.9	−36.0	−83.0

Note: Explanation of asterisks omitted from the original document.

Source: Compstat Citywide Report Covering the Week 3/10/2014 through 3/16/2014, vol. 21, no. 11, http://www.nyc.gov/html/nypd/downloads/pdf/crime_statistics/cscity.pdf.

formally a performance monitoring system, OASIS takes citizen ideas and suggestions that are clearly related to overall government performance. The system takes in ideas through a web-based portal—as mundane and simple as sidewalk cracks destroying high-heeled shoes—and vets them through online citizen votes and online discussion by bloggers. Ideas that make it through the voting stage and the blogging discussion are then forwarded to the government research think tank for evaluation, including cost-benefit analysis. Certainly performance information is collected and considered during this process to the extent it is available. The result is a recommendation to the mayor.

Recommendations are reviewed during monthly televised sessions where the mayor takes decisive action on the recommendation. Not all ideas are approved, and not all action is taken at the recommended level, but citizens feel that they have a role to play in government, that their voices matter, and the result is a feeling of increased satisfaction and trust.

Systems like this offer a glimpse of the future for performance monitoring systems. They conceptualize performance in a way that goes beyond tracking daily outputs and yearly outcomes to get to the heart of what citizens care about. This system does not replace traditional performance monitoring systems; they are up and running in city departments at a magnitude that would startle most municipal leaders in the United States. Transportation system performance is tracked in real time in a command-center type of environment. Call center performance is tracked on key performance indicators on an ongoing basis, right down to the individual level, and displayed on screens in the call center in real time. But OASIS tackles a dimension of performance that is often overlooked yet is at the very heart of democratic systems: aspects of government services that affect and frustrate citizens daily.

Taking lessons from other large-scale municipal performance management systems, CitiStat provides a citywide statistical performance monitoring framework. CitiStat, the original city "stat" program, was launched in Baltimore, Maryland, in 1999. The program was modeled after CompStat by initiating regular meetings with managers responsible not only for police services but for all municipal functions. While known commonly as CitiStat programs, these approaches are also referred to as "Performance-Stat" systems or approaches (Behn, 2008). The system was designed to foster accountability by requiring agencies to provide CitiStat analysts with performance data. Then, during regular meetings with the mayor's office, each agency is required to identify, acknowledge, and respond to performance at levels below expectation with targeted solutions. In large part, these programs work under the philosophy of the old adage that "the squeaky wheel gets the grease," meaning that problem spots are warranted attention and smooth-functioning components are left alone so as not to disrupt strong performance.

Central to the success of CitiStat is the formation of a core group of performance-based management analysts charged with monitoring, and continually improving, the quality of services provided by the City of Baltimore. Their charge extends to evaluating policies and procedures used by city departments to deliver services. These analysts examine data and identify areas in need of improvement. Each city agency participates in a strictly structured presentation format; they must be prepared to answer any question that the mayor or a cabinet member raises. The nature of the CitiStat model is such that it emphasizes multiple dimensions of performance simultaneously; hierarchical control, or controllability (Koppell, 2005) is achieved through the regular meetings, and the substantive focus of those meetings on performance addresses the accountability dimension of responsiveness. A quick glance at Baltimore's success with CitiStat explains why the model has been adopted by cities all around the world (http://www.baltimorecity.gov/Government/AgenciesDepartments/CitiStat/LearnaboutCitiStat/Highlights.aspx):

Baltimore CitiStat Performance Results

> *Year 1:* CitiStat helps the City of Baltimore save $13.2 million, including $6 million in overtime pay.

> *Year 3:* Overtime is reduced by 40 percent; absenteeism is reduced by 50 percent in some agencies.

> *Year 4:* CitiStat saves the City of Baltimore over $100 million.

> *Year 5:* CitiStat receives the Harvard Innovation in Government Award.

> *Year 7:* CitiStat saves the City of Baltimore $350 million.

> *2014:* The CitiStat approach has become institutionalized. The model covers broad multiagency goals such as keeping Baltimore clean. CitiStat has been incorporated into the budgeting process to hold recipients of city funds accountable for their performance. Control and accountability are ensured by employee knowledge that subpar performance levels will be addressed at CitiStat meetings.

The city is open and transparent about department performance. Reports are made available to the public through an online portal. (Reports are available at https://data.baltimorecity.gov/browse?q=CitiStat&sortBy=relevance.) Table 10.4, from Baltimore's parking management program, offers a simple example of the format of CitiStat reports.

TABLE 10.4 BALTIMORE CITISTAT REPORT: PARKING MANAGEMENT PROGRAM

Last Five Two-Week Periods (last ten weeks)

| Two-Week Reporting Periods | Start Date | 9/28/13 | 10/12/13 | 10/26/13 | 11/9/13 | 11/23/13 | Year-to-Date | | | | |
| | End Date | 10/11/13 | 10/25/13 | 11/8/13 | 11/22/13 | 12/6/13 | Average | Minimum | Maximum | Fiscal Year to Date | Periods |
		14.08	14.09	14.10	14.11	14.12	(year-to-date stats as of most recent two-week period)				
Dollars collected from Multi-Space Parking Meter program		$422,494	$419,843	$422,741	$432,839	$361,664	$423,010	$361,664	$445,761	$5,076,121	12
Number of residential permit parking permits issued/renewed		961	946	1,456	522	826	937	522	1,456	11,247	12
Number of vehicles parked in city-owned or st facility/space		119,099	98,674	106,725	105,891	86,634	106,922	82,423	167,347	1,283,069	12
Number of reserved residential handicap permits issued/renewed		16	12	5	14	11	11	5	16	134	12
Number of reserved residential handicap permits/spaces removed after investigation		10	1	3	3	4	4	1	10	50	12

Source: https://data.baltimorecity.gov/CitiStat/CitiStat-DOT-121313/t9yj-j28x, page 7.

These programs offer examples of what the Center for American Progress refers to as governing by the numbers—a trend in public sector management that focuses management attention on performance in areas of strategic focus or concern (Esty & Rushing, 2007). Central to their success is monitoring of key indicators, analysis and breakout by units, and identification of problems, areas of poor performance, or trends out of sync with expectations. By highlighting problems, such systems are able to reorient management attention to correct deficiencies immediately to limit potential damage.

While a number of cities and large departments have adopted CitiStat-like programs that are similar in form and function, there are important qualitative differences at work in such systems, particularly with respect to management and leadership style. The Baltimore example is very confrontational—almost to the point of the mayor or mayor's executive leadership team taking the part of frustrated citizens demanding improvement. Other cities administer their programs in a more collegial and collaborative fashion, such as that of Providence, Rhode Island.

Like most other performance management systems or approaches, the key to success is to first determine the purpose for which the system is being adopted. The purpose frames the approach and shapes the selection of measures, the frequency of measurement and so on. Behn (2008, p. 202) provides a list of eight steps that leaders of the adopting agency or government need to follow:

1. Specify the performance purpose they hope to achieve by using the strategy.
2. Determine what performance data will be collected and analyzed.
3. Build administrative capacity by allocating staff to be responsible for the analysis function.
4. Assemble necessary infrastructure.
5. Determine how they will conduct leadership meetings.
6. Assemble the necessary operational capacity.
7. Create an explicit mechanism to follow up on any problems that have been identified, solutions that have been proposed, and decisions made at those meetings.
8. Carefully think through how to adapt features of other Performance-Stat systems to their own purpose and situation.

The importance of purpose should be clear. It shapes every decision about the structure and operation of the system. As with many other policy or program adoptions, replication is often the goal. Managers, mayors, and other leaders see an example like Baltimore and want to adopt the approach. Bardach (2004) tells us that there are three things that can be done with someone else's idea: adopt it (which is akin to replication), adapt it (meaning that key features are preserved but adaptations are made to better suit it to local context and purpose), or be inspired by it (which means that a completely new, and potentially better, approach might be inspired by these systems). Whatever the case, it is almost always easier to adopt but wiser to adapt. Similar issues are experienced in another tool that managers use to manage programs—evidence-based practice.

Evidence-Based Practice

The use of evidence-based practice as an approach to choosing programs, policies, and practices has become commonplace in governance as a way to preemptively ensure performance, and thus accountability. By picking programs that have already been shown to work in other implementing environments, managers limit the level of risk they incur from trying new or untested programs, ensuring greater returns on investment. In the way of program management, evidence-based practice offers managers a tool for selecting high-performing strategies before or during implementation. Following on the lessons of CitiStat, evidence-based practice might be employed when a performance problem is identified during regular monitoring. Managers could use the evidence-based practice approach to select a proposed solution to introduce during monthly management meetings with the mayor. Like most other tools, there are limitations and criticisms to evidence-based practice as well. Among them are the potential to stifle innovation, the homogenization of public services across places, and concerns resulting from disagreement about what constitutes evidence.

As a subset of the field of best practices (Hall & Jennings, 2008), evidence-based practice is subject to the flawed interpretation that it is a mechanism for identifying the best possible way to do something. That it is not. Rather, it examines the available evidence to recommend a strategy or approach—a mechanism, if you will—that brings about the greatest level of some specified outcome. The outcome of choice is subjective, not universally accepted, and remains within the purview of program administrators. One program might emphasize efficiency, for example, while another emphasizes effectiveness. Evidence-based practice could easily lead to different recommended approaches for each of these implementation settings.

Evidence-based practice can be used systematically at the highest levels. For example, in Oregon, the legislature passed a law requiring all agencies to expend their program budgets on evidence-based practices. It can also be used within divisions or programs (where resources are sufficient) as a method of coping with bounded rationality. Much like policy analysis, the use of evidence-based practice requires establishing a set of values and criteria, searching for a set of practices intended to address the stated problem, collecting evidence on the effectiveness of each practice relative to the selected criteria, and adopting the alternative that results in the highest expected outcome, allowing for sensitivity to weighting across the identified criteria. It is an approach for organizing information, and like all other rational approaches, it will be limited by time and resources to continue the search. Most managers will attenuate their search when little new information is emerging.

Jennings and Hall (2012) reveal considerable differences in the extent to which scientific information is weighed among possible sources of information across different areas of public policy practice. This, of course, results partly from a lack of evidence in some fields (such as economic development) that do not present themselves readily for experimental research and partly from differences in opinion about what types of information are important in making policy decisions. For example, in areas where the questions are mostly instrumental—about how to achieve an already agreed-on goal—evidence may be weighted very heavily. In areas where questions are mostly political—about what should be done—values and ideology may dominate the policy debate. Managers can draw on evidence-based practice at all levels of governance from the legislature, where it can be used to influence broad policy action, to programs and departmental divisions where it can influence the adoption of standard operating procedures or approaches to implementing street-level practices that most directly affect citizens on a daily basis.

Let's look more closely at Oregon's case. Senate bill 267, now ORS section 182.525, not only mandates the use of agency resources on evidence-based practices but calls for agency performance assessment in their fulfillment of this requirement and links that performance to subsequent appropriations. Agencies must spend at least 75 percent of state funds received for programs on evidence-based programs. Agencies then submit biennial reports that delineate programs, the percentage of state funds expended on evidence-based programs, the percentage of federal or other funds expended on evidence-based programs, and a description of agency efforts to meet the requirements. The law defines evidence-based programs as those that incorporate significant and relevant practices based on scientifically based research and that are cost effective. It defines *scientifically based research* as follows:

> Scientifically based research means research that obtains reliable and valid knowledge by:
>
> (a) Employing systematic, empirical methods that draw on observation or experiment
> (b) Involving rigorous data analyses that are adequate to test the stated hypotheses and justify the general conclusions drawn
> (c) Relying on measurements or observational methods that provide reliable and valid data across evaluators and observers, across multiple measurements and observations and across studies by the same or different investigators. (ORS sec. 182.515)

This strict law was implemented incrementally, allowing agencies time to cope with the unfunded mandate. But it does not discuss or offer any interpretation regarding differences in the quality or availability of evidence across fields of practice. Oregon offers an interesting example of a state preemptively institutionalizing high-performance programs.

Program Evaluation

Evidence-based practice is a tool most suited for selecting a practice when the desired end is known or selecting a particular management or implementation strategy within the bounds of bureaucratic discretion. Program evaluation is a management tool used at the conclusion of the performance management cycle to assess program effectiveness and causality. In other words, program evaluation seeks to determine the extent to which the observed effects on selected outcomes are attributable to the program itself. Although performance measurement may be a more cost-effective alternative to program evaluation, particularly for answering the question, "What happened?" it does not allow users to address the deeper question: "Why did these results occur?" Other differences have been documented as well.

Program evaluation has many similarities to performance measurement, but seven key differences have been identified (McDavid, Huse, & Hawthorn, 2013, p. 324):

1. Program evaluations are episodic; performance measures are designed and implemented with the intention of providing ongoing monitoring.
2. Program evaluations are related to issues posed by stakeholders' (broadly defined) interests in a program. Performance measurement systems are intended to be more general information gathering and dissemination mechanisms.
3. Program evaluation requires at least partially customized measures and lines of evidence. Performance measures tend to rely heavily on data gathered through routinized processes.
4. Program evaluations are intended to determine the causal attributes of the actual outcomes of a program. Whereas in performance measurement attribution is generally assumed.
5. Program evaluation requires targeted resources. Performance measurement is usually part of a program or organizational infrastructure.
6. Program managers are not usually included in evaluation. In performance measurement program managers are key players in developing and reporting of results.
7. Program evaluation requires a statement of the intended purpose. Use of performance measurement will evolve over time to reflect needs and priorities.

Program evaluation has many similarities to performance measurement but also a number of key differences. In particular, program evaluation focuses on the causality between the program and outcomes of interest. To do this, it relies on evaluation methods and research designs to determine causation, which means greater cost and caution than one finds in routine performance measurement.

There are at least three advantages to integrating program evaluation with performance measurement in a performance management strategy:

• Program evaluation may be used to validate the measures and ensure overall data quality (Aristigueta, 1999).

- The data generated during performance measurement may be useful for the analysis conducted during program evaluation.
- Program evaluation is able to statistically validate the program theory expressed in the logic model.

These tools are widely used approaches to managing people, programs, and organizational units. Reflecting on the performance management model we presented in chapter 1, it should be clear that these approaches will be most effective when they are integrated carefully with the organization's strategic approach to performance management. Efforts to eliminate redundancy should be made, and the tools should be integrated into the overall management strategy rather than added as strictly symbolic layers of reform. This requires understanding the relevant role each tool can play. Whereas evidence-based practice is a tool most suited for selecting a practice when the desired end is known or selecting a particular management or implementation strategy within the bounds of bureaucratic discretion, program evaluation is a management tool that can assist in program performance management after a full implementation cycle by establishing or validating causal relationships. Program evaluation seeks to determine the extent to which the observed effects on selected outcomes are attributable to the program itself.

There are two advantages to integrating program evaluation with performance measurement in a performance management strategy. First, the data generated during performance measurement may be useful for the analysis conducted during program evaluation. Second, program evaluation is able to statistically validate the program theory expressed in the logic model. Understanding these relationships may lead to discoveries that require changing strategies or approaches in order to bring program implementation into conformity with the observed reality. Where program evaluation reveals that reality differs from the hypothetical relationships expressed in the program logic model, the model must be revised, which may alter the selection of performance measures and measurement strategy.

Understanding these relationships may lead to discoveries that require changing strategies or approaches in order to bring program implementation into conformity with the observed reality. Where program evaluation reveals that reality differs from the hypothetical relationships expressed in the program logic model, the model must be revised, which may in turn alter the selection of performance measures and measurement strategy.

References

Aristigueta, M. (1999). *Managing for results in states.* Westport, CT: Quorum Books.

Aristigueta, P. (2002). Reinventing government: Managing for results. *Public Administration Quarterly, 26,* 147–173.

Bardach, E. (2004). Presidential address—The extrapolation problem: How can we learn from the experience of others? *Journal of Policy Analysis and Management, 23,* 205–220.

Behn, R. D. (2008). Designing PerformanceStat: Or what are the key strategic choices that a jurisdiction or agency must make when adapting the CompStat/CitiStat class of performance strategies? *Public Performance and Management Review, 32,* 206–235.

City of Phoenix. (2001). *City manager's executive report: June 2001.* Phoenix: Author.

Esty, D. C., & Rushing, R. (2007). *Governing by the numbers: The promise of data-driven policymaking in the information age.* Center for American Progress. http://cdn .americanprogress.org/wp-content/uploads/issues/2007/04/pdf/data_driven _policy_report.pdf

Hall, J. L., & Jennings, E. T. (2008). Taking chances: Evaluating risk as a guide to better use of best practices. *Public Administration Review, 68*(4), 695–708.

Jennings, E. T., & Hall, J. L. (2012). Evidence-based practice and the use of information in state agency decision making. *Journal of Public Administration Research and Theory, 22,* 245–266.

Koppell, J. G. (2005). Pathologies of accountability: ICANN and the challenge of "multiple accountabilities disorder." *Public Administration Review, 65*(1), 94–108.

Marr, B. (2009). *Managing and delivering performance.* New York: Routledge.

McDavid, J. C., Huse, I., & Hawthorn, L. R. L. (2013). *Program evaluation and performance measurement: An introduction to practice.* Thousand Oaks, CA: Sage.

Morrisey, G. L. (1976). *Management by objectives and results in the public sector.* Boston, MA: Addison-Wesley.

Poister, T. H., & Streib, G. (1995). MBO in municipal government: Variations on a traditional management tool. *Public Administration Review,* pp. 48–56.

Rodgers, R., & Hunter, J. E. (1992). A foundation of good management practice in government: Management by objectives. *Public Administration Review,* pp. 27–39.

Swiss, J. E. (1991). *Public management systems: Monitoring and managing government performance.* Upper Saddle River, NJ: Prentice Hall.

## CHAPTER ELEVEN

PERFORMANCE MANAGEMENT IN GRANT AND CONTRACT PROGRAMS

In November 2013, President Barack Obama and his administration suffered an embarrassing blow in public opinion as his signature health care law, the Affordable Care Act, took effect. On October 1, the administration had just launched HealthCare.gov, the key Internet portal through which consumers could seek and purchase health insurance, to a host of debacles resulting from poor or incomplete system design and a lack of beta testing. The first few days were so bad—only six individuals nationwide actually purchased health insurance through HealthCare.gov on the first day—that the site had to be pulled down for extended maintenance, while the administration called in a blue-ribbon team of expert programmers and engineers from the top technology companies in the United States (Google, Red Hat, and Oracle) to help right the ship (FoxNews.com, 2013).

The contract with CGI Federal, a Canadian company filled with executives tied to a score of other botched government projects (Burke, 2013), was to build the web portal for HealthCare.gov. CGI Federal was confident six weeks prior to launch that the site would be fully functional in time for launch, but one week before launch in the "final 'pre-flight checklist'...41 of 91 separate functions that CGI was responsible for finishing by the launch were still not working" (Goldstein & Eiperlin, 2013). It was estimated that the number of lines of code that needed to be rewritten for the site to properly function could be in the millions. In the fallout from the HealthCare.gov debacle, CGI Federal immediately began to shift blame to other contractors and to the federal government (Morgan & Cornwell, 2013). In the aftermath of the launch, it came to light that CGI Federal had been the contractor for Canada's national gun registry, a project plagued by cost overruns, delays, privacy breaches, and dysfunction. Canada spent $2 billion on a list that still doesn't work after years of effort (Miller, 2013).

Why did this project fail so miserably? What steps could be taken to limit the risks of failure? How can performance measurement and management help to ensure accountability when relying on external providers for public services? These are the questions this chapter addresses.

Government Versus Governance: Challenges of the Transition to Third-Party Implementation

Over the past three decades, a movement has been afoot to shift production of public goods and services from government to the private sector, including nonprofit and for-profit firms. The New Public Management movement prioritized privatization of production to achieve greater efficiency and effectiveness. While government continues to provide such public goods and services, production has shifted outward. Frederickson and Frederickson (2006) referred to this as the "hollowing out of the state" and reflected on the host of implementation challenges it poses. Contracting out allows the government to enjoy cost savings through economy of scale and increased efficiency. Moreover, the trend has enjoyed bipartisan support, though it was largely promulgated by Republicans as a mechanism that was thought to make government more efficient through the adoption of businesslike public management approaches.

Contracting out is one example of a broader pattern of evolving government service delivery approaches that move away from single agency provision toward provision through grant making, contracting, networks, partnerships, collaboratives, and other multiagency forms of service delivery. Public agencies are increasingly working with private for-profit and nonprofit organizations as well as other agencies across multiple levels of government to deliver services in a more efficient and more effective manner. Public managers face new accountability challenges in this environment, particularly because the linkages that characterized control and controllability in traditional bureaucratic models were hierarchical and direct, whereas controllability is increasingly weakened through vertical relationships and indirect service provision involving multiple principals. Naturally, when multiple partners are engaged in any enterprise, even the delivery of contract goods and services, performance becomes more difficult to monitor and performance management more challenging to implement and maintain.

This chapter explores the application of performance measurement and management in the context of indirect service delivery, particularly in the context of grant making and contracting out. In the provision of public goods and services, it has become customary for governments to rely on external producers to deliver services they provide. This occurs in various forms, such as partnerships, including public-private partnerships, collaboration, grant making, and contracting out. But one common feature of such arrangements is their reliance on contractual agreements to specify the terms of the relationship, including the nature of products or services to be provided.

Outsourcing and privatization occur at all levels of government. As an article in *Governing* related, "The search for financial salvation is sweeping the country as local governments grapple with waning sales and property tax revenues" (Nichols, 2010). But contracting out services is no panacea. Nichols (2010) identifies a few concerns that limit the effectiveness of contracting out public services:

- Agencies don't have metrics in place to prove in advance that outsourcing a service will save money.
- Poorly conceived contracts can create cost increases beyond the costs of in-house services.
- Poor contract oversight can leave a government vulnerable to corruption and profiteering.

Nichols concludes that "the privatization of public services can erode accountability and transparency, and drive governments deeper into debt."

If we reflect on the extent to which this shift toward indirect service provision has occurred, a few numbers are worthy of consideration. Figure 11.1 reveals the level of US federal contract and grant spending by year. It highlights trends in both federal grant and contract spending over the past decade. Most notable in these trends is the fairly steady increase in both, the spike in grant spending as a result of the American Recovery and Reinvestment Act (ARRA) following 2008, and a tapering off of

FIGURE 11.1 FEDERAL GRANT AND CONTRACT SPENDING TRENDS, 2000–2011

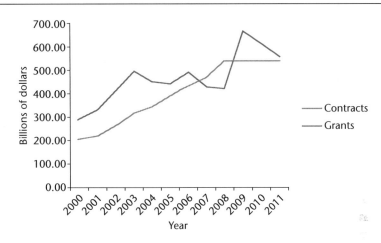

spending in both categories as a result of fiscal restraint brought on by the pressures of debt limits, sequestration, and fiscal stress.

With the transfer of production comes the transfer of control and accountability, the central concern of this chapter. How does one maintain control or hold contractors accountable when they are not directly answerable to policymakers? One of the strongest arguments against contracting out government services is the failure of private producers to embrace broader public values in the delivery of services. Another is the inability to control firms and organizations not directly in the control of government hierarchy. In particular, political principals lose control over program administration, and thus outcomes, because the linkages of control are weaker in contracted governance than in internal production. Government officials are unable to influence private producers in the same way they can government officials because they are not in their direct employ.

This chapter provides a glimpse into the role that performance management plays in grant and contract administration from both the grantor and grantee perspectives. We first distinguish grant making from contracting, then explore the purpose of performance management to both parties (purchaser and producer) in such contractual arrangements. We raise a number of special considerations that influence the use of performance management in contracted governance. Finally, we conclude with a look at problems that public and nonprofit professionals attempting to use performance management in grant making or grant administration settings are likely to encounter. Throughout the chapter there is an emphasis on both the grantor/contractor and the grantee/contractee in the relationship. When general concepts are introduced, we adopt the terms *purchaser* and *producer* instead of terms specific to grants or contracts to indicate the relationship. The goals of each party are potentially different, leading to the sort of tension that has been frequently observed when performance requirements have been imposed in grant and contract settings.

Distinguishing Contracts from Grants

In the grand scheme of things, contracts and grants are not that different. Both are mechanisms that government uses to facilitate the provision of public goods and services it does not directly produce. A grant is essentially a contractual obligation wherein one party agrees to produce or provide a good or service and another agrees to pay for those services. We distinguish between a grant and a contract in the following manner: a contract is used when the product or service to be provided is clearly defined and readily available off the shelf in the marketplace. Performance in contracts can often be clearly measured through outputs such as airplanes delivered. A grant is used when a problem exists but no clear identifiable solutions are available. Here the emphasis of performance— the goals of the program—is on activities that will take place and their intended outcomes. In a contract, the emphasis is on the output to be delivered; in a grant, the emphasis is on the process—the activities that will take place—and the expected outcomes to be generated.

A contract is almost always more constraining than a grant because grants require flexibility in implementation to address various uncertainties in the implementing environment, the subjects of the service, or the activities to be undertaken. Contracts are consequently negotiated on a price per unit basis, whereas grants offer fixed spending for a proposed set of activities to maximize the desired outcomes for the available funding. Grant applications are consequently far more descriptive with respect to the activities to take place, whereas contracts offer little description of those activities, focusing instead on the characteristics, timing, and price of the outputs to be delivered. In the end, the differences between the two forms of government spending are minimal because both parties are obligated through their acceptance of a contractual document.

A second meaningful distinction between contracts and grants is the role of the principal in each case. In a contract setting, the principal is making an outright payment for a good or service with no financial obligation from the agent. In grant settings, however, the exchange of goods or resources is often viewed as assistance and involves financial commitment and participation from both the principal and the agent, and sometimes multiple principals and agents in more complex programs that characterize cooperative endeavors across agencies on a single project.

One cannot engage in a thorough discussion of grants without considering federalism, and one cannot engage a discussion of contracting out without some mention of intersectoral management. Grants are one of many policy mechanisms at the disposal of governments, and they are effective tools when funding and expertise are mismatched. In other words, higher-level governments (usually federal but sometimes states) have broader tax bases and access to financial resources. But need may be local, and problems may require local knowledge and expertise that are available only at the local government level. Grants offer a mechanism through which federal policy goals may be carried out in a distributed fashion across numerous local governments across the country. Over time, dependence on federal funding has grown, leading to overreliance by local recipients on federal funds and a loss of local policy control as federal priorities are pursued rather than local ones. These relationships have enabled the federal government to increase in power relative to state and local counterparts over time. *Federalism* refers to the relationship between the federal government and the sovereign states; the term *intergovernmental relations* extends the discussion to include local governments as well.

Contracting goods and services necessitates working across sectors, that is, with organizations in the public sector, the private for-profit sector, and the nonprofit sector interchangeably from setting to setting. This promotes a host of challenges, not the least of which is the potential for goal multiplicity and, potentially, goal incongruence. The for-profit sector will be concerned primarily with profit as a motivating goal. Nonprofit organizations will likely be focused on institutional goals, such as budget and staffing needs, but they will certainly be driven by mission-oriented strategic goals with respect to programming. Public sector organizations share these concerns, but they must also adhere to broader democratic and nonmission-based goals such as transparency. In addition, contracting loosens the bonds of hierarchy and increases the potential for information asymmetry, both of which require the development of new mechanisms to provide for accountability.

As the federal government has transitioned from a producer to a contractor, its capacity and function have also changed. Rather than experts with high levels of program-related expertise, government agencies are now staffed with experts in accounting and contract management; essentially they are administrative experts rather than program experts. Consequently they demonstrate considerable administrative capacity amid declining substantive capacity. To the extent such substantive capacity has declined on the part of principals in grant relationships, they are forced to rely more directly on traditional mechanisms of accountability such as audit and evaluation. They exercise close control on the disbursement of funds or the transfer of funds across budget line items. They follow protocols for technical and financial reporting and freeze accounts when reports are late or incomplete to ensure compliance. As administrative experts, they are disconnected from the program and activities; there is a weak bond of professional accountability because of the lack of program expertise; shared professional norms with program implementers do not reinforce program goals.

When technical program expertise exists at the agent level but not the principal level, there is potential for information asymmetry, which allows agents to use greater discretion in program implementation. To summarize, the transition from involved participant to sterile administrator has implications for the dimension of accountability that is emphasized. If we think in terms of the five dimensions of accountability posed by Koppell (2005), we see that grant making and contracting are quite different from direct government service delivery (table 11.1). Notably, direct service

TABLE 11.1 ACCOUNTABILITY RELATIONSHIPS UNDER DIFFERENT DELIVERY MECHANISMS

	Contracts	Grants	Direct Delivery
Transparency	Weak	Moderate	Strong
Liability	Strong	Strong	Strong
Controllability	Weak	Moderate	Strong
Responsibility	Weak	Moderate	Strong
Responsiveness	Weak	Moderate	Strong

delivery offers stronger accountability in each of the five dimensions than does indirect delivery through grants or contracts.

Performance Measurement and Management in Grants and Contracts

The idea of performance contracting is not new. And over time, the performance requirements of contracts for standard services have become increasingly specific, addressing not only outputs but processes and not only quantity but quality. One example we find is in state highway contracts. Having dealt with projects that suffer considerable delays, states began to improve contracts to incentivize timely completion. To do so, they included performance clauses that focus on the timing of completion relative to the projected completion date. Where favor may be given to a contractor that promises to complete the project more quickly during the bid process, contractors face a moral hazard to promise more than they can deliver during the proposal process. Imposing penalties for delays in the contract helps to alleviate this problem. Likewise, adding performance bonuses for early completion minimizes disruption to the transportation system where projects can be completed ahead of schedule.

With respect to quality control, states routinely drill random core samples from newly constructed road projects to verify the composition, quality, and thickness of various layers of pavement that have been applied. Where roads and bridges have been specifically engineered, states must verify conformity with design in order to ensure public safety. For projects of this nature, it is now commonplace for contractual obligations to extend beyond the direct outputs to be delivered to also include secondary, or nonmission-based, aspects such as public safety. In other words, aspects of process are also managed, such as the use of safety mechanisms to protect both motorists and workers. Concrete barriers, signage, and barrels add to the cost of delivering the new road surface, but they are necessary to ensure safety, and failure to meet these process-based requirements could result in termination of a contract.

Grants are entirely different. In order to truly understand performance measurement within grant management, it is necessary to understand the differences in types of grants available. Grant types run a wide gamut from those in which the use of funds is highly constrained to those where the use of funds is subject to recipient discretion. Government grants were once characterized as categorical or noncategorical, where categorical grants were limited to use for particular functions and noncategorical grants were unrestricted in their use (Hall, 2010). Noncategorical grants, such as general revenue sharing, are a thing of the past. The most common categorical grant types include formula, block, and categorical, or project, grants. Over time grants have become more restrictive in general, buckling under the weight of considerable conditions, some of which are tied to the grant purpose and some of which focus on nonmission-based aspects of the recipient's work.

Formula grants offer the greatest flexibility in spending, as they support broad or general purposes. One example is federal funding to support public schools. Funds are allocated using a formula based on the number of students and student attendance; these funds support general operation of the school—personnel, equipment, capital, supplies, and so on. There are restrictions on the use of funds, but the recipient school has wide discretion in using them.

Block grants, like formula grants, have traditionally offered discretion to recipients within a categorical spending area. For example, in the category of community development, the Community Development Block Grant (CDBG) program has become one of the most widely known federal block grant programs. It makes available lump sums to states and entitlement cities, the use of which must simply be tied to a list of allowable project types and uses.

Finally, categorical project grants are the most restrictive of grant types. These grants fund a specific project for a specific period of time, and the use of funds is limited to the activities described in the proposal. Project grants might be used, for example, to build a senior citizens center or to rehabilitate a public housing development. They are used to develop sites for economic development projects or to fund vocational training programs in areas of targeted need. Project grants cover various activities across the gamut of federal agencies. They range from small technical assistance programs with $25,000 limits to massive projects in excess of $1 million. Project grants are tightly monitored to ensure compliance with the proposed activity and are the most restrictive grant type used. Over time most grant funding has shifted away from less restrictive forms toward project grant funding.

The differences highlighted so far typically characterize government grant types. When we look at foundation or corporate giving programs, there are similar distinctions. Categorical project grants characterize most of the funds awarded by foundations, especially to the extent they are competitive awards. That is, foundations have a strong interest in the outcomes to be delivered, and they work closely with grantees during implementation not only to ensure compliance but to offer substantive program assistance and participate in the learning process. These programs are closely monitored through reporting and audit just like their government counterparts. Some foundation giving and most corporate giving, however, is granted for general support of the organization with no strings attached, making it more like the noncategorical grant form. Such support comes with few strings attached and usually no monitoring or performance assessment. There is no longer a governmental counterpart to this type of assistance, though it would be similar in nature to general revenue sharing where funds were awarded with no restrictions on use.

Hall (2010) characterizes conditionality as an inverse relationship where increasing grantor conditions reduce local discretion. As a result, the efficacy of performance measurement and management will depend on the underlying purpose of the program. If federal (grantor) intent is to provide greater implementing flexibility for grantees, then performance measures must be flexible, or they might even be process-oriented measures that could capture the degree to which flexibility or discretion is preserved. These conditions, or strings, typically come in the form of matching requirements and restrictions on expenditure. Hall (2010) thus characterizes grant types on a spectrum ranging from unconditional to conditional and notes that the trend of conditionality is increasing in federal programs.

The method of allocation distinguishes among the grant forms as well. Formula grants are awarded on the basis of predetermined criteria on a formula basis, as are entitlement block grants. Project grants are awarded on a competitive basis. More and more grants take the competitive method of allocation and increasing conditions, consistent with greater targeting of effort to meet clearly defined goals.

While performance measurement may seem more straightforward in categorical or block grant programs, it also can play a role in formula grant programs. In fact, performance measurement can be central to the allocation of formula-based resources. It is often performance that justifies a recipient to qualify for assistance and that sets the amount of assistance. So without performance measurement, the formula would not function at all.

Let's consider one brief example: the Federal Transit Administration's Small Transit Intensive Cities (STIC) program, which makes grants to public transit systems in small urban areas that meet or exceed targets on selected performance measures. Those targets are established by taking the average performance of transit systems in larger urban areas on selected measures. STIC uses six performance targets: passenger-miles per vehicle-revenue-mile, passenger-miles per vehicle revenue hour, vehicle-revenue-miles per capita, vehicle revenue hours per capita, passenger-miles per capita, and passenger trips per capita. Notice that these indicators are all ratios, and they are all relative, so that if a shock occurs to the economy that has an adverse impact on ridership in large cities, the targets automatically compensate. Four of these measures heavily emphasize ridership, and the other two take service levels into account.

These differences are important to any consideration of performance management for two reasons. First, it is difficult to prescribe performance measures when the use of funds is itself neither restricted nor known, nor tied to specific outputs or outcomes. It violates the SMART principle for indicators—specific, measureable, ambitious, realistic, and time-bound—to adopt general measures. Second, performance measurement itself must conform to the purpose of the program. It is not realistic or necessary to assess specific performance outputs or outcomes for a program that is intended to preserve local spending discretion. Nonetheless, calls for accountability, and the adoption of government-wide performance management systems like the Government Performance and Results Act or the Program Assessment Rating Tool (PART) have imposed square peg solutions on the round hole of these more discretionary grant types. These have been met with implementation difficulty, frustration from recipients and grant program managers, and criticism of programs by political elites. The experience of CDBG offers a telling example of this trend (Hall & Handley, 2011).

The CDBG program is a longstanding federal block grant program situated within the US Department of Housing and Urban Development (HUD). The funding source has become a mainstay for state and local governments to support their community and economic development goals because of the considerable spending flexibility the grant offers. During the George W. Bush administration's tenure, PART was used to assess the extent to which almost one thousand federal programs were meeting their strategic goals. CDBG earned a PART rating of "Results Not Demonstrated," ultimately leading President Bush to issue a major legislative proposal to reorganize eighteen of the federal government's economic development programs, including CDBG, into one larger program (to be called the Strengthening America's Communities Initiative). The new program would consolidate these programs within the Economic Development Administration at a significantly lower total budget. The proposal was met with resistance from Congress and never passed, in large part due to widespread dissent from state and local government officials who relied heavily on the flexible funding to support their own local objectives.

In 2006 PART reported that CDBG contained inadequacies, including an unclear program purpose; an inability to address the specific stated problem of revitalizing distressed urban communities; a lack of targeting efforts to reach intended beneficiaries; a lack of long-term goals and performance measures to focus on outcomes; inadequate collection of grantee data in a timely, credible, and uniform manner; and an inability to provide public access to these data in a transparent manner (Center for Effective Government, 2006).

HUD nonetheless began to force CDBG to comply with the strategic planning and performance assessment goals of PART, reining in grant recipients by requiring them to demonstrate the connection of each funded local project to federally determined strategic goals. Hall and Handley (2011) characterize CDBG's history with performance measurement and reporting as ineffective and riddled with problems. Their research reports the problems encountered with the most recent implementation of performance measurement in CDBG. They find that local officials found the new requirements to be unworkable and to create an unnecessary administrative burden.

There are multiple lessons to be gleaned from this example. As Hall and Handley (2011) note, "A program with such diverse recipients and such broad functional areas provides a lesson for more effective implementation of future performance measurement initiatives" (p. 445). First, it is possible to measure the performance of grant programs, but the flexible design and discretion inherent in block grant programs preclude strict enforcement of grantor goals. Second, when grantor goals are contractually or administratively enforced, the net effect is reduced discretion for grantees, which may defeat the original purpose of the flexible program design. And finally, should that occur, the reduced flexibility may result in reduced grantee demand for grantor funding for the stated purposes as they lead grantee efforts further and further away from local priorities and toward grantor priorities. In particular, Hall and Handley found that local CDBG administrators who reported that the new CDBG regulations limited their city's CDBG mission were found to have significantly decreased satisfaction with performance measurement.

Hall and Handley (2011) also found that CDBG programs that received training or technical assistance on performance measurement from HUD, those with stronger relationships with HUD regional offices, and those receiving monitoring visits had increased satisfaction with the performance measurement effort. The light at the end of the tunnel is simple: even with flexible programs, where focus has traditionally been on activities and outputs rather than outcomes, the application of a clear process supported with training and development of performance measurement capacity can lead to successful implementation of performance measurement. The net effect of such a shift is greater responsiveness to federal program goals and stronger accountability in this dimension. Still of concern, however, is the problem associated with grantor/grantee goal incongruity in such programs. With strong performance measurement in place, grant recipients will be forced to conform closely to grantor goals or make the difficult choice to forgo funding. As Hall and Handley (2011) conclude, "Local administrators' lack of satisfaction may derive not just from the performance measures, but from the tension the measures create by increasing administrators' awareness that they are agents of local and federal principals with incongruent goals" (p. 463).

Contract Performance Management

Problems with procurement from third parties can result from two sources. One is weak or nonexistent procurement policies, including contract management. For example, contracts require sound practices to ensure accountability and prohibit waste or fraud. The first element of successful procurement is competition, which is generally attained through competitive bidding. The second is the elimination of bias, often established by identifying the criteria on which the award will be granted in advance and by blinding the identity of the bidders during the evaluation process. Third, it is necessary to clearly specify the goods or services to be solicited. Qualitative differences in products could lead to lower contract bids with less effective outcomes when the deliverables are not clear and consistent. Fourth, a clear basis of payment should be established in advance so as to ensure that payment is made only if deliverables are produced according to the agreement in both quantity and quality and in terms of timing. And a fifth premise of effective procurement is that production be monitored to validate quality control on an ongoing basis.

When we consider the opportunities for performance management with respect to indirect services like contracts, there are some clear parallels with direct service delivery but also some clear challenges. First, consider the simplicity of the logic model in contractual circumstances. Inputs are known insofar as procured services are within the available annual budget appropriation. Specification of contractual deliverables is actually identifying outputs. As contracting practices advance and partnerships become more elaborate and long term in nature, it is possible to move beyond simple outputs toward outcomes in some fields of practice. For example, when a state cabinet for families and children contracts for the management of services for individuals with developmental disabilities, the outcome of interest is providing for their health, economic security, and, insofar as possible, a high quality of life for individuals in the state's care. Attending to outcome performance is better aligned with program interests in this case than output performance because it provides greater flexibility to the contractors to determine and provide for individual needs and limits the incentive to game the system by generating unnecessary outputs, such as medical visits or behavioral evaluations.

In contract settings, the activities portion of the logic model may be handled in a few ways. If the process matters to outcome quality, activities may be specified in some detail in the contract. Highway contracts are a good example of this because they must fulfill engineering designs and standards to ensure public safety. At the other extreme, the purchaser may simply opt not to specify processes, choosing instead to leave strategy up to the producer. And in the way of a middle ground, the purchaser may choose to place limitations on strategy by prohibiting certain practices or limiting practice to a range of options.

The program goals and objectives must be established in advance with contracted goods and services because they are elements of the contract terms. But it is all too easy to set aside the obligation to monitor contract performance. In other words, if responsibility for producing public goods and services is exported, in whole or in part, to private firms or partner organizations, it is easy to assume that the responsibility for performance is transferred to the producer. That approach is naive, however, because producers are often motivated by profit or other goals rather than the public goals of equity, fairness, efficiency, and effectiveness. Performance monitoring is essential for in-house services, and so equal care should be taken with externally procured goods and services. It is necessary to examine the progress that producers are making with contracts they have been awarded to identify problems early on and endeavor to correct them before they evolve into more significant debacles.

To this end, it is important that an agency adheres to the SMART approach to identifying performance measures: specific, measurable, ambitious, realistic, and time-bound. Measures used to track contract performance should be tied directly to the program goals and objectives and should be readily observable and quantifiable. A monitoring plan should be in place to ensure that performance is tracked in a meaningful time frame and at an appropriate level of detail or aggregation. This information, of course, should be reported to appropriate managers, personnel, and stakeholders in a timely manner so that it can influence program management decisions. The issue with respect to measuring performance that is taking place in another organization is transparency. There has always been an information asymmetry between principals and agents within hierarchical organizations, and the same is true in contractual relationships. The producer, as the agent, has information that will be difficult for the purchaser to discern. The expectation of transparency will be lessened to the extent that efforts occur within private organizations.

In terms of responsible contract management, it is important to recognize that there are multiple forms of contracts designed to accommodate different needs. A competitive contract is used when there are multiple suppliers that can generate price competition. In some cases, time is of the essence, and so contracts may be let with fewer safeguards in place, preferring rather to use local suppliers that can act quickly. For example, when a mudslide closes an interstate highway, bottlenecking commerce and travel, a highway department might issue a noncompetitive contract to local firms to clear away the spoils and shore up the disrupted area. In other cases, there is a call for open-ended contracts where the deliverables are not clearly specified. For example, technical assistance may be needed, and so consulting contracts may be let for a specified number of hours at a particular rate to address problems not yet identified. And finally, there are some situations where the complexity of the problem itself limits the pool of potential bidders, often resulting in no-bid contracts.

In 2005 the US Army Corps of Engineers sought to issue a contract to repair the ailing Wolf Creek Dam that impounds Lake Cumberland in southern Kentucky. The dam was deemed at high risk of failure, which would have brought significant long-term economic distress to the region, not to mention the potential downstream flood damage in Nashville, Tennessee, situated on the Cumberland River. A global solicitation ultimately resulted in a $594 million contract issued to a partnership between two European firms (Treviicos-Soletanche, JV) formed explicitly to respond to the revised request for proposal, and construction began in March 2006

(US Army Corps of Engineers, 2013). In this case, the contract was awarded on the basis of expertise, not cost (Mardis, 2008).

In the way of perspective, "federal agencies awarded $115.2 billion in no-bid contracts in fiscal 2012, an 8.9 percent increase from $105.8 billion in 2009, even as total contract spending decreased by 5 percent during the period" (Hickey, 2013). Ironically, this jump followed President Barack Obama's 2009 promise that his administration would reduce "wasteful" and "inefficient" no-bid contracts and "dramatically reform the way we do business on contracts across the entire government" (Hickey, 2013).

The manner in which performance is tracked during contract implementation can range in sophistication from inputs to outcomes. This, of course, corresponds to similar observations in direct service delivery where better measures are outcome oriented. The simplest mechanism for tracking progress also reveals the least information about progress toward goals. The focus on inputs—often measured as dollars paid or the proportion of the total contract amount expended—is such an ineffective measure. A contractor can bill for services provided, leading to the impression that progress is being made, while in fact the work may be of poor quality or not in keeping with the expectations of the contract. In the Corps of Engineers example, such a performance measure would be indicated by the running total of funds expended or the proportion of the total contract amount expended to date. Again, this sort of measure provides opportunity for gaming and does not clearly identify key outcomes of interest.

Performance measures could relate to outputs as well such as personnel-hours of work completed or cubic yards of concrete poured. But these also fail to reflect the true outcome: the stability and safety of the dam. Performance could be tracked by identifying key milestones—objectives that represent significant achievement toward project completion. In other words, they provide information with meaning rather than just data. In the case of the dam rehabilitation, this might include phases of the project, such as preparation of the work platform; grouting work in the porous, cavernous rock beneath the structure; drilling of the secant piles; and pouring concrete for the final barrier wall. And finally, outcome measures could be used, such as readings from instruments designed to detect material shift within the structure, reductions in which would reveal improved safety. This is all to say that measurement in contract settings can be as simplistic or sophisticated as in direct service delivery, and better performance measures will provide better information to decision makers.

Ultimately the characteristic of contracting that permits increased accountability is the ability to tie payments to performance objectives. These instruments have become increasingly complex over time, for example, assessing penalties for substandard services or products, penalties for late delivery, and even bonuses and incentives for early completion. Performance contracts, though, require commitment to measurement and capacity to observe and measure the key elements of production and product quality.

Performance contracts have become commonplace in the public sector across levels of government and functions. In Hawaii, the legislature authorized the use of performance contracts to collect delinquent taxes in 1996. The following summarizes the requirements:

A contract under which compensation to the vendor shall be computed according to performance standards established by the department. Any performance-based contract entered into by the department for such purpose shall provide:

1. For the payment of fees based on a contractually specified amount of the increase in the amount of taxes, interests, and penalties collected and attributable to the implementation of automated tax systems; or

2. For the payment of fees on a fixed-fee contract basis to be paid from the increase in the amount of taxes, interest, and penalties collected and attributable to the implementation of automated tax systems. (Auditor of the State of Hawaii, 2010, p. 8)

As an example of how important contract provisions and management can be to agency performance, consider the following excerpt from the Hawaii Auditor's Report, demonstrating the breakdown of the requirements (the contractor is the same firm contracted to develop HealthCare. Gov):

In this environment of discord, the department modified the Delinquent Tax Collections Initiatives contract. We found that this 2009 modification was crafted independently by a former deputy director with no formal IT background or training. It removed the obligation of the vendor to complete the 2008 contract's 22 initiatives as well as a constraint limiting payment to the vendor to $9.8 million for work on the 2008 contract. Instead, the 2009 modification allowed the vendor to receive the remaining compensation of $15.2 million from new collections without first completing deliverables from the 2008 contract. In addition, the modification also deleted contract provisions that removed the department's ability to hold the vendor accountable for defects and system integration problems. (Auditor of the State of Hawaii, 2010)

This example reveals how lax contract management resulted in weak accountability on the part of vendors providing delinquent tax collection. It shows as well the importance of establishing clear performance measures and a clear performance measurement framework, and monitoring performance on an ongoing basis, even in contracted programs where service providers are contractually bound. Failure to monitor and provide oversight is a recipe for poor performance results.

In the case of Hawaii's delinquent tax collection contracts, significant changes occurred in 2009 that weakened accountability and performance (Auditor of the State of Hawaii, 2010). Under 2008 contract initiatives, performance (and payment) was assessed according to the completion of specific initiatives—activities—that were expected to lead, according to the program logic, to the desired outcomes. These twenty-two initiatives included, for example, automated address updates, risk modeling, a virtual call center and automation of collection calls, and collections business process improvements (Auditor of the State of Hawaii, 2010). But rather than improving, the system took a turn for the worse the following year.

A stronger system would have emphasized performance levels and institutionalized monitoring receipts of delinquent taxes. In this case, vendor performance could have been assessed using simple outcomes like the dollar value of delinquent taxes collected, the proportion of delinquent tax dollars collected, or breakouts of either measure by groups (such as business versus personal or residents versus nonresidents). Other measures might have focused on the number or proportion of delinquent accounts brought into compliance. Examining these data over time would have provided a ready check on the extent to which the contracted vendor was generating the desired outcomes and allowed time to make amendments or corrections.

Purpose of Performance Measurement in Grant and Contract Management

One guiding principle in performance measurement in grant or contract settings is that the parameters of the system will be determined primarily by whether one is the purchaser or the producer. Furthermore, purchasers' and producers' perceptions of the system will be colored by whether the system was developed internally in a bottom-up fashion or imposed externally or in a top-down fashion. The purpose will vary along this dimension, and so will the measures and processes established. External interests will focus on accountability, but the dimension emphasized may be controllability rather than responsiveness. Internal interests will likely focus on responsiveness and performance improvement. It is important to think along these differences as we examine performance management in grant and contract management settings.

The role of performance management in government has a number of possible dimensions. Behn (2003) identified eight, with an emphasis on improvement. In contracted settings, however, the contract or grant is negotiated in advance. The end results are specified, as is the time line for completion, and the role of government managers becomes one of oversight and enforcement. If the prescribed outputs are not delivered, payment is withheld. As such, there is no consideration on the part of either party for delivering more than has been negotiated in a contract setting. Program officers overseeing grant projects face similar dilemmas. Their role is one of oversight and enforcement of the proposed time line of activities. Outcomes are not guaranteed, so their focus is on implementation and ensuring consistency with the process described in the proposal, not with the traditional forms of accountability expected in public performance management. When the time is up, either the contract or grant has been fulfilled or it has not.

We can argue, then, that the purpose of performance management in grant and contract programs is one of ensuring conformity with the written agreements that set them into motion. The obligations of performance measurement will be weightier under grant management than under simple contracting. Grant making and contracting has been viewed as a top-down enterprise, and emphasis on performance management is naturally on the funding entity. However, in the case of contracting and grant making, it is now necessary to reflect on the role of not only the funder but also the recipient. The vast majority of grants are made from the federal government to state and local governments that may be operating their own performance management systems independent of any federal requirements. Likewise, nonprofit agencies have shown increased acuity in the use of performance measurement to demonstrate their effectiveness. Where these organizations are recipients of grants or contracts, they may find a meaningful role to play in measuring performance, and they may also find that the expectations of the funder do not align with their existing systems, processes, or structures.

Public managers in contracts may be obligated to ensure quality control, and report on quality, with the expectation that any substandard products or services will not be reimbursed. Public managers in grant programs, though, may be obligated to track and monitor performance on inputs, activities, outputs, outcomes, and impacts. This stems in part from the desire to identify programs that work and may be systematized over time into formal programs.

Performance-Based Grant Management

Recent trends in federal grant administration reveal a heightened focus on performance-based grant management. In light of the performance emphasis that pervades federal administration, this should not come as a great surprise. Two examples reveal the extent to which performance measurement has become central to the administration of grant funding programs in the United States. First, we explore the significant change brought about with implementation of the ARRA. Second, we explore the unique case of the US Centers for Disease Control's (CDC) National Breast and Cervical Cancer Early Detection Program (NBCCEDP).

The ARRA heralded a new approach to accountability in grant administration. The funding mechanism itself is not unique, especially considering that the funds were funneled through existing grant programs that Congress had previously authorized. ARRA was nevertheless unique in two ways. First, its sheer magnitude causes it to stand out amid the crowd of funding programs. Second, program implementation came with a strict concern for accountability brought about through three distinct mechanisms: performance measurement requirements that extend not just to grantees but to all subgrantees or contractors receiving funding from the program, clear goal orientation focused on jobs created or saved, and transparency through reporting of key funding and performance statistics for all awards, searchable by geography, program, or recipient. The web portal created for this program (www.Recovery.gov) did not use unique approaches but recombined them in a more effective manner that brought heightened attention to performance throughout the process (Hall & Jennings, 2011). It is interesting, though, that the intensive performance measurement and reporting focus was limited to the simple outputs and outcomes all awards had in common, while performance on the traditional mission-oriented focus of the programs went untracked, at least by the centralized repository.

The other example reveals how one program has not only used performance measurement to monitor key program outcome performance but tied performance to the allocation of grants. The CDC's NBCCEDP was created in 1990 to reduce morbidity and mortality due to breast and cervical cancer among medically underserved women. The program provides grant funding to health organizations in sixty-seven states, tribes, and territories; in 2013, nearly $150 million was allocated, with individual grants ranging from about $250,000 to over $8 million. These grantees contract with local health care providers for clinical service delivery and manage program data at the state, tribe, or territory level. Critical outputs for the program include women receiving quality screening and diagnostic services and referrals to treatment. Ample research has shown that these cancers can be prevented or treated more effectively when detected early, which directly links these outputs to the intended program outcomes (reduced morbidity and mortality among the target population) in the program logic model.

In 2005 NBCCEDP adopted a performance-based grant management system. Figure 11.2 presents the program logic from two perspectives—that of the grantee (panel A) and that of the grantor agency perspective (panel B) under this new system. Performance is assessed on twenty-six indicators, of which nine are central to the agency's data review process; these are key performance indicators that represent essential dimensions of performance. Performance information has been collected since the inception of the program, but with the adoption of the performance-based grant management system in 2005, the data were for the first time used to establish targets and linked to grants. As part of the semiannual data review, a summary report of the core measures is prepared and discussed by CDC and the grantee. This is made possible by the consistent grantee pool and stable geography. In other words, the performance measures are comparable over time because there are longstanding grantees serving the same service areas.

In panels A and B in figure 11.2, we see two unique perspectives that reveal the logic of how outcomes are realized. Panel A shows the grantee perspective; grantees are the organizations receiving federal grant funds in exchange for the services they provide or goods they produce. In this case, panel A shows the federal grant funds (received through the cooperative agreements) as inputs. The activities are focused on the substance of the program—delivering services. In panel B, we see program

FIGURE 11.2 PROGRAM LOGIC MODELS FROM TWO PERSPECTIVES: GRANTEE AND GRANTOR

A: Grantee Program Perspective

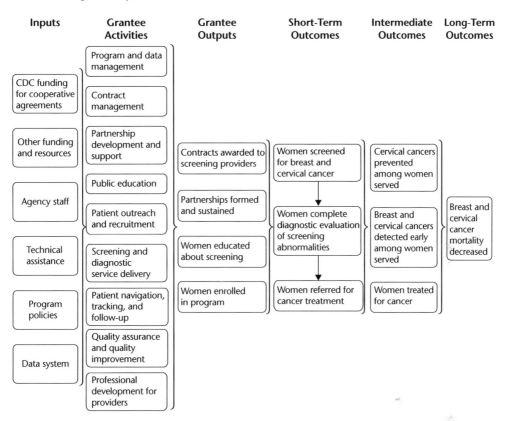

B: CDC Performance-Based Grants Management

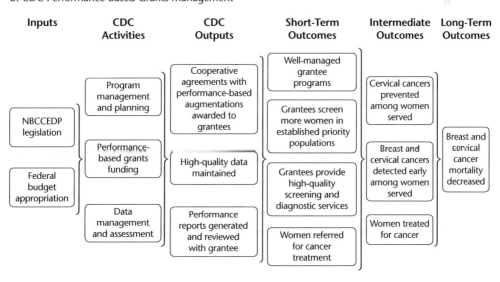

Source: US Centers for Disease Control and Prevention. Used with permission.

management from the administrative perspective, that is, the point of view of the grant-making agency. Here inputs are the legal constraints within which they must work, and activities are focused on the allocation of grant funds and management of cooperative agreements.

The outputs of the substantive process (panel A) focus on developing partnerships and establishing contracts with providers, and education and enrollment of women in the program for grantees. The outputs focus on administrative matters (panel B) for the grantor: cooperative agreements, data maintenance, and performance reporting drive outputs for the grantor agency. Notice, though, that when it comes to outcomes, the two models converge: both are working toward the same end goals, but their individual agency processes for doing so are unique. By mapping program logic in such a fashion, it becomes easier to understand how organizations bring about their results in a collaborative fashion. Similarities emerge in short-term outcomes, and in this case, the intermediate and long-term outcomes are identical between the two approaches.

Responsibility for performance, then, can be clearly attributed to the grantee and measurement over an extended time period is possible. The grantee's achievement of the established targets constitutes the criteria used to determine incremental changes in the grant amount. The targets are realistic and take measurement difficulties into consideration; the final targets are informed by medical expert opinion, stakeholder input, and the realities of program implementation. Program performance has been high overall, making it difficult to distinguish high performers from low performers within the program. In the case of this program, the implementation of performance-based grant management likely had little effect on overall performance because the targets set were already being met, were unambitious, and funding levels were at rates associated with achievement of the targets (Poister, Pasha, DeGroff, Royalty, & Joseph, 2013).

The challenge of such a performance-based grant management system, as with all other performance budgeting efforts, is that there is a subjective element to the funding allocation process. Objectively, better performance is associated with an expectation of higher funding, but there are certainly situations where this assumption would not be supported in the political arena. For example, when performance is high, the problem may be reduced, leading to a reprioritization of spending toward problems that are seen as needier. Moreover, in cases where performance is lower than expected, it may be the case that insufficient resources were available, calling for an increase in funding. While objective allocation of grants based on performance is a rational approach, it may not be appropriate as the sole allocation criterion in every instance.

Another example of innovative incorporation or performance measurement into grant administration comes from the Office of Rural Health Policy and, more specifically, the Medicare Rural Hospital Flexibility (FLEX) program. The FLEX monitoring group team is conducting a performance monitoring effort for the program to assess its impact on rural hospitals and communities and the role of states in achieving program objectives. The core of this initiative is a strong emphasis on the development of logic models that define linkages among resources, outputs, and outcomes and that facilitate the development of strong and meaningful measures of performance that can be tracked over time. Because the program focuses on state rural health plans, it is not strictly possible to establish federal standards for performance that would be appropriate to each state setting. The approach developed here, rather, is to focus on strong performance measurement within states by systematizing a strong performance measurement process that is able to track and report outcomes.

Other examples of performance-based grant management exist, and the incorporation of performance information into the application and funding allocation process is a key way to use performance information in decision making. Building performance targets and other requirements into grant awards is another way. And finally, institutionalizing performance measurement and reporting expectations for grant-funded programs is a key approach to building more performance-oriented grant management. These changes are taking place not only in the public sector through federal grants but also through major nonprofit organizations and foundations. It is not uncommon for foundations to request information on past performance as part of their request for proposals. In one major national example, the United Way recently revised its approach to making local funding decisions by requiring applicants to document their achievement of past strategic targets and setting aside points in the application review process for past success.

Problems and Special Considerations Using Performance Management in Grant Programs

When it comes to grant management, federal requirements have become a point of concern. The list of conditions to which a grantee must agree to adhere is ominous and ever expanding. These conditions are often not directly tied to the strategic program mission, but to other nonmission-based considerations. When it comes to accountability, documenting compliance for these conditions constitutes a significant administrative burden for grantees. Similarly, ensuring compliance with these conditions requires capacity and resources for the grantor agencies as well. Attention to these nonmission-based elements of program performance necessarily adds to the indirect costs of program administration and detracts from the efficiency of program delivery. Similar contractual conditions exist or can be incorporated.

The lesson is that those things that matter can be incorporated into the agreements that govern grant awards and contracts. If performance on mission-oriented strategic goals is important, performance requirements such as targets can be identified from the start, as can performance measurement and reporting expectations. It is equally possible to add a variety of nonmission-based considerations, including requirements to document performance with respect to those goals. Conditions have come under greater scrutiny by applicants, leading many to forgo federal funding to avoid the administrative burden and, ultimately, conformity with federal goals as opposed to local preferences. In many cases, such resistance is symbolic and temporary, such as Texas's refusal to accept federal stimulus funds (Condon, 2009). In others, such as Hillsdale College, federal funds come with conditional expectations that violate the institution's core values (Hillsdale College, 2013). For recipients of grants or contracts that accept the conditions and goals of the grantor or contractor, there is risk of mission creep over time away from those things deemed to be strategically important locally toward values or goals considered to be important by the funding agencies.

In a granted or contracted work environment, there are two levels of management. The purchaser is mostly interested in policy-level matters, whereas the producer is more concerned with day-to-day management. In networked collaborations, there may be multiple participants with further divergent goals and interests. Where multiple principals exist, the potential is strong for multiple goals that often find themselves in conflict. In these settings, it becomes a question of what to measure. The strictest constraint on performance measurement and management is resource availability; it takes time and effort to measure each additional indicator, and as the list of indicators grows, so grows the complexity associated with interpreting performance information. The trade-off becomes whether to develop a parsimonious model that would be useful to guiding implementation and management or an expansive model that incorporates the interests of all involved parties. When goals are not aligned, this effort may exacerbate the underlying conflict. When goals and outcomes are consistent and uniform from place to place, it may be easier to institutionalize measures and indicators from the top down. But collaborative settings are typically unique, precluding such a possibility.

Grant management has typically been about conformity to the process described in the scope of work provided in the application document. Quarterly technical reports are usually required to substantiate progress in implementing the proposed work plan. With many grant programs, particularly those that are categorical and competitive, the grant will have expired before outcomes have been realized. The contractual obligation between grantor and grantee would have been met, with no requirement or expectation to examine or report the extent to which the program actually realized its intended outcomes. In this way, the short time horizon of many grant programs limits the potential for performance measurement and management. Of course, where recipients and funders interact in repeated iterations on different projects, this information can be taken into consideration as a condition for future funding. The net result is a reluctance of agencies to focus on outcome goals in grant programs, preferring to focus on elements of process such as quality control and measures related to activities instead of outcomes.

References

Auditor of the State of Hawaii. (2010, December). Report 10–11. *Management and Financial Audit of Department of Taxation Contracts.* http://files.hawaii.gov/auditor/ Reports/2010/10–11.pdf

Behn, R. D. (2003). Why measure performance? Different purposes require different measures. *Public Administration Review, 63,* 586–606.

Burke, C. (2013, November 15). Obamacare contractor linked to 20 troubled government projects. Newsmax.com. http://www.newsmax.com/Newsfront/cgi -obamacare-ams-mishandled/2013/11/15/id/536988

Center for Effective Government. (2006). *OMB's 2006 PART performance measurements for community development block grant.* Washington, DC. http://www.foreffectivegov.org/ node/2436

Condon, S. (2009, July 16). Texas gov. who refused stimulus funds asks for loan. CBSNews.com. http://www.cbsnews.com/news/texas-gov-who-refused-stimulus -funds-asks-for-loan/

FoxNews.Com. (2013, November 11). *ObamaCare website contractor previously cited over security lapses.* http://www.foxnews.com/politics/2013/11/01/obamacare-website -contractor-previously-cited-over-security-lapses/

Frederickson, D. G., & Frederickson, H. G. (2006). *Measuring the performance of the hollow state*. Washington, DC: Georgetown University Press.

Goldstein, A., & Eiperlin, J. (2013, November 23). HealthCare.gov contractor had high confidence but low success. *Washington Post*. http://www.washingtonpost.com/national/health-science/healthcaregov-contractor-had-high-confidence-but-low-success/2013/11/23/1ab2c2b2–5407–11e3–9fe0-fd2ca728e67c_story.html

Hall, J. L. (2010). *Grant management: Funding for public and nonprofit programs*. Sudbury, MA: Jones & Bartlett.

Hall, J. L., & Handley, D. M. (2011). City adoption of federal performance measurement requirements: Perspectives from community development block grant program administrators. *Public Performance and Management Review, 34*, 443–467.

Hall, J. L., & Jennings, E. T. (2011). The American Recovery and Reinvestment Act (ARRA): A critical examination of accountability and transparency in the Obama administration. *Public Performance and Management Review, 35*, 202–226.

Hickey, J. G. (2013, November 14). No-bid contracts mark Obama administration. NewsMax.com. http://www.newsmax.com/Newsfront/Obama-administration-no-bid-contracts/2013/11/13/id/536496

Hillsdale College. (2013). *Financial aid: Scholarships, grants, and loans*. http://www.hillsdale.edu/aid/scholarships

Koppell, J. G. (2005). Pathologies of accountability: ICANN and the challenge of "multiple accountabilities disorder." *Public Administration Review, 65*, 94–108.

Mardis, B. (2008, July 25). Corps: Construction firm selected on merit. *Commonwealth Journal*. http://www.somerset-kentucky.com/local/x681548612/Corps-Construction-firm-selected-on-merit

Miller, E. (2013, November 6). How Obamacare contractor bungled Canada's gun registry. *Washington Times*. www.washingtontimes.com/news/2013/nov/6/miller-before-obamacare-a-record-of-failure/?page=all

Morgan, D., & Cornwell. S. (2013, October 23) *U.S. Contractors shift blame for Healthcare.gov problems*. http://news.yahoo.com/cgi-blames-another-contractor-healthcare-gov-bottleneck-211848670—sector.html

Nichols, R. (2010, December). The pros and cons of privatizing government functions. *Governing*. http://www.governing.com/topics/mgmt/pros-cons-privatizing-government-functions.html

Poister, T., Pasha, O. Q., DeGroff, A., Royalty, J., & Joseph, K. (2013). *Performance based grants management in the health sector: Evaluating effectiveness in the Centers for Disease Control and Prevention*. Unpublished paper.

US Army Corps of Engineers. (2013). *Wolf Creek Dam Safety Major Rehabilitation, Ky: Fact Sheet*. Washington, DC: US Army Corps of Engineers. http://www.lrn.usace.army.mil/Media/FactSheets/FactSheetArticleView/tabid/6992/Article/6242/wolf-creek-dam-safety-major-rehabilitation-ky.aspx

## CHAPTER TWELVE

IMPROVING QUALITY AND PROCESS

To what extent does performance measurement play a role in public and nonprofit agencies' drives to improve quality and productivity? What kinds of measures are typically used to track quality and productivity? What do these particular monitoring systems look like, and how are they different from the other kinds of measurement systems described in this book? How are such systems used to improve quality and productivity? Whereas previous chapters discuss measurement systems that are tied to other processes at higher management levels, this chapter discusses the use of performance measures at the operating level to help improve quality, productivity, and process improvement.

This chapter differentiates quality and process improvements from other types of measures in this book. The first part of the chapter focuses on quality and process improvements in general, while the latter provides specific tools from the quality movement. We begin by looking at the differences in the measures.

As the quality revolution has swept through government over the past three decades, it has made an indelible mark on the public management landscape (Carr & Littman, 1990; Berman & West, 1995; Hyde, 1997). Now more than ever before, managers of public programs are challenged to improve the quality of the services they deliver as well as increase customer satisfaction with those services. From a performance measurement perspective, this means they must track indicators of the quality of inputs and especially of the outputs produced and, as will be seen later in this book, customer satisfaction. Typically the dimensions of quality that are considered as being the most important in the quest for improving customer service are these:

- Timeliness, total time required, waiting time
- Accuracy, thoroughness, reliability, fairness
- Accessibility, hours of service, convenience
- Decor, cleanliness, and condition of facilities
- Personal safety and security
- Courtesy, politeness, professionalism

These and other dimensions of service quality can usually be measured with quantitative indicators, usually by defining what constitutes acceptable quality standards and then tracking the number or percentage of cases in which those standards are achieved or in which performance falls short of the standards. Looking at decentralized operations for renewing drivers' licenses, for example, managers might want to monitor (1) the percentage of customers who have to wait in line for more than twenty minutes before being served, (2) the average time required for a customer to complete the license renewal process, and (3) the percentage of renewals processed correctly the first time.

Monitoring Productivity for Process Improvement

In this book and throughout the public management literature, the term *productivity* is used at two levels. At a macrolevel, *productivity* is almost synonymous with overall performance, a kind of composite of efficiency, effectiveness, and cost-effectiveness. At this level, a productive organization is one that is functioning effectively and efficiently to deliver public services and produce desired outcomes. At a microlevel, *productivity* refers more specifically to the relationship between inputs or the factors of production and the immediate products, or outputs, produced. Thus, productivity monitoring is actually more output oriented, focusing on the amount of work completed, units of service provided, or number of clients served rather than looking at actual outcomes, the real impacts generated out in the field or in a target population as a result of services being delivered or clients being served. However, the two are directly related inasmuch as improving productivity will lead to increased outputs, which in turn will lead to greater impact, assuming a valid program logic and an effective intervention strategy.

At the microlevel as stated productivity is closely related to internal operating efficiency in that they both relate outputs to inputs. However, whereas efficiency indicators relate outputs to the overall direct cost of providing them, usually expressed as unit costs, productivity measures relate the outputs produced to the amount of specific kinds of resources needed to produce them. By far the most common type of productivity measure refers to labor productivity, but other types of productivity measures—such as those focusing on the use of equipment—are sometimes incorporated in productivity monitoring systems too. Productivity measures must also have a time dimension in order to be meaningful. In a government printing office, for example, labor productivity might be measured by the number of "images" produced per full-time equivalent (FTE) employee per week, and equipment productivity might be measured by the number of images produced per large press per hour.

Productivity analysis focuses on production processes or service delivery systems at the operating level and attempts to find ways to increase the flow of outputs per unit of inputs or resources. The most common approaches to improving productivity are setting productivity standards, training employees with better skills to work harder and smarter, streamlining methods and work processes, using new technology, improving workplace design, and implementing alternative service delivery systems (Berman, 1998; Holzer, 1992; Matzer, 1986). Thus, the most common kinds of performance measures tracked by systems designed to monitor productivity and the factors that influence it are these:

- Volume of output
- Labor productivity
- Equipment productivity
- Availability of resources, inventories
- Equipment downtime
- Cycle time, turnaround time
- Workloads or caseloads, client-staff ratios
- Pending workload, backlog of cases
- Use rates, flow of cases

For the purposes of productivity analysis, these kinds of factors are often monitored with respect to an operating system or service delivery system as a whole, but they may well also be applied to component processes that make up that system.

Standard Hours

Productivity is commonly measured in time frames such as hours, days, weeks, months, or years. It is also possible for agencies to measure their productivity in terms of billable hours, which are based on the estimated amount of time that will be spent on a particular job. This determination is made based on what management believes about the volume of work, difficulty in producing each unit of output, and required quality of each unit of output. In the case of hospitals owned by the Department of Veterans Affairs (VA), there is desire to minimize the risk of wrongful death and malpractice lawsuits, as well as repeat visits from the same patients that could be avoided. Management can nevertheless feel pressured to increase patient turnover if the volume of patients entering hospitals is high. In the recent VA scandal, patient wait time was decreased as found by the inspector general's report confirming press and whistleblower reports that employees of the VA in Phoenix, and apparently other VA hospitals around the country, kept a secret waiting list to make it appear that veterans were accessing care more quickly than they were in reality (see US VA Office of Inspector General, 2014). This type of gaming is one of the unintended consequences of performance measurement and ways to avoid it are discussed in chapters 5 and 15.

Output-Oriented Systems

Some monitoring systems are designed primarily as output-oriented systems because the management imperative that they are developed to support is principally concerned with increasing output, often through improving productivity. Sometimes it is possible to measure both the numerator and denominator of productivity indicators with the same scale. For example, although the varied outputs of a government printing office can be summarized in terms of images produced, they can also be measured in another common metric, the number of billable hours produced during a given time period. Each job coming into the plant is assessed in terms of volume of work and degree of difficulty, and from that is derived the number of billable hours, that is, the number of hours the job should require given the work standards in place. Productivity can then be measured as the ratio of billable hours produced by the plant in a week to the number of production hours worked that week (after subtracting out setup time, time spent in training, time spent in cleanup, and so on). If this ratio is less than one for any particular week, it signifies that the plant did not produce as many billable hours as it was expected to produce given the productivity standards in place.

Output-oriented monitoring systems are popular with agency management but do not seem to factor into legislative budgeting decisions (Sterck & Scheers, 2006). Output monitoring allows agencies to separate information about policy implementation from policy design. At the same time, it also provides agencies with a more complete understanding of the products and services they have delivered, allowing adjustments to practice in order to improve policy outcomes. Output-based monitoring and budgeting systems are popular in New Zealand, whereas outcome-oriented systems are popular in a greater range of countries such as Australia, Sweden, the Netherlands, and the United Kingdom (Sterck & Scheers, 2006).

These types of monitoring systems can be integrated into performance-based budgeting and greatly improve external accountability, allowing agencies to justify their activities to both their authorizing legislatures and the public. Agency officials rely on output-oriented measurement systems to demonstrate to the public the volume of their agency's performance with the intent of increasing public confidence in those agencies and, in the aggregate, the government (Sterck & Bouckaert, 2008). Output-oriented measurement systems have a distinct advantage over outcome-based systems due to the greater objectivity of the data produced, whereas outcome-based systems are subject to interpretation of outcomes (Sterck & Bouckaert, 2008).

Table 12.1 shows disability compensation and health care data for the US Department of Veterans Affairs. Disability compensation data show the amount of money paid by year to veterans who are considered disabled, but not outcome data regarding whether the veterans who were paid received enough to maintain a certain standard of living. Likewise, the health care statistics show the number of veteran and nonveteran patients treated in hospitals owned by the Department of Veterans Affairs but not any outcome data for those treated in those hospitals. The table shows the percentage change in expenditures from prior years and percentage change per year in the number of people who received services from the department. These output measures allow easy analysis of the yearly productivity of the department, so that managers and legislators can quickly detect deficiencies in service and take corrective action.

TABLE 12.1 DISABILITY COMPENSATION AND PATIENT EXPENDITURES: FISCAL YEAR 2000 TO FISCAL YEAR 2012

| | Disability Compensation | | | | VA Healthcare | | | | |
Fiscal Year	Expenditures	Recipients	Average Expenditure per Recipient	% Expenditure Change from Previous Year	% Change in Recipients from Previous Year	Patient Expenditures	Veteran Patients	Non-Veteran Patients	Average Expenditure per Patient	% Change in Recipients from Previous Year
2000	$14,773,382,340	2,308,186	$6,400	—	—	$16,806,577,327	3,427,925	312,810	$4,493	—
2001	$15,806,234,628	2,321,103	$6,810	6.99%	0.56%	$18,632,727,019	3,843,832	305,874	$4,490	10.93%
2002	$17,589,232,812	2,398,287	$7,334	11.28%	3.33%	$19,935,388,850	4,246,084	298,269	$4,387	9.51%
2003	$19,535,925,552	2,485,229	$7,861	11.07%	3.63%	$21,967,982,313	4,505,433	301,438	$4,570	5.78%
2004	$20,591,728,748	2,555,696	$8,057	5.40%	2.84%	$25,198,103,663	4,677,720	301,431	$5,061	3.58%
2005	$23,542,487,166	2,636,979	$8,928	14.33%	3.18%	$27,565,765,198	4,806,345	445,322	$5,249	5.47%
2006	$25,622,853,876	2,725,824	$9,400	8.84%	3.37%	$28,077,033,706	4,900,800	288,025	$5,411	−1.20%
2007	$27,969,259,960	2,844,178	$9,834	9.16%	4.34%	$29,036,286,719	4,950,501	283,225	$5,548	0.87%
2008	$30,274,152,913	2,952,285	$10,254	8.24%	3.80%	$33,962,036,284	4,999,106	300,539	$6,408	1.26%
2009	$34,102,951,214	3,069,652	$11,110	12.65%	3.98%	$39,348,043,535	5,139,285	308,778	$7,222	2.80%
2010	$36,485,965,838	3,210,261	$11,365	6.99%	4.58%	$40,586,657,907	5,351,873	286,731	$7,198	3.50%
2011	$39,373,549,773	3,354,741	$11,737	7.91%	4.50%	$42,265,215,266	5,499,498	295,667	$7,293	2.78%
2012	$44,358,737,799	3,536,802	$12,542	12.66%	5.43%	$43,028,963,249	5,598,829	297,680	$7,297	1.75%

Source: US Department of Veterans Affairs, Veterans Benefits Administration, Annual Benefits Reports, 2000 to 2012; Veterans Health Administration, Office of Policy and Planning, Table A: VHA Enrollment, Expenditures, and Patients National Vital Signs, September Reporting 2000 to 2012. Prepared by the National Center for Veterans Analysis and Statistics.

Note: "Patients" do not include veterans who have visits with the readjustment counseling service only; state nursing home patients; and non-veteran patients; or the associated cost.

The data shown in this example show both the productivity and efficiency of services offered by the department. Productivity is defined as the number of units of output created within a certain time frame, such as veteran patients per year. As can be seen in the table, productivity ranges anywhere from 2.3 million disabled veterans receiving compensation in 2000 to over 3.5 million disabled veterans receiving compensation in 2012, consistent with American military operations since September 11, 2001, which would result in some military personnel becoming disabled. Efficiency is defined as the amount of resources spent per unit of output, such as the average expenditure per veteran patient. This number declined between 2000 and 2002 and has steadily risen since the start of the Iraq war in 2003, except for a slight decline in 2010 from 2009 levels. This information is useful in determining overall trends in the department, but it does not allow microlevel analysis of individual department institutions. The data will have to undergo a process called disaggregation, discussed later in this chapter.

Monitoring Service Quality

Service quality measures are usually quantitative indicators, where acceptable quality standards are determined and statistics are compiled concerning the percentage of cases where standards are and are not met. This approach maintains the output-oriented philosophy of performance and quality measurement, as it measures only the immediate result of an action or inaction by the department rather than the effects of those outputs on the people affected. It also minimizes the need for interpretation of the data produced, allowing legislative overseers and the public to easily understand the state of service quality in the department.

The examples of disability benefits and hospital services provided by the Department of Veterans Affairs are also examples of how service quality and productivity are often seen as complementary performance measures. Management monitors productivity by assessing the number of disabled veterans who are paid disability benefits in a given year or by the number of patients treated at department hospitals. Service quality can be determined from this information as well by determining the number of disabled veterans who receive benefits compared to the number of veterans eligible to receive disability benefits, the length of time that nonemergency patients in department hospitals must wait to be treated, the turnaround time for adjudication on applications for disabled veteran status, the number of patients in department hospitals who develop infections from inside the hospital, and security incidents in department hospitals.

Rework

Rework refers to reprocessing products or services that were not of sufficient quality the first time they were produced. Since rework requires that resources be spent on an existing rather than a new product, it is often seen as an inefficiency as well as a service quality issue. In recent years, the public sector has experienced budget cuts that have placed a great deal of pressure on management to maximize efficiency with diminished resources, which makes avoiding rework critical in performance management. However, rework cannot always be avoided, especially if legislative policy changes affect the way agencies perform their functions. Statutory unemployment benefits extensions are an example of forced rework, since state unemployment compensation offices must process applications for extended benefits from those who were previously approved for an earlier tier of benefits.

Rework indicators are used in performance monitoring as a link between quality and productivity, since rework indicates quality issues and has a negative impact on productivity. Agencies differ in their definition of rework indicators due to the diversity of functions in which they are engaged. Common measures include the number of cases that must be reprocessed, the number of defective products that must be replaced, and the number of transactions that must be repeated (Poister, 2003). These indicators serve the purpose of saving the agency money by preventing the need for rerendering products and services while freeing up ever smaller amounts of money and other resources to be spent on new client needs.

Disaggregated Measures

Data are usually reported in aggregate form; that is, they show only the collective characteristics of the targets of measurement, such as averages. However, agency managers and interested members of the public often want to learn about the performance of particular parts of larger organizations, such as one particular post office. The disaggregation of data is crucial to identifying subunits of organizations that are performing atypically so that action can be taken if needed (Behn, 2003). One common form of data disaggregation is geographic so that agency performance in different parts of a region or country can be determined.

The use of disaggregated measures prevents the manipulation of aggregate data to misrepresent organizational characteristics, which can be influenced by the way that data are collected and presented (Enticott, Boyne, & Walker, 2008). Disaggregated data prevent the creation of false impressions of an agency by providing a comprehensive story, allowing legislators and agency executives to identify where room for improvement exists in an agency, organization, or community. By ensuring that public agencies are portrayed accurately, disaggregated data are vital in providing information necessary to address customer service and program improvements.

Quality and Productivity Improvement

Quality management and improvements are one of the most important tasks for agency management. In the public sector, agencies must not only consider the quality of the products or services provided for their direct clients, but also the effects of those products or services on the taxpaying public, which do not exist in private sector management (Van Dooren, 2008). The goal of quality management in the public sector is to ensure that the taxpayers are being provided an acceptable product or service in return for their payments. What had appeared to be perhaps a contradiction to some—process-measures-oriented Total Quality Management and outcome-oriented performance management—have found a way to integrate (Aristigueta, 2008). Quality and process measures usually thought of as organizational outputs are viewed as part of a comprehensive performance measurement initiative. The designers of Total Quality Management, Edward Deming and Joseph Juran, believed that the results or outcome would follow from a well-defined and well-executed process. The performance required a focus on outcomes or results with potential overlooking process to achieve the required results. Poister (2004, p. 237) found that quality and productivity are seen today as "mutually supportive or complementary performance criteria."

Table 12.2 shows statistics for disabled worker benefit claims between August 2012 and October 2013. One of the Social Security Administration's tasks is adjudicating applications for disabled worker status. The data shown in the table track the number of claims made, the number of claims awarded, the number of disabled workers currently receiving

TABLE 12.2 DISABLED WORKER BENEFICIARY STATISTICS, AUGUST 2012 TO OCTOBER 2013

Time Period	Awards				In Current Payment Status		Terminations		
	Number of Applications	Number	Number Increase over Prior Period	Percent of Applications	Number at End of Period	Increase over Prior Period	Number	Increase over Prior Period	Termination Rate
August-12	288,795	75,459	−9.15%	26.13%	8,767,941	0.16%	61,278	−2.35%	0.69%
September-12	222,777	82,687	9.58%	37.12%	8,786,049	0.21%	64,279	4.90%	0.72%
October-12	216,474	82,379	−0.37%	38.05%	8,803,335	0.20%	65,543	1.97%	0.73%
November-12	240,796	71,698	−12.97%	29.78%	8,805,353	0.02%	68,304	4.21%	0.76%
December-12	180,953	89,332	24.59%	49.37%	8,827,795	0.25%	66,398	−2.79%	0.74%
January-13	192,392	74,610	−16.48%	38.78%	8,830,026	0.03%	70,358	5.96%	0.78%
February-13	211,418	72,508	−2.82%	34.30%	8,840,427	0.12%	62,331	−11.41%	0.69%
March-13	276,482	81,804	12.82%	29.59%	8,853,614	0.15%	68,556	9.99%	0.76%
April-13	216,972	76,983	−5.89%	35.48%	8,865,586	0.14%	64,877	−5.37%	0.72%
May-13	259,760	73,508	−4.51%	28.30%	8,877,921	0.14%	61,280	−5.54%	0.68%
June-13	214,787	78,418	6.68%	36.51%	8,892,515	0.16%	63,639	3.85%	0.70%
July-13	196,952	76,207	−2.82%	38.69%	8,904,078	0.13%	64,701	1.67%	0.71%
August-13	271,235	73,058	−4.13%	26.94%	8,913,388	0.10%	63,623	−1.67%	0.70%
September-13	206,105	76,640	4.90%	37.18%	8,925,372	0.13%	64,199	0.91%	0.71%
October-13	199,340	70,800	−7.62%	35.52%	8,936,932	0.13%	59,479	−7.35%	0.65%

Source: US Social Security Administration (2014).

disability benefits, and the number of people who were terminated from disabled worker status. It also shows data on the percentage of claims awarded, the percentage increase in workers receiving benefits, and the percentage of disability recipients who were terminated from disabled worker status. This information is crucial to agency management and legislators who want to know how stringent the Social Security Administration is being in regard to adjudication of claims as well as the number of clients who are covered by disability insurance and those who have been terminated from disabled status.

Information shown in table 12.2 can help managers identify functional areas within the Social Security Disability Insurance program that are either not approving enough claims or are approving too many claims and whether a sufficient or insufficient number of people are being taken off disability status. The total number of people receiving benefits can be used by legislators to determine appropriate public policy concerning disability insurance, which is coming under increased scrutiny by elected officials who suspect that some unemployed workers who have exhausted their unemployment benefits are attempting to apply for disability insurance.

Tools Used for Quality Improvements

Total Quality Management. Edward Deming is credited with introducing quality control to industry; he used statistics to examine industrial production processes for flaws and believed that improving product quality depended on increased management-labor cooperation as well as improved design and production processes. Deming developed his management theory while working as an economic consultant in Japan. Eventually his ideas came to the United States, and organizations began to incorporate quality control into their practices through Deming's teachings. Although he did not use the term *Total Quality Management,* he is credited with its development. In his book, *Out of the Crisis,* Deming (1986) provides sixteen steps toward quality management:

1. Create constancy of purpose toward improvement of product and service, with the aim of becoming competitive, staying in business, and providing jobs.
2. Adopt the new philosophy. We are in a new economic age. Western management must awaken to the challenge, must learn its responsibilities, and take on leadership for change.

3. Cease dependence on inspection to achieve quality. Eliminate the need for massive inspection by building quality into the product in the first place.

4. End the practice of awarding business on the basis of a price tag. Instead, minimize total cost. Move toward a single supplier for any one item on a long-term relationship of loyalty and trust.

5. Improve constantly and forever the system of production and service, to improve quality and productivity, and thus constantly decrease costs.

6. Institute training on the job.

7. Institute leadership. The aim of supervision should be to help people, machines, and gadgets do a better job. Supervision of management is in need of overhaul, as well as supervision of production workers.

8. Drive out fear so that everyone may work effectively for the company.

9. Break down barriers between departments. People in research, design, sales, and production must work as a team in order to foresee problems of production and use that may be encountered with the product or service.

10. Eliminate slogans, exhortations, and targets for the workforce, asking for zero defects and new levels of productivity. Such exhortations only create adversarial relationships, as the bulk of the causes of low quality and low productivity belong to the system and thus lie beyond the power of the workforce.

11. Eliminate work standards (quotas) on the factory floor. Substitute with leadership.

12. Eliminate management by objective. Eliminate management by numbers and numerical goals. Instead substitute with leadership.

13. Remove barriers that rob the hourly worker of his right to pride of workmanship. The responsibility of supervisors must be changed from sheer numbers to quality.

14. Remove barriers that rob people in management and in engineering of their right to pride of workmanship.

15. Institute a vigorous program of education and self-improvement.

16. Put everybody in the company to work to accomplish the transformation. The transformation is everybody's job.

Joseph Juran is credited with adding the human dimension to quality management. He pressed for the education and training of managers and believed that human relations problems were the ones to isolate. He viewed resistance to change as the root cause of quality issues. Juran's concept of quality management extended outside the walls of the factory to encompass nonmanufacturing processes, especially those that might be thought of as service related. For example, in an interview he observed (Selden, 1997, pp. xxi–xxii):

> The key issues facing managers in sales are no different than those faced by managers in other disciplines. Sales managers say they face problems such as "It takes us too long...we need to reduce the error rate." They want to know, "How do customers perceive us?" These issues are no different than those facing managers trying to improve in other fields. The systematic approaches to improvement are identical... There should be no reason our familiar principles of quality and process engineering would not work in the sales process.

In practice, others adapted and shortened the requirements. For example, the strategy of Total Quality Management developed by a branch of the US Navy in the 1980s to help public sector agencies improve their productivity and service quality is guided by four principles: (1) that customers determine the needed quality of a product or service, (2) it is the responsibility of upper management to improve service or product quality to the level demanded by the customer, (3) quality should be improved by the study and improvement of work processes, and (4) quality improvement is a perpetual process and needs to be conducted throughout the entire organization (Houston & Dockstader, 1988). To fulfill these principles, management created quality management boards staffed by managers from departments that have been targeted for improvement. The improvement process is structured as a "plan-do-check-act" cycle that examines two categories of improvement: unexpected problems that arise during the creation and delivery of the agency's product or service and issues that have arisen from within the system (Houston & Dockstader, 1988).

Zu, Fredendall, and Douglas (2008) describe seven practices for Total Quality Management: top management support, customer relationship, supplier relationship, workforce management, quality information, product/service design, and process management. Nonetheless, Total Quality Management has developed into a mature field with sound definitional and conceptual foundations (Sousa & Voss, 2002), and new quality methods continue to grow (Chiarini, 2012; Maleyeff, 2007).

For example, Six Sigma, which is "an organized and systematic method for strategic process improvement and new product and service development that relies on statistical methods and the scientific method to make dramatic reductions in customer defined defect rates" (Linderman, Shroeder, Zaheer, & Choo, 2003, p. 194), has generated intense interest. Likewise, lean methods are focused on the "simplification of the mainstream with the intent of avoiding any kind of waste and accelerating the flow" (Chiarini, 2012, p. 29).

Two major categories of metrics are relevant to lean and Six Sigma in organizations: process metrics and organizational metrics (www.epa.gov/lean/government/pdf/Metrics_guide.pdf). *Process metrics* address a specific process or program and provide information on key attributes of the process such as time, cost, quality, outputs, and process complexity. *Organizational metrics* address characteristics of the broader organization or agency, providing information on the status of lean deployment and morale. Table 12.3 provides examples of the metrics used in the US Environmental Protection Agency.

TABLE 12.3 EXAMPLES OF PROCESS AND ORGANIZATIONAL METRICS

PROCESS METRICS

Time Metrics	Cost Metrics	Quality Metrics
• Lead Time	• Labor Savings	• Customer Satisfaction
• Best and Worst Completion Time	• Cost Savings	• Rework
• Percent On-Time Delivery	• Cost per Product	• Percent Complete and Accurate
• Processing Time		• Roiling First Pass Yield
• Activity Ratio		
• Value = Added Time		
• Non-Value = Added Time		
• Percent Value = Added Time		

Output Metrics	Process Complexity Metrics
• Production	• Process Steps
• Backlog	• Value = Added Process Steps
• Work in Process	• Decisions
• Inventory	• Delays
	• Handoffs
	• Loops
	• Black Holes

ORGANIZATIONAL METRICS

Lean Deployment	Morale Metrics
• Lean Events Conducted	• Employee Satisfaction
• Lean Event Participation	• Turnover
• Lean Training	

Source: http://www.epa.gov/lean/government/pdf/Metrics_guide.pdf.

Six Sigma. Six Sigma is an organizational change and quality improvement strategy originally designed to increase business profitability. The approach was developed in the mid-1980s by Mikel Harry, then a senior staff engineer at Motorola, and used by executives such as George Fisher and Richard Schroeder of that company to produce both improvements in quality and reductions in cost, with savings due to operations improvements alone of over $2.2 billion. From Motorola, Schroeder and Harry took the Six Sigma methodology to such companies as ABB (Asea Brown Bovari), an international engineering firm, and later to Texas Instruments, Allied Signal, and General Electric, in each case producing documented savings of hundreds of millions of dollars within a relatively short time period (one to two years). Having shown such impressive results, Six Sigma is being employed by hundreds of companies and public sector organizations throughout the world.

Six Sigma is a disciplined, data-driven approach and methodology for eliminating defects (driving toward six standard deviations between the mean and the nearest specification limit) in any process (http://www.isixsigma.com/new-to-six-sigma/getting-started/what-six-sigma/). It begins by employing statistical analysis to locate process errors that produce defects in a product line. A "sigma rating" is then determined, based on the number of defects per 1 million products. Strategies are developed for correcting errors and in turn improving quality and reducing cost. Six Sigma is a level of performance with 99.9997 percent perfection, meaning that the organization delivers its services with only 0.0003 percent defects among 1 million transactions. This means that only three or four customers are not satisfied by the service (or they receive services with defects). For example, a state-level office of cash and debt management could decide to implement Six Sigma methodology and establish a goal of achieving 99.9997 percent perfection with the domestic cash transactions. That would mean that the office would allow only three or four defective transactions out of 1 million total. This will reduce the extra costs that the unit is paying because of the errors that occur while doing the payments, and increase the satisfaction of customers because they would be paid on time and without any inconvenience.

Advocates of Six Sigma claim that their techniques and approaches can turn around poor performance, improve public perception of a company's products, develop an improved financial rating, create a competitive barrier, corner markets, and improve the cycle time of new product development. Six Sigma uses statistical tools, but it is important to note that "the measures of Six Sigma performance begin with the customer"

(Pande & Holpp, 2001, p. 214); it helps managers decide which data and information they need and how best to use these data and the information. The implementation of Six Sigma starts with a management decision on what the organization needs to achieve: a full-scale change (business transformation), strategic improvements limited to one or two critical needs, or solving persistent problems within the organization.

Once this decision has been made, many employees and managers in the organization are trained for different roles: Black Belt, Green Belt, Master Black Belt, Champion, and Implementation Leader. The people acting in these roles have specific tasks to implement. The Black Belt works with a team on a specific Six Sigma project and is "responsible for getting the team started, building their confidence, observing and participating in training, managing team dynamics, and keeping projects to successful results" (Pande & Holpp, 2001, p. 25). The Green Belt brings the new Six Sigma tools into day-to-day activities. Most employees in the organization are trained to perform this role. The Master Black Belt, an expert in Six Sigma analytical tools, trains Black Belts and their teams. The Champion is the person in the organization who provides the resources, informs management on the Six Sigma progress, and makes sure that ongoing projects are in accordance to the organizational goals. "The ultimate goal of the Implementation Leader is to drive Six Sigma thinking, tools, and habits across the organization and to help the effort reap financial and customer benefits" (Pande & Holpp, 2001, p. 25).

All Six Sigma roles can be successfully performed if the actors are adequately trained. Six Sigma involves cultural change as well, and the people in their new roles have to act to facilitate that change. These new roles require abandoning the well-rooted saying, "That's the way things are done here." Changing habits and establishing new statistical tools in order to improve the quality of processes and to achieve almost perfect performance are hard tasks. Management has to know how to energize the employees and, most of all, be persistent in meeting the high established goals. Some have found that if appropriately established and implemented, Six Sigma can be a powerful tool for employee motivation; "When the company is committed to improving its processes, to meeting customer expectations, to cutting cost, employees will naturally feel motivated to do better" (Brue, 2002, p. 30). In other words, the fact that they actively participate in the implementation of the changes and ultimately the goals of the organization motivates the employees to give their best to the organization.

The Six Sigma methodology follows five steps (DMAIC) in establishing goals, tools, and measures:

D—Defining the projects and goals. The project should be meaningful and manageable, which means that the team can get the project done.

M—Measuring the current performance. The units of measurements are the outputs or outcomes, the process itself, and the inputs.

A—Analyzing and determining the roots of the problems or defects.

I—Improvement of the outputs and outcomes, the process and the inputs.

C—Control, that is, "developing a monitoring process to keep track of changes," "creating a response plan for dealing with problems that may arise" and "helping focus management's attention on a few crucial measures" (Pande & Holpp, 2001, p. 54).

The DMAIC steps can be briefly explained by using our example of the office of cash and debt management transactions. Once the managers make the decision to use Six Sigma methodology, they have to define the goal. Let us suppose that the goal of the project is to reduce the number of errors made in their cash flow transactions to 3 or 4 in 1 million. After establishing the goal, a project team has to be formed and the people on that team trained. The other employees who will not be part of the project team have to be trained to perform day-to-day operations in order to achieve the goal. The next step is measuring the current performance. The project team gathers data, such as how many transactions a day this office is doing per certain time unit (daily, monthly, semiannually, or annually), how many defects are occurring, where in the process the defects occur, the amount of the fees that this office is paying because of the repeated transactions, whether there are any other consequences induced by these errors, and so on. The data then must be carefully analyzed in order to find the source of the problem. In our case, the analysis might show that one part of the problem is outdated software that cannot adequately support the increased number of transactions, and another part of the problem lies in the lack of employee training. The improvement step has to solve these two major problems by providing new software and organizing training for the employees. The final step of DMAIC is control, or the phase where the office of cash and debt management would ensure that the results of the project will last in the future.

The ultimate goal of Six Sigma is to reach almost perfect performance in the organization, satisfy customers, and save money by reducing the defects in the production phase and the delivery of goods and services. This is possible only if the whole organization is aware of the goal and is willing to implement the necessary changes in the organization. Successful implementation of Six Sigma requires the involvement of the whole organization in the new process and the full support from the managers who play the major role in the success of this new method.

The organizations that use Six Sigma methodology are faced with new challenges: they have to be prepared to implement all necessary steps, train employees on how to perform new roles, and be persistent with the established goals if they want to enjoy the benefits. Producing and delivering goods and services with the greatest customer satisfaction, avoiding the defects while saving money are desirable goals for the private companies and public organizations alike.

Lean. Another quality improvement tool, lean, started in manufacturing and has been adopted by government to enable agencies to work more effectively and efficiently by eliminating waste in processes. Numerous government agencies, including the US Environmental Protection Agency (EPA), are using lean improvement methods to improve the quality, transparency, and speed of their processes (http://www.epa.gov/lean/government/). EPA headquarters and regional offices have employed lean methods to shorten process time frames by as much as 82 percent and reduce the number of process steps by more than 63 percent. About thirty state environmental agencies are using it to dramatically improve permitting and other processes. Agencies have reduced administrative review times by over 50 percent and slashed permitting backlogs.

Lean is based on five steps: (1) specify value from the customer's perspective, (2) identify the stream of processes used to provide value, (3) remove non-value-added activities from the value stream, (4) create pull by having all work initiated by customer demand, and (5) strive for perfection (Maleyeff, 2007). The EPA uses three common methods applied in lean: value stream mapping, 5S, and kaizen rapid process improvement events (http://www.epa.gov/lean/government/methods.htm).

Value Stream Mapping. Value stream mapping (VSM) refers to the activity of developing a visual representation of the flow of the processes, from start to finish, involved in delivering a desired outcome, service, or product (a "value stream") that customers value. In the context of housing agencies, a value stream could be the process of approving new affordable housing developments or hiring new agency staff. VSM examines information flows and systems, as well as the flow of the product or service product (e.g., housing permits) through an agency's processes. It can increase understanding of actual decision-making processes and identify sources of non-value-added time (e.g., documents waiting to be reviewed). The typical products of a two- to five-day VSM workshop are two maps—a map of the current state of targeted processes and a future state map of the desired process flow—and an associated implementation plan for future process improvement activities. Value stream mapping refers to the activity of developing a visual representation of the flow of the processes, from start to finish, involved in delivering a desired outcome, service, or product (a value stream) that customers value.

The Delaware Department of Natural Resources and Environmental Control (DNREC) conducted a VSM workshop to identify ways to make air construction permitting processes more efficient. In this case, the future state goals focused on improving permitting processing times by significantly reducing rework and waiting periods and increasing early communication with permit applicants. As a result of process changes, the following benefits were achieved: (1) backlog reduced from 199 to 59 natural minor permits in three months and to 25 in one year; (2) natural minor air construction permits issued within 76 days of application submittal; (3) Delaware DNREC staff time allocated more effectively to "mission-critical work"; (4) rework reduced by 45 percent; (5) devotion of FTE employees half-time to VSM efforts during project planning and implementation stages; (6) improved communication with industry applicants; (7) a process improvement culture integrated into the division; and (8) staff gained ownership of the process, empowering them to identify and address improvement opportunities (http://www.epa.gov/lean/government/state-initiatives/delaware.htm).

5S. This methodology, named after the Japanese words sort (*Seiri*), *set in order* (*Seiton*), *shine* (*Seiso*), *standardize* (*Seiketsu*), and *sustain* (*Shitsuke*), is useful to "reduce waste and optimize productivity through maintaining an orderly workplace and using visual cues to achieve more consistent operational results" (http://www.epa.gov/lean/environment/methods/fives.htm). Typically this is the first lean method that organizations implement. Before engaging in housekeeping practices, the 5S process may need the establishment of a cross-functional team, a revision of the work area, and a brainstorming session to envision a "future state" (Productivity Press Development Team, 1996).

The Minnesota Department of Health conducted a 5S event to remove fifteen hundred pounds of trash, paper, and surplus items from a work area (http://www.lean.state.mn.us/LEAN_pages/results.html). In addition to improving the aesthetics and efficiency of the workplace, "5S places" can make the environment safer for customers and employees.

Kaizen Events. Kaizen, which combines two Japanese words that mean "to take apart" and "to make good," refers to an approach to continuous improvement founded on the belief that small, incremental changes routinely applied and sustained over a long period result in significant performance improvements. It focuses on eliminating waste in a targeted system or process of an organization, improving productivity, and achieving sustained improvement. Kaizen activity is often focused in the form of rapid improvement events (sometimes called a kaizen blitz) that bring together a cross-functional team for two to five days to study a process and begin implementation of process changes.

The Iowa Department of Natural Resources (DNR) used kaizen events to improve fifteen projects. As a result of these events, Iowa DNR observed improved time efficiency of processes, increased the overall quality of permit applications, increased the ability to focus on "mission-critical" work, experienced continuous cultural improvement in the department, and improved relationships with the regulated community and permit applicants (http://www.epa.gov/lean/government/primer/resources/LeanGovtPrimer.pdf). Table 12.4 summarizes Iowa DNR projects' improvement.

Lean Six Sigma. The fusion of the Japanese and American methods, lean and Six Sigma, has rendered a well-established system for process improvement (Chiarini, 2012). Lean Six Sigma encompasses many common features of lean and Six Sigma, such as an emphasis on customer satisfaction, a culture of continuous improvement, the search for root causes, and comprehensive employee involvement. In addition to the adoption of the core principles of lean and Six Sigma, organizations that implement the combined approach use other tools such as visual controls and root cause analysis.

Together these systems can tackle issues of quality and efficiency by reducing variability and optimizing process flows. In each case, "a high degree of training and education takes place, from upper management

TABLE 12.4 RESULTS OF IOWA'S PROJECT IMPROVEMENTS

Kaizen Event Projects	Before Process Improvement	After Process Improvement
Air quality complex permit	214 days	180 days
Air quality new source construction	62 days	6 days
Animal feeding operations construction permits	66 days	36 days
Clean water construction permits	28 months	4.5 months
Floodplain permits	Implemented: Predesign meeting and outreach strategy, database design, and permit redesign	
Landfill permits	187 days	30 days
Land acquisition: best case	24 months	9 months
Land acquisition: worse case	22 years	6.3 years
Leaking underground storage tanks corrective action decision	38 months	3 months
Legal services: administrative orders	Consent orders Unilateral orders Attorney General referrals	40%–90% improvement in lead time reduction
Manure management plans	Incomplete submittals reduced by 50%	
National Pollution Discharge Elimination System (NPDES) wastewater permitting	425 days	15 days
Sovereign land permits: environmental reviews	163 days	86 days
State Revolving Fund (SRF) cross-cutters	Delays reduced by 40% Steps reduced by 23%	
SRF cross-cutters	Delays reduced by 40% Steps reduced by 23%	
Vehicle dispatch	Pool vehicles reassigned to Department of Administrative Services—General Service Enterprise	
Magazine production	Allows on-time quality production while meeting day-to-day communication needs	

Source: http://www.epa.gov/lean/government/primer/resources/LeanGovtPrimer.pdf.

TABLE 12.5 KAIZEN EVENT

Day 1: Training Day	Day 2: Discovery Day	Day 3: Do Day	Day 4: Do, Redo, Document Day	Day 5: Celebration Day
Begin mapping and measuring current work process	Measure and analyze current work process	Create and map new process	Finalize new process design, estimate benefits, develop action plan	Present results and celebrate

Source: http://www.epa.gov/lean/government/starterkit/resources/Lean-Starter-Kit.pdf.

to the shop floor" (Maleyeff, 2007, p. 8) with impressive results. For example, Southcoast Health System, a three-hospital system in Massachusetts with six thousand employees, began implementing Lean Six Sigma at the start of 2009 and in two years had realized about $20 million in cost benefits, according to Patrick Gannon, vice president and chief quality officer for Southcoast Hospitals Group (http://www.southcoasttoday.com/apps/pbcs.dll/article?AID=/20101022/SCBULLETIN/11010316/1036).

Lean methods can be developed and implemented in a short period of time, while Six Sigma requires a longer analytic process. For instance, a kaizen event can be developed over a five-day agenda (table 12.5).

As suggested by the activity scheduled on the fifth day, the ability to focus on action-oriented projects is a good way to simultaneously achieve short-term material outputs and positively engage employees in a culture of continuous improvement. Six Sigma's more systematic approach provides a unique role structure, a long-term improvement procedure, and a focus on metrics (Zu et al., 2008). Such features are considered improvements to previous management systems and are oriented toward the achievement of long-term outcomes. Example of projects in the US Department of Agriculture that use both are streamlining existing physical work flow to eliminate redundancy, reviewing staff alignment and duties to recommend improvements in efficiency, and improving customer service through more efficient processing (http://www.ocfo.usda.gov/lssprojects.htm).

Monitoring the Nuts and Bolts

This chapter has examined the kinds of performance measures used most frequently to monitor service quality and productivity in public and nonprofit agencies and to illustrate how they are used. As compared with performance measurement systems that are intended to support strategic management processes or budgeting systems that work with annual data, for example, systems designed to monitor quality and productivity tend to focus on more detailed indicators of performance at the operating level and often very frequently, perhaps on a monthly, weekly, or even daily basis. Governmental and nonprofit entities that manage to sustain a comprehensive quality and productivity improvement program over many years appear to have some common characteristics: "(1) they initiated and continue to preach a constancy of purpose based on a consistent underlying methodology; (2) their key leadership positions have been in place for lengthy periods of time; (3) they guarantee that employees will not lose their jobs as a consequence of an improvement project; and (4) they measured their time to success in years rather than weeks or months" (Maleyeff, 2007, p. 6).

References

Aristigueta, M. P. (2008). The integration of quality and performance. In P. De Lancer Julnes, F. Berry, M. Aristigueta, & K. Yang (Eds.), *International handbook of practice-based performance management*. Thousand Oaks, CA: Sage.

Behn, R. D. (2003). Why measure performance? Different purposes require different measures. *Public Administration Review, 63*(5), 586–606.

Berman, E. M. (1998). *Productivity in public and nonprofit organizations: Strategies and techniques*. Thousand Oaks, CA: Sage.

Berman, E. M., & West, J. P. (1995). Municipal commitment to total quality management: A survey of recent progress. *Public Administration Review, 55*(1), 57–66.

Brue, G. (2002) *Six Sigma for managers*. New York: McGraw-Hill.

Carr, D. K., & Littman, I. D. (1990) *Excellence in government: Total quality management in the 1990s*. Arlington, VA: Coopers & Lybrand, 1990.

Chiarini, A. (2012). *From total quality control to lean Six Sigma: Evolution of the most important management systems for the excellence*. Milan: Springer.

Deming, E. (1986) *Out of the crisis*. Cambridge, MA: MIT Press.

Enticott, G., Boyne, G. A., & Walker, R. M. (2008). The use of multiple informants in public administration research: Data aggregation using organizational echelons. *Journal of Public Administration Research and Theory, 19*, 229–253. doi:10.1093/jopart/mun017

Holzer, M. (Ed.). (1992). *Public productivity handbook*. New York: Dekker.

Houston, A., & Dockstader, S. L. (1988). *A total quality improvement process model*. http://www.dtic.mil/dtic/tr/fulltext/u2/a202154.pdf

Hyde, A. (1997, July). A decade's worth of lessons in continuous improvement. *Government Executive*, pp. 58–68.

Linderman, K., Shroeder, R., Zaheer, S., & Choo, A. (2003). Six sigma: A goal theoretic perspective. *Journal of Operations Management, 21*(2), 193–203.

Maleyeff, J. (2007) *Improving service delivery in government with lean Six Sigma.* Washington, DC: IBM Center for the Business of Government.

Matzer Jr., J. (Ed.). (1986). *Productivity improvement techniques: Creative approaches for local government.* Washington, DC: International City Management Association.

Pande, P. S., & Holpp, L. (2001). *What is Six Sigma?* New York: McGraw-Hill.

Poister, T. H. (2003). *Measuring performance in public and nonprofit organizations.* San Francisco: Jossey-Bass.

Poister, T. H. (2004). Monitoring quality and productivity in the public sector. In M. Holzer & S. H. Lee (Eds.), *Public productivity handbook* (2nd ed., pp. 231–245). New York: Marcel Dekker.

Productivity Press Development Team. (1996). *5S for operators: 5 pillars of the visual workplace.* Portland, OR: Productivity Press.

Selden, P. H. (1997). *Sales process engineering: A personal workshop.* Milwaukee, WI: ASQ Quality Press.

Sousa, R., & Voss, S. A. (2002). Quality management revisited: A reflective review and agenda for future research. *Journal of Operations Management, 20,* 91–109.

Sterck, M., & Bouckaert, G. (2008). Performance information of high quality: How to develop a legitimate, functional, and sound performance measurement system. In P. L. Julnes, F. S. Berry, M. P. Aristigueta, & K. Yang (Eds.), *International handbook of practice-based performance management* (pp. 433–453). Thousand Oaks, CA: Sage.

Sterck, M., & Scheers, B. (2006). Trends in performance budgeting in seven OECD countries. *Public Performance and Management Review, 30*(1), 47–72. doi:10.2753/PMR1530-9576300103

US Social Security Administration. (2014). Selected data from Social Security's Disability Program. http://www.socialsecurity.gov/OACT/STATS/dibStat.html

US Veteran's Affairs Office of Inspector General. (2014). *Review of patient wait times, scheduling practices, and alleged patient deaths at the Phoenix Health Care System.* http://www.va.gov/oig/pubs/VAOIG-14–02603–178.pdf

Van Dooren, W. (2008). Quality and performance management: Toward a better integration? In P. L. Julnes, F. S. Berry, M. P. Aristigueta, & K. Yang (Eds.), *International handbook of practice-based performance management* (pp. 413–432). Thousand Oaks, CA: Sage.

Zu, X., Fredendall, L. D., & Douglas, T. J. (2008). The evolving theory of quality management: The role of Six Sigma. *Journal of Operations Management, 26,* 630–650.

CHAPTER THIRTEEN

SOLICITING STAKEHOLDER FEEDBACK

Who are the stakeholders of a public agency or program? What tools are available to identify stakeholders? Why should we be concerned with soliciting their feedback? What tools are available to solicit their feedback? What type of measures should be used? How may this feedback improve our services?

What used to be referred to as citizen participation has matured into contemporary public engagement—and stakeholder involvement—and broadened in its definition to include those who had not previously had a voice in policymaking and implementation (Thomas, 2013). Other democracies around the world, from Brazil to the Netherlands, have experienced similar trends (Ackerman, 2004; Fung & Wright, 2001). Others also identify stakeholder concerns as crucial to the success of public organizations, nonprofit organizations, and communities (Bryson, 2011; Light, 1998; Fernandez & Rainey, 2006; Rainey, 2009).

Stakeholder engagement requires the identification of the roles the public plays in public management in order to maximize resources and address needs. According to Thomas (2013), the roles of the public in relation to the government take the following form:

- *Customers* receiving specific services from the government, nonprofit agency, or contract. Examples include garbage pickup, issuing of drivers' licenses, and health care provided by public health clinics.

- *Partners* joining with the public managers in coproducing services or pursuing public goals. In this form, individuals work with government, as in the example of sorting recyclables from other waste prior to collection by government or contracted service.
- In the most important role, that of *citizens,* managers deliberate with the public to answer larger questions about what services to provide or how to exercise governmental authority. Examples include the one later in this chapter regarding the selection of crosswalks, or it may take, as another example, the form of discussing whether to adopt a new recycling program.
- Public managers must work with members of the public in more than one of these roles at a time, for example, when people expect to be treated courteously and helpfully (as customers), as they voice opinions (as citizens), and on the nature of public programs in which they might assist (as partners). The United Way example later in this chapter demonstrates the role of citizen and partner in action.

Beyond customers and the public at large, however, it is important to note that an agency's stakeholders may include many other groups. First, governing bodies such as congressional offices, state legislatures, county commissions, and city councils are obviously important stakeholders from an operating agency's perspective, as are boards of directors of nonprofit organizations. In addition, central executives such as governors and mayors and their administrative agencies are important stakeholders, as are regulatory agencies that have purview over programs managed by line agencies. Second, since programs are delivered so often through networked environments, one agency's stakeholders are likely to include an array of other governmental agencies and jurisdictions in the intergovernmental system with which they must work effectively in order to provide services. Third, government agencies often rely heavily on grantees, contractors, and service providers (usually for-profit private firms or nonprofit organizations) to deliver services. And state and local governmental agencies are often dependent on higher-level government agencies to provide them with resources through grant programs, just as nonprofit organizations often rely on public agencies or private foundations for funding. Finally, business groups, civic and community or neighborhood associations, and interest groups often represent important stakeholders who are concerned with particular public agencies and programs.

These collaborations also provide new challenges. Bryson (2004), for example, discusses the importance of stakeholders regarding a public agency's viability and performance and identifies several techniques for analyzing various stakeholders' interests and influence over relevant issues with an eye toward managing relations with those stakeholders more effectively. In examining the Georgia Department of Transportation's partner agencies, Thomas, Poister, and Ertas (2010) find that various stakeholders assess agency performance from different perspectives and that satisfaction in one role does not necessarily equate with satisfaction in another. Using the roles of stakeholders identified by Thomas (2013), this chapter provides examples of stakeholder involvement in measuring and managing performance in nonprofits and government agencies while keeping in mind that satisfaction in one role does not necessarily transfer to satisfaction in another.

Identifying Stakeholders: The Stakeholder Audit

How do we know who our stakeholders are, and how are they identified? Often authors refer to brainstorming techniques to identify stakeholders (see Bryson, 2011) or perhaps to client or customer surveys for services (Hatry, Marcotte, Van Houten, & Weiss, 1998). Thomas and Poister (2011) expand the process for identification by developing for the Georgia Department of Transportation (GDOT) a technique to identify stakeholders consisting of three tasks: (1) defining the stakeholder universe of the agency, (2) defining the information the agency lacks on various stakeholders, and (3) prioritizing those information needs in terms of degree of urgency. In order to accomplish these tasks, they recommend the extensive interviewing of agency personnel using the snowballing technique, which allows the interviewee to identify others who would be relevant to interview so as to include all personnel with relevant perspectives. Thomas and Poister (2011) also suggest that stakeholders themselves might be useful to interview as part of a stakeholder audit.

The stakeholder audit offers two principal benefits over other techniques for identifying stakeholders: "First, the stakeholder audit produces a map of the full range of an agency's stakeholders where most other techniques focus only on specific stakeholder groups or publics" (Thomas & Poister, 2011, p. 80). The broader focus is preferable because most agencies work with multiple stakeholder groups at the same time, as illustrated by the GDOT stakeholder map, shown in figure 13.1, that was created from the stakeholder audit. The paragraph after the figure includes explanation of the categories used in the figure.

FIGURE 13.1 GEORGIA DEPARTMENT OF TRANSPORTATION STAKEHOLDER MAP

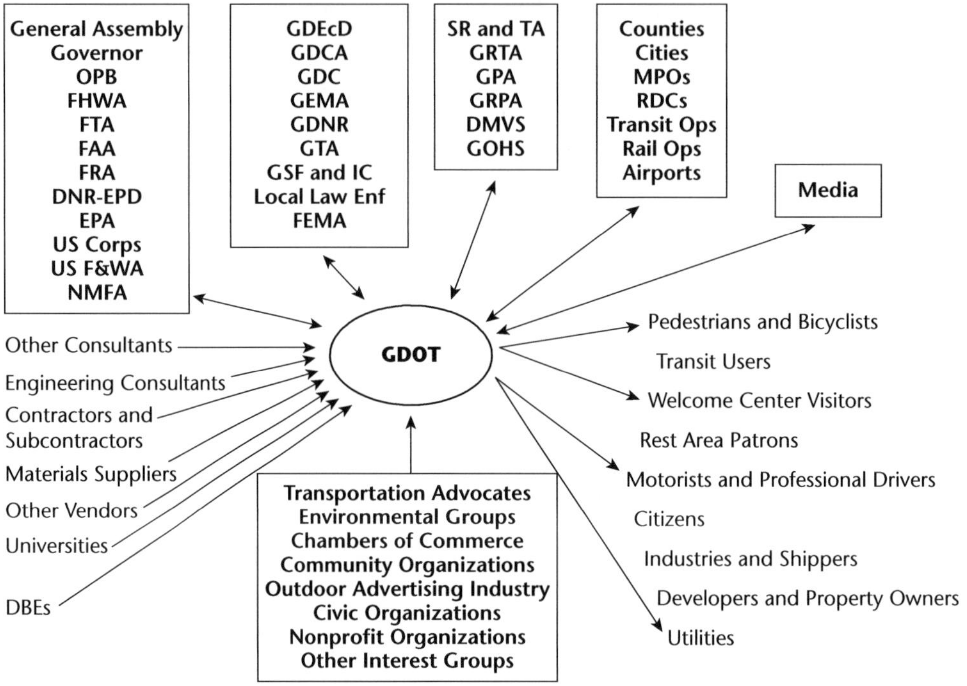

| General Assembly
Governor
OPB
FHWA
FTA
FAA
FRA
DNR-EPD
EPA
US Corps
US F&WA
NMFA | GDEcD
GDCA
GDC
GEMA
GDNR
GTA
GSF and IC
Local Law Enf
FEMA | SR and TA
GRTA
GPA
GRPA
DMVS
GOHS | Counties
Cities
MPOs
RDCs
Transit Ops
Rail Ops
Airports |

Media

Other Consultants
Engineering Consultants
Contractors and Subcontractors
Materials Suppliers
Other Vendors
Universities

DBEs

GDOT

Pedestrians and Bicyclists
Transit Users
Welcome Center Visitors
Rest Area Patrons
Motorists and Professional Drivers
Citizens
Industries and Shippers
Developers and Property Owners
Utilities

**Transportation Advocates
Environmental Groups
Chambers of Commerce
Community Organizations
Outdoor Advertising Industry
Civic Organizations
Nonprofit Organizations
Other Interest Groups**

Source: Poister, Thomas, and Berryman (2013). Used with permission.

According to Poister, Thomas, and Berryman (2013), "The stakeholders on the right side of the map include customer groups such as public transit users, property owners, and motorists in addition to citizens at large. On the left side are partners and suppliers, such as consultants, contractors, and vendors. Across the top of the stakeholder map are five clusters: (1) entities that provide oversight and resources to GDOT, such as the Governor's Office and the General Assembly, (2) nontransportation government agencies whose missions overlap with GDOT in some way, such as the Department of Community Development and the Department of Natural Resources; (3) other agencies of state government whose missions also focus on strengthening Georgia's transportation system, such as the State Road and Tollway Authority and the Department of Driver and Motor Vehicle Services, (4) other entities that are also involved in planning and delivering transportation services in the state, such as units of local government and public transit authorities, and (5) the media, such as newspapers and local television stations" (p. 307).

The second benefit to a stakeholder audit is that it recommends information gathering and only limited involvement of stakeholders in contrast to the emphasis of other techniques on extensive involvement (Thomas & Poister, 2011). Once the agency's stakeholders have been identified, it is important to understand their roles as related to the agency's performance and to systematically assess their rating of and satisfaction with services produced by the agency and the results generated by it or the quality of the interactions with the agency in various respects.

Obtaining Customer Feedback

Most public agencies that emphasize quality improvement are also concerned at the same time with customer service and customer satisfaction with the services they provide. Thus, they are often interested in regularly soliciting customer feedback. Although that feedback might well focus for the most part on the same performance criteria addressed by the quality indicators, obtaining satisfaction measures directly from customers themselves provides feedback from a different source that might or might not be consistent with the results generated with the programmatic data. In general, agencies solicit or receive direct input and feedback from customers through the following mechanisms: advisory groups, customer councils, focus group sessions, complaint systems, customer surveys, and response cards. In addition, agencies invite feedback in the form of questions, comments, suggestions, and recommendations regarding performance from customers and other stakeholders who visit their websites, and increasingly they are using social media such as Facebook and Twitter to solicit this kind of feedback as well.

The latter three of these channels are good means of accumulating data on a regular, ongoing basis so as to facilitate monitoring performance indicators over time. Although complaint systems principally record negative feedback from customers and therefore cannot be expected to provide a balanced picture of customer attitudes, they can be useful in tracking the extent to which customer dissatisfaction and perceived problems change over time. Surveys can be conducted on a systematic basis by public and nonprofit organizations to solicit unbiased customer feedback, and if they are replicated regularly, they also allow managers to track trends in customer satisfaction over time. Ongoing use of response cards, which are very brief surveys focusing attention on specific instances of service delivery, can also indicate trends over time (Hayes, 1997; Hatry et al., 1998; for in-depth discussions of customer satisfaction measurement and analysis, see Hayes, 1997; Vavra, 1997; Allen & Rao, 2000).

Customer Surveys: Girl Scout Council of Northwest Georgia

Broad-based customer or client surveys have become a favored method of soliciting feedback on services offered by public and nonprofit agencies. A good example is provided by the Girl Scout Council of Northwest Georgia, one of three hundred local chapters of the Girl Scouts of the USA. This council, which covers the metropolitan Atlanta areas and twenty additional counties, provides a range of programming to girls at four levels (Brownies, Junior Girl Scouts, Cadettes, and Senior Girl Scouts) aimed at producing seven generalized outcomes. The first four of these are national goals (developing individual potential, relating to others, developing values, and contributing to society); the remaining three have been added by the local council (safe activities, productive activities, and structured activities outside of school hours).

To assess the extent to which the program produces the expected outcomes, the council conducts annual surveys of each of three groups that include girls at each of the four levels, leaders who staff the program, and parents. The sample sizes employed are large enough to generate 95 percent confidence intervals of only plus-or-minus 5 percentage points in the final results. Drawing from a logic model of the program, the short-answer questions contained in the three parallel survey instruments are keyed directly to attitudes and behaviors that represent accomplishment of the seven goals.

For each level of girl scouting, the survey responses to various items are combined to compute indexes for each of the seven goals. Furthermore, they are combined across the three surveyed populations—girls, leaders, and parents—as weighted specifically for each goal. The results from this survey for 2002 are summarized in table 13.1 (Girl Scout Council of Northwest Georgia, 2002), basically in terms of the percentage of favorable responses, suggesting that particular goals are being met for the different levels of girl scouts in the program. This example is instructive because it is methodologically rigorous and sophisticated, breaks the results down by clientele groups, and uses customer feedback to track overall program effectiveness in producing desired outcomes.

TABLE 13.1 GIRL SCOUT COUNCIL PROGRAM OUTCOMES

Girls' Age Level	Program Outcomes	Met Criteria (%)
Brownie	Developing Individual Potential	81
	Relating to Others	87
	Developing Values	92
	Contributing to Society	83
	Safe Activities Outside of School Hours	94
	Productive Activities Outside of School Hours	87
	Structured Activities Outside of School Hours	72
Junior	Developing Individual Potential	83
	Relating to Others	88
	Developing Values	90
	Contributing to Society	83
	Safe Activities Outside of School Hours	93
	Productive Activities Outside of School Hours	85
	Structured Activities Outside of School Hours	74
Cadette	Developing Individual Potential	79
	Relating to Others	80
	Developing Values	85
	Contributing to Society	72
	Safe Activities Outside of School Hours	88
	Productive Activities Outside of School Hours	78
	Structured Activities Outside of School Hours	75
Senior	Developing Individual Potential	82
	Relating to Others	85
	Developing Values	91
	Contributing to Society	77
	Safe Activities Outside of School Hours	89
	Productive Activities Outside of School Hours	80
	Structured Activities Outside of School Hours	72

Customer Service

As part of their overall quality improvement processes, public and non-profit agencies often focus on improving customer service. Thus, in addition to monitoring customer feedback on overall program effectiveness, measurement systems also track feedback from customers about how they were treated by service delivery processes. Such indicators focus on detailed, individual parts of the process, and collectively they can paint a composite picture of customers' perceptions of the quality of service they received.

For example, as we discussed in chapter 4, state child support enforcement offices work to ensure adequate financial support for children from broken families by locating absentee parents, establishing paternity when necessary, obligating support payments through the courts system, collecting support payments from absentee parents on a regular basis, and disbursing the payments to custodial parents. In Georgia, the Office of Child Support Enforcement carries out this program through 107 local field offices that work with both custodial and absentee parents. The office periodically conducts operational audits of the local offices to make sure that they are complying with prescribed procedures regarding program delivery, general administration, financial management, public outreach, and security, as well as customer service in terms of responding to complaints, resolving problems, and providing access to information.

To complement these data on customer service, the Office of Child Support Enforcement also conducts periodic surveys of its principal customers, including both custodial and absentee parents who have made visits to a local office or contacted one by telephone. The survey solicits reaction to several statements concerning various components of customer service, including visits to the office, service provided in the office, service provided over the telephone, use of the customer hot line, and the office itself. Customers are asked to rate the importance of each item as well as its actual performance. The indicators can be tracked separately for each individual local office. Thus, these data facilitate tracking measures of customer service locally or on a statewide basis over time; they can also be used to compare the quality of service as perceived by the customer across the 107 local offices.

Washington, DC, government is using Grade DC as an innovative analytical tool to improve customer service in participating agencies. Feedback is collected from the website and combined with data from comments posted on social media sites like Twitter and Facebook (see figure 13.2).

These data allow the district to form a grade for each agency. The goal is for customers to easily offer actionable feedback and help district agencies improve the quality of customer services. At the same time, internal reports are generated each month to aggregate public comments into a single report. The Office of the City Administrator (OCA) monitors these reports and, if necessary, will hold a session on a topic brought up in Grade DC. For example, if residents increase the number of complaints about

FIGURE 13.2 GRADE.DC.GOV: PROVIDING FEEDBACK BY AGENCY

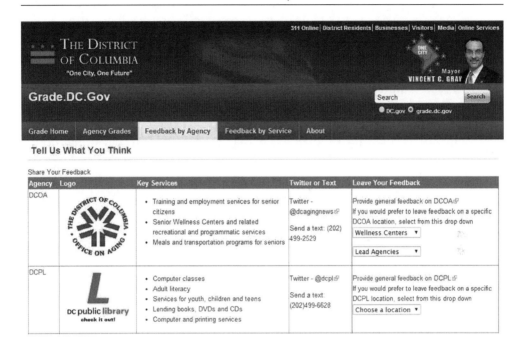

Source: Government of the District of Columbia. http://grade.dc.gov/page/tell-us-what-you-think. Used with permission.

long lines at the Department of Motor Vehicles and the agency's grade decreases from an A to a B, the OCA might hold a session to discuss the issue with the agency and identify appropriate remedies to improve performance (Jason Yuckenberg, personal communication, January 15, 2014).

These sessions use DC Stat, a measurement and communication tool like those found in Baltimore CitiStat, CitiStat Buffalo, and numerous other cities, and used by the office of the city administrator to improve performance and accountability. Formerly known as CapStat, DC Stat is a focused, hour-long public process aimed at driving performance improvements and efficiencies in the city government. During the session, the mayor or city administrator (or both) and other senior staff from relevant agencies take an in-depth look at key issues. Data for the sessions are often derived from the performance plans and key performance indicators for each agency, available for public view on the Track DC website (DC STAT/OCA).

Feedback from Partners and Other Stakeholders

Performance measurement often involves soliciting feedback from stakeholders other than customers on a systematic basis. For example, working from the stakeholder map shown in figure 13.1 as a starting point, Poister et al. (2013) developed a multichannel process of obtaining feedback from a number of key stakeholders of the Georgia Department of Transportation (GDOT). The process was conceived as applying a 360-degree assessment process, a well-known approach to evaluating the capabilities and performance of individual managers, to assess overall organization performance (Testa, 2002) from a variety of perspectives including supervisor, direct reports, and colleagues or counterparts.

The 360-degree assessment model developed and piloted by GDOT, as reflected in figure 13.3, focused on soliciting systematic feedback from motorists, professional drivers, and the public at large as customers. On the partner side, the model sought feedback from the professional consulting community that helped the department develop transportation plans, project designs, and environmental impact studies, as well as the contractors who build new highway and other projects. The model also included elected officials and managers who both work with GDOT in developing, funding, and implementing transportation improvements and constitute customers as the recipients of GDOT local government financial and technical assistance. Finally, the 360-degree assessment

FIGURE 13.3 GDOT'S 360-DEGREE ASSESSMENT MODEL

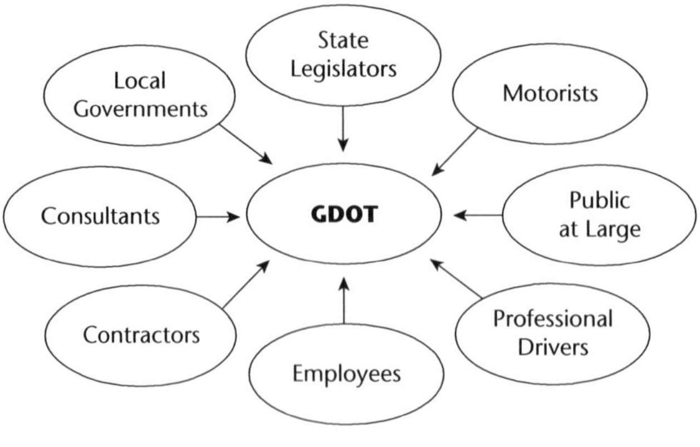

Source: Poister et al. (2013). Used with permission.

process also included feedback from members of the state legislature as resourcing and oversight bodies and from GDOT employees as internal customers.

GDOT conducted a mix of telephone, mailed hard copy, and online surveys of these stakeholder groups, focusing primarily on issues of particular concern to a given stakeholder but also including some questions that are common to all (Poister et al., 2013). For example, the consultants' survey focuses in part on GDOT's consultant selection, contract negotiation, project management, consultant evaluation, payment, and auditing processes, while the contractors' survey focuses more on the department's letting process, project design, construction management, contract modifications, and closeout practices. In contrast, the surveys of local government officials emphasize feedback on transportation planning and programming, project delivery, right-of-way acquisition, permitting, and an array of GDOT local assistance programs.

In addition to tracking the responses to individual substantive survey items such as, "The time it takes to move from initial award to a contract is usually reasonable," on the consultant survey, indexes were developed for common process dimensions such as responsiveness to stakeholder concerns, timeliness in responding to questions, fairness, clarity of requirements, and consistency in decisions and working with stakeholders.

Figure 13.4 summarizes the feedback obtained from four stakeholder groups: consultants, contractors, local government administrators, and state legislators on GDOT's performance along these dimensions. In brief, these ratings indicated that while the department received relatively high marks for responsiveness, fairness, and burden imposed on partners, its grades regarding consistency and timeliness were generally lower. In addition, the 360-degree assessment process showed that overall satisfaction with their working relationships with GDOT ranged from 57 to 77 percent among the five partnering stakeholder groups included in the model.

Beyond such process measures, the 360-degree assessment focused on stakeholder feedback concerning outcomes produced by GDOT such as pavement condition and ride quality on state highways, traffic flow and congestion, highway safety, environmental preservation, and meeting transportation needs in Georgia. Figure 13.5 is a data display presenting stakeholder feedback on GDOT's performance in the area of highway safety. In general, while the highest grades on this score came from the public at large, followed by the consultants and contractors, the lowest grades by far regarding highway safety came from motorists and

FIGURE 13.4 SURVEY RESULTS REGARDING SELECTED PROCESS DIMENSIONS

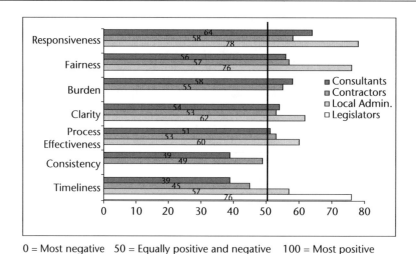

0 = Most negative   50 = Equally positive and negative   100 = Most positive

Source: Poister et al. (2013). Used with permission.

FIGURE 13.5 GRADES FOR HIGHWAY SAFETY

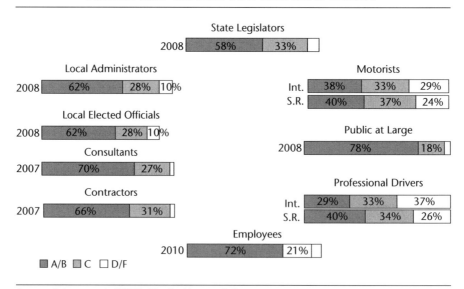

Source: Poister et al. (2013). Used with permission.

professional drivers, which is not surprising inasmuch as they are the groups that drive on state highways the most.

The Commitment to Ongoing Regulatory Excellence Process

A second example of performance measurement and management in the form of monitoring feedback on agency performance from a well-rounded set of external stakeholders is the Commitment to Ongoing Regulatory Excellence (CORE), conducted by the National Council of State Boards of Nursing. CORE is designed to facilitate the use of performance management practices on state boards of nursing, monitor national trends in performance in the field of nursing regulation at large, facilitate benchmarking of an individual state's performance against the field as a whole, and provide a basis for identifying promising practices on the part of high or improving agencies that might be imported or adapted by others.

Because it is a comparative performance measurement and benchmarking process, CORE is discussed in greater detail in chapter 14 (see figure 14.6 for a nursing regulation program logic model), but since it is based in large part on feedback obtained from external stakeholders, it can be instructive in this chapter as well. Like other public agencies, state boards of nursing have numerous external relationships, but the most important stakeholders tend to be the public (patients in particular), employers of nurses (e.g., hospitals, clinics, nursing homes), and nursing education programs in the state as well as nurses themselves.

The CORE process entails conducting surveys of nurses, employers, and nursing program directors periodically, for the most part every two years, to solicit feedback on the performance of all the state boards of nursing in the United States. The sample sizes in the nurse and employers surveys are sufficiently large to provide a reasonable level of statistical reliability at the state level, and while the number of nursing education programs in most states is relatively small, the response rate of the program directors is high and so can be taken as representative of the predominant views of that stakeholder group. While each of these survey instruments is tailored to the concerns and interests of that particular stakeholder group, they also contain common items such as one asking the respondents to provide a rating of the nurse practice act in their state in terms of being current and reflecting the state-of-the-art of nursing practice.

Although some of the performance measures used in the ongoing CORE process come from hard data sources such as cycle times in resolving complaints or reports of nurses violating regulations, or pass rates on

FIGURE 13.6 PATIENT FEEDBACK ON HOSPITAL CARE

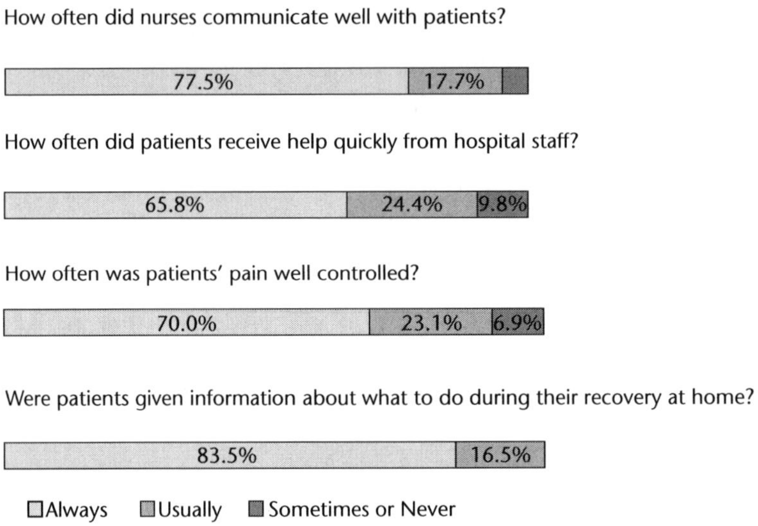

How often did nurses communicate well with patients?

| 77.5% | 17.7% | |

How often did patients receive help quickly from hospital staff?

| 65.8% | 24.4% | 9.8% |

How often was patients' pain well controlled?

| 70.0% | 23.1% | 6.9% |

Were patients given information about what to do during their recovery at home?

| 83.5% | 16.5% |

☐ Always   ☐ Usually   ■ Sometimes or Never

Source: Centers for Medicare and Medicaid Services (2013).

the national nurse licensure exam, the majority of the measures use survey data from these stakeholders. For example, data on patient feedback regarding the care they received in hospitals are accessed from the Hospital Consumer Assessment of Health Care Providers and Systems (HCAHCPS) conducted by the US Centers for Medicare and Medicaid. Figure 13.6 shows responses to four of the survey questions that relate closely to nurses' responsibilities; patients nationwide give more positive responses to the questions regarding communication with nurses and information regarding follow-up care at home than to the items concerning pain control and receiving help quickly when needed. These same data can be broken down on at state-by-state basis as well.

Analyzing Stakeholder Feedback

As is the case with other kinds of performance data, analysis of the data beyond summaries in the aggregate can make stakeholder feedback much more meaningful. As discussed in chapters 6 and 7, this kind of analysis is often based on, or at least begins with, comparisons of particular performance data over time, against targets or budgets, across organizational or programmatic reporting units, and against external benchmarks. For example, the patient feedback data shown in figure 13.6 can be broken down by states whose boards of nursing are structured as independent agencies versus states with umbrella boards that are structured as one part of much larger umbrella organizations. In addition, the data can be compared among small, medium-sized, and large boards of nursing as represented by the number of licensed nurses within their purview.

The CORE process involves biennial surveys of nurses, employers, and nursing program educators, and while many of the items on those surveys are tailored to each of those three stakeholder groups, other items are common questions included in all surveys. For example, a question asking respondents to rate their state's nurse practice act in terms of being current and reflecting state-of-the art nursing practice is relevant to all three surveys. Thus, it might be helpful to compare the percentages of respondents rating their nurse practice acts as good or excellent, for instance, across the three stakeholder groups. In addition, it is often helpful to analyze associations between two or more of the measures incorporated in stakeholder surveys. For instance, data provided by state boards of nursing on their mean average cycle times may be much more informative if they are broken down by whether these boards have delegated authority regarding decisions to open investigations to staff.

Quality-Importance Matrixes

Some public and nonprofit agencies solicit feedback from customers and clients regarding the importance of the services they provide, as well as their quality or effectiveness. The results can yield a customer-based perspective on the strategic context of the agency. For example, nearly seven thousand Pennsylvania residents rated Pennsylvania's Department of Transportation services. Figure 13.7 shows a quality-importance matrix in which those ratings are cross-plotted against the average importance level assigned to each service by the respondents. This survey asked respondents to rate the quality of each of these services with the kind of grades typically used in schools: A = Excellent, B = Good, C = Fair, D = Poor, and F = Failing. Respondents were also instructed to indicate how important each service was to them on a scale of 1 to 10 in which 1 means "Not at All Important" and 10 means "Very Important."

This kind of plot can be particularly revealing in that some services, though highly rated, may not be seen as particularly important, and

FIGURE 13.7 PENNSYLVANIA DEPARTMENT OF TRANSPORTATION QUALITY-IMPORTANCE MATRIX

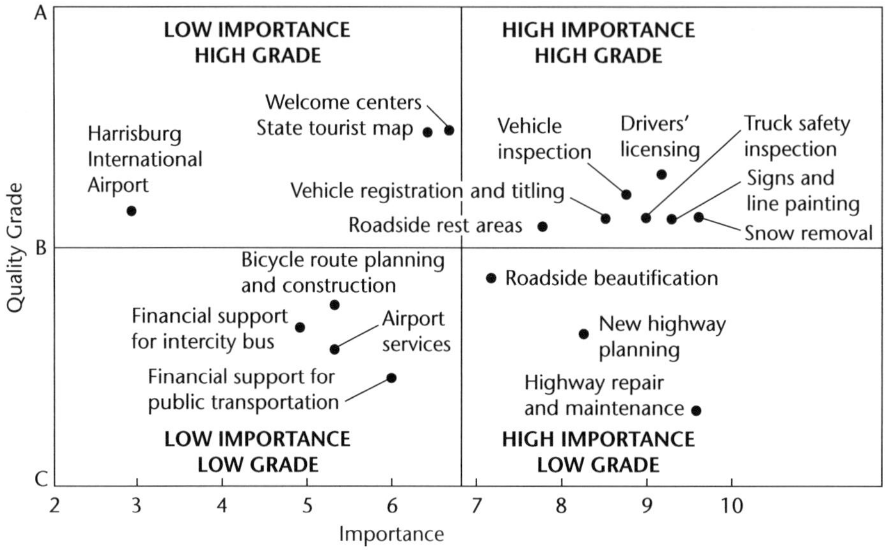

services that are perceived as being much more important may receive lower ratings. In this example, although Department of Transportation customers see the department as doing a good job with respect to such services as driver licensing, truck safety inspections, and snow removal, all rated as being very important, they rated other very important services, such as highway construction and highway repair and maintenance, as still needing improvement.

While the importance ratings shown in figure 13.7 represent "stated importance" because they are based directly on ratings stated in response to questions in a survey, customer satisfaction analysts often use measures of "derived importance" instead because they more accurately reflect the importance of a given public service to customers, given their current levels of performance as perceived by the customers. These derived importance scores are most often derived from multiple regression models in which the overall perceived performance scores or satisfaction levels are regressed on the perceived performance levels or satisfaction measures for each individual service. Assuming that the performance scores or satisfaction levels for each individual service use the same metric or unit of measurement, their regression coefficients provide an indica-

FIGURE 13.8 LOCAL PUBLIC SERVICES IN THE ATLANTA AREA PERFORMANCE: IMPORTANCE MATRIX

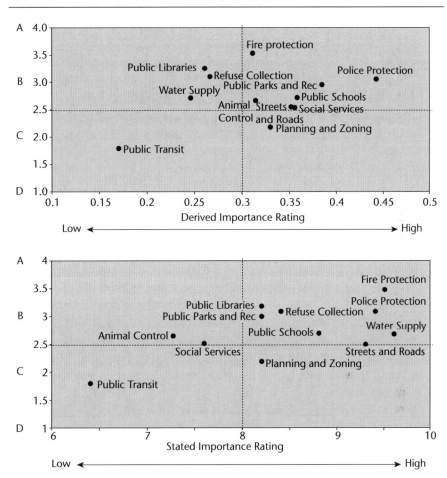

tion of the extent to which each service influences the overall performance of a variety of services or satisfaction with them.

Figure 13.8 shows performance-importance matrixes for a number of local public services in the Atlanta metropolitan area, based on stated importance scores in the lower panel and derived importance scores in the upper panel. Similar to the Pennsylvania Department of Transportation example, the performance of each service was graded on a scale of A to F, while a single summary question asked respondents to assign a grade to a whole set of services provided in their local areas as well.

The location of some services, such as police protection, remain the same or almost the same, while for other services, such as fire protection, it changes dramatically.

As it happened, on the one hand, there was substantial variation in the performance ratings for police protection that correlated strongly with overall grades for these local service as a whole when all the other service ratings were taken into account. Thus, perceived performance of police protection is a strong driver of overall perceived performance. On the other hand, the performance grades for fire protection did not correlate strongly with overall service ratings, and thus its derived importance as a driver of the overall performance ratings on these public services is substantially less than its stated significance.

Thus, derived importance scores provide a more useful indication than do stated importance scores of the relative importance of individual public services in influencing overall performance ratings or satisfaction with public services overall in a given local jurisdiction (Van Ryzin & Immerwahr, 2004). While fire protection is almost certain to be considered of the utmost importance in a local community, as indicated by its high stated importance score shown in figure 13.8, the context of derived importance implies a magnitude of impact or leverage on performance ratings of or satisfaction with a set of services. It should also be understood that this kind of analysis can also be applied to a single public service, with performance ratings of individual dimensions of service delivery—waiting time, transaction time, responsiveness, and accuracy for instance—being regressed on overall satisfaction with the delivery of that service to derive measures of the extent to which each dimension of the process influences customer satisfaction with the service.

Customer Satisfaction and Objective Performance Measures

Analysis of customer satisfaction data often focuses on the relationship between satisfaction and more objective measures of service delivery and results. There has been a stream of research in this area over the past three decades, focusing in part on the question of whether customer satisfaction measures, as strictly perceptual indicators, correlate to some degree through correlations with other performance measures based on transactional data, administrative records, direct observation, testing, and clinical examinations (Stipak, 1979; Brown & Coulter, 1983; Parks, 1984; Kelly & Swindell, 2002). In the more recent research on this issue, Van Ryzin, Immerwahr, and Altman (2008) found a strong correlations between citizen perceptions and hard performance data on street cleanliness in New York City, but in a related study on road smoothness, Van Ryzin (2008) found no correlations between the soft perceptual data solicited from citizens and the hard engineering data on pavement smoothness. Looking at a variety of local public services, Kelly and Swindell (2002) found some correlations between the subjective citizen feedback and measures based on operating data, although much less so than expected, and they concluded that the variation in results might be due to differences in service areas and the fact that some of the performance measures focused more on outputs while others focused more on outcomes.

The view taken here is that agencies should have a multiple indicator approach in their performance measurement systems in any case and that these will often include measures of program outputs, service quality, and outcomes on the one hand and measures of customer satisfaction with service delivery and results on the other hand. Such complementary measures would often be expected to be associated since satisfaction would in part be a reaction to actual and perceived performance, but they really are measuring different dimensions of performance and in some cases may not be correlated.

Figure 13.9 shows the percentage of motorists who report being satisfied with ride quality on a number of road segments on the Pennsylvania state highway system, plotted against the international roughness index (IRI) values for these same roads (Poister, Garvey, Zineddin, Pietrucha, & Smith, 2005). Since lower IRI values represent smoother roads and higher values indicate rougher roads, the statistical association between motorist satisfaction and IRI is negative. Furthermore, the regression lines in figure 13.9 show that the negative slope for the interstate highways in the sample is steeper than those for the two other types of roads observed, indicating that satisfaction declines more sharply as roughness increases on these high-speed, limited-access roads. And the drop-off in satisfaction with ride quality is the slightest on the secondary roads.

This kind of analysis is useful because it presents a view of two different measures of performance, a customer satisfaction measure and a more tangible objective measure at the same time, as well as describing and assessing the association between them. It can also be used to set standards. For instance, if the general goal is to maintain 80 percent customer satisfaction rates on these kinds of highways, then the state's highway maintenance program would have to keep IRI scores at 80 or below on interstate highways, 90 or lower on other national highway system roads,

FIGURE 13.9 SATISFACTION WITH RIDE QUALITY AND ROUGHNESS BY ROAD TYPE: PENNSYLVANIA HIGHWAYS

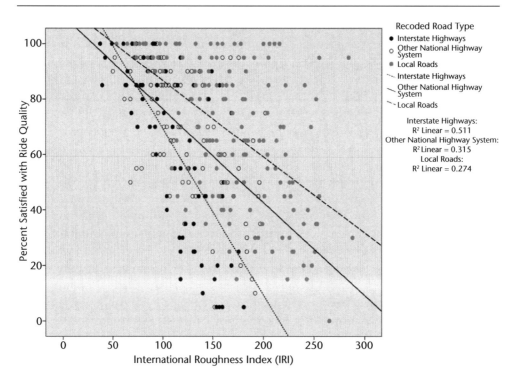

and at 126 or lower on the secondary roads included in that state's highway system.

Expectations, Satisfaction, and Confirmation and Disconfirmation Models

The analysis of customer satisfaction data can also be placed in the context of the larger cognitive structure of which it is part. Research applying the American Customers Satisfaction Index Model to public sector programs over the past decade has generally found that the expectations that customers or citizens at large have regarding the delivery of public services, in addition to their perceptions of how well they perform, influence their satisfaction with those services (Van Ryzin, Muzzio, & Immerwahr 2004; Van Ryzin, 2006; James, 2009). Whereas more positive perceptions about performance lead to greater satisfaction with a program, higher expectations regarding its performance tend to dampen satisfaction with the

FIGURE 13.10 EXPECTATIONS AND SATISFACTION WITH TRAFFIC FLOW AND CONGESTION

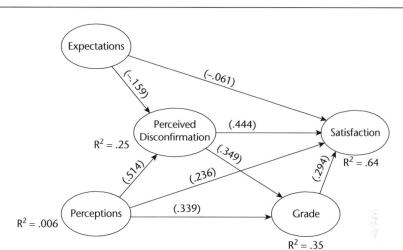

program. And perhaps more important, the confirmation or disconfirmation of expectations, whether and the extent to which perceived performance meets or exceeds expectations (confirmation) or falls short of expectations (disconfirmation), also has a direct effect on customer satisfaction.

Figure 13.10 shows an example of the model as applied to traffic flow and congestion on state highways in Georgia (Poister & Thomas, 2011). (In this example, a grade of the highway program's effectiveness is used along with perceptions of traffic flow taken together to represent perceived performance of the state roads that motorists drive on in their local areas.) The results of the structural equation modeling indicate that the grades motorists assign to traffic flow and congestion lead to increased satisfaction with it and that perceptions exert a positive influence on motorists' satisfaction with the traffic flow on their roads both directly and indirectly through grades. Motorists' expectations, however, have a negative effect on their satisfaction with traffic flow both directly and indirectly through the confirmation or disconfirmation measure.

Thus, performance measurement systems focusing on customer feedback or, for that matter, other stakeholders as well, might benefit from including questions regarding expectations and grades in addition to perceptions and satisfaction in order to develop a more complete understanding of how they view public services. In some cases the results might suggest that managers and policymakers attempt to influence citizen and customer expectations regarding particular public services, in some cases trying to make those expectations more realistic within the context of available resources and capacities, in addition to working to improve performance.

Furthermore, monitoring feedback on all of these dimensions on a regular basis over time (annually, for instance) would allow managers to determine the extent to which perceptions of service levels and quality and grades given to a service go up or down along with their more objective measures of service delivery. In addition, they could monitor the extent to which satisfaction with a service increases or decreases in conjunction with changes in perceptions and grades. Finally analysts could examine whether customer expectations increase as actual service delivery improves over time, in effect raising the bar or standard to which customers want to hold agencies accountable, and whether heightened expectations resulting from improved service levels might actually dampen satisfaction or suppress increases in customer satisfaction even as service delivery has gotten better.

Stakeholder Involvement as Citizens and Partners to Address Community Issues

It is important to keep in mind that performance management entails establishing clear goals, developing strategies and plans to realize them and manage effectively in order to achieve them. Thus, stakeholder engagement is an often important part of the process by involving citizens and other stakeholders at the front end in terms of setting goals and developing plans as well as soliciting feedback from them at the back end once the plans have been implemented.

In the most common scenario, public managers must work with members of the public in more than one of these roles at a time, as demonstrated in the example provided by United Way. United Way, an international nonprofit organization with eighteen hundred agencies in forty-one countries, partnered with the Harwood Institute to develop a method for conducting "Community Conversations" for stakeholder engagement. The questions are structured to solicit participants' aspirations for the community. These conversations provide valuable feedback about how United Way is addressing issues in their neighborhoods and the residents who participate in them feel engaged in the larger process because they are contributing to the organization's understanding of the community (Kline, 2013).

This concept of communicative planning affirms that decisions are "an inter-subjective effort at mutual understanding...[that] refocuses the practices of planning to enable purposes to be communicatively discovered" (Healey, cited in Fainstein, 2010, pp. 26–27). For example, the Community Conversations for United Way of Metropolitan Dallas focused on the issue of high school graduation because the community had high dropout rates: 40 percent of high school freshmen do not graduate. Partnering with more than thirty public, voluntary, and corporate sector community partners, United Way developed an initiative customized for individual schools focusing on specific strategies and outcomes (http://www.unitedway.org/our-work/graduate-from-high-school-on-time):

- College preparation and SAT training
- Parental involvement
- Mentoring and counseling

In 2006–2007, program participants advanced to the next grade level at a rate 19 percent higher than that of peers not participating in the Dallas program.

In the country of Georgia, citizen involvement resulted in the unexpected benefit of young people becoming involved in local government. "As part of a project to help improve public services, five local governments in Georgia sought volunteers to undertake ratings of service quality. Announcements were posted in schools asking youth to participate in a training session" (Mark, 2008, p. 245). This resulted in more applicants than needed and youth were selected on previous volunteer experience and basic familiarity with local government.

As a result of the monitoring, fairly significant improvements in cleanliness were noted in most of these cities (Nayyar-Stone & Bishop, 2004). All five cities in the original study showed visible improvement in ratings and in citizen satisfaction. Once the first five cities had visible results, a number of other cities asked to become involved. Youth groups sponsored "Cleaning Days" on International Youth Day, drawing on other citizens to help clean the city, with the equipment provided by the city (Mark, 2008). The experience broadened the youth perspective on civic responsibility, providing a relatively "high insight in a country still in transition from an autocratic communist rule" (Mark, 2008, p. 247). The trained observer perspective from citizens in the community had the added benefit of raters as users of the services, which provided greater credibility to the recommendations and initiatives.

E-Government and Stakeholder Involvement

The evolution of stakeholder involvement in public management and measurement has been "facing a new phase as many government agencies have initiated electronic government (e-government) development and taken advantage of internet-based applications to communicate with constituents and to provide online application services" (Kim & Lee, 2012, 6). For example, South Korea goes as far as to say that "Seoul's rapidly increasing international competitiveness is in large part due to the city's use of information and communication technology (ICT) to improve the delivery of public services" (Korean Ministry of Public Administration and Security, 2011).

Also in Washington, DC, the Track DC website allows the public to monitor agency performance. The website provides the public with agency budget information (such as spend rates), personnel information (such as number of agency vacancies), performance data (such as key performance indicators), and other useful information. With access to this information, the public may then contact the government with inquiries, complaints, or concerns, which help to inform topics for future DC Stat sessions. This information is shared with the District government by e-mail, hard-copy mail, phone, social media, or in person at community meetings.

In Buffalo, New York, the CitiStat meetings are streamed live on the City of Buffalo website and filed for availability at a later date. In addition the CitiStat meetings are aired on the Government Channel on Time Warner Cable (Martha Meegan, personal communication, January 27, 2014).

Measuring and Evaluating Stakeholder Engagement

It is important to have goals and develop measurement tools for stakeholder involvement in order to determine the success of the engagement. Defining performance measures in conjunction with deciding who should be invited to participate will help managers anticipate what kind of results participation will produce, articulate participation process goals, and align their design and management strategies accordingly (Nabatchi, 2012; Bryson, Quick, Slotterback, & Crosby, 2013). Effective and operable measures of participation can help policymakers learn from implementation so that they can enhance the effectiveness of the remainder of the participation efforts they are currently working on and build long-term institutional capacity for future participation (Rowe & Frewer, 2004; Laurian & Shaw, 2009).

Monitoring and evaluation may use a combination of process criteria to determine how well an organization is implementing its proposed stakeholder participation program and impact criteria to measure the consequences of participation for decision outcomes (Nabatchi, 2012). Surveys are also useful to determine customer satisfaction and for strengthening relationships with consultants, contractors, and a wide range of other stakeholders. Designing a logic model will be useful in determining these measures. Figure 13.11 shows a logic model for soliciting

FIGURE 13.11 LOGIC MODEL FOR STAKEHOLDER FEEDBACK

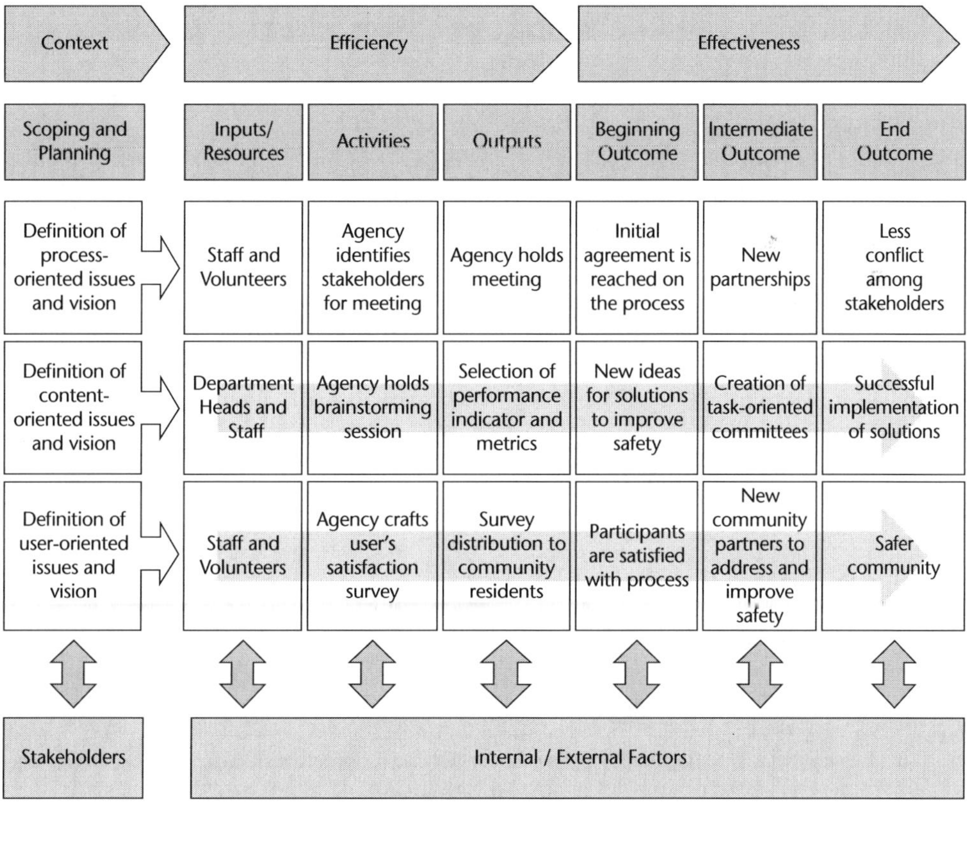

Context	Efficiency			Effectiveness		
Scoping and Planning	Inputs/ Resources	Activities	Outputs	Beginning Outcome	Intermediate Outcome	End Outcome
Definition of process-oriented issues and vision	Staff and Volunteers	Agency identifies stakeholders for meeting	Agency holds meeting	Initial agreement is reached on the process	New partnerships	Less conflict among stakeholders
Definition of content-oriented issues and vision	Department Heads and Staff	Agency holds brainstorming session	Selection of performance indicator and metrics	New ideas for solutions to improve safety	Creation of task-oriented committees	Successful implementation of solutions
Definition of user-oriented issues and vision	Staff and Volunteers	Agency crafts user's satisfaction survey	Survey distribution to community residents	Participants are satisfied with process	New community partners to address and improve safety	Safer community

Stakeholders	Internal / External Factors

stakeholder feedback that uses the indicators discussed in the next paragraph.

Existing research and practice models support measuring a combination of different types of outcomes, for example (Deyle & Slotterback, 2009; Innes & Booher, 1999; Laurian & Shaw, 2009; Mandarano, 2008; Margerum, 2002; Milward & Provan, 2000; Schively, 2007; Poister & Thomas, 2009; Bryson et al., 2013):

- *Process-oriented outcomes* (e.g., building trust among participants, incorporating a diverse group of stakeholders)
- *Content-oriented outcomes* (e.g., improving safety or environmental quality)
- *User-oriented outcomes* (e.g., participants' satisfaction with the process, recognizing that different stakeholders have different criteria for success)

These may be measured at different units of analysis:

- *Individual-level outcomes* (e.g., individuals' increased knowledge of a policy issue, effects on citizenship behavior)
- *Group-level outcomes* (e.g., mutual learning within the group about others' perspectives)
- *Community-level outcomes* (e.g., the development of new options not previously considered, overall measures of community betterment)

And, at different outcome levels:

- *Beginning, intermediate, and end outcomes,* which are, respectively, the immediately discernible effects of the process (e.g., the quality of initial agreements), impacts that unfold once the process is under way (e.g., the formation of new partnerships), and long-term impacts (e.g., less conflict among stakeholders in the future)

References

Ackerman, J. (2004). Co-governance for accountability: Beyond "exit" and "voice." *World Development, 32,* 447–463.

Allen, D. R., & Rao, T. R. (2000). *Analysis of customer satisfaction data.* Milwaukee, WI: ASQ Quality Press.

Brown, K., & Coulter, P. B. (1983). Subjective and objective measures of police service delivery. *Public Administration Review, 43,* 50–58.

Bryson, J. M. (2004). What to do when stakeholders matter: Stakeholder identification and analysis techniques. *Public Management Review, 6*(1), 21–53.

Bryson, J. M. (2011). *Strategic planning for public and nonprofit organizations* (4th ed.). San Francisco: Jossey-Bass.

Bryson, J. M., Quick, K. S., Slotterback, C. S., & Crosby, B. C. (2013). Designing public participation processes. *Public Administration Review, 73*, 23–34. doi:10.1111/j.1540-6210.2012.02678.x

Centers for Medicare and Medicaid Services. (2013). *Hospital Consumer Assessment of Health Care Providers Systems.* http://www.cms.gov/Medicare/Quality-Initiatives-Patient-Assessment-Instruments/HospitalQualityInits/HospitalHCAHPS.html

Deyle, R. E., & Slotterback, C. S. (2009). Empirical analysis of mutual learning in consensual planning processes: An exploratory analysis of local mitigation planning in Florida. *Journal of Planning Education and Research, 29*(1), 23–38.

Fainstein, S. S. (2010). *The just city.* Ithaca, NY: Cornell University Press.

Fernandez, S., & Rainey, H. G. (2006). Managing successful organizational change in the public sector: An agenda for research and practice. *Public Administration Review, 66*, 1–25.

Fung, A., & Wright, E. O. (2001). Deepening democracy: Innovations in empowered participatory governance. *Politics and Society, 29*, 5–41.

Girl Scout Council of Northwest Georgia. (2002). *2002 outcomes study report.* Atlanta: Author.

Hatry, H. P., Marcotte, J. E., Van Houten, T., & Weiss, C. (1998). *Customer surveys for agency managers: What managers need to know.* Washington, DC: Urban Institute

Hayes, B. E. (1997). *Measuring customer satisfaction: Survey design, use, and statistical analysis methods.* Milwaukee, WI: ASQ Quality Press.

Innes, J. E., & Booher, D. E. (1999). Consensus building and complex adaptive system: A framework for evaluating collaborative planning. *Journal of the American Planning Association, 65*(4), 412–423, 806.

James, O. (2009). Evaluating the expectations disconfirmation and expectations anchoring approaches to citizen satisfaction with local public services. *Journal of Public Administration Research and Theory, 19*, 107–123.

Kelly, J., & Swindell, D. (2002). A multiple-indicator approach to municipal service evaluation: Correlating performance measurement and citizen satisfaction across jurisdictions. *Public Administration Review, 62*(5), 610–621.

Kim, S., & and Lee, J. (2012, June 7–9) *Citizen participation and transparency in local government: An empirical analysis.* Paper prepared for the Second Global Conference on Transparency, Utrecht University Netherlands.

Kline, A. (2013). Unpublished class paper, Fall. University of Delaware.

Korean Ministry of Public Administration and Security. (2011). *E-government plans for the 21st century.* Seoul: Korean Ministry of Public Administration and Security.

Laurian, L., & Shaw, M. M. (2009). Evaluation of public participation. The practices of certified planners. *Journal of Planning Education and Research, 28*, 293–309.

Light, P. C. (1998). *Sustaining innovation: Creating nonprofit and government organizations that innovate naturally.* San Francisco: Jossey-Bass.

Mandarano, L. (2008). Evaluating collaborative environmental planning outputs and outcomes: Restoring and protecting habitat and the New York New Jersey Harbor estuary program. *Journal of Planning Education and Research, 27*(4), 456–469.

Margerum, R. D. (2002). Collaborative planning: Building consensus and building a distinct model for practice. *Journal of Planning Education and Research. 21*(3), 237–253.

Mark, K. (2008). Experience with trained observers in transition and developing countries: Citizen engagement in monitoring results In P. Julnes, F. Berry, M. Aristigueta, & K. Yang (Eds.), *International handbook of practice-based performance management.* Thousand Oaks, CA: Sage.

Milward, H. B., & Provan, K. G. (2000). Governing the hollow state. *Journal of Public Administration Research and Theory, 10,* 359–380.

Nabatchi, T. (2012). Putting the "public" back in public values research: Designing. *Public Administration Review, 72*(5), 699–708.

Nayyar-Stone, R., & Bishop, L. (2004). *Georgia Customer Survey 2004.* Washington, DC: Urban Institute.

Parks, R. B. (1984). Linking objective and subjective measures of performance. *Public Administration Review, 44,* 118–127.

Poister, T. H., Garvey, P. M., Zineddin, A. Z., Pietrucha, M. T., & Smith, C. L. (2005). Developing roadway standards for ride quality from the customer's perspective. *Transportation Research Record,* 1940, 43–51.

Poister, T. H., & Thomas, J. C. (2009) GDOT's consultant and contractor surveys: An approach to strengthening relationships with government's business partners. *Public Performance and Management Review, 33,* 122–140.

Poister, T. H., & Thomas, J. C. (2011). The effect of expectations and expectancy confirmation/disconfirmation on motorists' satisfaction with state highways. *Journal of Public Administration Research and Theory, 21,* 601–617.

Poister, T. H., Thomas, J. C., & Berryman, A. F. (2013). Reaching out to stakeholders: The Georgia DOT 360-Degree Assessment Model. *Public Performance and Management Review, 17,* 302–328.

Rainey, H. G. (2009). *Understanding and managing public organizations* (4th ed.). San Francisco: Jossey-Bass.

Rowe, G., & Frewer, L. R. (2004). Evaluating public-participation exercises: A research agenda. *Science, Technology, and Human Values, 29,* 512–556.

Schively, C. S. (2007). A quantitative analysis of consensus building in local environmental review. *Journal of Planning Education and Research, 27*(1), 82–98.

Stipak, B. (1979). Citizen satisfaction with urban services: Potential misuse as a performance indicator. *Public Administration Review, 39*(1), 46–52.

Testa, M. R. (2002). A model for organization-based 360 degree leadership assessment. *Leadership and Organization Development Journal, 23,* 260–268.

Thomas, J. C. (2013). Citizen, customer, partner: Rethinking the place of the public in public management. *Public Administration Review, 73,* 786–796.

Thomas, J. C., Poister, T. H., & Ertas, N. (2010). Customer, partner, principal: Local government perspectives on state agency performance in Georgia. *Journal of Public Administration Research & Theory, 20*(4), 779–799.

Thomas, J. C., & Poister, T. H. (2011). The effect of expectations and expectancy confirmation/disconfirmation on motorists' satisfaction with state highways. *Journal of Public Administration Research and Theory, 21*(4), 601–617.

Van Ryzin, G. G. (2006). Testing the expectancy disconfirmation model of citizen satisfaction with local government. *Journal of Public Administration Research and Theory, 16,* 599–611.

Van Ryzin, G. G. (2008). Validity of an on-line panel approach to citizen surveys. *Public Performance and Management Review, 32*(2), 236–262.

Van Ryzin, G. G., & Immerwahr, S. (2004). Derived importance-performance analysis of citizen survey data. *Public Performance and Management Review, 27,* 144–173.

Van Ryzin, G. G., Immerwahr, S., & Altman, S. (2008). Measuring street cleanliness: A comparison of New York City's scorecard and results from a citizen survey. *Public Administration Review, 68*(2), 286–294.

Van Ryzin, G. G., Muzzio, D., & Immerwahr, S. (2004). Drivers and consequences of citizen satisfaction: An application of the American Customer Satisfaction Index Model to New York City. *Public Administration Review, 64,* 331–340.

Vavra, T. G. (1997). *Improving your measurement of customer satisfaction.* Milwaukee, WI: ASQ Quality Press.

## CHAPTER FOURTEEN

USING COMPARATIVE MEASURES TO BENCHMARK PERFORMANCE

What is benchmarking, and how do public agencies and programs use it to compare their performance against that of others? What are the uses of statistical benchmarking, and how is it done? What are the pitfalls inherent in interagency or interprogram comparisons, and how can they be avoided? This chapter discusses the benchmarking of performance measures in the public and nonprofit sectors, challenges in designing and implementing such systems, and strategies for using them effectively.

Public Sector Benchmarking

Chapter 6 makes the point that performance data need to be compared to something in order to provide useful information; it discusses four bases of comparisons: (1) current performance against past performance, (2) actual performance against standards or targets, (3) performance among subunits within an agency or program, and (4) an agency's or program's performance against that of other similar agencies or programs. Probably the most frequent type of comparison is tracking trends over time, but with the general movement toward results-oriented management in the public and nonprofit sectors, comparisons of actual performance against targets and standards are becoming more common. In addition, particularly in decentralized service delivery systems, more detailed performance reports also break performance data down by subunits, such as organizational divisions, field offices, or grantees in an intergovernmental program.

One of the most exciting developments in the move toward managing for results is the growing interest in using external comparisons to gauge the performance of one agency or program against other counterpart agencies or programs, such as other local jurisdictions or similar agencies in other states. The term *benchmarking* is used increasingly now to refer to making such comparisons among agencies or programs with an eye toward managing performance more effectively. Although public managers have often resisted external comparisons on the grounds that their programs and operating contexts were unique and that therefore such comparisons would be misleading, increased pressures for accountability, the drive for improved performance, and more sensitive approaches to implementing such systems have led to greater interest in the potential of benchmarking.

As defined in a report on benchmarking practices in federal agencies produced by the consulting firm Accenture (Howard & Kilmartin, 2006, p. 3), *benchmarking* refers to "the routine comparison with similar organizations of administrative processes, practices, costs and staffing, to uncover opportunities to improve services and/or lower costs." It can serve several purposes for public and nonprofit organizations, as follows:

- It allows an agency to gauge its performance against other similar organizations—both to see the range of performance within the parameters of its particular public service industry and where it fits in that range and to see how its performance stacks up against counterpart programs elsewhere.
- By comparing its performance data against counterpart agencies or industry leaders, an organization can develop a framework for establishing challenging but feasible objectives, performance targets, or service delivery standards for the near or midterm future.
- By identifying apparent star performers among counterpart programs, an agency can seek out and adopt or adapt leading-edge practices, adapt strategies, and generally learn lessons from peer organizations to improve its own performance.

As Keehley and Abercrombie (2008) pointed out, a variety of activities fall under the umbrella label of benchmarking in the public sector. One form of activity—as exemplified by the Oregon Benchmarks, Florida Benchmarks, Minnesota Milestones, and Texas Tomorrow programs—has been called benchmarking, but the term is a misnomer. As discussed in chapter 8, these and similar efforts in other states, as well as local government versions (such as Life in Jacksonville and Sustainable Seattle), are macrolevel strategic planning initiatives created to develop a vision of the future and chart progress in moving toward that future. Although numerous performance measures are monitored by these programs and compared against targets that have been set for the "out years," they are rarely compared directly to similar measures for other comparable jurisdictions. Thus, these efforts do not really constitute the kind of external benchmarking discussed here.

Another form of benchmarking is perhaps most relevant to the subject of this book; it might be best termed *statistical benchmarking or comparative performance measurement.* This involves collecting data on the same set of performance measures for a number of similar organizations or programs in order to peg the performance of a particular agency in relation to comparable programs. Although this approach can lead to follow-up searches for best practices on the part of the high performers, comparative performance measurement is a more surface-level approach that simply provides comparative data. However, by virtue of focusing on a particular process or the overall performance of an agency or program with a common set of measures, thus facilitating one agency's efforts to compare its performance against a number of counterparts, statistical benchmarking is also a more comprehensive approach that is useful for interpreting performance in a larger context.

Another approach is corporate-style benchmarking, which focuses directly on so-called best practices. In this approach, the organization usually focuses on a particular service delivery process, such as recruitment of employers in a welfare-to-work program or case management in a crisis stabilization unit and attempts to learn about the practices of agencies that are high performing in that area—the benchmarking partners—and adapt them. Although public and nonprofit managers have always tried to borrow or steal effective practices and approaches from cutting-edge agencies in their particular service industries through consultation, site visits, information exchanges, and so forth, corporate-style benchmarking, emphasizing the best-practices approach, has become more carefully structured in recent years to capitalize more fully on the potential of this particular form of benchmarking to help public and nonprofit agencies strengthen their own performance (Keehley & Abercrombie, 2008).

It is also useful to point out that benchmarking in general can be carried out at multiple levels. For instance, Georgia's Office of Child Support Enforcement delivers services through 107 local offices, and it regularly collects comparable performance data from each of these offices. From the perspective of the central office, these comparisons among subunits constitute a form of internal benchmarking. From the viewpoint of an individual local office, however, these same comparative performance measures afford an opportunity for external benchmarking. Similarly, the federal Social Security Administration monitors the performance of all state agencies with which it contracts to adjudicate claims for disability benefits on a set of common performance measures and uses these data to help manage the program and make budget allocations. Although this constitutes internal benchmarking from the federal perspective, it also affords an opportunity for each state agency to engage in some external benchmarking. Thus, the term *benchmarking* most often connotes external comparisons, whereas the less frequently used *internal benchmarking* refers to the comparison of performance measures among subunits within programs or agencies.

Statistical Benchmarking

Statistical benchmarking or comparative performance measurement, then, is the collection and comparison of performance data across a set of similar agencies or programs (Hatry, 1999; Morley, Bryant, & Hatry, 2001). It comes about in different ways. Sometimes groups of organizations or programs voluntarily agree to initiate a program of collecting and sharing a common set of performance indicators on a regular basis. In many states, for example, public hospitals benchmark their performance in terms of patient satisfaction and other criteria against other hospitals using common measures that are collected through the auspices of a statewide association. Similarly, municipal governments in at least two states have cooperative agreements to implement common sets of performance indicators on the same cycle and share the data among themselves (Ammons & Rivenbark, 2008; Boyer & Martin, 2012).

In other cases, the collection or reporting of common performance measures is mandated or even carried out from outside the agencies in question. As discussed in chapter 5, for instance, federal agencies maintain large databases on crime rates, health statistics, environmental quality, transportation systems, and other information. Typically these data are reported by or for states and local governments and contain elements that lend themselves to comparing performance across these jurisdictions. In addition, state and federal agencies that manage grants programs often impose reporting requirements on the public and nonprofit organizations receiving these grants. Furthermore, associations of particular kinds of agencies such as the International City/County Management Association (Ammons, Coe, & Lombardo, 2001), the American Association of State Highway and Transportation Officials (2006), and the National Council of State Boards of Nursing are increasingly taking the lead in developing comparative performance measurement systems. The data generated by these systems tend to be designed principally for program management purposes, but they are also often used, or are available for use, in benchmarking some grantees against others.

Whether initiated by a number of counterpart agencies, facilitated by an association of governmental units or agencies, or mandated by some higher level of authority, the statistical benchmarking process usually proceeds through four major steps:

1. *Identifying the measures to be used—that is, what is to be measured and what those measures will be.* Most often organizations emphasize output, efficiency, and cost-effectiveness measures, but others include indicators of effectiveness, service quality, and customer satisfaction as well. Note that because the purpose of benchmarking is to make comparisons across other agencies or programs, the measures will almost always be defined as *standardized* measures in terms of percentages, rates, ratios, or averages rather than raw numbers.

2. *Developing precise definitions of the operational indicators to be used by all participants, along with clear guidelines for implementing them and uniform procedures for collecting and processing the data and computing the measures.* Participants will have to agree on specified procedures for operationalizing indicators—for instance, allocating costs to activities, outputs, or programs and defining the stages of process to be included in computing cycle times—and then report their data on that basis.

3. *Collecting and reporting the data on a periodic, often annual, basis.* It might be advantageous to collect raw data from the participating agencies and then compute the measures centrally in order to flag suspicious-looking numbers and ensure consistency in how the measures are computed. In addition, it will often be essential to conduct spot checks or data audits to verify reliability and ensure consistency of data collection procedures among participating agencies.

FIGURE 14.1 CHILD CARE SPACES

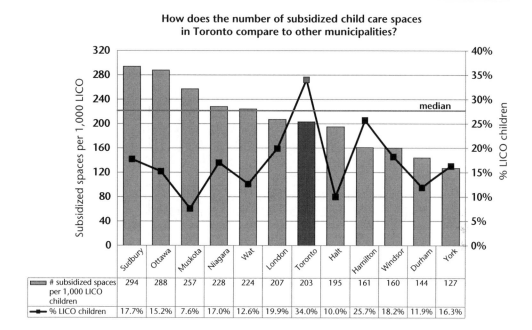

How does the number of subsidized child care spaces
in Toronto compare to other municipalities?

	Sudbury	Ottawa	Muskota	Niagara	Wat	London	Toronto	Halt	Hamilton	Windsor	Durham	York
# subsidized spaces per 1,000 LICO children	294	288	257	228	224	207	203	195	161	160	144	127
% LICO children	17.7%	15.2%	7.6%	17.0%	12.6%	19.9%	34.0%	10.0%	25.7%	18.2%	11.9%	16.3%

Note: LICO children = low-income children

Source: Toronto, City Manager's Office (2013, p. 108). Used with permission.

4. *Using the comparative data to assess the performance of an agency or program, set targets for particular entities or more general standards for the field at large, or identify star performers and industry leaders and investigate leading-edge practices, as appropriate. Benchmarking agreements should specify times and processes for reviewing the data and interpreting the results collectively in order to promote learning and the search for promising practices.*

As an example, figure 14.1 shows the number of subsidized child care spaces per 1,000 low-income children twelve years or younger in in 2011 for twelve municipalities in Ontario, Canada. Data on the percentage of children under age twelve who are in low-income families are reported annually by these municipal jurisdictions to the Ontario Municipal CAO's Benchmarking Initiative along with measures on the number of subsidized child care spaces available, the size of the waiting list for subsidized spaces, and the average annual cost of providing regulated child care service for one child. At just under the median of 205 spaces per 1,000 low-income children, the City of Toronto ranks seventh among the twelve municipalities. The highest performers on this measure are Sudbury and Ottawa, with 280 or more spaces per 1,000 children, while the lowest performers are Durham and York with only 150 or fewer subsidized child care spaces per 1,000 low-income children. Figure 14.1 also shows the number of low-income children as a percentage of all children in each of these communities on the right axis. As an indicator of need or demand for child care services, this measure shows that Toronto has the highest percentage of low-income children, at over 30 percent, as compared with Muskoka, with under 10 percent low-income children at the low end of the scale.

Problems and Challenges in Benchmarking

The benchmarking process is quite straightforward, but like performance measurement itself, the process is not always as simple as it looks. In addition to concerns about how the comparative data will be used and whether a program might be penalized somehow for relatively poor performance, there are also a number of more methodological issues that create special challenges for would-be benchmarkers. These include questions regarding the availability of common data elements, problems concerning data reliability, and variation in programs and their operating environments.

Availability of Data

Agencies engaged in benchmarking efforts often attempt to rely on readily available data, which tend to come from such traditional sources as agency records. These data lend themselves primarily to measures of resources, outputs, and efficiency, but often not to measures of real outcomes or customer satisfaction. Although it is certainly understandable to want to limit the expenditure of additional time and resources in what is an already demanding data collection effort, doing so will constrain the usefulness of the comparative data. As discussed in chapter 3, measures of outcomes and customer satisfaction tend to be more ambitious, often involving new procedures that require going out into the field for data collection; they are expensive and time consuming to implement. The most obvious examples are customer surveys designed to determine whether certain outcome conditions have improved or the extent to which respondents are satisfied with the services they have received.

When an individual agency decides to initiate or strengthen its performance measurement system, it need concern itself only with committing time and resources to collect data for its own needs. For successful benchmarking, however, two or more agencies must decide that these additional data collection efforts are worth the cost, and this agreement is not always easily reached. Sometimes, therefore, benchmarking partners begin on a more limited basis, sharing data that are relatively easy to generate and then perhaps moving to flesh out the system with more demanding data as the partners become convinced that the comparative performance measures are beneficial.

Reliability of Comparative Data

As discussed in chapter 5, data reliability is a critical issue in performance measurement. In looking at changes in performance over time, evaluating actual performance against targets, or comparing performance across organizational units or clientele groups, for example, managers want to be assured that any differences they see are real and not simply artifacts of sloppy data collection. With benchmarking, this concern is elevated because comparisons among agencies or programs are valid only to the extent that all participants employ consistent data collection procedures. Suppose, for example, that a number of municipalities want to compare their cost per mile of road maintained, but some are using data on lane-miles of local road to compute this ratio while others using centerline-miles. If this inconsistency is compounded by variation in the extent to which the cost figures incorporate overhead costs, then the resulting measures are likely to be all over the place, and comparisons among these jurisdictions will be between apples and oranges.

Because these data are usually self-reported by the individual agencies or programs, ensuring consistency can be challenging. Where possible, it is far preferable to use the same instrument to collect data from different jurisdictions or programs. For instance, rather than relying on grades earned by students in various school systems around the country, the National Assessment of Educational Progress generates state comparisons of student achievement in science, math, and reading based on standardized tests administered to samples of fourth graders and eighth graders in schools in each state.

Even when benchmarking participants use standardized instruments, it is critical for them to follow uniform procedures in collecting the data—for instance, using the same sampling procedures, enforcing the same time limits in administering standardized tests, or counting things the same way in an observational survey. Obviously the more that different agencies use uniform accounting standards and management information systems, the more likely they are to provide comparable performance measures. When participants do not employ standardized instruments for collecting primary data—for example, when the constituent data elements already reside in existing information systems—it is all the more important for there to be unambiguous definitions of the data elements to be used and clear guidelines for including some categories or cases and excluding others in tallying up counts.

In such circumstances, it may be worthwhile to provide for a system of reviews, at least of a sample, by outside professional data auditors to ensure data reliability. On the front end of the process, if there are staff, analysts, or consultants who have been assigned to support the benchmarking project, they should be readily accessible to the agencies or programs when they are reporting data in order to field questions and provide guidance on how the performance measures should be observed and reported. As the data come in, staff supporting the project should review them on a case-by-case basis, looking for inconsistencies among the various measures reported as well as completeness. Then as the database begins to build up with data reported by multiple programs or agencies, they should be looking for possible outliers and questionable data that do not seem to fit the patterns taking shape. When these kinds of issues pop up, staff can make calls or send e-mails to the source of the data to try to verify that the data are in fact correct or to help correct problems with faulty data. Occasionally, particularly in the early stages of a benchmarking enterprise, site visits to the reporting entities may be necessary in order to track back data trails to confirm the accuracy of the data.

Variation in Operating Conditions

One of the most critical problems in benchmarking performance measures across different agencies or programs is that these entities often function in very different operating environments. Some may feel that they are being subjected to unfair comparisons because they operate in more difficult conditions than others. For example, some human service programs work with more difficult clientele, some juvenile justice departments work in communities that are less supportive, and some welfare-to-work programs operate in local labor markets that are much weaker than elsewhere. Such differences in operating context can generate highly distorted comparisons of program performance. Because the purpose of benchmarking is not to penalize weak performers or make some programs appear inferior to others, it is important to take differences in operating conditions into account in interpreting benchmarking data.

Strategies to Improve Comparative Measures

Remedies to account for contextual differences that can distort comparative performance measures include descriptive interpretation of explanatory variables and the use of peer groups, recalibrated measures, and adjusted performance measures.

Explanatory Variables

As discussed in chapter 3, it is important to identify critical environmental variables—external factors beyond a program's control that can influence its performance—in developing logic models. If benchmarking partners are notably different in terms of critical environmental variables, these may need to be taken into account as explanatory factors in interpreting comparative performance data. For example, the incidence and prevalence of sexually transmitted diseases (STDs) are significantly greater in areas with high poverty rates. Thus, comparing incidence and prevalence rates to assess the effectiveness of various state and local STD prevention programs can be misleading. Prevention programs in poverty-stricken urban areas in the Midwest, for instance, may in fact be quite effective in relative terms in containing the spread of these diseases even though the residual rates of syphilis and gonorrhea are still substantially higher there than in more affluent areas. One response to this difficulty is simply to include comment fields in the report formats presenting these data and provide an explanatory comment to the effect that the incidence and prevalence rates in certain of the areas observed would be expected to be greater due to their higher poverty rates.

Another approach is to take the environmental variable that may have a strong influence on an agency's performance into account by examining the statistical relationship between that variable and the relevant measure of performance. For example, figure 14.2 is a scatter plot of the high school graduation rates of 176 local school systems in Georgia, plotted on the percentage of students who are eligible to participate in the federally funded free lunch program. The free lunch program eligibility variable is

FIGURE 14.2 HIGH SCHOOL GRADUATION RATES BY PERCENTAGE
STUDENTS ELIGIBLE FOR THE FREE LUNCH PROGRAM

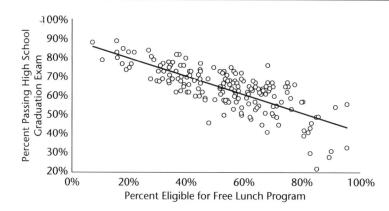

being used as a proximate measure of poverty, which is generally known
to have a negative effect on academic achievement. As expected, the
scatter plot along with the regression line show that graduation rates tend
to be substantially lower in school districts in higher poverty areas. In
comparing the performance of any given school district with other systems
in terms of graduation rates, then, it will be helpful to interpret the data
within the context of the percentage of students who are eligible for the
free lunch program. For example, while most of the school districts
on the right side of figure 14.2 have lower graduation rates than do the
school systems on the left side of the chart, those differences can be largely
attributed to this statistical relationship, suggesting that the poorer
performance in some districts may be a result of higher poverty levels in
those areas rather than mismanagement, a lack of effective leadership, or
inferior educational processes.

Peer Groups

A second approach is also straightforward: limit comparative performance
measures to a relatively few agencies or programs that are fairly similar in
terms of operating conditions. Rather than including all possible counterpart agencies, which may vary widely in terms of important environmental
factors, it may be preferable to construct a "peer group" consisting of
relatively few programs that are more comparable in terms of operating contexts. For example, an analysis designed to assess the current

FIGURE 14.3 CRIMES PER 1,000 CAPITA BY PERCENTAGE OF THE POPULATION BELOW THE POVERTY LEVEL

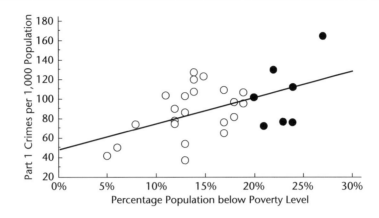

Source: Urban Institute and International City/County Management Association (1997).

performance and future prospects of a particular local public transit system might benchmark that system against a set of other systems of the same size operating the same modes of transportation (rail, bus, paratransit) in similar service areas in terms of demographics, population density, and land use patterns (Ryus et al., 2010).

Figure 14.3 shows crime rate data for twenty-nine large cities participating in the Comparative Performance Measurement Consortium, which was created in conjunction with the International City/County Management Association for the purpose of benchmarking service delivery. One of the participating jurisdictions, the City of Atlanta, Georgia, was interested in using these data to compare the performance of its police department against other similar cities. As shown in figure 14.3, there is a fairly pronounced statistical relationship between total crime rates and the percentage of the population living below the poverty level; cities with higher poverty rates also tend to have higher crime rates. The City of Atlanta (near the upper right corner of the scatter plot) has the highest crime rate among all these jurisdictions, and it also has the highest poverty rate. Because both of these factors might also be expected to influence police department performance in responding to reported crimes, the six other cities with the next highest poverty rates (represented with black markers) were selected as benchmark cities for Atlanta. Selected comparative indicators of police performance are shown in table 14.1 for these seven cities.

TABLE 14.1 COMPARATIVE POLICE PERFORMANCE

City	FTE Sworn Officers per 1,000 Population	Arrests per Sworn Officer	Percentage Part 1 Crimes Cleared	Crimes Cleared per Officer	Expense per Crime Cleared
Atlanta	3.6	42.7	25.5%	11.6	$5,671
Baltimore	4.2	22.6	18.9%	5.8	$10,336
Cincinnati	2.6	38.8	31.9%	9.2	$8,644
Houston	2.6	19.5	19.4%	5.3	$14,670
San Antonio	1.7	33.2	15.2%	6.9	$11,066
Shreveport	2.4	28.5	17.2%	7.9	$6,231
Tucson	1.6	68.4	16.4%	10.4	$8,169

Source: Urban Institute and International City/County Management Association (1997).

The data suggest that relative to these other jurisdictions, the City of Atlanta performs favorably for the most part in terms of the number of arrests made per police officer, the percentage of Part 1 crimes that are cleared, the number of crimes cleared per officer, and the overall expense per crime cleared.

Recalibrated Measures

Sometimes performance indicators can be recalibrated to take into account the environmental variable of concern. For instance, in comparing crime rates against other cities, City of Atlanta officials wanted to take into account the number of visitors and persons commuting into and out of the city for work. They felt that because Atlanta has more people who live elsewhere but work inside the city and because it is a large convention center with large numbers of overnight guests staying in hotels, crime rates based only on the resident population would put Atlanta in a negative light in such comparisons. Thus, the average daytime population was estimated for each of these cities by adding in the number of people living elsewhere in the respective metropolitan area who report commuting into the central city to work, subtracting the number of central city residents who report working somewhere outside that city, and adding in the estimated number of daily hotel guests in each city.

The number of reported crimes per 1,000 residents and the number of crimes per 1,000 estimated daytime population are shown for each of the seven cities in figure 14.4. Although Atlanta has by far the highest number of Part 1 crimes per 1,000 residents, when the indicator is

FIGURE 14.4 CRIMES PER 1,000 RESIDENTS AND ESTIMATED DAYTIME POPULATION

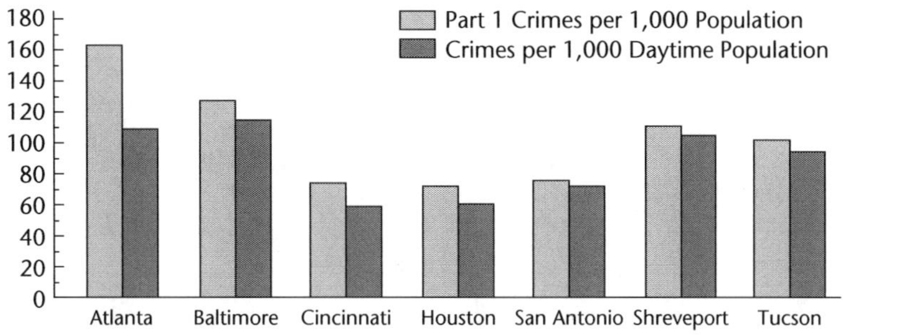

Source: Figures computed based on data reported in Urban Institute and International City/County Management Association (1997).

recalibrated on the basis of estimated daytime population, it is in line with Baltimore, Shreveport, and Tucson, thus changing somewhat the impression of Atlanta as a city with an inordinately high crime rate relative to other areas with high percentages of people living below the poverty level. Organizations cannot often use the environmental variables that affect performance measures to recalibrate the original indicators, but when they can, it is a direct approach to addressing the impact of such variables.

Adjusted Performance Measures

Currently there is substantial interest in statistically adjusting performance measures to account for the influence of one or more environmental or explanatory variables. For example, public hospitals may want to adjust comparative data on measures of inpatient length of stay and mortality rates to take into account differences in the severity of illnesses their patients are treated for. Some hospital administrators may fear that otherwise their facilities will appear to be inferior in terms of both efficiency and the quality of care provided when the real reason for their longer average stays and higher mortality rates is that they are caring for patients with more serious illnesses. Similarly, local schools whose performance is being compared on standardized achievement tests may want to adjust the data by some measure of the socioeconomic status of the communities they serve in order to be evaluated on a level playing field (Stiefel, Rubenstein, & Schwartz, 1999).

FIGURE 14.5 COUNTY HIGHWAY MAINTENANCE COST PER MILE OF SURFACE TREATMENT

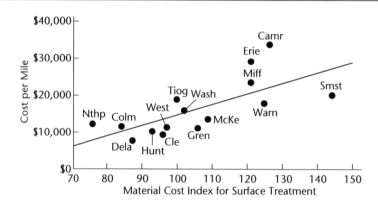

Briefly, to create adjusted performance measures, regression models are developed to predict values of the performance indicator in question as a function of the environmental variable or variables. These predicted values represent what the performance level of each case would look like if performance were solely determined by those explanatory factors. Residual values are then computed as the difference between the observed and predicted values of the performance indicator to represent the direction and extent to which actual performance deviates from what it would be expected to look like based on the explanatory variable(s) alone. These residual values are then considered to constitute adjusted performance measures that represent each unit's performance relative to industry averages adjusted for the environmental variable(s).

For example, figure 14.5 shows the unit cost of surface treatment for a number of county highway maintenance operations, plotted against an index of the cost of materials required to do this work. Generally counties with lower unit costs appear to be more efficient in performing this work, whereas those with higher unit costs appear to be less efficient. However, local prices for the necessary materials vary widely from county to county, as represented by the material cost index, and they have a direct bearing on the cost per mile of surface treatment. The regression line shown in figure 14.5 summarizes the expected unit cost for each county based on the materials cost index. Therefore, counties that fall above the regression line are incurring higher costs than would be expected, whereas those below the line appear to be performing surface treatment work more efficiently than would be expected given the cost structure.

TABLE 14.2 ADJUSTED PERFORMANCE MEASURES: COST PER MILE OF SURFACE TREATMENT

County	Actual Cost per Mile	Material Cost Index	Predicted Cost per Mile	Adjusted Cost per Mile
Erie	$29,254	121	$21,049	$8,205
Warren	$18,030	125	$22,209	$4,179
Clearfield	$9,566	96	$13,798	$4,233
Cameron	$33,843	126	$22,499	$11,344
McKean	$13,841	109	$17,569	$3,728
Mifflin	$23,736	121	$21,049	$2,688
Columbia	$11,619	84	$10,318	$1,301
Tioga	$19,224	100	$14,958	$4,266
Northumberland	$12,248	76	$7,998	$4,250
Delaware	$8,116	87	$11,188	$3,072
Huntingdon	$10,468	93	$12,928	$2,460
Somerset	$20,571	144	$27,719	$7,148
Greene	$11,478	106	$16,699	$5,220
Washington	$16,106	102	$15,539	$567
Westmoreland	$11,508	97	$14,088	$2,581

Table 14.2 shows the predicted cost per mile for each county based on the regression model (with an R^2 of .51), along with the actual unit cost and the material cost index value on which the predicted value is based. Then an adjusted cost per mile is computed as the residual, that is, the difference between the actual and predicted unit costs. Adjusted cost measures less than one (negative numbers) indicate counties that appear to be more efficient than would be expected by taking the material cost index into account. These adjusted performance measures provide a different interpretation of which counties exhibit more or less operating efficiency. For example, with a cost of $20,571 per mile resurfaced, Somerset County would appear to be one of the least efficient counties. But when the inordinately high cost of materials in that county is taken into account, Somerset County is shown to be quite efficient, spending $7,148 less per mile than would be expected given the cost of materials in that area.

Potentially, adjusted performance measures offer a means of providing "fair" comparisons by subtracting out the influence of contextual factors beyond management's control that might have substantial bearing on comparative program results. However, the usefulness of the adjusted performance measures depends heavily on the validity of the contextual factors employed. If these variables are inappropriate, incomplete, or in fact not causally related, the adjusted measures may indeed yield more distorted data rather than a fair basis for comparison.

Identifying Best Practices

In order to move beyond comparative performance measurement to a systematic approach to actually improving performance, agencies using benchmarking programs often try to identify what are often called "best practices," which are strategies, policies, interventions, practices, or processes that have been found to be, or at least are thought to be, approaches that can produce significant improvements in performance. While Keehley and Abercrombie (2008) note that such practices may come from a variety of sources—existing reports, professional contacts or associations, in-house staff or volunteers, awards programs, as well as other organizations—they also point out that the practices suggested by these sources are not automatically best practices in effectively generating improved performance. Thus, it makes more sense to think of them as promising practices that can be experimented with and possibly validated.

With respect to comparative performance measurement, the principal focus of this chapter, the data generated by such systems often provide a good starting point in the search for promising practices. Most typically those involved in benchmarking efforts use the data to identify the programs or agencies that are the leading performers on the performance measures of interest and then attempt to learn from them, assuming that their success is not due solely to operating in more facilitative or benign environments, about practices they employ that might contribute to their success. When the benchmarking efforts have accumulated substantial data over time, it often makes sense to include programs or agencies that have shown substantial improvement over past time periods in the search for promising practices even when they are not yet leading-edge performers.

When such high-performing or improving programs or agencies have been identified from the performance monitoring data, they can be approached through messaging, site visits, or focus groups to try to identify the keys to their success that might be transferable to others. As Keehley and Abercrombie (2008, p. 83), suggested, the line of questioning to probe for practices that might be responsible for their high performance could proceed as follows:

1. Have you experienced the performance problem or challenge that we are concerned with?
2. How did you solve that problem? What practices did you initiate or change?
3. To what extent has performance improved as a result of this approach?
4. What evidence is available to link that improvement with the promising practice?
5. Does that evidence match our own criteria for success in our case?
6. Are there unique circumstances in your case that might limit the transferability of the promising practices identified here to other similar programs or agencies?

While the promising practices identified through this benchmarking process may well appear at face value to be responsible for the high level of performance or the improved performance on the part of the benchmarking partner, it is usually wise to assess them and validate them with evidence, as suggested by the questions above, before bestowing the status of "best practice" on them. They may be validated in part by the evidence provided by the benchmarking partner, which may have time series or other comparative data from ongoing performance monitoring systems that support their causal impact on performance. In addition, the agencies importing a given practice may experiment with it using pretest-posttest data to evaluate its effectiveness in strengthening their own performance.

In a benchmarking project conducted by the American Association of State Highway and Transportation Officials along these lines, comparative performance measurement data were used to initiate the process of identifying high-performing state transportation departments and the promising practices they used with respect to both highway construction (Crossett & Hines, 2007) and pavement management (Harrison & Park, 2008). Furthermore, at the local government level, evidence shows that this kind of benchmarking activity can be effective in bringing about performance improvements in the public sector, at least in some cases. For example, commissioners in one county participating in the Florida Benchmarking Consortium were convinced by the comparative performance data to increase user fees in order to strengthen the financial viability of their parks and recreation program, a move they had been philosophically opposed to by seeing the data on user fees as a percentage of operating expenses in other participating jurisdictions (Boyer & Martin, 2012). And in the North Carolina Benchmarking Project, several of the fifteen participating cities have used the comparative performance data to identify problems and then identify and implement best practices, thereby improving their own performance in such service areas as residential refuse collection, recycling programs, and fire protection (Ammons & Rivenbark, 2008).

The results of benchmarking have been mixed to date, and not all comparative performance measurement initiatives have led to the identification of promising practices and use of these practices by other agencies to improve their performance. A review of the National Benchmarking Project in Sweden, for example, found that there was little action-oriented follow-up to the comparative performance data generated by participating municipalities and that some "excellent performers used the results as a reason to reduce performance," creating a leveling effect toward average performance levels rather than promoting best practices as the norm (Knutson, Ramberg, & Tagesson, 2012).

A Regulatory Benchmarking Example

While most of the examples in this book are oriented to service delivery programs, performance measurement and benchmarking are equally relevant for regulatory agencies as well. As a case in point, the National Council of State Boards of Nursing (NCSBN) initiated a comparative performance measurement process called CORE (Commitment to Ongoing Regulatory Excellence) in 2005 to promote and facilitate performance measurement by the member boards and provide a basis for member boards to gauge their own performance. The process involved conducting surveys to solicit feedback on the boards of nursing in each state from three principal stakeholder groups—nurses, employers of nurses, and nursing education program directors—as well as collecting data from the member boards themselves regarding their own processes and operations.

Prior to the 2012 round of data collection, NCSBN engaged in a major effort to enhance the CORE process in order to make it more meaningful for the member boards. This effort began with the development of a program logic model showing the activities, outputs, and intended outcomes of the four components of nursing regulation (practice, education, licensure, and discipline) as shown in figure 14.6. This model provided a

FIGURE 14.6 BOARD OF NURSING PROGRAM LOGIC MODEL

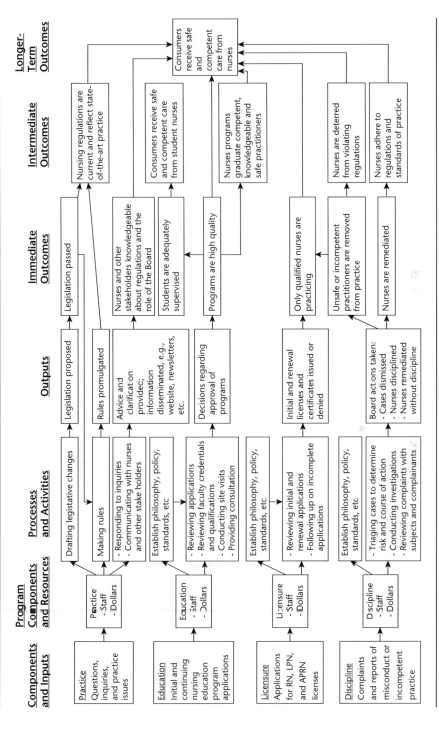

Source: National Council of State Boards of Nursing. Used with permission.

compelling performance framework that led to defining additional performance measures, revising others, and incorporating additional data sources such as the Hospital Consumer Assessment of Health Care Providers and Systems survey conducted nationally by the Centers for Medicare and Medicaid, the Nursys database on licensure and disciplinary data regarding nurses maintained centrally by NCSBN in-house, and the NCLEX examination process that is also maintained by NCSBN and required for licensing nurses in all US states. All of this led to a much more balanced, comprehensive, and outcome-oriented set of performance measures that focused more on results all along the way.

The performance data from all of these sources are provided in customized state reports developed for each board of nursing. Two external control variables that are likely to influence the performance of state boards of nursing are (1) structure, as either an independent board versus a board operating within the structure of a larger umbrella agency, and (2) size, in terms of the number of practicing nurses within a board's purview. Thus, the structure variable is used to define peer groups within which individual boards are compared, and size is also taken into account when it is thought to be relevant.

Each individual state report provides comparisons of that board's performance with the aggregate as well as boards of similar size and structure, but states are not given data pertaining to other individual boards. For example, table 14.3 shows the responses to an item in the HCAPHS survey asking whether patients received help quickly from hospital staff in Idaho as compared with all independent boards as well as against all

TABLE 14.3 PATIENT FEEDBACK ON HOW OFTEN PATIENTS RECEIVE HELP QUICKLY FROM HOSPITAL STAFF

Survey Responses	Idaho	Independent	All States
Always	71.00%	68%	67%
Usually	22.00%	23%	24%
Sometimes or never	7.00%	9%	9%
Total	100%	100%	100%
Number of states	1	28	51

Source: Centers for Medicare and Medicaid Services, *Hospital Consumer Assessment of Health Care Providers and Systems.* https://data.medicare.gov/Hospital-Compare/Survey-of-Patients -Hospital-Experiences-HCAHPS-Sta/fhk8-g4vc, retrieved April 25, 2014.

FIGURE 14.7 NUMBER OF ACTIONS TAKEN TO REMOVE NURSES FROM PRACTICE BY TOTAL LICENSEES

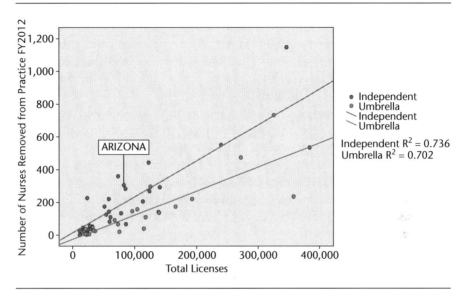

Source: National Council of State Boards of Nursing. Used with permission.

boards of nursing in the United States. The data indicate that a higher percentage of hospital patients in Idaho reported that they always received help quickly as compared with other states, while a lower percentage in Idaho reported that they received help quickly either sometimes or never.

Figure 14.7 shows the number of actions taken to remove nurses from practice in fiscal year 2012 for all boards of nursing identified as independent versus umbrella boards. This scatter plot also shows, for each type of board, the linear association between the number of such actions taken against nurses and size of the board as represented by the number of licensed nurses within its jurisdiction. This plot shows that the independent boards tend to take more such action against nurses than do the umbrella boards. Focusing on Arizona in particular, the plot also indicates that the Arizona board took more such actions against nurses in FY 2012 than would be expected given its relatively small size. Furthermore, it indicates that the Arizona Board of Nursing took more such actions leading to the removal of nurses from practice, than did many other independent boards, including both smaller and larger independent boards.

Because the CORE process incorporates such a wide array of performance measures regarding resources, program outputs, outcomes, efficiency and productivity, service quality, and customer satisfaction,

NCSBN develops four customized reports for each state board of nursing that focus on nursing practice, education, licensing, and discipline. This allows for more in-depth presentation of results and makes the performance information they contain more readily digestible. More of the exhibits have cross-sectional data from the most recent round of surveys in statistical tables, bar graphs, and scatter plots as shown above, but others show trends in performance over time. One critical measure of efficiency from earlier rounds of data collection that was retained in the enhanced CORE process concerns the cycle time in processing disciplinary cases, defined as the average number of calendar days between receipt of cases or complaints to resolution of those cases by the board in question. The Idaho Board of Nursing, for instance, which reported a substantially lower average cycle time than most other boards in 2007, reported longer cycle times in 2009, although significantly lower than the average of the other boards, and then decreased at about the same rate as did the other boards between 2009 and 2012.

It was this measure of cycle time, with state boards of nursing taking on the order of two hundred days to resolve disciplinary cases, that was identified as one of the most pressing performance challenges facing the boards. Thus, in order to begin identifying evidence-based practices to address issues in this area, NCSBN conducted two focus groups in the latter part of 2012 designed to explore promising practices regarding the discipline function of nursing regulation. The state boards that were invited to participate in these focus group sessions had been identified as strong performers in the 2009 round of data collection or as improving performers between 2007 and 2009.

These focus groups concentrated on decreasing cycle time in the discipline process and identified several promising practices that various states had implemented with resulting decreases in cycle times. To flesh these out further and move toward validating them, some participants in the focus groups transitioned into an ongoing working group to lead the effort to find effective approaches to reducing cycle times. Early on, the group defined a set of criteria for promising practices as follows. They must be

- Innovative or unique
- Able to reduce cycle times in the disciplinary process
- Linked to CORE performance measures
- Efficient in the use of resources and be economically feasible
- Adaptable to other boards of nursing

The working group then segmented the overall disciplinary process into three major steps—initial intake and triage, investigation, and resolution and monitoring—and searched within the participating states, having already been identified as high-performing or improving state boards for promising practices in each of these stages. A number of promising practices were put forth through this process, consisting of policies and ongoing work processes as well as management practices. States that had been using these practices were then asked to bring evidence, if possible, to show that implementing a particular practice had indeed led to reduced cycle times. In most cases, state boards that were championing these practices were able to provide evidence in the form of time series data or simple before-and-after comparisons that supported their contentions that these practices had in fact been responsible for decreases in cycle times, which tended to validate them as promising practices.

Follow-up steps are to develop clear descriptions of these promising practices and how they work, along with requirements for using them successfully and guidance for implementing them with other boards. As part of the CORE process, NCSBN plans to sponsor a process for piloting these promising practices in other state boards of nursing that have not been using them to determine how readily they can be adapted by other states and the extent to which they can help reduce cycle times in other boards. Thus, benchmarking comes full circle inasmuch as ongoing performance measurement can be used to identify leading-edge and improving performers to facilitate efforts in identifying promising practices, which can then be adapted by similar agencies and tested with data coming out of continuing performance monitoring activity, and the effectiveness of the CORE process will be measured by whether, and the extent to which, it leads to improved performance in the field of nursing regulation over time.

More generally, recommended approaches for developing comparative performance measurement and benchmarking processes, as reflected in the CORE projects at NCSBN, include the following:

- Identify and recruit benchmarking partners on a voluntary basis. It is okay to start small and build over time.
- Develop a common performance framework, and identify the principal areas of concern.
- Define the comparative performance measures to be monitored, and develop consensus on specific indicators that all benchmarking partners can observe and report.

- Develop definitions of indicators and common data collection procedures, and build commitment on the part of all programs or agencies to maintain the fidelity of the data.
- Provide guidance and assistance to benchmarking partners reporting the data, when necessary, and have some kind of verification process to ensure the reliability of the comparative data
- Respect proprietary interests on the part of the benchmarking partners and reach agreement early on regarding the level of confidentiality to be maintained, focusing in particular on the extent to which the data reported by an individual program or agency will be shared with others.
- Develop report formats to present the results as meaningfully as possible, focusing on the performance issues of interest to the participating entities, analyzing differences across groups of participants where relevant, and maintaining the confidentiality limits that have been imposed.
- Review the results collectively and encourage discussion of the factors that both facilitate and impede performance, focusing especially on external possibilities and constraints versus internal policies and practices that influence performance.
- Identify leading-edge and improving performers, and work to distill promising practices from the data and discussion, Provide assistance to other agencies in adapting these practices, and evaluate their effectiveness with additional and sometimes more detailed data from the programs or agencies that import them.

Prospects for Benchmarking

Comparative performance measurement and benchmarking efforts have gained momentum in the public sector over the past ten years in the United States and elsewhere, and the idea of comparing measures against other agencies or programs in order to help gauge performance, and possibly help improve it, would seem to be a commonsense one. Identifying other organizations or programs as potential benchmarking partners should not be too difficult for most state and local agencies, as they often have counterparts in other governmental jurisdictions. The same is true for many nonprofit agencies at the state and local level. However, issues concerning data reliability and differences in programs or operating conditions create methodological challenges in developing useful benchmarking systems.

Furthermore, in terms of political and managerial contexts, the prospect of statistical benchmarking carries both problems and opportunities. Obviously, comparing the performance of individual agencies or programs on a set of common measures is a sensitive issue simply because some may "look bad" in comparison with others whether or not the indicators have been adjusted for contextual factors. Yet the comparative data may be useful in a number of ways, not the least of which is to provide an incentive for less efficient and effective programs to improve their performance. Indeed, just participating in efforts to define and report common measurements on a uniform basis may spur some agencies to upgrade their own measurement systems and use them more productively. Thus, the prospects for increased benchmarking will depend on the extent to which its usefulness outweighs the costs. This in turn will depend largely on the extent to which benchmarking can be used as an opportunity for improving performance through incentives and sharing information about leading-edge practices rather than as a basis for penalizing poorly performing programs.

References

American Association of State Highway and Transportation Officials. (2006). *Measuring performance against state DOTs*. Washington, DC: AASHTO.

Ammons, D. N., Coe, C., & Lombardo, M. (2001). Performance-comparison projects in local government: Participants' perspectives. *Public Administration Review, 61*, 100–111.

Ammons, D. N., & Rivenbark, W. C. (2008). Factors influencing the use of performance data to improve municipal services. *Public Administration Review, 68*, 304–318.

Boyer, S. R., & Martin, L. L. (2012). The Florida Benchmarking Consortium. *Public Performance and Management Review, 36*, 124–137.

Crossett, J., & Hines, L. (2007). *Comparing state DOTs' construction project cost and schedule performance: 28 best practices from 9 states*. Washington, DC: American Association of State Highway and Transportation Officials.

Harrison, F., & Park, H.-A. (2008). *Comparative performance measurement: Pavement smoothness*. Washington, DC: American Association of State Highway and Transportation Officials.

Hatry, H. P. (Ed.). (1999). Mini-symposium of intergovernmental comparative performance data. *Public Administration Review, 59*, 101–134.

Howard, M., & Kilmartin, B. (2006). *Assessment of benchmarking within government organizations*. Accenture. Accenture.com/SiteCollectionDocumentsPDF/Assessment_of_Benchmarking_Within_Gov_Org.pdf

Keehley, P., & Abercrombie, N. N. (2008). *Benchmarking in the public and nonprofit sectors* (2nd ed.). San Francisco: Jossey-Bass.

Knutson, H., Ramberg, U., & Tagesson, T. (2012). Benchmarking impact through municipal benchmarking networks. *Public Performance and Management Review, 36,* 1021–1023.

Morley, E., Bryant, S. P., & Hatry, H. P. (2001). *Comparative performance measurement.* Washington, DC: Urban Institute Press.

Ryus, P. Coffel, K., Parks, J., Perk, V., Cherrington, L., Arndt, J.,…Gan, A. 2010. *A methodology for performance measurement and peer comparison in the public transportation industry* (TCRP Report 141). Washington, DC: Transportation Research Board.

Stiefel, L., Rubenstein, R., & Schwartz, A. E. (1999). Using adjusted performance measures for evaluating resource use. *Public Budgeting and Finance, 19,* 67–87.

Toronto, City Manager's Office. (2013, March). *2011 performance measurement and benchmarking report.* www.toronto.ca/legdocs/mmis/2013/ex/bgrd/backgroundfile -57525.pdf

Urban Institute and International City/County Management Association. (1997). *Comparative performance measurement: FY 1995 data report.* Washington, DC: Author.

PART FOUR

DESIGN AND IMPLEMENTATION OF PERFORMANCE MANAGEMENT SYSTEMS

Implementing a performance management system in a public or nonprofit agency involves the process of managing organizational change. This means that in addition to the more technical issues inherent in defining and evaluating performance measures, managerial challenges are likely to arise in trying to implement them effectively. Managers need to recognize that resources are required to develop, implement, and maintain measurement systems, and they should view this as an investment, with the objective of maximizing the rate of return in terms of generating useful information.

Part 4 consists of a single chapter, which identifies critical elements of successful approaches to developing and implementing management systems, emphasizing the importance of strong leadership and stakeholder involvement as well as the need to manage the overall developmental effort as a deliberate process using a project management approach. The chapter concludes by presenting thirty-three strategies for the successful implementation of performance management systems. These strategies are intended to respond to such issues as resource requirements, lack of use, lack of stakeholder buy-in, internal resistance, goal displacement and gaming the system, and potential system abuse. Building these strategies into the process of designing and implementing performance measures in your public or nonprofit agency can help you substantially in installing a worthwhile, cost-effective measurement system.

## CHAPTER FIFTEEN

DESIGNING AND IMPLEMENTING EFFECTIVE MANAGEMENT SYSTEMS

What is the best way to manage the process of designing and implementing a performance management system? Who should be involved in this process? How can you overcome the resistance that often builds up against such systems and build support for them instead? What are the most frequent problems that plague efforts to implement measurement systems, and how can you avoid or surmount them? This chapter discusses organization and management issues involved in designing and implementing performance management systems and suggests strategies for success in developing systems that are useful and cost-effective.

Expectations that performance management should contribute to higher levels of organizational performance and, in particular, better outcomes is almost universal among both proponents and critics of the performance movement (Ammons, 1995; Behn, 2003; Epstein, 1984; Halachmi & Bouckaert, 1996; Hatry, 2006; Heinrich & Marschke, 2010; Moynihan, 2008; Poister, 2003; Radin, 2006; Wholey & Hatry, 1992). While interest in performance management is largely predicated on the assumption that it will lead to performance improvement, however, empirical research testing this relationship has been relatively sparse to date. A few celebrated cases of effective performance management have been documented, such as CompStat in New York City (Bratton & Malinowski, 2008) and CitiStat in Baltimore (Behn, 2007), and a growing number of case studies demonstrate great potential for using performance information to manage for results (Sanger, 2008; Ammons & Rivenbark, 2008; Gore, 1993; Holzer & Yang, 2004; de Lancer Julnes, Berry, Aristigueta, & Yang, 2007; Barnow & Smith, 2004). For example, New York City's CompStat, a data-driven system, has been credited with effectively fighting crime (Smith & Bratton, 2001), and Baltimore's CitiStat, which expanded the concept to a wide array of municipal services fostering program improvements, won the 2004 Kennedy School of Government's Innovations in American Government Awards (Behn, 2006). Similarly, the ongoing North Carolina municipal benchmarking program has been credited with enabling individual cities participating in the project to make significant improvements in terms of efficiency and service delivery (Ammons & Rivenbark, 2008).

However, Ammons and Rivenbark (2008) contend that "most claims of performance measurement's value in influencing decisions and improving services tend to be broad and disappointingly vague," and they point out that "hard evidence documenting performance measurement's impact on management decisions and service improvements is rare" (p. 305). Poister, Pasha, and Edwards (2013) state "the fairly meager empirical research to date on the impact of performance management practices has produced decidedly mixed results, with four of the eight studies employing cross-sectional analysis across comparable public organizations showing positive effects on performance. Therefore, the question of the effectiveness of performance measurement or management practices in actually improving performance is very much still at issue" (p. 628).

Beyond case studies, a small but growing stream of quantitative research has examined the impact of performance management–related approaches on performance itself, and that work has produced mixed results. Some of these studies have produced evidence that performance management can make a positive difference. The study by Poister et al. (2013) is a recent example finding evidence that both strategic planning and performance measurement, the principal components of performance management in public organizations, "do contribute to improved performance in small and medium-sized transit systems in the United States" (p. 632). Earlier, Walker, Damanpour, and Devece (2011) found that elements of performance management such as building ownership and understanding of organizational mission and goals, specification of appropriate performance measures and targets, devolution of control to service managers, and taking corrective action when results deviate from plans in English local government authorities led to higher core service performance scores constructed by the British Audit Commission. In the field of education, on the one hand, similar research has found positive effects of performance management practices on student test scores in England (Boyne & Chen, 2007) and Denmark (Andersen, 2008), as well as the United States (Sun & Van Ryzin, 2014). On the other hand, a recent longitudinal review of a large number of US cities "at the forefront" of performance measurement activities found significant advancement in the reporting of performance data but little support for the proposition that it has been a catalyst for improved performance. Clearly additional empirical research is needed to identify the kinds of contextual factors and implementation strategies that facilitate the ability of performance management systems to make a difference in government and nonprofit organizations.

Managing the Process

In designing and implementing an effective performance management system, we need to consider the elements that are key for its success. Wholey (1999), an early proponent of performance management, attributed three essential elements to effective performance-based management:

1. Developing a reasonable level of agreement among key stakeholders regarding agency mission, goals, and strategies
2. Implementing performance measurement systems of sufficient quality
3. Using performance information to improve program effectiveness, strengthen accountability, and support decision making

This chapter begins by discussing ways to manage the process and implement these essential elements.

Mission, Goals, and Strategies

The practice of strategic planning is often used to develop reasonable agreement among key stakeholders regarding agency mission, goals, and strategies. Strategic planning is concerned with optimizing the fit between an organization and the environment in which it operates, and, most important, for public agencies that means strengthening performance in providing services to the public (Poister et al., 2013). Goal setting drives performance and serves as a motivator because it diverts energy and attention away from goal-irrelevant activities toward goal-relevant efforts and energizes people to put forth greater effort to achieve these goals (Latham, 2004; Fried & Slowik, 2004). This is especially important in the public sector, where problems of goal ambiguity can impede performance (Chun & Rainey, 2005). Therefore, setting goals, objectives, or targets regarding organization or program performance will keep the organization focused on priorities, outcomes, and results and thereby facilitate improvements in performance (Ammons, 2008; Kelly, 2003; Poister, 2003; Van Dooren, Bouckaert, & Halligan, 2010). Strategic planning establishes goals and objectives, many of which are likely to be performance related, and creating and implementing strategies designed to achieve them is expected to lead to improved performance (Bryson, 2011; Niven, 2003; Poister, 2010; Walker et al., 2011). (More on this process has been previously discussed in chapter 8 of this book.)

Quality Performance Measures

Good performance measures, particularly outcome measures, signal what the real priorities are, and they motivate people to work harder and smarter to accomplish organizational objectives. Tools like the balanced scorecard and logic models explored in chapter 8 help organizations decide on measures. For example, Neely and Bourne (2000) found that as more organizations started to use the balanced scorecard, they found enormous value in the act of deciding what to measure.

Quality performance measures require a balance between cost of data collection and the need to ensure that the data are complete, accurate, and consistent to document performance and support decision making at various organizational levels (Wholey, 2006). The technical quality of performance measurement systems will require the measures to be valid and reliable. Validity will mean that the performance indicators measure what is important to the recipients of the information, measure what they claim to measure, and are shared in a timely manner. Reliability requires consistency in that repeated measurements yield similar results.

Sterck and Bouckaert (2008) find the major challenges to collecting quality performance measures when (1) objectives are not specific enough and measurable; (2) there is high dependence on secondary data collection; (3) there is no established causal relationship between input, activities, outputs, and outcomes; (4) information on unit costs is missing; (5) difficulties arise in consolidating information; (6) data collection practices are expensive; and (7) time lags arise between inputs, activities, outputs, and outcomes. In order to alleviate these challenges, quality standards should be established, data quality monitored, and problems in data quality addressed. The last should be included in the process as outlined by Wholey (1999) in the previous section and number 2 on his list: implementing performance measurement systems of sufficient quality.

Measurement systems provide managers and decision makers with information regarding performance that they use to manage agencies and programs more effectively, redirecting resources and making adjustments in operations and service delivery systems to produce better results. And the performance data generated by measurement systems provide information to elected officials that can be useful in setting goals and priorities, making macrolevel budget decisions, and holding public agencies and managers accountable.

In the nonprofit sector as well, outcome measures can help agencies improve services and overall program effectiveness, increase accountability, guide managers in allocating resources, and help funding organizations make better decisions. At an operational level, performance measures provide feedback to staff, focus board members on policy and programmatic issues, identify needs for training and technical assistance, pinpoint service units and participant groups that need attention, compare alternative service delivery strategies, identify potential partners for collaboration, recruit volunteers, attract customers, set targets for future performance, and improve an agency's public image (Plantz, Greenway, & Hendricks, 1997).

Program Improvement

Behn (2003, p. 586) counts eight purposes for performance measurement but contends that one of the eight, fostering improvement, is "the core purpose behind the other seven." Those other seven—evaluate, control, budget, motivate, promote, celebrate, and learn—are means to the desired end and core purpose, which is to improve.

In studying the CitiStat programs, Behn (2006) found that to foster an improvement in performance, the meetings had to produce some decisions and some commitments. But unless there is follow-up, these decisions and commitments did not significantly improve agency operations.

The follow-up needs to have five critical traits:

1. Subsequent assignments phrased as performance targets with due dates
2. Assignments made by the authority figure running the meeting

3. Assignments communicated at the meeting and may include written communication
4. Agencies that prepare for CitiStat meetings with AgencyStat
5. Review of the results of the assignment at the next CitiStat meeting

Fostering improvements benefits from providing incentives. For example, Hatry (2006) recommends the use of rewards in performance contracts—rewards for meeting or exceeding targets and reduction of fees for failing to meet targets. The Food and Nutrition Services uses a variety of cash and nonmonetary awards to reinforce its desired results. It has unique internal peer and spirit awards, certificates of merit, spot awards, and time-off awards. In its quarterly newsletter, the region lists the names of award recipients for the quarter and includes information about the recipient and his or her contribution to performance (https:// www.opm.gov/policy-data-oversight/performance-management/ reference-materials/more-topics/what-a-difference-effective-performance -management-makes/).

Barriers to Success

But success does not come easily. It is a grand understatement to say that designing and implementing a performance measurement system in a public or nonprofit agency is a challenging process. Obviously the technical aspects of identifying appropriate performance criteria, defining valid and reliable indicators that are resistant to goal displacement and gaming, deciding on useful comparisons and reporting formats, and developing workable software support present many challenges from a methodological perspective, and these are largely the focus of this book. However, installing a system in an organization and building commitment to it, using it effectively on an ongoing basis, and embedding it in other management and decision-making processes present an even more daunting challenge.

Many governmental agencies and nonprofit organizations have set out to design a performance monitoring system but abandoned the effort before it was completed, or they completed the design but failed to move on to the implementation stage; still others have gone through the motions of installing a system but to no avail. Sometimes a promising measurement system is implemented in an agency but fails to take hold or be used in any meaningful way; then it may be maintained in a halfhearted way or be abandoned at some point. Still others are installed and maintained, but they never make a significant contribution to improved management, decision making, or performance.

Moynihan (2009) also points out that in contrast to purposeful use of the data by public managers and decision makers to improve performance, some actors in these performance regimes are likely to make passive use of performance data—minimally complying with procedural requirements without actually working to improve performance—or political use or even perverse use of performance information to support self-serving interests, which might actually work against achieving the kinds of results a program is intended to produce.

There are numerous reasons that these things happen. In some cases, the measurement system as designed does not meet the needs of the managers it is intended to serve. Or implementing the system and maintaining it on an ongoing basis may consume too much time and too many resources, and the information the system provides is not viewed as being worth the effort. There may be considerable resistance from within the organization to a new system, and the resulting lack of support and cooperation may stifle its effective implementation. Sometimes such systems wither before they get off the ground for lack of champions who can build support for them and persistently guide the organization through the process of system design and implementation.

In yet other cases, the public programs do not lend themselves readily to performance measurement (Bouckaert & Balk, 1991; Leeuw, 2000; Radin, 2006) because of complexity and or goal ambiguity or outputs and outcomes that are difficult to measure and difficult to control (Jennings & Haist, 2004). The problem may exist with the choice of measures as they may not generate useful information, may lack validity and reliability, are not actionable, focus on past performance and therefore are not timely, or are descriptive rather than prescriptive (Hatry, 2006; Heinrich, 2007; Marr, 2012; Poister, 2003).

Resource constraints also often present barriers to performance improvement (Boyne, 2003) by "limiting training and development activities, discouraging innovation and experimentation with newer programmatic approaches, or preventing implementation of new strategies aimed at generating increased outcomes" (Poister et al., 2013, p. 626). Finally, an organization may not have the kinds of performance-oriented management systems, such as performance budgeting processes, performance contracting or grant management, process improvement, or customer service processes, that may be required to make meaningful use of the performance data (Poister et al., 2013).

Elements of Success

Installing a performance measurement system and embedding it in management processes involve bringing about organizational change, and this can be difficult. Even technically sound systems may face substantial problems in effective implementation. Obviously successful design and implementation will not occur automatically, but several factors can elevate the probability of success significantly. Best practices among both public agencies and private firms reveal the following ingredients for successful performance measurement programs:

- Leadership is critical in designing, deploying, and maintaining effective performance measurement and management systems. Clear, consistent, and visible involvement by senior executives and managers is a necessary part of successful performance measurement and management systems.
- A conceptual framework is needed for the performance measurement and management system. Every organization needs a clear and cohesive performance measurement framework that is understood by all levels of the organization and that supports objectives and the collection of results.
- Effective internal and external communication and participation of key stakeholders are the keys to successful performance measurement. Effective communication with employees, process owners, customers, and stakeholders is vital to the successful development and deployment of performance measurement and management systems.
- Performance measures should be developed primarily by the program that will be responsible for the data with input from upper management. Input and feedback should also be obtained from citizens, customers, and other stakeholders to make sure the measures include those of importance to the citizens.
- Agencies and their programs need to track and distinguish types of measures. The logic models and the balanced scorecard discussed throughout this book are a useful technique for this discussion.
- Accountability for results must be clearly assigned and well understood. High-performance organizations make sure that all managers and employees understand what they are responsible for in achieving organizational goals.
- Data processing and analytic support are critical, and data processing personnel should be brought into the planning stages early. Data must

be analyzed by knowledgeable individuals to ensure reliability and validity of data.

- Performance measurement systems must provide intelligence for decision makers, not just compile data. Measures should be limited to those that relate to strategic goals and objectives and yield timely, relevant, and concise information that decision makers at all levels can use to assess progress in achieving goals.
- Compensation, rewards, and recognition should be linked to performance measurements. Such a linkage sends a clear and unambiguous message to the organization as to what is important.
- Performance measurement systems should be positive, not punitive. The most successful measurement systems are not "gotcha" systems, but rather are learning systems that help identify what works and what does not so as to continue with and improve what is working and repair or replace what is not working.
- Results and progress toward program commitments should be openly shared with employees, customers, and stakeholders.

In working to build these elements of success into a performance measurement program, public and nonprofit managers should (1) ensure strong leadership and support for the effort by involving a variety of stakeholders in developing the system, (2) follow a deliberate process in designing and implementing it, and (3) use project management tools to keep the process on track and produce a suitable measurement system.

Leadership and Stakeholder Support and Involvement

In a small agency, a performance measurement system could conceivably be designed and implemented by a single individual, but this approach is not likely to produce a workable system in most cases. A wide variety of stakeholders usually have an interest in, and may well be affected by, a performance measurement system—for example:

Stakeholders in the Performance
  Measurement Process

Governmental agencies	**Nonprofit organizations**
Agency or program managers and staff	Agency or program managers and staff
Employees	Employees

Labor unions	Volunteers
Contractors, grantees, and suppliers	Contractors, grantees, and suppliers
Elected officials	Governing board members
Clients and customers	Clients and customers
Advocacy groups	Advocacy groups
Other governmental units	Local chapters
Citizens and community organizations	Community organizations and the public
Funding organizations	Funding organizations
Management analysts and data specialists	Management analysts and data specialists

Including at least some of these stakeholders in the design and implementation process will have two big advantages. First, they will raise issues and make suggestions that might not otherwise surface, and ultimately this will result in a better system. Second, because they have had a chance to participate in the process, voice their concerns, and help shape a system that serves their needs or at least is sensitive to issues that are important to them, they will be more likely to support the system that emerges. Thus, although it may be somewhat more cumbersome and time consuming, involving a variety of stakeholders in the process is likely to produce a more effective system and build ownership for that system along the way.

In a public or nonprofit organization of any size and complexity, therefore, it usually makes sense at the outset to form a working group to guide the process of designing and implementing a performance measurement system. Normally this group should be chaired by the top manager—the chief executive officer, agency head, division manager, or program director—of the organizational unit or program for which the system is being designed or another line or staff manager whom that individual delegates. Although the makeup of this working group, task force, or steering committee may vary, at a minimum it needs to include managers or staff from whatever agencies, subunits, or programs are to be covered by the performance measurement system. In the case of agencies or programs where service delivery is highly decentralized, it is advisable to include managers from field offices or local chapters in addition to those from the central office or headquarters. As Swiss (1991, p. 337) notes, a measurement system should be "designed to bring the most usable information to bear on the most pressing problems facing managers. Only the managers of each agency can say what their most pressing problems are and what kinds of information would be most useful in attacking them." In addition, public agencies might well be advised to include an elected official or staff representative from the appropriate legislative body on the steering group; nonprofit agencies should include members of their governing boards in such a group.

The following are some other internal stakeholders who might be included in this steering group:

- A representative of the central executive office (e.g., the city manager's office, the secretary or commissioner's office)
- Representatives from central office administrative or support units, such as the budget office, the personnel department, or a quality or productivity center
- A systems person who is knowledgeable about information processing and the agency's existing systems
- A representative from the labor union if the employees are unionized

The steering committee also needs to have a resident measurement expert on board. In a large organization, this might be someone from a staff unit such as an office of planning and evaluation or a management analysis group. If such technical support is not available internally, this critical measurement expertise can be provided by an outside consultant, preferably one who is familiar with the agency or the program area in question.

In addition, it may be helpful to include external stakeholders in the steering group. With respect to programs that operate through the intergovernmental system, for example, representatives from either sponsoring or grantee agencies, or other agencies cooperating in program delivery, might make significant contributions. Private firms and or nonprofits working as contractors in delivery services should perhaps also be included. Furthermore, it may be helpful to invite consumer groups or advocacy groups to participate on the steering committee to represent the customer's perspective or the field at large.

Finally, if it is anticipated that the performance measurement issues may be particularly difficult to work through or that the deliberations may be fairly contentious, it may be advisable to engage the services of a professionally trained facilitator to lead at least some of the group's meetings.

The primary role of the steering committee should be to guide the process of developing the measurement system through to a final design and then to oversee its implementation. As is true of any such group process, the members need to be both open-minded and committed to seeing it through to the successful implementation of an effective system.

Deliberate Process

A recommended process for designing and implementing a performance management system was discussed in chapter 2 and is presented here again. Although these steps and the sequence can be modified and tailored to fit the needs of a particular agency or program, all the tasks listed, with the exception of the optional pilot, are essential in order to achieve the goal of implementing and using an effective measurement system on an ongoing basis. Thus, very early on in its deliberations, the steering group should adopt, and perhaps further elaborate, an overall process for designing and implementing a performance measurement system like the one shown here.

Process for Designing and Implementing Performance Management Systems

Step One: Clarify the purpose of the system.

Step Two: Assess organizational readiness.

Step Three: Identify relevant external stakeholders.

Step Four: Organize system development process.

Step Five: Identify key purposes and parameters for initiating performance management.

Step Six: Define the components for the performance management system, performance criteria, and use.

Step Seven: Define, evaluate, and select indicators.

Step Eight: Develop data collection procedures.

Step Nine: Specify system design.

- Identify reporting frequencies and channels.
- Determine analytical and reporting formats.
- Develop software applications.
- Assign responsibilities for maintaining the system.

Step Ten: Conduct a pilot if necessary.

Step Eleven: Implement the full-scale system.

Step Twelve: Use, modify, and evaluate the system.

Step Thirteen: Share the results with stakeholders.

Developing such systems can be an arduous undertaking, and it is easy to get bogged down in the details of data and specific indicators and to lose sight of what the effort is really about. Thus, having agreed on the overall design and implementation process can help members of the steering group keep the big picture in mind and track their own progress along the way. It will also help them think ahead to next steps—to anticipate issues that might arise and prepare to deal with them beforehand. Along these lines, one of the most important steps in this process is the first one: clarifying the purpose and scope of the measurement system to be developed.

Clearly identifying the purpose of a particular system—for example, the tracking of the agency's progress in implementing strategic initiatives, as opposed to the monitoring of the effectiveness of a particular program or the measuring of workforce productivity on an ongoing basis, establishes a clear target that can then be used to discipline the process as the committee moves through it. In other words, for the steering group to work through the process deliberately and thus accomplish its objective more efficiently and effectively, it would do well to ask continually whether undertaking certain steps or approaching individual tasks in a particular way will advance its objective of developing a measurement system to serve this specific, clearly established purpose.

Project Management

A clearly identified purpose will help the steering committee manage the design and implementation process as a project, using standard project management tools for scheduling work, assigning responsibilities, and tracking progress. Although in certain cases it may be possible to get a system up and running in fairly short order, more often it will take a year or two to design and implement a new system, and more complex systems may require three or four years to move into full-scale operation, especially if a pilot is to be conducted. This is a complicated process, and over the course of that period, the steering group (or some subgroup or other entity) will have to develop several products, including the following:

- A clear statement of the scope and purpose of the measurement system
- A description of the performance criteria to be captured by the system
- Definitions of each measure to be incorporated in the system and documentation of constituent elements, data sources, and computations
- Documentation of data collection procedures
- A plan for ensuring the quality and integrity of the data
- A plan for reporting particular results to specified audiences at certain frequencies
- Prototype analytical and reporting formats
- Software programs and hardware configurations to support the system
- Identification of responsibilities for data collection and input, data processing, report preparation, system maintenance, and utilization
- A plan for full-scale implementation of the measurement system

The committee will also conduct and evaluate the pilot, if necessary, and be responsible for at least early-stage evaluation and possible modification of the full-scale system once it is being used. It usually helps to sketch a rough schedule of the overall process over a year or multiyear period, stating approximate due dates when each of these products, or deliverables, will be completed. Although the schedule may change substantially along the way, thinking it through will give the steering group a clearer idea of what the process will involve and help establish realistic expectations about what will be accomplished by when.

Managing the project also entails detailing the scope of work by defining specific tasks and subtasks to be completed. The steering group might elaborate the entire scope of work at the outset, partly in the interest of developing a more realistic schedule; alternatively, it may detail the tasks one step at a time, projecting a rough schedule on the basis of only a general idea of what will be involved at each step. Detailing the project plan sooner rather than later is advantageous in that it will help clarify what resources, what expertise, what levels of effort, and what other commitments will be necessary in order to design and implement the system, again developing a more realistic set of expectations about what is involved in this process.

The project management approach also calls for assigning responsibilities for leading and supporting each step in the process. It may be that the steering group decides to conduct all the work by committee as a whole, but it might well decide on a division of labor whereby various individuals or subgroups take lead responsibility for different tasks. In addition, some individual or work unit may be assigned responsibility for staffing the project and doing the bulk of the detailed work between committee meetings. Furthermore, the steering group may decide to work through subcommittees or involve additional stakeholders in various parts of the process along the way. Typically the number of participants grows as the project moves forward and particular kinds of expertise are required at different points along the way, and a number of working groups may spin off the core steering committee in order to get the work done more efficiently and effectively. A further advantage of involving more participants along the way is that they may serve as "envoys" back to the organizational units or outside groups they represent and thus help build support for the system.

Finally, project management calls for monitoring activities and tracking progress in the design and implementation process along the way. This is usually accomplished by getting reports from working groups or subcommittees and comparing progress against the established schedule. It also means evaluating the process and deliverables produced, noting problems, and making adjustments as appropriate. The overall approach should be somewhat pragmatic, especially when members of the steering group have little experience in developing such systems, and no one should be surprised to have to make adjustments in the scope of work, schedule, and assignments as the group moves through the process. Nevertheless, managing the overall effort as a project from beginning to end will help the steering committee keep the process on track and work in a more deliberate manner to install an effective measurement system.

Software is available to track projects. For example, Microsoft Project tracks projects with due dates and the person responsible. The main modules of Microsoft Project are project work and project teams, schedules, and finances. It allows its users to create projects, track tasks, and report results.

Networks and Collaborations

As the work of governments and nonprofits continues to include multiple partners or networks, thought must be given to managing the performance of these networks and collaborations. Milward and Provan (2006) describe four uses for performance management in networks: service implementation, information diffusion, problem solving, and community capacity building. Understanding the kinds of networks and role of leaders in the networks is essential to developing a performance management system. For example, managing the accountability of a network should include determining who is responsible for which outcomes, but accountability for those delivering service in a network would be monitoring one's own agency involvement and accomplishments.

The Government Accountability Office (2014) studied the best practices in collaborative approaches in the federal government and found the key considerations and implementation approaches in table 15.1.

In setting up a system that involves collaborations whether intergovernmental, with private contractors, or nonprofits, it will be useful to plan for the measurement of these accomplishments. The key considerations and implementation approaches found by the Government Accountability Office in interagency collaborations will be a useful starting point.

Strategies for Success

Structuring the design and implementation effort with committee oversight, using a deliberate process, and using project management tools constitutes a rational approach to installing an effective measurement system, but by no means does this approach guarantee success. Implementing any new management system is an exercise in managing change, and a performance measurement system is no different. This places the challenge of designing and implementing a measurement system outside a technical sphere and in the realm of managing people, the culture, organizations, and relationships. Indeed, research finds that even though decisions by public organizations to adopt measurement systems tend to be based on technical and analytical criteria, the ways in which systems are implemented are influenced more strongly by political and cultural factors (de Lancer Julnes & Holzer, 2001).

Clearly both technical and managerial issues are important in designing and implementing performance measurement systems. Proponents and observers of performance measurement in government have noted a number of problems in implementing such systems and proposed strategies to overcome them (Kamensky & Fountain, 2008; Poister, 2003; Aristigueta & Zarook, 2011; Hatry, 1999, 2002, 2006; Kassoff, 2001; Wholey, 2002). Others have summarized lessons learned by nonprofit agencies in developing measurement systems and made suggestions for ensuring success in implementing such systems in the nonprofit sector (Plantz,

TABLE 15.1 IMPLEMENTING INTERAGENCY COLLABORATIONS

Key Considerations for Implementing Interagency Collaborative Mechanisms	Implementation Approaches from Select Interagency Groups
Outcomes • Have short-term and long-term outcomes been clearly defined?	• Started group with most directly affected participants and gradually broadened to others • Conducted early outreach to participants and stakeholders to identify shared interests • Held early in-person meetings to build relationships and trust • Identified early wins for the group to accomplish • Developed outcomes that represented the collective interests of participants • Developed a plan to communicate outcomes and track progress • Revisited outcomes and refreshed interagency group
Accountability • Is there a way to track and monitor progress?	• Developed performance measures and tied them to shared outcomes • Identified and shared relevant agency performance data • Developed methods to report on the group's progress that are open and transparent • Incorporated interagency group activities into individual performance expectations
Leadership • Has a lead agency or individual been identified? • If leadership will be shared between one or more agencies, have roles and responsibilities been clearly identified and agreed on?	• Designated group leaders exhibited collaboration competencies • Ensured participation from high-level leaders in regular, in-person group meetings, and activities • Rotated key tasks and responsibilities when leadership of the group was shared • Established clear and inclusive procedures for leading the group during initial meetings • Distributed leadership responsibility for group activities among participants
Resources • How will the collaborative mechanism be funded? • How will the collaborative mechanism be staffed?	• Created an inventory of resources dedicated toward interagency outcomes • Leveraged related agency resources toward the group's outcomes • Pilot tested new collaborative ideas, programs, or policies before investing resources

Source: US Government Accountability Office (2014, p. 1).

Greenway, & Hendricks, 1997; Sawhill & Williamson, 2001; Newcomer, 2008). Ammons and Rivenbark (2008, p. 307) suggest three factors that effectively encourage the productive use of performance information: "the collection of and reliance on higher-order measures—that is, outcome measures (effectiveness) and especially measures of efficiency—rather than simply output measures (workload); the willingness of officials to embrace comparison with other governments or service producers; and the incorporation of performance measures into key management systems."

Although the process of developing performance measurement systems is similar for both public and nonprofit organizations, such efforts may be even more challenging for nonprofit managers because of several factors:

- Many nonprofit agencies rely heavily on the work of volunteers to deliver services, who may be particularly leery of attempts to evaluate their performance.
- Local chapters often have a high degree of autonomy, and it may be more difficult to implement uniform reporting procedures for roll-up or comparison purposes.
- Nonprofit agencies are often funded by a variety of sources and are often highly dependent on a changing mix of grants for funding, creating a more fluid flow of services that may be more difficult to track with ongoing monitoring systems.
- Funders may provide nonprofits with the indicators, providing very little freedom for selection of measures and stakeholder involvement.
- Many nonprofit agencies have relatively limited managerial and analytical resources to support performance measurement systems.

At the same time, because most nonprofit agencies are governed by boards of directors that are more closely focused on the work of their particular agencies than is the case with legislatures and individual public agencies, they may have an advantage in terms of ensuring alignment of the expectations of the managerial and governing bodies regarding performance as well as building meaningful commitments to use the measurement system.

Despite these differences between public and nonprofit agencies, for the most part both face similar kinds of issues in developing a measurement system, including problems concerning the information produced, the time and effort required to implement and support the system, the

lack of subsequent use of the measurement system by managers and decision makers, the lack of stakeholder support for it, internal resistance to
it, undesirable consequences that might arise from putting certain measures in place, and possible abuses of such a system. Thus, this concluding
section presents thirty strategies that address these problems and help
ensure the successful design and implementation of performance measurement systems in both public and nonprofit agencies.

Usefulness of the Information Produced

Performance management systems will be used only if they provide worthwhile information to managers and decision makers, but many systems do
not provide relevant and useful information. Sometimes they are simply
not well conceived in terms of focusing on the kinds of results that are of
concern to managers. If, for example, the measures are not consistent with
an agency's strategic agenda, they are unlikely to be relevant to managers.
In other cases, measures are selected on the basis of what data are readily
available, but this approach rarely provides decision makers with a well-
rounded picture of program performance. To ensure that measurement
systems do provide relevant information that will help manage agencies
and programs more effectively, those who commission measurement
systems as well as those who take the lead in designing them should be
sure to

1. Clarify mission, strategy, goals and objectives, and program structure as a prelude to measurement. Use this strategic framework to focus
the scope of the performance measurement system on what is truly important to the organization and its stakeholders.
2. Establish the purpose of the performance management system and
the mechanisms through which performance information will be used to
improve management and decision making regarding strategy, resource
allocation, quality and process improvements, grants and contract management, stakeholder engagement, or other similar uses. Clearly define
the critical elements with respect to how the information will be used to
inform management and decisions aimed at improving performance.
3. Develop logic models to identify the linkages between programmatic activity and outputs and outcomes, and use this framework to define
appropriate measures. These logic models help sort out the myriad variables involved in a program and identify what the important results really
are. When the focus is on agency rather than programmatic performance,

develop balanced scorecards or use other goal structures as the performance framework. When the focus is on quality or process improvement, develop flowcharts and use them as performance frameworks.

4. Be results driven rather than data driven in the search for relevant measures. Do not include measures simply because the data are already available. Use need and usefulness rather than data availability or ease of measurement as the principle criteria for selecting measures.

5. Work toward omnidirectional alignment across various management processes. Ensure that programmatic and lower-level goals and objectives are consistent with strategic objectives, that budget priorities are consistent with strategic objectives, and that individual and organizational unit objectives derive ultimately from higher-level goals and objectives. Then develop performance measures that are directly tied to these objectives.

6. Periodically review the measures and revise them as appropriate. Performance measurement systems are intended to monitor trends over time, which is why it is important to maintain consistency in the measures over the long run. However, this should not be taken to mean that the measures are cast in stone. Over time, the relevance of some measures may diminish substantially, and the needs for other indicators may emerge. In addition, the reliability of some indicators may erode and require adjustment or replacement. It is therefore imperative to review both the quality and the usefulness of the measures and make changes as needed.

Resource Requirements

Performance management systems may require too much time and effort, especially when they require original data collection instruments, new data collection procedures, or substantial data input from the field. Measurement systems are not free, and they should be viewed as an investment of resources that will generate worthwhile payoff. The objective is to develop a system that is cost-effective, but at the beginning of the development process, system planners often underestimate the time, effort, and expenditures required, which then turn out to be much greater than expected. This leads to frustration and can result in systems whose benefit is not worth the cost. To avoid this situation, system planners should take the following into consideration:

7. Be realistic in estimating how long it will take to design and implement a particular measurement system. The design and implementation

process itself involves a substantial amount of work, and creating realistic expectations at the outset about what it will require can help avoid disillusionment with the value of performance measurement overall.

8. Develop a clear understanding of the full cost of supporting and maintaining a measurement system, and keep it reasonable in relation to the information produced. Conversely, try to ascertain your resource constraints at the outset and then work to maximize the information payoff from available resources. This approach creates fair expectations regarding what investments are necessary and is more likely to result in a system whose benefits exceed its costs.

9. Use existing or readily available data whenever appropriate, and avoid costly new data collection efforts unless they are essential. Some potentially expensive data collection procedures may need to be instituted, but only when it is clear that they add real value to the measurement system.

Lack of Use

Even when they are relevant, performance measures can be ignored. They will not be used automatically. Although in some cases this is due to a lack of interest or outright resistance on the part of managers, it may also result from poor system design. Managers often feel overwhelmed by systems that include too many measures and seem to be unnecessarily complex. Another problem is that some systems track appropriate measures but do a poor job of presenting the performance data in ways that are understandable, interesting, and convincing. More generally, some systems simply are not designed to serve the purpose for which they were intended. The following guidelines are aimed at maximizing the useful content of performance data:

10. Be clear about why you are developing performance measures and how you will use them. Tailor the measures, reporting frequencies, and presentation formats to the intended use so as to encourage use.

11. Provide regular review sessions to engage select policymakers or managers at various levels to discuss the performance information and its implications for policy, programming, and management. Focus the discussion in part on identifying weak or eroding areas of performance, identifying the causes of problematic performance, and develop plans for corrective action.

12. Focus on a relatively small number of important measures of success. Managers often feel inundated by large numbers of measures and

by detailed reports and thus will often disregard them. There is no magic number of measures to include, and sometimes you will need additional measures to provide a more balanced portrait of performance or to balance other measures in the effort to avoid problems of goal displacement. Everything else being equal, though, it is preferable to have fewer measures rather than too many.

13. Keep measures and presentations as simple and straightforward as possible. The KISS principle (Keep It Simple, Stupid) applies here because so many higher-level managers who are the intended audiences for the performance data will not have the time or the inclination to wade through complex charts, tables, and graphs.

14. Emphasize comparisons in the reporting system. Showing trends over time, gauging actual performance against targets, breaking the data down across operating units, comparing results against other counterpart agencies or programs, breaking results out by client groups, or some combination of these is what makes the performance data compelling. Make sure that the comparisons you provide are the most relevant ones, given the intended users.

15. Develop multiple sets of measures, if necessary, for different audiences. The data might be rolled up from operating units through major divisions to the organization as a whole, providing different levels of detail for different levels of management. Alternatively, different performance measures can be reported to managers with different responsibilities or to different external stakeholders.

16. Identify "results owners," the individuals or organizational units with responsibility for maintaining or improving performance on key output and outcomes measures. Holding particular people accountable for improving performance on specific measures encourages them to pay attention to the system.

17. Informally monitor the usefulness and cost-effectiveness of the measurement system itself and make adjustments accordingly. Again, the system design is not cast in stone, and getting feedback from managers and other intended users helps you identify how the measurement system might be improved to better serve their needs.

Lack of Stakeholder Buy-In

A wide variety of stakeholders have interests in performance measurement systems, and the perceived legitimacy of a system depends in large part on the extent to which these stakeholders buy into it. If stakeholders fail to buy into a measurement system because they don't think the measures are meaningful, the data are reliable, or the results are being used appropriately, it will lose credibility. The system will then be less than effective in influencing efforts to improve performance or in demonstrating accountability. Thus, in developing a measurement system, the agency should

18. Build ownership by involving stakeholders in identifying performance criteria, measures, targets, and data collection systems. This can be done by including some internal stakeholders, and even some external stakeholders, on the steering group developing the system and on subcommittees or other working groups it establishes. The steering committee can solicit input and feedback from other stakeholder groups as well.

19. Consider clients, customers, and other relevant stakeholders throughout the process, and involve them when practical. In addition to ensuring that the resulting system will include measures that are responsive to customer needs and concerns, this will also develop buy-in from these important stakeholders.

20. Generate leadership to develop buy-in for the measures, and demonstrate executive commitment to using them. One of the best ways to develop buy-in on the part of internal stakeholders, and sometimes external stakeholders as well, is to show that the agency's top managers are committed to the measurement system and that they are personally involved in developing and then using it.

21. Develop and nurture a performance culture within the organization through leadership, incentive systems, and ongoing management processes to emphasize involvement with performance measures and commitment to using them with an eye toward maintaining and improving performance.

Internal Resistance

Managers and employees may resist the implementation of performance measures because they feel threatened by them. Employees often view performance monitoring systems as "speed-up" systems intended to force them to work harder or allow the organization to reduce the workforce. Middle-level managers may see such systems as attempts to put increased pressure on them to produce added results and hold them accountable for standards beyond their control. Even higher-level managers may resist the implementation of measurement systems if they perceive them as efforts to force them to give up authority to those above and below them. Because the success of measurement systems depends on the cooperation of managers at all levels, and sometimes of rank-and-file employees as well, in feeding data to the system and working to register improvement on the measures, avoiding or overcoming this kind of internal resistance is critical. Thus, administrators wanting to install measurement systems should

22. Be sure to communicate to managers and employees how and why measures are being used. Take every opportunity to educate internal stakeholders about the purpose of a new system and explain what kinds of measures will be monitored and how they will be used to improve the performance of agency programs; doing so will serve to reduce fear of the unknown and help build credibility for the new system and a higher level of comfort with it in the organization.

23. Provide early reassurance that the system will not produce across-the-board punitive actions such as budget cuts, layoffs, or furloughs. This is often a very real fear among managers and employees, and alleviating it early on will help preempt opposition and gain greater acceptance of any new management system. If reductions in force do in fact result from productivity gains, they can probably be accomplished through attrition rather than firing.

24. Consider implementing the system in layers, or by division or program, to work out problems and demonstrate success. In addition to allowing time to work out the bugs before going full scale, implementing the system incrementally—and perhaps beginning in parts of the organization that are most likely to readily accept it—can also be an opportunity to show not only that the performance measures really can be useful but also that they are not harmful to the workforce.

25. Make sure that program managers and staff see performance data first and have a chance to check and correct them before sending reports up to the executive level. Asking program managers to verify the data first not only strengthens the accuracy and integrity of the reporting system but also helps reinforce their role as process owners rather than self-perceived victims of it.

26. Include fields in the reporting formats for explanatory comments along with the quantitative data. The use of such comment fields gives higher-level managers a much fuller understanding of why performance is going up or down while also giving program managers and staff a safeguard—that is, allowing them the opportunity to shape realistic

expectations and point out factors beyond their control that might be negatively affecting performance.

27. Delegate increased authority and flexibility to both program managers and staff administrators in exchange for holding them accountable for results. This is a critical mechanism for allowing monitoring systems to translate into positive action: holding managers responsible for bottom-line results while giving them wider discretion in how they manage to achieve those results. The added flexibility can also help managers accept a system that they may view as putting more pressure on them to perform.

28. To the extent possible, tie the performance appraisal system, incentive system, and recognition program to the measurement system. Tying these rewards systems to the performance measures puts more muscle in the monitoring system by giving managers and employees added incentive to work harder and smarter in order to perform well on the measures. In tying rewards directly to measures, top management can build additional credibility for the system and positively reinforce improved performance.

Goal Displacement and Gaming

Performance measurement systems can encourage undesirable behavior. As discussed in chapter 5, unbalanced sets of measures can focus undue attention on some performance criteria to the detriment of others, producing undesirable consequences. When managers and employees strive to perform well on less-than-optimal measures while ignoring other more important goals because they are not reflected in the measures, goal displacement occurs and overall performance suffers. In other instances, performance standards or incentives are poorly specified in ways that also allow certain entities to game the system in order to look good on the measures while not really achieving the true goals. Thus, in designing performance measurement systems, it is important to

29. Anticipate possible problems of goal displacement and gaming the system and avoid them by balancing measures. The most systematic approach here is to probe the likely impact of measures by asking the following question: If people perform to the extreme on this particular measure, what adverse impacts, if any, are likely to arise? Usually the antidote to goal displacement and gaming the system is to define additional measures that will counterbalance whatever potential adverse impacts are identified in this way. Along these lines, managers would do well to heed

the adage, "Measure the wrong things, and that's what you will be held accountable for."

30. Install quality assurance procedures to ensure the integrity of the data, and impose sanctions to minimize cheating. Problems with the reliability of data can arise for a variety of reasons, ranging from sloppy reporting to willful cheating. Installing quality assurance procedures, perhaps tracing the data trail in a quality audit on a very small sample basis, is usually sufficient to keep the system honest in most cases, particularly when everyone knows there is a policy in place to impose serious sanctions when anyone is found to have falsified data or otherwise tried to cook the books.

System Abuse

Performance measurement systems can also be abused. Data indicating suboptimal performance, for example, can be used to penalize managers and staff unfairly, and performance data in general can be used either to reward or penalize certain managers and employees on a selective basis. Or, less blatant, authoritarian-style managers can use performance measures and the added power they provide over employees to micromanage their units even more closely in ways that are unpleasant for the employees and counterproductive overall. In order to avoid such problems, higher-level managers should

31. Be wary of misinterpretation and misuse of measures. Higher-level managers should not only review the performance data that are reported up to their levels and then take action accordingly, but also monitor in informal ways how the measurement system is being used at lower levels in the organization. If they become aware that some managers are making inappropriate use of the measures or manipulating the system to abuse employees, they need to inform the abusers that behavior of that kind will no longer be tolerated.

32. Use measurement systems constructively, not punitively, at least until it is clear that sanctions are needed. Top managers need to model this constructive use of performance measures to their subordinates and others down through the chain of command, relying on positive reinforcement to provide effective inducements to improve performance; they must also insist that their subordinates use the system to work with their employees in the same manner. When the data show that performance is subpar, the most productive response is to engage managers in an

assessment of the source of the problem and approaches to remedying it rather than punishing people because they failed to achieve their goals.

33. Above all, recognize and use the measures as indicators only. Although measures can be invaluable in enabling managers and others to track the performance of agencies and programs, they cannot tell the whole story by themselves. Rather, they are intended to serve as one additional source of information on performance; the data they generate are purely descriptive in nature and provide only a surface-level view of how well or poorly programs are actually doing. Thus, managers should learn to use performance data effectively and interpret the results within the fuller context of what they already know or can find out about a program's performance, but they should not let measures themselves dictate actions.

Prospects for Progress in Performance Management

At this point in its evolution, prospects for performance management abound with the speculation that measurement is here to stay as the work of government become more complex and the delivery of services includes multistakeholders. The following list includes our expected changes to the performance management landscape:

- *Broader stakeholder engagement to include those who were not previously able to participate in the process.* Chapter 13 has examples of how technology is facilitating and expanding participation. It is important to note that while the United States is a leader in the development of tools for citizen engagement, other countries are making greater investments in institutionalizing the engagement (Lukensmeyer & Hasselblad Torres, 2006). Kamensky and Fountain (2008) note that the European Union is investing 100 million euros in experimentation with engagement, and the Canadian federal government spends about $1 million a year in citizen engagement efforts.
- *Expanding the use of collaborative networks for achieving performance across organizations and multiple sectors.* The complexity of government is requiring boundary spanning beyond the sector. Collaborations for the delivery of services are appearing not only across organizational boundaries but also across sectors. This requires an understanding of the outcomes for the collaborative network, the leadership, the accountability infrastructure and responsibilities, and resources.

- *Make distinction and resolution for use of performance information for program improvement, accountability to stakeholders, and decision making.* Care must be taken to not use punitive measures for accountability purposes that will have a negative impact on program improvement and use for decision making. Ways to improve accountability and performance must guard against inclinations for gaming, particularly when budget and pay are at risk.
- *Increased improvement in quality of measures will contribute to greater use of measures for decision making.* Performance information needs to be audited for accuracy and relevance of the information in measuring the desired results.
- *Finally, as all of these changes are occurring, care must be taken not to overbureaucratize the performance management process:*

> The performance orientation of public management is here to stay. It is essential for successful government. Societies are now too complex to be managed only by rules of input and process and a public-spirited culture. The performance movement has increased formalized planning, reporting and control across many governments. This has improved the information available to managers and policy makers. But experience shows that this can risk leading to a new form of bureaucratic sclerosis. More attention needs to be given to keeping performance transactions costs in check, and to making optimal use of social and internalized motivators and controls. (Organisation for Economic Co-operation and Development, 2005, p. 81)

A Final Comment

Performance management is essential to managing for results in government and nonprofit organizations. Although measurement can aid greatly in the quest to maintain and improve performance, it is by no means a panacea. High-quality performance measures can provide managers and policymakers with valid, reliable, and timely information on how well or how poorly a given program is performing, but then it is up to those managers and policymakers to respond deliberately and effectively to improve performance.

Clearly the time for performance management in the public and nonprofit sectors has arrived, and agencies are installing new measurement systems and fine-tuning existing systems on an ongoing basis. Yet a substantial amount of skepticism remains about both the feasibility and the utility of measurement systems (Radin, 2006; Moynihan, 2008), and numerous fallacies and misperceptions about the efficacy of performance measurement still prevail in the field (Ammons, 2002; Hatry, 2002, 2006). Nevertheless, tracking the results produced by public and nonprofit programs to include collaborative networks and using the information produced to attempt to improve performance as well as provide accountability to higher-level authorities is a commonsense approach to management based on simple but irrefutable logic.

Although many public and nonprofit agencies have developed and implemented performance management systems in recent years solely in response to mandates from elected chief executives, legislative bodies, and governing boards, many of these systems have proved to be beneficial to the agencies themselves, and many public and nonprofit managers have become converts. We can expect to see efforts continue to proliferate along these lines, and that should be good news for those who are interested in promoting results-oriented management approaches. However, it must always be understood that performance measurement is a necessary but insufficient condition for results-oriented management or results-oriented government. For measurement to be useful, it must be effectively linked to other management and decision-making processes, as discussed in chapter 1 of this book.

Thus, public and nonprofit managers at all levels, in cooperation with elected officials and governing bodies, must build and use effective measurement systems as components that are carefully integrated into processes for strategic planning and management, operational planning, budgeting, performance management, quality and productivity improvement, and other purposes. Without strong linkages to such vital management and decision-making processes, performance measurement systems may generate information that is nice to know but will not lead to better decisions, improved performance, or more effective accountability and control, which are necessary to engage in performance management.

This book has dealt with a number of components of performance management systems from a technical design perspective, and this concluding chapter has discussed issues concerning the implementation of such systems from an organizational and managerial perspective, all with an eye to helping you install the most effective system you can. Yet you need to understand that difficulties abound in this area, that real challenges are likely to persist, and that the perfect measurement system doesn't exist. Although you should work to implement the best measurement system possible and address the kinds of problems discussed in this chapter, you will also need to make the necessary pragmatic trade-offs regarding system quality and usefulness versus cost and level of effort in order to install a workable, affordable, and effective measurement system. Although this may not produce the perfect system, it will clearly be preferable to the alternatives of not having a workable system or having no system at all.

References

Ammons, D. N. (1995). Overcoming the inadequacies of performance measurement in local government: The case of libraries and leisure services. *Public Administration Review, 55*, 37–47.

Ammons, D. N. (2002). Performance measurement and managerial thinking. *Public Performance & Management Review, 25*(4), 344–347.

Ammons, D. N. (Ed.). (2008). *Leading performance management in local government.* Washington, DC: International City/County Management Association Press.

Ammons, D. N., & Rivenbark, W. C. (2008). Factors influencing the use of performance data to improve municipal services: Evidence from the North Carolina Benchmarking Project. *Public Administration Review, 68*, 304–318.

Andersen, S. C. (2008). The impact of public management reforms on student performance in Danish schools. *Public Administration, 86*(2), 541–558.

Aristigueta, M. P., & Zarook, F. N. (2011). Managing for results in six states: Progress in over a decade demonstrates that leadership matters. *Public Performance and Management Review, 35*, 177–201.

Barnow, B., & Smith, J. (2004). Performance management of US job training programs: Lessons from the Job Training Partnership Act. *Public Finance and Management, 4*, 247–287.

Behn, R. D. (2003). Why measure performance? Different purposes require different measures. *Public Administration Review, 63*, 586–606.

Behn, R. D. (2006). The varieties of CitiStat. *Public Administration Review, 66*, 322–340.

Behn, R. D. (2007). *What all mayors would like to know about Baltimore's CitiStat performance strategy.* Washington, DC: IBM Center for the Business of Government.

Bouckaert, G., & Balk, W. (1991). Public productivity measurement: Diseases and cures. *Public Productivity and Management Review, 15*, 229–235.

Boyne, G. A. (2003). Sources of public service improvement: A critical review and research agenda. *Journal of Public Administration Research and Theory, 13*, 367–394.

Boyne, G., & Chen, A. A. (2007). Performance targets and public service improvement. *Journal of Public Administration Research and Theory, 17*(3), 455–477.

Bratton, W. J., & Malinowski, S. W. (2008). Police performance management in practice: Taking Compstat to the next level. *Policing, 2*, 259–265.

Bryson, J. M. (2011). *Strategic planning for public and nonprofit organizations: A guide to strengthening and sustaining organizational achievement.* San Francisco: Jossey-Bass.

Chun, Y. H., & Rainey, H. G. (2005). Goal ambiguity and organizational performance in US federal agencies. *Journal of Public Administration Research and Theory, 15,* 529–557.

de Lancer Julnes, P., Berry, F. S., Aristigueta, M. P., & Yang, K. (2007). *International handbook of practice-based performance management.* Thousand Oaks, CA: Sage.

de Lancer Julnes, P., & Holzer, M. (2001). Promoting the utilization of performance measures in public organizations: An empirical study of factors affecting adoption and implementation. *Public Administration Review, 61*(6), 693–708.

Epstein, P. D. (1984). *Using performance measurement in local government: A guide to improving decisions, performance, and accountability.* New York: Van Nostrand Reinhold.

Fried, Y., & Slowik, L. H. (2004). Enriching goal-setting theory with time: An integrated approach. *Academy of Management Review, 29,* 404–422.

Gore, A. (1993). *From red tape to results: Creating a government that works better and costs less: Report of the National Performance Review.* Darby, PA: Diane Books Publishing Company.

Halachmi, A., & Bouckaert, G. (Eds.). (1996). *Organizational performance and measurement in the public sector: Toward service, effort, and accomplishment reporting.* Westport, CT: Quorum Books.

Hatry, H. P. (1999). *Performance measurement: Getting results.* Washington, DC: Urban Institute Press.

Hatry, H. P. (2002). Performance measurement: Fashions and fallacies. *Public Performance & Management Review, 25*(4), 352–358.

Hatry, H. P. (2006). *Performance measurement: Getting results.* Washington, DC: Urban Institute Press.

Heinrich, C. J. (2007). Evidence-based policy and performance management challenges and prospects in two parallel movements. *American Review of Public Administration, 37,* 255–277.

Heinrich, C. J., & Marschke, G. (2010). Incentives and their dynamics in public sector performance management systems. *Journal of Policy Analysis and Management, 29,* 183–208.

Holzer, M., & Yang, K. (2004). Performance measurement and improvement: An assessment of the state of the art. *International Review of Administrative Sciences, 70,* 15–31.

Jennings, E. T., & Haist, M. P. (2004). Putting performance measurement in context. In P. W. Ingraham & L. E. Lynn Jr. (Eds.), *The art of governance: Analyzing management and administration* (pp. 173–194). Washington, DC: Georgetown University Press.

Kamensky, J., & Fountain, J. (2008). *Creating and sustaining a results-oriented performance management framework.* In P. DeLancer Julnes, F. Berry, M. Aristigueta, & K. Yang (Eds.), *International handbook of practice-based performance management* (pp. 489–508). Thousand Oaks, CA: Sage.

Kassoff, H. (2001). Implementing performance measurement in transportation agencies. In *Performance measures to improve transportation systems and agency operations.* Washington, DC: National Academy Press.

Kelly, J. M. (2003). Citizen satisfaction and administrative performance measures. *Urban Affairs Review, 38,* 855–866.

Latham, G. P. (2004). The motivational benefits of goal-setting. *Academy of Management Executive, 18,* 126–129.

Leeuw, F. L. (2000). Unintended side effects of auditing: The relationship between performance auditing and performance improvement and the role of trust. In W. Raub & J. Weesie (Eds.), *The management of durable relation.* Amsterdam: Thelathesis.

Lukensmeyer, C., & Hasselblad Torres, L. (2006). *Public deliberation: A manager's guide to citizen engagement.* Washington, DC: IBM Center for the Business of Government.

Marr, B. (2012). *Managing and delivering performance.* New York: Routledge.

Milward, B., & Provan, K. (2006). A manager's guide to choosing and using collaborative networks. Washington, DC: IBM Center for the Business of Government.

Moynihan, D. P. (2008). *The dynamics of performance management: Constructing information and reform.* Washington, DC: Georgetown University Press.

Moynihan, D. P. (2009). Through a glass, darkly. *Public Performance and Management Review, 32*(4), 592–603.

Neely, A., & Bourne, M. (2000). Why measurement initiatives fail. *Measuring Business Excellence, 4*(4), 3–6.

Newcomer, K. (2008). *Assessing performance in nonprofit service agencies.* In P. de Lancer Julnes, F. Berry, M. Aristigueta, & K. Yang (Eds.), *International handbook of practice-based performance management* (pp. 25–44). Thousand Oaks, CA: Sage.

Niven, P. R. (2003, April 22). *Adapting the balanced scorecard to fit the public and non-profit sectors.* Primerus Consulting Report.

Organisation for Economic Co-operation and Development. (2005). *Modernising government: The way forward.* Paris: Author.

Plantz, M. C., Greenway, M. T., & Hendricks, M. (1997). Outcome measurement: Showing results in the nonprofit sector. In K. E. Newcomer (Ed.), *Using performance measurement to improve public and nonprofit programs.* New Directions for Evaluation, no. 75. San Francisco: Jossey-Bass.

Poister, T. H. (2003). *Measuring performance in public and nonprofit organizations.* San Francisco: Jossey-Bass.

Poister, T. H. (2010). The future of strategic planning in the public sector: Linking strategic management and performance. *Public Administration Review, 70,* 246–254.

Poister, T. H., Pasha, O. Q., & Edwards, L. H. (2013). Does performance management lead to better outcomes? Evidence from the US public transit industry. *Public Administration Review, 73,* 625–636.

Radin, B. A. (2006). *Challenging the performance movement: Accountability, complexity, and democratic values.* Washington, DC: Georgetown University Press.

Sanger, M. B. (2008). From measurement to management: Breaking through the barriers to state and local performance. *Public Administration Review, 68,* S70–S85.

Sawhill, J. C., & Williamson, D. (2001). Mission impossible? Measuring success in nonprofit organizations. *Nonprofit Management and Leadership, 11*(3), 371–386.

Smith, D. C., & Bratton, W. J. (2001). Performance management in New York City: CompStat and the revolution in police management. In D. W. Forsythe (Ed.), *Quicker, better, cheaper? Managing performance in American government* (pp. 453–482). Albany, NY: Rockefeller Institute.

Sterck, M., & Bouckaert, G. (2008). Performance information of high quality. How to develop a legitimate, functional and sound performance measurement system?

In P. de Lancer Julnes, F. Berry, M. Aristigueta, & K. Yang (Eds.), *International handbook of practice based performance management* (pp. 433–454). Thousand Oaks: Sage.

Sun, R., & Van Ryzin, G. G. (2014). Are performance management practices associated with better public outcomes? Empirical evidence from New York public schools. *American Review of Public Administration, 44*(3), 324–338.

Swiss, J. E. (1991). *Public management systems: Monitoring and managing government performance.* Englewood Cliffs, NJ: Prentice-Hall.

US Government Accountability Office. (2014). *Implementation approaches used to enhance collaboration in interagency groups* (GAO-14-220). Washington, DC: Author.

Van Dooren, W., Bouckaert, G., & Halligan, J. (2010). *Performance management in the public sector.* New York: Routledge.

Walker, R. M., Damanpour, F., & Devece, C. A. (2011). Management innovation and organizational performance: The mediating effect of performance management. *Journal of Public Administration Research and Theory, 21,* 367–386.

Wholey, J. S. (1999). Performance-based management: Responding to the challenges. *Public Productivity & Management Review, 22,* 288–307.

Wholey, J. S. (2002). Making results count in public and nonprofit organizations: Balancing -performance with other values. In K. E. Newcomer, E. T. Jennings, C. A. Broom, & A. Lomax (Eds.), *Meeting the challenges of performance-oriented government.* Washington, DC: Center for Accountability and Performance of the American Society for Public Administration.

Wholey, J. S. (2006) Quality control: Assessing the accuracy and usefulness of performance measurement systems. In H. P. Hatry, *Performance measurement: Getting results* (pp. 267–286). Washington, DC: Urban Institute Press.

Wholey, J. S., & Hatry, H. P. (1992). The case for performance monitoring. *Public Administration Review, 52,* 604–610.

NAME INDEX

A

Abercrombie, N. N., 385, 386, 400
Ackerman, J., 355
Ackermann, F., 220
Allen, D. N., 240
Allen, D. R., 360
Altman, S., 11, 372
Ammons, D. N., 121, 175, 387,
   388, 402, 413, 414, 416, 430,
   441
Andersen, S. C., 415
Aristigueta, M. P., 212, 301, 339,
   414, 428
Arkin, M., 121

B

Balk, W., 419
Bardach, E., 298
Barnow, B., 414
Behn, R. D., 11, 12, 13, 194, 294,
   297, 322, 338, 413, 414, 417
Berliner, D. C., 148
Berman, E. M., 5, 29, 331, 333
Berry, F. S., 414
Berryman, A. F., 358
Bevan, G., 149
Bishop, L., 377
Booher, D. E., 380
Bouckaert, G., 38, 335, 413, 416,
   419
Bourne, M., 416

C

Caiden, N., 237
Carr, D. K., 331
Carroll, S. J., 94
Chen, A. A., 415
Chiarini, A., 343, 344, 350
Choo, A., 344
Chun, Y. H., 410
Coe, C., 388
Condon, S., 328
Cook, T., 269
Cornwell, S., 305
Coulter, P. B., 372
Crittenden, S., 121
Crosby, B. C., 378
Crossett, J., 401

Boyer, S. R., 387, 402
Boyne, G. A., 109, 339, 415, 419
Brass, C. T., 20, 21, 22
Bratton, W. J., 23, 292, 413, 414
Breul, J. D., 231
Broom, C., 54, 94
Brown, K., 372
Brue, G., 346
Bryant, S. P., 387
Bryson, J. M., 200, 203, 205, 206,
   220, 355, 356, 357, 378, 380,
   416
Bugler, D. T., 145
Burke, C., 304
Burnett, J., 240

D

Damanpour, F., 414
de Lancer Julnes, P., 414,
   428
DeGroff, A., 326
Deming, E., 339, 341–342
Devece, C. A., 414
DeVellis, R. F., 127
Deyle, R. E., 380
Dixon, D. R., 118
Dockstader, S. L., 343
Douglas, T. J., 343
Dubnick, M. J., 4, 14, 15–17

E

Eden, C., 220
Edwards, L. H., 414
Eiperlin, J., 304
Enticott, G., 339
Epstein, P. D., 413
Ertas, N., 357
Esty, D. C., 297

F

Fainstein, S. S., 377
Fernandez, S., 355
Fisher, G., 345
Fountain, J., 41, 428, 439
Frechtling, J. A., 54, 76, 85
Fredendall, L. D., 343

447

SUBJECT INDEX

Page references followed by *fig* indicate an illustrated figure; followed by *t* indicate a table.

450

Printed and bound by CPI Group (UK) Ltd, Croydon, CR0 4YY

17/04/2025

14658876-0001